D1825808

Senescence and Rejuvenescence

SENESCENCE AND REJUVENESCENCE

THE UNIVERSITY OF CHICAGO PRESS
CHICAGO, ILLINOIS

Agents

THE CAMBRIDGE UNIVERSITY PRESS
LONDON AND EDINBURGH

THE MARUZEN-KABUSHIKI KAISHA
TOKYO, OSAKA, KYOTO

KARL W HIERSEMANN
LEIPZIG

THE BAKER & TAYLOR COMPANY
NEW YORK

SENESCENCE

AND

REJUVENESCENCE

By

CHARLES MANNING CHILD

Of the Department of Zoölogy
The University of Chicago

THE UNIVERSITY OF CHICAGO PRESS
CHICAGO, ILLINOIS

Copyright 1915 By
The University of Chicago

All Rights Reserved

Published October 1915

Composed and Printed By
The University of Chicago Press
Chicago, Illinois, U S A

PREFACE

The following study of senescence and rejuvenescence is primarily a register of progress along certain lines of a research program on which I have been engaged during the last fifteen years. This program began with the attempt to analyze experimentally the simpler reproductive processes, but it at once became evident that the whole problem of the organic individual, its origin, development, physiological character, and limiting factors, was involved. In the study of the organic individual the importance of the physiological age changes soon became apparent and it was found necessary to devote considerable time to their analysis, for the origin of new individuals by reproduction is in many cases very closely associated with physiological aging And since the conclusions reached concerning the age cycle finally attained a definite, positive form, differing to some extent from commonly accepted views, but seeming to throw some light upon various other biological problems, it has seemed desirable to attempt a general consideration and synthesis of the subject of age changes from the point of view which has grown out of the research program mentioned above

It will appear clearly in the following pages that the problems of individuation, reproduction, and age are all closely connected. For that reason it has been necessary to devote a chapter—chap ix —to the problem of individuation and reproduction This chapter is merely a brief statement of some of the more important evidence and the conclusions reached concerning the nature of the organic individual, a full consideration of the subject being left to another time.

About half the book is a presentation of results of my own investigations and the larger part of these have not been published elsewhere. Consequently the book stands as a record of research as well as an attempt at a general survey. No attempt has been made to present a complete bibliography of the subject of age The references are to a large extent intended to serve rather as guides or aids in obtaining further knowledge of the literature than as an

v

86431

exhaustive bibliography. The matter of selection has often been
a difficult one and doubtless references have been omitted which
should have been included. For such errors of judgment or of
ignorance I must accept the full responsibility.

At various points in the book it has seemed necessary to extend
the consideration into fields more or less remote from those with
which I am most familiar. I must frankly acknowledge, however,
that some of these ventures into other fields have been attended by
the feeling that discretion would perhaps have been the better part
of valor, for any venture very far outside one's own little garden plot
of scientific thought is likely to be attended by a very decided feeling
of strangeness, one realizes that one is not at home. Nevertheless
such ventures are necessary if different lines of investigation and
thought are to be co-ordinated and synthesized into a harmonious
whole   I can only hope that in this particular case the excursions
into neighboring gardens and fields have not been wholly fruitless
or mistaken. As regards actual errors of statement or reference
and other similar matters which may have escaped correction, I
can only plead human fallibility.

It has been necessary, particularly in those chapters which are
concerned with the various reproductive processes and with the
morphology of the gametic cells, to use figures from various other
authors and I wish to acknowledge my obligations for such figures.
Figs 102, 103, 104, 105, 106, 107, $A-C$, 108, 125, 128, 132, 133, 134,
135, 136, 137, 138, 139, 141, $A-E$, are reproduced from *A Text-
book of Botany* by Coulter, Barnes, and Cowles, by permission of
the American Book Company, publishers, and Dr Coulter, the
senior author   I am greatly indebted both to the publishers and
to Dr. Coulter for permission to use these figures of characteristic
morphological and reproductive features of plant life   Figs. 111
and 112 are reproductions in slightly modified form from Minot's
The Problem of Age, Growth and Death, by permission of the publishers, Messrs G. P. Putnam's Sons. For other figures which are
not original acknowledgment is made in the legends, and since it
is often highly desirable to know, not only the author of a particular
figure, but the publication in which it originally appeared, a reference number, as well as the author's name, is given and the full

reference is included in the list at the end of the chapter in which the figure appears

For permission to cite unpublished data I am indebted to Dr. S. Tashiro, of the Department of Biochemistry, to Miss L. H. Hyman, of the Department of Zoology, and to Mr. M. M. Wells, formerly of the Department of Zoology, of the University of Chicago. For the redrawing of all figures from other authors and for a number of original drawings from preparations I am indebted to Mr Kenji Toda, the artist of the Department of Zoology, and I wish to express my appreciation of his work. For the reading of parts of the manuscript and proofs and for various suggestions and criticisms my thanks are due to my colleagues, Dr. A. P. Mathews and Dr. C. J. Herrick. To my wife, Lydia Van Meter Child, I am deeply indebted for her unfailing co-operation and assistance in the preparation of the manuscript and proofs. And, lastly, I wish to express my appreciation of the manner in which the University of Chicago Press has done its part as publisher.

C. M. CHILD

HULL ZOOLOGICAL LABORATORY
UNIVERSITY OF CHICAGO
May, 1915

TABLE OF CONTENTS

INTRODUCTION

The succession of generations and the repetition of the life cycle in the individual are the two great facts about which biological thought centers. The problems of reproduction, growth, development, inheritance, and evolution, as well as many other special problems, are concerned with one aspect or another of these fundamental characteristics of life   Life as we know it exists only in the form of individuals of various degrees and kinds which pass through a definite series of changes and give rise to other individuals, and these in turn repeat the process more or less exactly.

At the beginning of a new generation the size of the organism is usually only a fraction of that to which it finally attains.   Various substances are taken up by the organism as food and transformed in part into the energy of its activity and in part into the material substratum in which the dynamic activities occur   Under the usual conditions this material substratum which constitutes the visible organism increases in amount or grows during a large part of the life of the organism

In all except perhaps the very simplest organisms another series of changes occurs which we call morphogenesis or differentiation   Localized differences in constitution, form, or structure appear, and we say that the organism undergoes differentiation   Under natural conditions this process of differentiation is very commonly associated with growth, but the fact that it may occur in the complete absence of growth shows that the association is by no means a necessary one.

Sooner or later and in one way or another the organism gives rise to one or more new organisms, which like their parent are at first relatively small and simple, and like it also undergo a process of growth and differentiation.   This is reproduction   In some of the simpler forms of reproduction the parent organism divides into two or more parts which constitute the new generation, and there is nothing which corresponds to death in the usual sense. The old individuality is replaced by new individualities, but nothing

I

D. H. HILL LIBRARY

is left behind.   In such cases there is, as Weismann has aptly put it, no death because there is no corpse

We see, however, that in certain other forms of reproduction, as in various types of sporulation in plants and budding in lower animals, and in sexual reproduction also if we take the facts at their face value without reference to the germ-plasm theory, only a circumscribed part of the parent organism is directly involved in reproduction   In such cases the parent organism either remains alive for a longer or shorter time, perhaps with periodic or continuous reproduction, or it dies almost at once   In short, death of the non-reproductive or somatic parts of the organism is apparently the final result in at least most of these cases

In the higher animals which reproduce only sexually, and in at least many of the higher plants, certain physiological and morphological changes accompany growth and development of the somatic parts   The rate of growth decreases, in many cases irritability and the rate of metabolism have also been found to decrease, a relative and later an absolute decrease in the percentage of water occurs, the structural elements become less plastic and in some cases undergo more or less atrophy in later stages, and the organism in general appears to be gradually losing its vigor   In many plants these changes occur rapidly in certain parts and may be long, perhaps indefinitely, delayed in others, and it will be shown in Part III that the same is true for many of the lower animals, but in the higher animals the whole of the body is apparently involved, though even here the facts indicate that these changes may occur more rapidly in one part or another according to various conditions.

These changes, which constitute a gradual deterioration of the organism, a gradual decrease in the intensity of its living, are commonly designated as aging or senescence. The question whether certain changes are properly to be regarded as senescence or not may often be raised with respect to particular cases, but in general there can be no doubt that in at least many organisms a process of senescence does occur   the organism grows old. Moreover, there is no doubt that in at least many forms this process of senescence leads to the cessation of the processes of life, i.e., to what we call death.

The occurrence of senescence in the organic world raises many questions of great interest and importance, not only for the scientist, but in certain aspects for the human race in general. How do young and old organisms differ from each other, and what is the nature of senescence? Is it a feature of the fundamental processes of life or the result of incidental conditions? Does it occur in all organisms or only in the more complex, more highly differentiated forms? Does it inevitably lead sooner or later to death, or is a rejuvenescence of old organisms or parts possible? Is the process of senescence in a given organism always of the same character, or does it depend upon the environmental conditions? Is the rate of senescence always the same in a particular species, or does it differ in different individuals according to the action of internal or external factors. Many of these questions can be summed up in the one, Can we control senescence?

In nature the organism resulting from the union of the two sexual cells is young This fact raises another series of questions Does rejuvenescence occur somewhere in the course of sexual reproduction, or does the germ plasm from which the sex cells arise not grow old? Are the organisms which result from asexual reproduction also young, or is sexual reproduction the only process which gives rise to young organisms? If rejuvenescence occurs, upon what does its occurrence depend and what is its nature? Does it occur in all organisms, or only in certain of them? Is complete rejuvenescence possible, or is the species and the organic world in general undergoing a senescence which will lead to extinction?

These are a few of the most important questions which the occurrence of senescence and the processes of reproduction lead us to ask. In the following chapters these and some other questions will be considered in the light of the experimental and observational evidence which we possess. To some of these questions we shall be able to give a definite answer, to some others the answer must be provisional, and some we must leave open for the future to answer, though even here we can indicate the direction in which the facts point

The problem of senescence has been discussed many times in the history of biology, and many hypotheses as to its nature have been elaborated   Unfortunately by far the greater part of the work along this line has dealt chiefly with the process of senescence as it appears in man and the higher mammals.   Only now and then has an attempt been made even to formulate a general theory of senescence, and analytic investigation of senescence in the lower organisms has scarcely been attempted.   This limitation in the investigation of the problem of senescence is due to the fact that in the past interest in the problem has been very largely confined to the medical profession.

It is of course true that we are most familiar with the phenomena of senescence in man and other mammals, the most complex of all organisms.   But man is a member of the organic world and a product of evolution, and, as we have traced the development of his structure from lower forms, so we must look to the lower forms for adequate knowledge of his physiological processes.   Before we can understand senescence in man we must determine what it is in its simplest terms.

The present book finds its chief reason for existence in the fact that it has been possible with the aid of certain experimental methods of investigation to obtain some definite knowledge concerning the processes of senescence and rejuvenescence in the lower animals.   The facts discovered afford, as I believe, a basis for the further investigation of senescence and rejuvenescence in general, and for an analytic consideration and interpretation of various phenomena in plants and animals which are more or less closely associated with these processes.   Since the most important result of these investigations is, in my opinion, the demonstration of the occurrence of rejuvenescence quite independently of sexual reproduction, the book differs to some extent from most previous studies of senescence in that it attempts to show that in the organic world in general rejuvenescence is just as fundamental and important a process as senescence   In the higher forms the possibilities of rejuvenescence are apparently very narrowly limited, but in the simpler organisms it is a characteristic feature of life, and the nature of the process here enables us to understand more clearly certain changes which occur in the higher forms.

My investigation of senescence and rejuvenescence has been closely connected with an attempt to determine the physiological nature of the reproductive processes in organisms, and I believe that some such conception of senescence and rejuvenescence as that presented here is essential for the physiological analysis of reproduction, since senescence, reproduction, and rejuvenescence are very closely connected. But while some discussion of the nature of various reproductive processes will be necessary in the course of the present study, a full consideration of the problem of reproduction is postponed to another time.

Our conception of the nature of these various processes, growth, differentiation, senescence, reproduction, and rejuvenescence, must depend upon our conception of the organism. It seems necessary, therefore, to consider briefly in certain of its aspects the problem of the constitution of the organism by way of clearing the ground for consideration of the particular features of organic constitution which form the subject of the book.

PART I

THE PROBLEM OF ORGANIC CONSTITUTION

CHAPTER I

VARIOUS THEORIES OF THE ORGANISM

NEO-VITALISTIC THEORY

To the primitive man all the phenomena of nature were determined and controlled by some agent or agents essentially similar to himself, but as his knowledge of the world increased, the contrast between living and non-living things forced itself upon him and the idea of a special vital principle of some sort arose. In the mind of different thinkers this principle has taken various forms, and the attempt has been made again and again in the history of thought to show that some such principle is absolutely indispensable for any adequate conception of life. A century ago the idea of vital force dominated biological thought.

Within recent years the same idea has reappeared in a somewhat changed though not essentially different form Particularly in Germany a group of investigators has arisen who believe that they have found new evidence in the facts of experimental biology for the existence of a vital principle. The chief exponent of these ideas is Driesch ('08) who has developed the Aristotelian idea of entelechies in a somewhat modified form. The entelechy is something which acts in a purposive way and constructs the organism for a definite end and controls its functioning after it is constructed The physico-chemical processes are simply means to the end

Since the neo-vitalistic hypotheses profess to find their foundation to a greater or less extent in the facts of experimental biological investigation, they have a claim on the attention of biologists which purely speculative hypotheses do not have. But a critical examination of the works of Driesch and other neo-vitalists discloses the fact that their hypotheses actually rest, not upon facts, but upon certain undemonstrated and at present undemonstrable assumptions. Driesch's so-called "proofs of the autonomy of vital processes" are not proofs at all, because each of them involves in one way or another the assumption of what it is supposed to prove. At present it is as impossible to prove as to disprove the existence of a vital principle, because our knowledge of the organism is insufficient. Only when we have exhausted physico-chemical possibilities and found them to be inadequate shall we be justified in searching elsewhere for the basis of life.

But there is one point of particular interest in connection with the neo-vitalistic hypotheses. They are a logical consequence of the corpuscular theories of heredity and organic constitution and development, such as the theory of Weismann. These theories were widely current at the time when the neo-vitalistic school arose. They themselves are fundamentally "vitalistic" in character, whatever their assertions to the contrary. An orderly progressive development of a definite character is inconceivable in an organism composed of a very large number of independent ultimate units each capable of growth and reproduction, except under the influence of some controlling and directing principle distinct from the ultimate units themselves If such theories represent the last word of science concerning the physico-chemical constitution of the organism, then we must all be vitalists, whether we admit it or not. But if the controlling and determining principle, entelechy or whatever we choose to call it, is indispensable, why must we complicate matters by assuming the existence of a multitude of discrete ultimate units of one kind or another? Why not give the entelechy a task worthy of it and assume that all parts of the organism are essentially alike and equipotential? This is practically what Driesch has done. The entelechy determines localization and development and uses physico-chemical processes to effect its ends.

The trend of biological thought has undergone change during the past twenty years The development of experimental methods on the one hand and the development of the physical sciences on the other have contributed to alter our conception of the organism and today there is less basis for vitalistic theory than ever before. Even the theory of Weismann and other morphological theories of the organism are giving place to theories of a different type, and while many other attempts will undoubtedly be made in future to demonstrate the indispensability of some sort of vital principle, the analysis and synthesis of science, proceeding step by step, testing and retesting the supposed facts, adopting and discarding hypotheses, will continue to be the basis of our advance in knowledge.

CORPUSCULAR THEORIES

During the latter half of the nineteenth century, biology, and particularly zoology, was to a large extent dominated by the corpuscular theories of heredity and organic constitution These theories postulate some sort of a material particle or corpuscle consisting of more than one molecule as the ultimate basis of life. The organism is built up in one way or another from a number, often very large, of such corpuscles, and the corpuscles are the "bearers of heredity " The gemmules of Darwin, the pangenes of DeVries, the physiological units of Spencer, the biophores and determinants of Weismann, and various other hypothetical units have played an important part in biological thought during almost half a century

This group of theories may be called the morphological or static group. They all postulate a complex morphological structure as the basis of inheritance and development, and they are all attempts to answer the question as to how the characteristics of the species are maintained from one generation to another Among them the theory of Weismann has been more completely developed and has influenced biological thought and investigation to a greater extent than any other.

All of these theories possess certain characteristic features in common. The ultimate elements, whatever they may be called, are not alike, but each possesses certain definite characteristics and plays a definite part in the development of the individual. The organism is in short essentially a colony of such units According to Weismann, DeVries, and others, the ultimate units are each capable of growth, and each reproduces its own kind.

It is scarcely necessary to call attention to the fact that these theories do not help us in any way to solve any of the fundamental problems of biology; they merely serve to place these problems beyond the reach of scientific investigation. The hypothetical units are themselves organisms with all the essential characteristics of the organisms that we know; they possess a definite constitution, they grow at the expense of nutritive material, they reproduce their kind In other words, the problems of development, growth, reproduction, and inheritance exist for each of them and the assumption of their existence brings us not a step nearer the solution of any of these problems. These theories are nothing more nor less than translations of the phenomena of life as we know them into terms of the activity of multitudes of invisible hypothetical organisms, and therefore contribute nothing in the way of real advance. No valid evidence for the existence of these units exists, but if their existence were to be demonstrated we might well despair of gaining any actual knowledge of life.

But these theories possess another fundamental defect in that they do not provide any adequate mechanism for the control and co-ordination or dominance and subordination of the activity of the ultimate units. It is absolutely inconceivable that a multitude of these units, such as is assumed to constitute the basis of the cell or the organism, should always in a given species arrange themselves in a perfectly definite manner so as to produce always essentially the same total result In other words, these theories do not account satisfactorily for the peculiarly constant course and character of development and morphogenesis. If we follow them to their logical conclusion, which their authors have not done, we find ourselves forced to assume the existence of some sort of controlling and co-ordinating principle outside the units themselves, and superior to them. If the units constitute the physico-chemical basis of life, as their authors maintain, then this controlling principle, since it is an essential feature of life, must of necessity be something which is not physico-chemical in nature. In short, these theories lead us in the final analysis to the same conclusion as that reached by the neo-vitalists. If we are not content to accept this conclusion we must reject the theories.

The development within recent years of the experimental method of investigation and the consequent approach of morphology and physiology toward a common ground have accomplished much in inducing biologists to turn their attention in other directions for interpretation and synthesis of the facts. But the Weismannian germ plasm as an entity distinct from the soma and governed by different laws still plays no small part in interpretation and speculation, and we have heard much of unit characters within the last few years. The chromosomes and their hypothetical constituent elements still serve their purpose as safe repositories of unsolved problems, and doubtless will long continue to do so. And in Rignano's theory of centro-epigenesis ('06) we have a corpuscular theory in a new dress, but still with the same characteristic features

But all of these theories and conceptions bear the stamp of the study rather than of the laboratory. Many of them show great ingenuity, but they all fail to show us how the things are done that they assume to be done: they ignore almost entirely the dynamic side of life. At present we can neither prove nor disprove them, for they are entirely beyond the reach of science. No facts can overthrow them, for it is always possible to make the hypothetical units behave as the facts demand. But we can at least look in other directions for a more satisfactory basis for interpretation of the facts of observation and experiment and for guidance in our thinking.

CHEMICAL THEORY

The synthesis in the laboratory of organic substances which began in 1828 with the synthesis of urea by Wohler led to the overthrow of the doctrine of vital force current before that time. The formulation of the law of conservation of energy by Robert Mayer, its establishment by Helmholtz, and its application to organisms by both of these investigators as well as by others, contributed still further to the belief that the dynamic processes in organisms, instead of being unique and governed by special laws, are not fundamentally different from those which occur independently of life. And, finally, the acceptance of the theory of evolution gave a breadth of outlook never before attained, in that it permitted us not only to regard the organic world as one great whole, but also afforded a firm foundation for the belief that the living must have arisen from the lifeless and that the fundamental laws governing both are the same.

With the attainment of this point of view the problem of the nature of the processes in the living organism was fully established as a scientific problem. And since it was evident that chemical reactions play a very large part in life processes it became essentially a chemical problem. From this time on our knowledge of the chemistry of organisms increased rapidly, and certain investigators have been so sanguine as to believe that we were on the threshold of the synthesis in the laboratory of living matter. During the same period the visible structural basis of life was being studied under the microscope. In 1837–39 the cell theory was formulated by Schleiden and Schwann, and in the half-century following the problems of cellular and protoplasmic structure claimed the attention of biologists to a large extent.

These investigations soon made it evident that life is closely associated in some way with the substances which we call proteids. These are found in all organisms and so far as we know nowhere else. Excepting water, they are the chief constituent of the visible substance characteristic of organisms, i.e., protoplasm. It was also demonstrated that life is associated with a complex of chemical activities. Certain substances are taken up by the organism and others are eliminated. Between ingestion and elimination a complex series of chemical reactions was found to occur, and the whole process was called metabolism.

The conception of the metabolic process and its relation to protoplasm, which was most widely accepted during this period of chemical and morphological investigation in the latter half of the nineteenth century, was that metabolism consisted fundamentally of two parts. Of these one, the anabolic or assimilative process, was in its essential features the recombination and synthesis of the nutritive substances into extremely complex proteid molecules which constituted the "living substance." These proteid molecules were regarded as highly labile chemically, or "explosive," so that they were able to respond to stimulation of various kinds by decomposition and the very rapid liberation of energy. The various steps in the decomposition of these living proteid molecules constituted the process of katabolism or dissimilation. Investigation showed that the molecular weight of the proteids was in general very high, and this was believed to indicate very great complexity of the molecules. The highly unstable or labile character of the

living proteid was believed to be connected with its great complexity Of course many differences of opinion existed with respect
to the details of the process, but the essential feature of this conception of the organism is that life consists in the building up and
the breaking down of proteid molecules. The energy developed
by living forms is the energy contained in these molecules

The necessity for the distinction between living and dead proteid
was pointed out by Pfluger ('75), and in later years Verworn ('03)
has developed the idea further in his "biogene hypothesis," of which
the essential feature is that certain complex labile proteid molecules are the biogenes, the "producers of life." These molecules
are not necessarily entirely decomposed in metabolism, but the
source of energy probably lies in certain chemical groups which
break down and are replaced by synthesis from the nutritive substances. According to this hypothesis the dynamic processes in
the organism are connected with the breakdown and synthesis of
these labile molecules. The molecule is not itself "alive," but its
constitution is the basis of life and life results from the chemical
transformations which its lability makes possible The "living
substance" is then not a substance of uniform definite molecular
constitution: such a substance would not be alive. It is rather a
substance in which some of the labile molecules are continually
undergoing transformation, i e., life itself consists in chemical
change, not in chemical constitution

This theory of the organism leaves us very much in the dark on
many points. In the first place, most of the proteids as we know
them in the laboratory are relatively stable and inert chemically
and show no traces of the extreme lability or explosiveness which
the theory postulates as their most important characteristic in the
living organism. This difficulty was solved theoretically by assuming that the lability is a property of living proteids only and disappears with death Death in fact was regarded as resulting from
this change from lability to stability. The proteids *in vitro* are
of course dead proteids, therefore we should not expect to find them
possessing the property of lability. This assumed distinction between living and dead substance has the further disadvantage of
practically removing the "living substance" from the field of

investigation, for as soon as we attempt to determine how it differs from dead substance death occurs.

Moreover, if death results from change from extreme lability to relatively high stability we should expect at least many of the proteids of the body to undergo marked changes in appearance and physical properties at the time of death. Some changes of this sort, such as coagulation, do occur, but coagulation does not necessarily involve chemical transformation, and in general the visible changes in the proteids with death are not very great. Certainly they are not as great as would be expected if such a profound chemical change occurs

If the energy of the organism is due to the explosive transformation of highly labile molecules into more stable conditions and if death also results from a more extreme change of the same sort in the substance of the organism, we should expect to find a very large amount of energy developed at the time of death   If all the living substance changes into dead substance in the course of a few moments or a few hours, or even a few days, what becomes of the energy liberated?   The amount of energy developed by such a change would necessarily be greater than that resulting from the most extreme stimulation which did not kill, for such stimulations are supposed always to leave some part of the hypothetical living substance intact. Such a liberation of energy could scarcely fail to produce profound changes of some sort, either mechanical, electrical, or thermic, but death is not necessarily accompanied by any energetic changes of such magnitude as might be expected to occur according to the hypothesis.

How, we must also ask, are we to account for growth on this basis?   What peculiar property of the living substance determines not only that the molecules which break down shall again be built up or replaced, but that other new molecules shall be added? Various highly hypothetical answers have been given to this question, but the fact remains that so far as we know no similar process exists elsewhere in the world. The growth of crystals has often been compared with that of organisms, but the resemblance is at best only very remote, for growth in the organism is certainly closely associated with chemical reaction of a complex character, while in the crystal it results from a physical relation between like molecules.

The solution of the problem of differentiation has scarcely been attempted. It is manifestly closely associated with the metabolic process, but what is the origin and significance of the different kinds of proteid substance and how is their localization at different points of the organism accomplished? If the "labile" biogene molecules all possess the same constitution, then they must undergo different transformations in different parts of the organism; if they differ in constitution in different parts we must find some basis for the difference. It is an established fact that the basis of differentiation exists within the organism and not in environmental factors: it must then depend in some way upon the labile proteid molecule which according to the hypothesis is the basis of life. But it is difficult to understand how such molecules can serve as a foundation for localization and differentiation.

If we accept this hypothesis we must after all conclude that the processes in the living organism differ very widely from those in the inorganic world, for nowhere except where there is life do we find anything approaching in any degree the synthesis of so complex and highly labile a substance as the living substance is assumed to be. But even if we should ever succeed in producing in the laboratory a proteid with the degree of lability postulated for the living substance, it would be likely, in the absence of the delicate mechanism regulating its transformation in the organism, to die or "explode" at once.

From this point of view it is also difficult to account for the capacity of organisms to continue alive when subjected to the never-ceasing changes in the world about them. We should scarcely expect such extremely delicate and sensitive mechanisms as these highly labile molecules to withstand the shocks to which organisms in nature are constantly subjected. The facts indicate that organisms have existed continuously for millions of years and during this time have given rise to inconceivable amounts of "living substance." How could such a labile substance ever have persisted long enough in the first instance to form an organism?

The only way in which we can account for these facts without discarding the hypothesis of a highly labile living substance is by the assumption that in some way a part of the energy liberated by the breakdown of these labile molecules must serve for the synthesis of new molecules from the nutritive substances   In other words, the living substance once produced is self-perpetuating, at least within a very wide range of external conditions.   But if the ability to perpetuate itself in this way is a property of the living substance, then it is in this respect also very different from any other substance with which we are acquainted.

It appears then that when we analyze this hypothesis of a labile proteid substance which gives rise to the manifestations of life by its chemical transformations we find that it does not help us to any great extent in bridging the gap between the organism and the inorganic world.   The self-perpetuating substance or substances which constitute the basis of life remain unique in character. They are highly labile, yet persist under a great variety of conditions, and "die" in most cases without the liberation of any very great amount of energy.   During life they regulate their own chemical changes in some way, they determine the formation of new molecules like themselves, and they are responsible somehow for an orderly sequence of differentiation of parts of the organism Evidently they are very different from other chemical substances, even highly labile ones, with which we are familiar.

The numerous difficulties which arise in connection with hypotheses of this character must at least raise the question whether the point of view on which they are based is fundamentally correct. Is life at bottom simply a complex of chemical reactions or is there some other factor involved which the hypothesis of a labile molecule as the basis of life fails to take into account ?   In the following sections an attempt is made to answer this question.

PHYSICO-CHEMICAL THEORY

A few years ago the existence of a living substance as a more or less definite chemical compound was very generally accepted, and only rarely were criticisms and questionings heard.[1]

[1] See for example A P Mathews, '99, '05, Driesch, '01 (pp 140–52). Mathews pointed out that living matter must be a mixture of many substances among which various chemical reactions occur   Driesch denies very positively the existence of a definite living substance, but for him this is merely one point in the argument for the autonomy of vital processes

In his book on the physical chemistry of the cell and tissues, Hober ('11, pp. 553–55) asserts that we have absolutely no grounds for believing that the metabolic process is based on the lability of a complex organic component of the protoplasm.   When we attempt to solve the problems of metabolism with the aid of this hypothetical labile molecule, we find ourselves in a *cul de sac* from which the only possible way out is retreat.   According to Hober, and most authorities now agree with him, there is no kind of proteid essentially different from that with which we are familiar in the laboratory.   If proteids are readily broken up in the organism, it is not because in some way they have acquired a peculiar property of lability which they do not possess elsewhere, but for very different reasons, the conditions in the organism are different from those in the test-tube   Hober maintains that the fundamental characteristic of the process of metabolism is to be found in the combined and correlated activity of certain definite substances in certain definite quantitative relations.

This conception of metabolism has gained ground rapidly of late and for various reasons.   In the first place, evidence in its favor has been rapidly accumulating, and there is not a shred of experimental evidence in support of the labile molecule hypothesis. It is all the time becoming more evident that life does not consist in any one process nor depend on a particular kind of molecule, but that it is the result of many processes occurring under conditions of a certain kind and influencing each other.   Moreover, such a conception has a logical advantage over the hypothesis of the labile molecule in that it does not involve assumptions which are outside the range of scientific investigation and which we can therefore never hope to prove or disprove.

If we accept this idea we must abandon the assumption of a living substance in the sense of a definite chemical compound. Life is a complex of dynamic processes occurring in a certain field or substratum.   Protoplasm, instead of being a peculiar living substance with a peculiar complex morphological structure necessary for life, is on the one hand a colloid product of the chemical reactions, and on the other a substratum in which the reactions occur and which influences their course and character both physically and chemically. In short, the organism is a physico-chemical system of a certain kind.

One point should perhaps be emphasized. The importance of the proteids for life is no less according to this theory than on the assumption of the labile proteid molecule. But the proteids are physical as well as purely chemical factors in the result. We know also that metabolism is not simply a process of building up and breaking down of proteids, and that the proteids of the protoplasm are only one of the products of the reaction-complex and may or may not play an important chemical rôle after their formation. Since the investigations of recent years point more and more clearly to some such physico-chemical conception of the organism as this as the only satisfactory working hypothesis, it is necessary to consider certain features of the organism in the light of this conception

THE COLLOID SUBSTRATUM OF THE ORGANISM

The classical investigations of Kossel and Emil Fischer have established a firm foundation for the belief that the complexity of the proteid molecule is not as great as was formerly believed. The proteids are apparently built up from certain relatively simple chemical compounds, the amino-acids and their derivatives, together with certain other substances, and the proteid molecule, though very large, apparently consists essentially of a number of these components linked together. Of course such a constitution affords the possibility of a very great variety of chemical reactions, but it does not afford a basis for the assumption of extreme lability in the proteids of the living organism. On the contrary the results of chemical as well as of morphological investigation indicate that at least many of the proteids are relatively stable in the living organism as well as in the test-tube.

The proteids exist in the colloid condition Graham ('61) distinguished two groups of substances, the colloids and crystalloids, and although we now know that no sharp distinction exists between the two groups and that any substance may, at least theoretically, exist in the colloid condition, certain substances usually appear as colloids and others as crystalloids. In general the more complex the constitution of a substance the more likely it is to exist in the colloid condition.

The colloids are disperse heterogeneous systems, i.e., they consist essentially of particles larger than molecules of a substance or substances in a medium of dispersion which may be water or some other fluid   In the colloid solution, or "sol," the particles are suspended and separated from each other by the medium, while in the coagulated condition, or "gel," they are more or less aggregated. As regards the size of the particles, the colloid may range from a suspension or emulsion in which the particles are visible to the naked eye to the molecular true solution at the opposite extreme. The colloids are usually divided into two groups, the suspensoids, in which the particles are solid, and the emulsoids, in which they are fluid or, more properly, contain a high percentage of fluid.

The suspensoids are comparatively unstable as regards the colloid condition, are readily precipitated or coagulated by salts, carry a constant electric charge of definite sign, are not viscous, usually do not swell, do not show a lower surface tension than the pure medium of dispersion, and are mostly only slightly reversible.

The emulsoids, however, are comparatively stable as colloids, less readily coagulated by salts, may become either positively or negatively charged, are usually viscous and possess a lower surface tension than the medium of dispersion, form membranes at their limiting surfaces, and are reversible to a high degree [1]

Most of the organic colloids together with some other substances belong to the second group, the emulsoids, and it is demonstrated beyond a doubt that many of the characteristic features of living organisms are due to the presence of a substratum composed of these colloids. The viscosity, the reversible changes in aggregate condition through all gradations from sol to gel and back again, the ability to take up water and swell, and the formation of membranes as well as the other properties are of great significance

[1] Books on colloids are rapidly becoming numerous   See for example Freundlich, '09, and Wolfgang Ostwald, '12, as general works on the subject   Bechhold, '12, Hober, '11, and Zanger, '08, consider the significance of the colloids for the living organism.

for the phenomena of life. The organic colloids are chiefly proteid or fatty in nature, and the present state of our knowledge indicates that the properties of these substances as colloids are no less important for the living organism than their chemical constitution.

In every living organism known to us the chemical processes of metabolism take place in a complex colloid field or substratum, and many of the peculiarities of the metabolic processes are unquestionably due to this fact. Within recent years the significance of colloids for the phenomena of life has been pointed out again and again. Bechhold in his recent book ('12) goes so far as to assert that life is inconceivable except in a colloid system. Doubtless "colloid chemistry" is at present the fashion, but it is also true that this fashion has a certain justification. The study of the behavior and properties of colloids has thrown new light, not only on many problems of chemistry and physics, but on many problems of biology as well. Attention may briefly be called to a few of these biological problems.

The problems of localization and morphogenesis assume a new form in the light of our knowledge of colloids. In the course of development of the organism certain processes become localized at certain points and morphological structure and differentiation result. The visible basis of morphogenesis is the protoplasm, and in it the structural features arise. The definiteness and persistence of organic structure in a substance like protoplasm which presents all conditions between a concentrated and a very dilute gel or a sol has always presented many difficulties, and the problem is at present by no means solved. The attempt has been made repeatedly to find in the process of crystallization and the definiteness of form in the crystal a basis for organic form and structure, but without any very satisfactory results. The resemblance between the physical process of crystallization in a substance of uniform constitution and the development of form and structure in connection with chemical reaction in the complex organism is certainly not very close.

Under proper conditions it is possible to produce more or less definite forms by means of chemical reaction, but in all such cases we find that the form is not directly dependent upon the reaction but upon particular osmotic or other physical conditions which are present in the experiment. Structures so produced are often evanescent and disappear as the conditions in the medium change, for the chemical processes do not remain localized in the ordinary media of chemical reaction, though where the substance of the structure is insoluble they may persist

Within recent years it has been shown that the production of form and structure in connection with chemical reaction is much more readily accomplished when the reaction occurs in the presence of colloids. The colloids in such cases are not necessarily involved in the chemical reaction in any way, but act primarily as a physical substratum in which the reaction occurs. By altering the course and rate of diffusion they serve to establish or maintain differences of concentration; in consequence of the great amount of surface of the colloid particles adsorption may play an important part, and the formation of membranes may also affect the course of the re-action. The effect of the colloid as a localizing factor, as a means of producing form and structure, is greater in the gel than in the sol state of aggregation [1]

Many have not been slow to call attention to the resemblance between form and structure thus produced and organic form and structure, and more or less adventurous hypotheses of the nature of life have been one result of such researches On the other hand, many biologists have been inclined to regard experimentation of this sort as of little value for the problem of morphogenesis, but this attitude seems to arise in part from a misconception. The most important point in connection with such experiments is not the resemblance between the forms and structures produced and those of living organisms. Actually of course the resemblances are in many cases very remote and superficial and of minor importance. But the fact that morphological form and structure can be made to arise in such physico-chemical systems is of great importance for biology, for it affords at least a basis for the scientific investigation and interpretation of morphogenesis in the organism. Earlier attempts to formulate theories of morphogenesis have consisted in

[1] Examples of investigation along this line are the work of Leduc, '08, '09a, '09b, '10, Liesegang, '09, '11, '14, and other earlier papers, and Kuster, '13.

most cases simply in the postulation of a complex invisible morphological structure of one kind or another as the basis of the visible
structure which develops, with such theories the problem of structure remains and is less accessible than before.

The experiments mentioned above demonstrate that such a complex invisible structure is quite unnecessary as a basis for visible
morphogenesis. In the case of many of the artificial structures the
determining conditions are not at all complex and the process is
readily analyzed   It is certainly not too much to say that these
experiments in the production of form constitute a real and important step toward the solution of the problem of organic morphogenesis   From them we can at least see the possibility and even
the probability of reducing the problem of structure to other and
simpler terms, that is to say, terms of dynamic processes, and that
must be reckoned as no slight advance.

But the colloid substratum in the organism is of importance in
many other ways. The capacity of many of the organic colloids
for taking up water is of very great importance in determining and
maintaining· the water content of organisms. A certain water
content is indispensable for the normal activity of every organism
and every part. We know, moreover, that various inorganic
substances alter the capacity of colloids to take up or hold water
and evidence is rapidly accumulating that many normal and pathological variations in water-content are at least in part determined
by changes in the colloids which in turn result from changes in the
content of certain inorganic salts and other substances.

The content and distribution of the salts themselves is also
influenced by the colloids. Changes in the colloids alter the salt-
content, as regards either amount or kind. The permeability of
colloid membranes to the ions of salts and other substances and the
changes which they undergo with changes in conditions is believed
by many to be of great importance for many of the processes of
life. Authorities are not fully agreed as to the part played by
colloid surface membranes in organisms. While the theory of semi-
permeable membranes and of changes in permeability has been
very widely accepted, there are some facts which indicate that
other factors besides membranes are concerned in the penetration

of substances, and that differences in the aggregate condition of different parts are important factors in the process

But even if membranes play the important part which the membrane theory assigns to them, there is no general agreement as to the nature of the conditions which determine permeability, semi-permeability, and impermeability Some maintain that these properties of membranes depend upon their chemical constitution, and that most substances to enter the cell must combine chemically with the substance of the membrane Others believe that the entrance of substances into the cell is a matter of solubility in the membrane-substance According to the familiar theory of Overton and Meyer, the chief constituents of the cell membrane are lipoids, and the passage of at least many substances depends on their solubility in these lipoids There is, however, considerable evidence against this view that lipoids are in all cases the chief or only factors concerned. Still another hypothesis is that the selective capacity of the membrane depends in one way or another upon its colloid condition It may well be that many different factors are involved in the permeability of membranes in living organisms, but it seems certain that whatever the nature of these factors may prove to be, the peculiarities of the so-called living substance in this respect are very closely connected with its colloid condition. And when we recall the slight diffusibility of colloids through each other, it becomes evident that the colloid condition of the substratum is an important factor in determining the accumulation and localization of colloids themselves.

It has been shown that various inorganic colloids, such for example as colloid platinum, resemble to some extent in their action as catalyzers the enzymes or ferments of the organism. All the known organic enzymes are apparently colloids, and while there is still difference of opinion as to the nature of their action, yet the resemblance between them and inorganic catalyzers is at least highly suggestive.[1] We know that enzymes are absolutely essential factors in the processes of life, and if enzyme action is in any way associated with the colloid condition the significance of this condition for organic life will be still further demonstrated.

[1] See Bredig, '01; Hober, '11, pp. 553–614.

The transmission of stimuli in living tissues is also very commonly regarded as dependent in some way upon the colloid condition, although here again there are differences of opinion as to the exact nature of the process

Our knowledge of the colloids and particularly of the organic colloids is far from complete, undoubtedly the future will clear up many points which are now obscure, but even now it is clear that the colloid substratum in which the chemical reactions of metabolism occur is an essential factor in making the phenomena of life what they are. Bechhold ('12), referring to the possibility of life on other planets, asserts that whatever the substances may be which make up such organisms they must be colloids   In fact, the more we know concerning colloids the less possible it becomes to conceive of anything similar to what we regard as life apart from them. Whatever else it may be, it seems certain that the organism is a colloid system.   From this point of view our definition of a living organism must be somewhat as follows: A living organism is a specific complex of dynamic changes occurring in a specific colloid substratum which is itself a product of such changes and which influences their course and character and is altered by them

THE RELATION BETWEEN STRUCTURE AND FUNCTION

The definition of the organism given above leads us to very definite conclusions concerning the relation between structure and function.

The dynamic processes which occur in organisms do not and cannot constitute life in the absence of the colloid substratum, nor is the colloid substratum alive without the dynamic processes. But since the colloids characteristic of the organism are among the products of the dynamic processes, it is also evident that the processes cannot go on in their entirety without producing the colloid substratum.   In other words, neither structure nor function is conceivable except in relation to each other.

The beginning of life is to be sought neither in a particular complex of chemical reactions nor in a special morphological structure.   Both the reactions and the colloid substratum are necessary for life.   But since the substratum is formed in the course of the reactions, it is evident that the association between the reaction-complex and the substratum must continue as long as the reaction-complex continues. It is probable that if we could duplicate the reaction-complex in the laboratory it would be impossible to designate any particular point in the process as the point where life begins. Life is not any particular reaction nor any particular substance, but a great system of processes and substances. Structure and function are then indissociable. And yet in the broad sense function produces structure and structure modifies function. At first glance it may appear that this relation is quite unique, that nothing like it exists in the inorganic world. As a matter of fact, however, the same relation exists everywhere in dynamic systems in nature

Various authors have from time to time compared the organism with one or another inorganic system Roux ('05), for example, has carried out in some detail the comparison between the organism and the flame. Although this analogy contains much that is valuable, especially on the chemical side, it is imperfect morphologically because the morphology of the flame is much less stable and persistent than that of the organism. Some years ago (Child, '11) I found the analogy between the organism and a flowing stream useful for purposes of illustration. While as regards metabolism the river is much more widely different from the organism than the flame, yet as regards the relation between structure and function there are certain resemblances between the two which are of value for the present purpose. Such analogies serve merely to call attention to certain points. The flow of water—the current of the stream—is the dynamic process and is comparable in a general way to the current of chemical energy flowing through the organism. On the other hand, the banks and bed of the stream represent the morphological features. Wherever such a system exists, certain characteristic developmental changes occur which, though much less definite and fixed in localization and character than in the organism, are nevertheless of such a nature that we can predict and control them.

Neither water alone nor the banks and bed alone constitute the system which we call a river; and in nature the banks and bed and the current have been associated from the beginning. Here also structure and function are connected as in the organism the configuration of the channel modifies the intensity and course of the current and the current in turn modifies the morphology of the channel by deposition at one point, giving rise to structures such as bars, islands, flats, and by erosion at another. And besides this, the river possesses a considerable capacity for self-regulation Where the channel is narrower the rate of flow is higher, and vice versa. A dam raises the level until equilibration results and the flow continues. It is of course true that only in the lower reaches does the river resemble the organism in the accumulation of structural material: over most of its course it is primarily an erosive agency It does, however, exhibit what we may call a physical metabolism on which its morphogenesis depends. The current carries certain materials and the character of these differs with the current. When the energy of the current is no longer able to carry them they are deposited and take part in the building up of structure. Certain materials are more readily carried by the stream than others, and these may be eliminated from the river and take no part in its morphogenesis

But the most important point for present purposes is that in the river, as in the organism, structure and function are indissociable and react upon each other. From the moment the current begins to flow it is a constructing agent, i e., it determines form along its channel, and from the same moment the structure already existing affects the flow of the current It is evident then that the relation between structure and function in the living organism is not fundamentally different from that in the flowing stream. Structure and function are indissociable and mutually determining as long as the river exists and the organism lives In a very interesting series of papers Warburg[1] has recently demonstrated the close interrelation between function and structure for the oxidation processes and the fundamental structure of the cell, the occurrence of the oxidations being very directly dependent upon the existence of the cell structure.

[1] Warburg, '12a, '12b, '13, '14a, '14b.

The living organism has often been compared to a machine made by man, such as the steam engine, which converts a part of the energy of the fuel into function as the organism transforms the energy of nutrition into functional activity. This analogy is a very imperfect one, for in the steam engine and in all other machines constructed by man structure and function are separable. Moreover, the man-made machine does not construct itself by its functional activity, but is completely passive as regards its construction, being built up by an agent external to itself for a definite purpose, and being unable to function until its structure is completed. The organism, on the other hand, functions from the beginning and constructs itself by its own functional activity; and the structure already present at any given time is a factor in determining the function, and the function at any given time is a factor in determining the future structure. The organism is then a very different thing from a man-made machine, and comparisons between the two are likely to lead to incorrect conclusions concerning the organism. The machine corresponds more closely to a fully developed morphological part of the organism which constitutes a definite functional mechanism. But the structure and function of such a part give us no conception of the organism as a whole and of its action as a constructive and activating agent.

The comparison between the living organism and the man-made machine completely ignores the relation between structure and function in the former. And any conception of the organism which does not take into account its ability to construct its own mechanism is very far from adequate. The whole living organism may be compared with the machine plus the constructing and activating agent, the intelligence that makes and runs it. It may appear at first glance that this view leads necessarily to the assumption that an intelligence more or less like that of man is concerned in the development of every organism. This, however, is far from being the case. In the broad sense, the man building and running a machine is an organism constructing a part with a definite functional mechanism which functions under the control of the whole.

If intelligence is a function of the human or any other organism, then the same laws must hold for its activity as for that of organisms

in general. The facts show clearly enough that different degrees
of intelligence exist in different organisms, and we cannot deny
that even the simple organisms show something remotely akin
to intelligence. On the other hand, many of the supposed fundamental differences between the organism and the inorganic world
have disappeared in the light of scientific investigation. But
even supposing that we shall some day demonstrate the essential
unity of the universe from the simplest inorganic system to the
highest organism, when that is done there is no reason to believe
that the real problem of teleology will be eliminated; it will doubtless still be before us as a problem concerned, not with any single
group of organisms, nor with all organisms, but with the world as a
whole. In other words, on the basis of such a conception there is
not merely an analogy but a fundamental similarity between the
river with its current and channel, the organism constructing itself
by its own functional activity, and the man constructing and
running a machine. And this remains true whatever the final
solution of the teleological problem.

But as the complex structure of the human organism and also
the machine which it has constructed have constituted essential
factors in the development of human intelligence, so also in other
organisms the approach to anything like intelligence in the broadest
sense is manifestly associated with the development of structure
The more complex the structure, particularly of the nervous system, the closer the approach to intelligence. This is again merely
a special case under the general relation between structure and
function: the more complex the structure the greater the possibilities of function Moreover, even in man a very complex
structure is developed before we can find any evidence of intelligence. In short, all the evidence along this line indicates that
anything which we are able to recognize as intelligence is not a
primary function of the organism, but one which becomes apparent
only in a highly complex structure. Just as clearly does the evidence indicate that there is no real break in the series between the
simplest morphogenetic activity of the organism and the man
building and controlling the machine. But because the man builds
and runs the machine with a definite purpose in mind, it does not

at all follow that a similar idea of purpose underlies morphogenesis, even though the dynamic processes may be more or less similar in both cases The foundations from which purposive action arises must be sought in the constitution of the world in general, but it does not follow that purposive action is everywhere present.

The various attempts made within recent years to interpret the organism in terms of memory (Semon, '04), behavior (Schultz, '10, '12), entelechy (Driesch, '08), or other more or less psychological or teleological terms, are interesting to every biologist, if only as indications of a reaction from theories current a few years ago, but they rather obscure than illuminate the problem. More-over, purposive action and intelligence in various degrees of complexity are all features of organic life, but any attempt to show that they are fundamental or universal features is, to say the least, premature and merely a matter of personal opinion. The close association between complexity of structure and complexity of behavior in organisms should lead us to search for terms common to both, rather than to attempt to translate either into terms of the other.

REFERENCES

BECHHOLD, H.
    1912. *Die Colloide in Biologie und Medezin.* Dresden.
BREDIG, G
    1901 *Anorganische Fermente.* Leipzig.
CHILD, C. M.
    1911 "A Study of Senescence and Rejuvenescence Based on Experiments with Planarians," *Arch. f. Entwickelungsmech.,* XXXI
DRIESCH, H.
    1901. *Die organischen Regulationen.* Leipzig
    1908 *The Science and Philosophy of the Organism.* London.
FREUNDLICH, H.
    1909. *Kapillarchemie.* Leipzig.
GRAHAM, T.
    1861. "Liquid Diffusion Applied to Analysis," *Phil. Trans ,* CLI.
HOBER, R.
    1911. *Physikalische Chemie der Zelle und der Gewebe.* Dritte Auflage. Leipzig.
KUSTER, E
    1913. *Über Zonenbildung in kolloidalen Medien.* Jena

LEDUC, S.

    1908   "Essais de biologie synthétique," *Biochem Zeitschr*, Festband fur H J Hamburger

    1909a. *Les Croissances osmotiques et l'origine des êtres vivantes.* Bar-le-Duc

    1909b. "Les bases physiques de la vie et la biogenèse," *Presse medicale*, VII.

    1910. *Théorie physico-chimique de la vie.* Paris

LIESEGANG, R E

    1909   *Beitrage zu einer Kolloidchemie des Lebens.* Dresden.

    1911.   "Nachahmung von Lebensvorgangen I, Stoffverkehr, bestimmt gerichtetes Wachstum; II, Zur Entwicklungsmechanik des Epithels," *Arch f. Entwickelungsmech.*, XXXII

    1914   "Eine neue Art gestaltender Wirkung von chemischen Ausscheidungen," *Arch. f. Entwickelungsmech.*, XXXIX.

MATHEWS, A P

    1899.   "The Changes in Structure of the Pancreas Cell," *Jour. of Morph.*, XV (Supplement).

    1905.   "A Theory of the Nature of Protoplasmic Respiration and Growth," *Biol. Bull*, VIII.

OSTWALD, WOLFGANG.

    1912   *Grundriss der Kolloidchemie.* Dresden.

PFLÜGER, E. F. W

    1875   "Über die physiologische Verbrennung in den lebendigen Organismen," *Arch. f d. ges Physiol*, X

RIGNANO, E

    1906   *Sur la Trasmissibilité des caractères acquis: Hypothèse d'une centroépigénèse* Paris

ROUX, W.

    1905   "Die Entwickelungsmechanik ein neuer Zweig der biologischen Wissenschaft," *Vortr. und Aufs u Entwickelungsmech*, I

SCHULTZ, E

    1910   *Prinzipien der rationellen vergleichenden Embryologie.* Leipzig.

    1912   "Über Periodizität und Reize bei einigen Entwicklungsvorgängen," *Vortr. und Aufs u Entwickelungsmech*, XIV.

SEMON, R.

    1904   *Die Mneme als erhaltendes Prinzip im Wechsel des organischen Geschehens.* Leipzig.

VERWORN, M.

    1903.   *Die Biogenhypothese* Jena

WARBURG, O.
  1912a. "Untersuchungen uber die Oxydationsprozesse in Zellen II,"
     Munchener med Wochenschr., LVIII.
  1912b. "Über Bezichungen zwischen Zellstruktur und biochemischen
     Reaktionen," *Arch. f. d. ges. Physiol*, CXLV.
  1913. *Über die Wirkung der Struktur auf chemische Vorgange in Zellen*
     Jena.
  1914. "Über die Empfindlichkeit der Sauerstoffatmung gegenüber in-
     differenten Narkotika," *Arch. f d. ges. Physiol.*, CLVIII
  1914b. "Beitrage zur Physiologie der Zelle, insbesondere uber die Oxyda-
     tionsgeschwindigkeit in Zellen," *Ergebn. d. Physiol*, XIV
ZANGGER, H.
  1908. "Über Membranen und Membranfunktion," *Ergebn. d. Phy-
     siol*, VII.

CHAPTER II

THE LIFE CYCLE

GROWTH AND REDUCTION

Definitions of growth and reduction.—One of the most characteristic and striking features of the living organism is its ability to add to its own substance. In most organisms an enormous increase in size and weight occurs during the earlier part of the life cycle. This is commonly known as growth. But different authorities are not entirely agreed as to what constitutes growth. The differences of opinion seem to center chiefly about the question whether growth consists simply in increase in size, or whether change in form is the essential feature. Davenport,[1] following Huxley and others, defines organic growth as increase in volume The plant physiologist Pfeffer ('01), on the other hand, says that in general all formative processes which lead to a permanent change of form are to be regarded as growth. Most authorities have regarded the addition of material, or of certain kinds of material, or the increase in size as the essential feature of growth To make change of form the basis of growth is certainly a wide departure from the commonly accepted meaning of the word, and also fails, I think, to recognize the significance of accumulation of material in the organism. Increase in size or the addition of material may occur without appreciable change in form, and change in form may occur without increase in size or amount of material, and most of those who have attempted to define growth have recognized this fact The capacity of the organism to add to its own substance and to increase in size is evidently closely connected with the fundamental processes of metabolism, and even organisms which do not undergo appreciable changes of form do nevertheless grow in the usual sense of the word.

But any consideration of the problem of growth which does not take into account the process of reduction is incomplete Under the usual conditions of existence the healthy active organism is not

[1] In Davenport's *Experimental Morphology* ('97, pp. 281–82) a number of the definitions of growth which have been given are cited.

only adding new material, but is at the same time breaking down and eliminating material previously accumulated The total result as regards size or bulk is simply the difference between the two processes. Some of the substances accumulated within the organism break down less rapidly than others, but even such substances may be more or less completely removed In the more complex organisms also some of the substances of the substratum are apparently more stable, i e., inactive chemically, under physiological conditions, and the processes of breakdown are therefore less conspicuous as a factor in the total result than in the simpler forms. Under conditions where the breakdown of material overbalances the increment, as for example in starvation, the higher organisms soon die with a considerable portion of their substance intact, but in many of the simpler forms the material previously accumulated serves to a large extent as a source of energy and the organism remains alive and active, but undergoes reduction until it represents only a minute fraction of its original size Various species of the flatworm *Planaria* may undergo reduction from a length of twenty-five or thirty millimeters (Fig. 1) to a length of three or four millimeters (Fig. 2) with a corresponding change in other proportions before they die, and many others among the simpler organisms are capable of undergoing great reduction without death Since the addition of material and increase in size play a much more conspicuous part in the life of organisms in nature, and particularly in the higher organisms, than do the reductional processes, it has come about that the term growth has usually been applied to the incremental, or productive, factors, and the significance of reduction in the life cycle has scarcely been considered.

Various authors have laid stress upon the permanency of the changes involved in growth. As a matter of fact, these changes are not necessarily permanent, although they are more stable in the higher than in the lower organisms. To say that growth consists in permanent increase in volume or change of form is to ignore entirely the phenomena of reduction which are, it is true, most striking in the lower organisms, but which may occur to some extent in all.

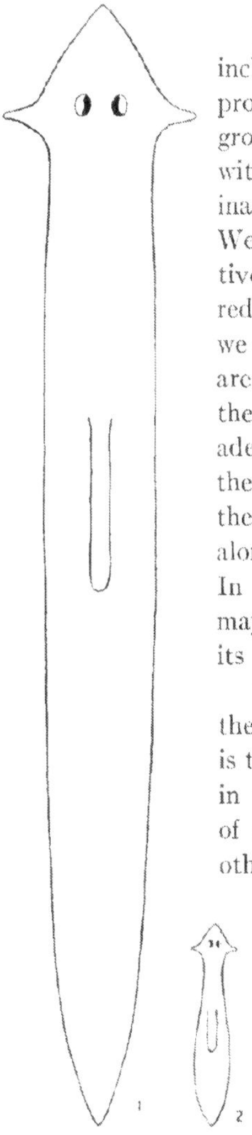

Logically our definition of growth might well include both positive and negative growth, or production and reduction, but since the word growth has come to be so generally associated with an increase in substance it is perhaps inadvisable to attempt to change its meaning. We may then retain the word growth for positive growth or production, and use the term reduction for negative growth. But in so doing we must not forget that both these processes are in the broad sense, though not necessarily in the chemical sense, reversible, and that any adequate conception of the relation between the substratum and the dynamic processes in the organism must be based, not on growth alone, but upon both growth and reduction. In other words, the activity of the organism may either increase or decrease the amount of its substance according to conditions.

The question has often been raised whether the increase in the water-content of the organism is to be regarded as growth, or only the increase in the structural substance. Some definitions of growth have taken the one view, some the other, but if water is included among the substances concerned in growth we have then to determine whether increase in water-content is in all cases to be regarded as growth, or whether we shall make a distinction between growth and passive distension due to external factors. Here again views differ. As a matter of fact, various investigators have shown that the imbibition of water is a very characteristic feature during at least certain stages of what we are accustomed to call growth: on the other hand, loss of water is a

FIGS. 1, 2.—*Planaria dorotocephala:* Fig. 1, a well-fed animal 25 mm. in length; Fig. 2, an animal reduced by starvation from 25 to 4 mm.

characteristic feature of certain other stages of the life cycle Moreover, there is evidence that water is produced by chemical action in the organism (Babcock, '12), and it is a familiar fact that water is absolutely essential to life

But an adequate definition of organic growth must also take account of the fact that it is a process of the living organism A passive distension of the organism or any part of it by water or other substances, or a passive loss of water, is not properly growth or reduction, because it is not due to the activity of the organism or part.

If we admit then, first, that organic growth and reduction consist essentially in changes in the amount of substance, secondly, that water as well as other substances may be involved in growth, and thirdly, that growth is a process of the living organism, our definitions of growth and reduction must read somewhat as follows: organic growth is an increase, organic reduction a decrease, in the amount of the substance of a living organism or part, resulting directly or indirectly from its specific metabolic activity This definition does not any more than others avoid all difficulties, for sharp lines of distinction do not necessarily exist in natural phenomena Whether we call a certain process growth or not must often depend upon whether we are considering the whole organism or a part; moreover, it is impossible to separate the activity of the organism completely from external factors.

Although growth in its simplest terms consists in large measure in the synthesis of proteid molecules, it is evident that growth is not always the same chemical process Under different conditions different proteid molecules may be formed, and very often growth results from the synthesis of various substances other than proteids. Recent investigations seem to indicate that from the point of view of nutrition growth in recovery from starvation is not the same as developmental growth with continuous feeding and that growth in adult life is not the same as growth during youth[1] Doubtless many other differences will appear as investigation proceeds, but there seems at present to be no adequate reason for limiting the

[1] See the papers by Osborne and Mendel, in the references appended to chap xi, particularly the recent general discussion of the subject by Mendel ('14)

term growth to one or the other of the particular processes as some authors incline to do. Growth results primarily from the ability of the cell to synthesize certain substances which, once formed, remain as relatively permanent constituents of the cell. Under different conditions the nutritive substances necessary, the course of synthesis, and the substances formed must differ widely, but growth is a complex organic process rather than this or that particular chemical reaction.

The nature of growth and reduction —The question why the organism grows is one of great interest, and while we cannot at present answer it fully, we can at least reach certain provisional conclusions. On the basis of the chemical hypothesis of the labile proteid molecule, growth remains a mystery. We cannot conceive how these labile molecules are able to build up others like themselves. Reduction, however, is readily enough accounted for as the result of breakdown of the labile molecules. But if we regard the organism as a complex of reactions in a colloid substratum, the problem of growth assumes a different form and is open to attack. Certain aspects of the problem require brief consideration from this point of view.

The reversibility of the growth process leads us at once to ask whether or to what extent reversible chemical reactions are concerned. If we could regard growth and reduction as the two terms of a reversible chemical reaction it would simplify our conceptions very greatly. Unfortunately, however, this seems to be impossible. Reversible chemical reactions are undoubtedly concerned in the synthesis and breakdown of the various molecules which make up protoplasm, but the growth-reduction process is something more than such a reaction. Apparently the course of synthesis and of breakdown and the character of the end products may differ widely. Many or all of the component reactions in growth and reduction may be reversible, but it does not by any means follow that reduction is a reversal in the chemical sense of growth. During a considerable part of life under the usual conditions the synthesis of certain substances overbalances their breakdown, they accumulate in the organism, and growth occurs. Evidently conditions in the organism are such that certain substances once formed are not as readily or as rapidly decomposed and eliminated.

It is evident that synthesis of proteid molecules is a factor of great importance in growth, since proteids form the chief constituents of protoplasm, but there is no reason to believe, as various authorities have maintained, that the metabolic process consists wholly or chiefly in the synthesis and decomposition of proteid molecules All the facts indicate that much of the energy of the organism comes from substances other than proteids, and that proteid synthesis is only one of many chemical transformations occurring in the organism.

Moreover, according to physico-chemical laws, the accumulation of colloids and other substances as a substratum in the organism or in the cell must depend upon what we may call their physiological stability A physiologically stable substance is one which, when once formed, cannot readily escape from the living cell or organism under the existing conditions, unless it undergoes chemical change, and which, under the usual physiological conditions, does not undergo this change or undergoes it less readily than other substances. Physiological stability depends then, not only on the constitution of the substance concerned, but also and probably to a large extent on the conditions to which it is subjected. Different substances differ in stability under the same conditions, and the same substance may differ very greatly in stability under different conditions. Moreover, physiological stability does not necessarily imply complete chemical stability There is good reason to believe that many substances in the cell are undergoing more or less continuous partial chemical breakdown and reconstitution, but so long as they do not undergo complete breakdown and elimination they constitute parts of the cell which are relatively stable physiologically. In most plants, for example, proteid molecules once formed never undergo decomposition to the point where the nitrogen which they contain is eliminated in any form, yet there can be no doubt that these proteids, or some of them, take part in the chemical reactions within the cell and that their molecules are often partially decomposed and reconstituted They are then physiologically, though not necessarily chemically, stable constituents of the plant cell

The visible substratum of the organism, i e , the protoplasm, must consist fundamentally of such physiologically stable substances, for if this were not the case we should have merely a system of chemical reactions, and no permanency of form or structure could exist. Theoretically, at least, a distinction must be made between the substratum of the cell or organism and the substances which are decomposed and eliminated and which constitute the source of energy. Practically, however, such a distinction cannot be clearly made in most cases, for physiological stability is relative rather than absolute and it is impossible to say in a given case to what extent the substratum is itself involved in the chemical reactions. Still it is evident that the substances which accumulate within the cell under given conditions as its visible or structural substratum must be in general and under the existing conditions less subject to decomposition into eliminable form than those substances which undergo breakdown and elimination.

The organic colloids are in general physiologically stable substances When once formed within the cells they do not diffuse readily and cannot ordinarily escape except as they are decomposed into eliminable substances. We know from studies of the metabolism of the higher animals and from the amount of nitrogen-containing food which is necessary for maintenance that in these forms at least the breakdown of proteid molecules into completely eliminable form constitutes only a fraction of the metabolic process at any given time Moreover, some of the nitrogenous substances excreted may come from proteids of the food which have been decomposed without forming a part of the substratum of the cells Undoubtedly also many chemical changes occur in the colloid substratum which involve merely the transformation or exchange of certain chemical groups and not the complete disruption of the molecule Chemical changes of this sort do not necessarily involve the disintegration of the substratum as a whole, and it is probable that cellular structures are often the seat of such changes without undergoing any conspicuous morphological change.

The fact that emulsoid colloids and particularly proteids are the fundamental constituents of the substratum of living organisms is a necessary consequence, first, of the formation of these substances ın the course of the reactions which constitute metabolism, and, secondly, of their physico-chemical properties. The substratum once formed in the course of chemical reactions affords a basis for the continuation of the reactions and for the further addition of colloids. So far as the metabolic reactions are enzyme reactions, the structural substratum of the organism must consist of the substances which for one reason or another are less susceptible to enzyme action than other substances which are transformed without forming a part of the structure.

According to this view the colloid substratum and the morphological structure of the organism represent, so to speak, the sediment from the metabolic process. They are, in short, by-products of the reactions which do not readily escape from the cell unless they undergo decomposition and which are relatively stable Therefore they must constitute the more permanent constituents of the cell and appear as a visible substratum or more or less permanent structure of some sort   The constitution of the structural substratum developed in different organisms differs because the metabolic processes and the substratum already existing at the beginning of development differ. The visible organism is then the sediment left behind by the metabolic current: ıt consists of the substances which the current is unable to carry farther.   It does not represent life any more than the sand-bar represents the river; it ıs simply a product of past activıty which may ınfluence future activity.   Sixty years ago Huxley said concerning the cells: "They are no more the producers of the vital phenomena than the shells scattered along the sea-beach are the instruments by which the gravitative force of the moon acts upon the ocean   Like these, the cells mark only where the vital tıdes have been and how they have acted" (Huxley, '53)   And yet since Huxley's words were written how many attempts have been made either to show that this or that structural element of the organism represents something fundamental to life or to translate the phenomena of life into terms of an invisible hypothetical structure[1]

The visible structural features of the organic substratum possess very different degrees of stabılity: some are evanescent, while others persist throughout the life of the cell in which they arise.

This is true, not only as regards the different structures in a cell, but also as regards different cells of an organism, and the cells of different organisms. Many of the more or less evanescent structural appearances in protoplasm are perhaps nothing more than visible indications of differences in the aggregations of the colloid. The more highly aggregated portions, which form more or less dense colloid gels, appear as more or less definite structures, the less aggregated portions as indefinitely granular, alveolar, or fluid   But even in such cases the denser portions of the protoplasm are probably for the time being less subject to chemical change than the more fluid portions because of their physical condition. It is evident, however, that many of the more permanent structural features result from the accumulation in the cell of specific substances which possess a relatively high degree of physiological stability under the existing conditions   But there is little doubt that in at least most organic structures which are not mere inclosures in the protoplasm or extra-cellular secretions a greater or less degree of chemical breakdown, of degradation of the structural substance, is more or less constantly occurring while life continues   In some cases this may be very slight in amount or may involve only certain components, in others it may involve the whole structural basis of the organ or organism. When the conditions are such that the new material added exceeds in amount that undergoing breakdown, growth occurs, but when the rate of breakdown exceeds that of accumulation, reduction is the result

According to the theory of the labile proteid molecule, functional activity results primarily from the breakdown of the structural substratum itself, or at least of its proteid constituents. But if the substratum consists of comparatively stable by-products of metabolism, as the facts seem to indicate, then it is clear that the energy of functional activity must ordinarily come chiefly from other sources, i e , from the breakdown of other substances which do not constitute an essential structural part of the protoplasm. Under the usual conditions the structural substratum is probably to a large extent a field in which the reactions occur rather than the reacting substance or substances, but in the absence of other nutritive substances, i.e., in starvation, it may itself become the chief source of energy, especially in the lower animals As already pointed out, different constituents of the substratum show very different degrees of stability, some being evanescent and disappearing at once with slight change in conditions, while others once formed persist for a long time or through life It is therefore impossible to distinguish sharply between what constitutes the substratum and what does not We can only say that the substratum consists in general of more stable substances than those which do not appear in it

As our knowledge of the great complex of reactions which we call metabolism increases, it becomes more and more evident that the different reactions of the complex are not entirely independent of each other, but constitute a reaction system In this system the oxidations appear to be the most important or dominant factor, the independent variable, as Loeb and Wasteneys ('11) express it, upon which the other reactions depend more or less closely. Rate of oxidation is a more fundamental factor in growth than the amount of nutritive material in excess of a certain minimum From this point of view the term "metabolism" loses some of its vagueness It is not simply a hodgepodge of chemical reactions in which now one, now another, component is most conspicuous, as external conditions change, but rather an orderly correlated series of events in which certain reactions play the leading rôles. The rate or character of component reactions may change very widely with external conditions, but nevertheless the reaction system retains in general certain definite characteristics and the relation between its component reactions persists. Anabolism and katabolism, the synthesis and the breakdown of the substance of organisms, are not independent processes, but the syntheses are apparently associated with, and in greater or less degree dependent in some way upon, the oxidations

From this point of view functional hypertrophy loses its peculiar character It is not in any sense a "regeneration in excess" or an "over-compensation," as it is so generally assumed to be, but is simply the result of increased metabolism in the presence of an adequate nutritive supply. Increased metabolism under these conditions means increased production of structural substances

The organism does not construct itself *for* function as the vitalistic and chemical theories maintain: it constructs itself *by* function.

When the supply of nutritive material from without is insufficient, the previously accumulated structural material may serve as a source of energy to a much greater extent than when nutritive material is present in excess, and under these conditions the new structural material, if any is formed, may be insufficient to cover the loss and reduction results. Such reduction may involve the whole organism to a greater or less extent, as in the flatworms and other simple animals, or it may involve only or chiefly certain parts, but in all cases we find that some parts or substances are involved to a greater extent than others. In a starving flatworm, for example, certain organs may disappear entirely before death occurs, while others retain more nearly their usual proportions. Much has been made of this fact in a teleological sense (see, for example, E. Schultz, '04), and it has been repeatedly pointed out that the organs least affected are those most essential to the life of the organism. But a teleological interpretation seems to be quite unnecessary. In general it is very evidently the case that those organs which are most constantly, most frequently, or most intensely active in the life of the organism undergo least reduction during starvation. There is some reason to believe that the structural substratum of the cells of such organs is more stable than that of cells which possess in general a low rate of metabolism. The nervous system undergoes least reduction during starvation, and during the earlier stages of development it certainly has the highest metabolic rate of any part of the body, and in many cases, if not in all, this condition persists throughout life. Furthermore, during the later stages of life its special functional activity is certainly almost if not quite continuous. In such organs energy must be derived to a much greater extent from nutritive substances than from the substratum of the cells itself. Consequently, during starvation their losses are less and are more completely repaired than in organs where the substratum is less stable. Thus the more active and therefore the more persistent organs maintain themselves largely at the expense of other less active parts in which the degradation of the structural substratum occurs more readily.

And it is these more continuously or more intensely active organs which are more essential to life. But according to this view they undergo less reduction in starvation, not because they are more essential in life, but because they are more active.

Reduction in an organ or part may also occur when conditions change so that a decrease in the average rate of its metabolism below a certain level occurs and synthesis of structural substances does not compensate the gradual loss. The atrophy of organs from disuse is a case in point. And, finally, reduction may occur in a part when the correlative conditions which were an essential factor for its continued existence as a part undergo change. In such cases it is difficult to determine whether the change in metabolism is primarily qualitative or quantitative. In the lower organisms extensive reduction of this kind occurs when pieces are isolated and undergo reconstitution. Previously existing organs may be reduced and disappear and others be formed anew. In the higher organisms such processes of reduction are narrowly limited.

If we accept the general conception of growth and reduction here outlined, then it is no longer necessary to assume the existence of a mysterious growth-impulse which gradually decreases in intensity during development, for growth is primarily the accumulation of certain substances formed in the course of the metabolic reactions which are physiologically more stable than other substances that break down, furnish energy, and are eliminated. Reduction occurs when the breakdown and elimination of the cell substance is not balanced by the synthesis of new substance. Some such conception of growth and reduction seems to be forced upon us by the facts, for certainly there is every reason to believe that the different constituent substances of the cell show very different degrees of stability and that the stability of a given substance may differ with different conditions. Organic growth remains a complete mystery unless certain fundamental constituents of protoplasm are relatively stable under the conditions of their production in the cell.

DIFFERENTIATION AND DEDIFFERENTIATION

Differentiation—The process of development in the organism is also a process of differentiation, of apparent complication, but we find that differences in reaction or in capacity to react very commonly exist in different parts even before visible differentiation occurs, or in cases where it never occurs. The term "specification" is often used for these differences which appear only in physiological activity, and "differentiation" for the visible structural differences. The distinction is of course arbitrary, for the visible differences result from differences in physiological activity An orderly sequence of differentiation during development is characteristic of at least all except the very simplest organisms and probably in these also some degree of differentiation exists.

In its biological sense the term "differentiation" is purely descriptive: broadly speaking, differentiation includes all perceptible changes in structure or behavior from the primitive embryonic or "undifferentiated" condition, which occur either in the cells or parts of an organism during its developmental history, or in different organisms in the course of evolution. It is, in short, a becoming different, but since the process of becoming different in cells and organisms is a change from a generalized to a specialized condition—a progressive development of particular kinds of structure and activity in different parts of the whole—differentiation in organisms is a process of specialization.

The problem of differentiation has long been one of the great biological problems Biological thought has always been divided upon the question of preformation versus epigenesis. To what extent does the differentiation of the fully developed organism actually exist as something preformed in the germ, so that development is strictly an unfolding, a becoming visible, of what already exists, and to what extent is there a real increase in complexity during development? The corpuscular theories are an attempt to answer the question from the point of view of preformation, but they, like the vitalistic theories, succeed merely in placing the problem beyond the reach of investigation It is evident that if the organism is a physico-chemical system, at least some differentiations must arise in the course of development. The adult organism is represented, not in the morphological structure nor in the physical and chemical changes of the reproductive cell or cell-mass, but rather in its capacities. The experimental investigation of recent years has shown that different degrees of differentiation exist in different reproductive cells, but has not afforded any real support to the view that the morphological characters of the adult are represented in some way by distinct entities in the germ [1] But even if we admit that organic differentiation is, at least to a large extent, an epigenetic process, the real problem still remains The orderly and definite character of the process, the variety of structural features, and their apparent adaptation to the function which they are to perform, all combine to render the problem one of the greatest interest and significance

At present, however, it must suffice to call attention only to certain aspects of the problem In the first place, in so far as differentiation is really a progressive or epigenetic process, it must depend on changes of some sort in the dynamic processes in different regions of the developing organism. We know that differentiation in its specific features is to a large extent independent of external conditions; therefore the internal conditions must determine these changes. And this brings us to the important question: How can such localized differences in the dynamic processes arise in the developing organism? The corpuscular theories have accustomed us to regard different morphological parts of the organism as qualitatively different, and it is evident that in many cases they are, but it does not necessarily follow that the qualitative differences are primary, or that all differentiations are qualitative It is a well-known fact that quantitative differences in the conditions existing in a chemical reaction may result in qualitatively different products, and this is demonstrated for many reactions which occur in the metabolic complex It cannot then be doubted that qualitative differences may result from quantitative differences in the processes occurring in the organism. We also know that many morphological differences are differences of size, shape, or quantity of some

[1] In view of the present vogue of the factorial hypothesis among investigators in the field of genetics, and particularly of certain attempts to apply it to the chromosomes, such a statement may appear to many as at least unwarranted, if not incorrect The factorial hypothesis, however, does not necessarily involve the assumption of factors as distinct entities in the germ, and the attempts to connect particular factors with particular chromosomes or parts of chromosomes are not at present, properly speaking, scientific hypotheses.

other kind, which are not necessarily qualitative in any sense. And, finally, we are able to determine experimentally the development of very different morphological characters by changes in conditions which affect primarily the rate and not the character of the metabolic reactions (Child, '11). To what extent quantitative differences in the dynamic processes actually serve as a basis for specialization and differentiation we do not know, although it is certain that they are a much more important factor than most biologists have been accustomed to believe.

But, supposing that quantitative or qualitative differences arise or exist in different regions of the developing organism, how can they persist in a substance of the physical consistency of protoplasm? It is here that the colloid condition of the substratum plays a very important part   The organic colloids with their slight diffusibility, their effect on the diffusion of other substances, their viscosity and differences of aggregate condition, afford possibilities for the localization as well as the origination of different processes which do not exist in any other known medium   The experiments on the production of form and structure by means of chemical reactions in a colloid substratum outside the organism demonstrate how readily even complex morphological features may arise under such conditions, and in such cases we are often able to analyze the process of differentiation.   We have then in the colloid substratum a real basis for differentiation, and the problem of morphogenesis becomes accessible to scientific investigation and analysis, instead of being merely restated in terms of some "vitalistic" principle or of determinants or other ultimate units.

The embryonic or undifferentiated cell is distinguishable from the specialized or differentiated cell rather by the absence than by the presence of definite morphological features   It represents the cell of the species reduced to its simplest morphological terms, consisting essentially of nucleus and relatively homogenous cytoplasm.[1]   It is of course true that cells which are not morphologically

[1] Embryonic cells are shown in Fig 113 (p 285), and in the smaller cells of Fig. 187 (p. 347), and in Fig. 194, *em* (p. 348).   Cells which are embryonic in appearance are represented more or less diagrammatically in various other figures, e.g., Figs 71–74 (pp. 206, 208) and Fig. 192, *pc* (p. 348).

different in any visible way may show themselves by their behavior to be physiologically different, so that the absence of visible differentiation in the cell is not proof that the cell is completely unspecialized.

The substance of the undifferentiated cell is the general metabolic substratum of the organism, and it is the chemical or physical transformations of this substratum, or the addition of substances to it, that constitutes morphological differentiation. Physiological differentiation consists in the progressive development of certain activities at the expense of others.

While we know too little at present of the nature of the various metabolic processes and of the relation between metabolism and the cellular substratum to permit us to reach positive conclusions concerning the nature of differentiation, the facts at hand suggest certain probabilities. In the first place the embryonic cell very evidently has in general a higher metabolic rate, or capacity for a higher rate, independent of external stimulation, than do differentiated cells. Apparently the mere continuation of life in the cell without cell division brings about changes which decrease the metabolic rate Such changes may conceivably result from gradual atomic rearrangements or from changes in aggregate condition of the colloids. It is a well-known fact that emulsoid sols outside the organism undergo slow changes in the direction of coagulation, even when kept under as nearly as possible constant conditions, and there is good reason to believe that similar changes occur in the colloids of the living organism. In the coagulation of proteids by high temperatures time is a factor, i.e , the occurrence of coagulation depends, not only upon the actual temperature, but on the time of exposure to it: the lower the temperature, the longer the time necessary to bring about perceptible coagulation From the character of this relation between time of exposure and temperature it is inferred that, theoretically, coagulation must occur at all temperatures above the freezing-point of the sol, its rate being infinitely slow at low temperatures and increasing rapidly as the temperature rises. The fact that coagulation changes do occur slowly in colloid sols at ordinary room temperatures supports this view. Lepeschkin ('12) has found that the relation between temperature, time of exposure, and occurrence of coagulation as indicated by death is the same in living plant cells as in proteid sols outside the organism, and he therefore concludes that the protoplasmic sol is slowly undergoing changes in the direction of coagulation even at temperatures where continued life is possible If this view is correct, then a slow increase in aggregation is occurring continuously in protoplasm, but the formation of new sol and the gradual chemical breakdown of the older partially coagulated substance may serve to delay the final result for a long time, or indefinitely.

The accumulation and apparent gelification of protoplasm in the course of growth and differentiation suggest that changes of this sort are characteristic of the developmental history of all organisms. If this is true, they must result in increasing physiological stability of the protoplasm or parts of it, and so lead to decrease in the rate of metabolism, and the decrease in metabolic rate may in time lead to changes in the character of the metabolic complex and so to further changes in structure which may again alter metabolic conditions, and so on

It is probable then that mere continued existence may in many cases result in gradual progressive changes in protoplasm which become evident sooner or later as some degree and kind of differentiation   Such a process is a self-differentiation in the strictest sense. Its occurrence or non-occurrence must depend upon the absence or presence of changes which balance or compensate in some way the progressive changes, and these are the changes which lead to dedifferentiation (see following section).

Where all cells or parts are alike, self-differentiation must produce the same result in all, but where differences of any sort exist, such, for example, as differences in metabolic rate between external surface and interior or between other parts, then the different parts may influence each other and differentiation becomes a correlative process which may result in the production of many different parts. In correlative differentiation the parts may influence each other in various ways   Dynamic changes of one kind or another may be transmitted from one part to another; quantitative or qualitative differences in the chemical substances produced by different parts may affect the course of metabolism in other parts, and differences in the rate of growth of different parts may produce mechanical effects. Since the action of external factors is variable, both in time and in space, it is impossible for a cell or cell-mass to exist for any considerable length of time under natural conditions without local differences of some sort, temporary or permanent, quantitative or qualitative, appearing in it in consequence of the differential action of external factors

Differentiation of some degree and kind is then a necessary and inevitable result of continued existence except where the progressive changes are balanced or compensated in some way, and we must distinguish self-determining, correlative, and external factors in the process   In general, as I have pointed out above, the gradual accumulation and increase in physiological stability of the protoplasm, either through change in chemical constitution or aggregate condition or both, is self-determined and results from the nature of metabolism and the constitution of protoplasm, while the correlative and external factors play a part in determining the character of the structural substratum thus produced

The process of differentiation once initiated, each step becomes a factor bringing about further changes. For example, the character of the substances accumulated in a cell seems to depend to a greater or less extent upon the conditions in the cell which affect metabolic rate, such as aggregate condition of protoplasm, enzyme activity, etc   In embryonic, undifferentiated cells, where the internal conditions permit a high metabolic rate, only those substances which form the general metabolic substratum, i e , protoplasm, remain as constituents of the cell, but as the self-determined metabolic rate decreases, other substances begin to appear and remain in the cell.   Undifferentiated protoplasm is protoplasm reduced morphologically to its lowest terms. Apparently the metabolic rate in the cell, or the internal conditions on which the metabolic rate depends, are factors in determining the physiological stability of substances.   Substances which are either not formed or are broken down and eliminated after formation in cells with a high metabolic rate appear as more or less permanent structural components in cells with a lower rate. As the self-determined metabolic

rate decreases, new features appear as relatively stable components of the structural substratum, and these become factors in
further changes.   Probably also substances which were sufficiently
stable physiologically to become components of the structural substratum at the higher metabolic rate become more stable as the
metabolic rate decreases, not necessarily because of changes in
themselves, but because of the decrease in rate, or the conditions
which determine it.   Thus the visible substratum of the cells
becomes more and more altered from its original condition, and
apparently the farther these changes go the less the ability of the
cell to synthesize protoplasm—i e , the general metabolic substratum of the organism—and the less "protoplasmic" does its
structure become.

   The non-protoplasmic substances which appear in the cell,
either in definite morphological form or as granules, droplets, or
inclosures in the protoplasm, have very commonly been grouped
together under the head of metaplasm   Kassowitz ('99), for example, makes a sharp distinction between protoplasm and metaplasm and believes that only the accumulation of the latter is
responsible for decrease in metabolic rate in the cell   The distinction is doubtless of value theoretically, but practically it is impossible to say what is protoplasm and what is metaplasm.   And
there can be no doubt that the so-called metaplasmic substances
often take more or less part in the metabolic activity of the
cell instead of being inactive, as Kassowitz and others have
maintained.   It seems therefore more in accord with the facts
to regard the cellular substratum as showing all gradations from
the purely protoplasmic condition of the embryonic cell to the
highly differentiated cell which may be loaded with substances
obviously non-protoplasmic in nature.

   Differentiation is very generally, though not necessarily, associated with growth.   It is probable that growth cannot proceed
very far without bringing about some degree of differentiation, for
the accumulation in the metabolic substratum of substance, whatever its nature, must result sooner or later in altering metabolic
conditions.   On the other hand. change in conditions external to a
cell or part may bring about differentiation without growth

According to the theory of differentiation developed here, the self-determined rate of metabolism of the cell must be to some extent an index of its degree of differentiation. This is to be expected, since the metabolic rate must depend upon the condition of the metabolic substratum. It is important to note that it is the metabolic rate, as determined by conditions existing within the cell independently of external stimulation, which is thus related to the degree of differentiation. Many highly differentiated cells with a low, self-determined metabolic rate are capable temporarily of a very high rate when stimulated from external sources. Such increases in rate are evidently the result of changes in the cellular substratum which are largely or wholly reversible. What their nature is we do not know certainly, although various theories of stimulation have been advanced. As differentiation proceeds beyond a certain stage, even the metabolic rate following stimulation decreases and the cell becomes less and less capable of performing its special function as a differentiated cell.

In general, a greater degree of differentiation of cells is one of the features which distinguish the so-called higher organisms from the lower. A comparison of the cells of higher and lower forms and of their course of differentiation seems to indicate very clearly that the physiological stability of the substratum must be greater even in the embryonic cells of the higher than in those of the lower forms in order to serve as a basis for the more rapid and greater differentiation which the higher forms show. Whether the rate of metabolism per unit of weight and under similar conditions of temperature, etc., is lower in the higher than in the lower forms is not at present known, but there is some evidence that it is. If increase in physiological stability of the cellular substratum has occurred during the course of evolution, it must have been an essential factor in determining the increase in structural complexity which is so characteristic a feature of evolution, and structural evolution must then be regarded as in some degree an equilibration process, a change from a less stable to a more stable condition.

The orderly sequence of the process of organic differentiation and the constancy of the results in a given species must result from certain definite characteristics of the organic individual. My own experimental investigations have forced me to the conclusion that the organic individual consists of a dominant and of subordinate parts and that dominance and subordination in their simplest terms depend upon rate of metabolism (see chap. ix) Not only does the evidence indicate that this is the case, but it is impossible to conceive of a definite, orderly process of differentiation attaining a definite constant result in a complex physicochemical system without some sort of dominance and subordination in the processes involved In a complex system consisting of coordinate parts the process of differentiation must differ widely in character according to conditions, and the orderly character of development and constancy of result which we find in organisms would be impossible.

Most theories of the constitution of the organism have failed to recognize the necessity for such a relation of dominance and subordination between parts as a fundamental feature; consequently they have failed to account satisfactorily for the orderly course and definite result of differentiation Driesch is one of the few who have seen clearly that the organic individual is impossible without a controlling and ordering principle of some sort, and not finding any physico-chemical basis for such a principle, he has vested the control in entelechy. As regards plants, the dominance of the vegetative tip over other parts has been clearly demonstrated, but no such relation of parts in animal development has been generally recognized by zoologists Nevertheless such a relation exists and must exist, for without it development, as we know it, is impossible.

Dedifferentiation —Dedifferentiation is a process of loss of differentiation, of apparent simplification, of return or approach to the embryonic or undifferentiated condition Zoologists have been slow to admit its occurrence. According to Weismann—and many agree with him—development proceeds always in one direction and dedifferentiation is impossible. Whenever a new development of a part or a whole occurs, it originates from cells or parts of cells which have not undergone differentiation beyond the stage at which the new development begins. Whenever cells which are visibly differentiated give rise to new wholes or parts, as they often do in cases of regeneration, it is assumed that they contain either some of the undifferentiated germ plasm or those elements of the germ plasm which are necessary for the formation of the new part. Such assumptions are not only unsatisfactory because they cannot be proved or disproved, but they are wholly unnecessary. We have seen that the organism can not only accumulate structural material of various kinds, but under other conditions can remove to a greater or less extent the material previously accumulated. Since reduction occurs in organisms, we must at least admit the possibility of dedifferentiation. Consideration of the data of observation and experiment is postponed to later chapters:[1] at present only certain general features of the process need be considered

In the case of self-differentiation (see pp. 50, 51) the gradual changes in the substratum may be reversed in direction under altered conditions, the gel may again become a sol. But the synthesis of new colloid molecules and the formation of new sol, on the one hand, and the gradual breakdown and elimination of the old gel, on the other, is also possible. Apparently nuclear and cell division are or may be factors in dedifferentiation. With the occurrence of division the progressive changes in the cell, since the preceding division, disappear more or less completely and the cell returns to or approaches its original condition. An increase in metabolic rate is also apparently associated with division[2] If the changes in one direction balance those in the other, cells which divide may remain indefinitely embryonic, like the vegetative tissues of plants and the growing regions of certain animals. But if the nucleus or cell does not divide, or if division does not bring the cell back to its original condition, then a progressive change must occur in the cell or from one cell generation to another, and this change appears sooner or later as differentiation and may go so far that the cell finally becomes incapable of division. Where differentiation has been a correlative process, isolation of a part from the influence of the correlative factors which have determined the course of its differentiation may result, if the part is capable of reacting to the altered conditions, in metabolic changes of such a

[1] See particularly chap. v, and chap. x, pp 245–47.

[2] See chap. vi, pp 141–42, and also Lyon, '02, '04; Spaulding, '04, Mathews, '06.

character that substances previously accumulated as structural components of the part are now broken down and eliminated, and this is dedifferentiation

If the cell is a physico-chemical system and not an entity *sui generis*, the occurrence of dedifferentiation is no more difficult to account for than the reappearance of a certain kind of chemical reaction in a non-living chemical system when conditions which altered the character of the reaction have ceased to act. The occurrence of both differentiation and dedifferentiation is exactly what we should expect from the physico-chemical point of view. The assumptions of the germ-plasm theory merely complicate and befog the whole problem, and not only that, but, as pointed out in the preceding chapter, the theory is essentially "vitalistic" and even pluralistic in its logical implications.

Within the last few years, however, many cases of dedifferentiation have been recorded and various authors, among them Lillie, Loeb, Driesch, Schultz, and others, have suggested that development in animals is a reversible process But reversibility of development, so called, is not necessarily reversibility in the chemical sense. Dedifferentiation may conceivably result from the breakdown and elimination of the differentiated substratum or certain components of it, and the synthesis of new undifferentiated substances from nutritive material, as well as by the reversal of the reactions which occurred in the differentiation. As in the case of growth and reduction, it would certainly simplify our conception of the process of development if we could regard it as a reversible chemical reaction, but such a conception can only lead us astray Undoubtedly many reversible reactions are concerned in development, but development itself is not a reversible reaction. In fact, it is not simply a chemical reaction of any kind, but an exceedingly complex series of interrelated physical and chemical changes. Reversal of development may result from relative changes in the rate of certain reaction components of the metabolic complex as well as from reversal of reaction. In fact, it is probable that reversal of development occurs at least as frequently in this way as by reversal of reaction. A change in metabolism, for example, such that a substance which has previously been accumulated as a structural component of the cell is now broken down, oxidized, and eliminated, may bring about dedifferentiation, but it is not necessarily a reversal of reaction in the chemical sense, for the breakdown and elimination of the substance may be a different process dependent upon different factors from its synthesis out of nutritive substances.

In order then to avoid the possibility of confusion, it is preferable to regard development, not as reversible, but as regressible Differentiation is a progression from one condition to another, dedifferentiation a regression, but perhaps through stages very different from the stages of progression.

Apparently not all differentiated cells are capable of dedifferentiation to the embryonic condition, at least dedifferentiation fails to occur in many cases under any conditions with which we are familiar. In general, less highly differentiated cells undergo dedifferentiation more readily and more completely than more highly differentiated, consequently dedifferentiation is much more conspicuous in the lower than in the higher forms, although even in man some cells are capable of more or less dedifferentiation This limitation of dedifferentiation, as well as the advance of differentiation, in the course of individual development and evolution, suggests again an increase in the physiological stability of the cellular substratum.

Dedifferentiation may be brought about in cells capable of it either by forcing the cell to use up its own substance as a source of energy and so undergo reduction, as in starvation, or by isolating the cell from the action of the correlative factors which have brought about differentiation, and in some cases, and to a certain degree, simply by increasing the rate of metabolism of the cell by stimulation or otherwise. Reduction, except perhaps in embryonic cells, is probably impossible without some degree of dedifferentiation, but dedifferentiation may occur without reduction. Since the differentiated cell has in general a low rate of metabolism as compared with the embryonic cell, and since the decrease in rate is associated with differentiation, we should expect that an increase in rate would occur during dedifferentiation, and this, as will appear, is apparently the case.

If the suggestions of the preceding section concerning the nature of differentiation are correct, we should expect the most recently developed morphological features of the cell to disappear first in dedifferentiation, since these are, under the conditions existing in the cell, the least stable of the substratal constituents. As these are removed the rate of metabolism rises and other parts of the substratum become relatively unstable and disappear, and so on, until the cell once more approaches the embryonic condition So far as the course of morphological dedifferentiation has been followed, it seems in general to proceed in this way and so to reverse the course of differentiation. But this does not necessarily involve a reversal of reaction any more than the removal of a previously deposited sand-bar, by acceleration or change of course of the current of a river, involves a reversal of its flow.

The dedifferentiating cell is apparently capable at any stage of resuming the process of differentiation, and if dedifferentiation proceeds far enough it may, under altered correlative conditions, begin a new course of differentiation and become a different kind of a cell from that which it was originally As the sand-bar formed in the stream under certain conditions may under others be removed and its place taken by a deep channel, and again the channel may give place to a mud flat or a beach, so the original morphological differentiation of the cell may disappear and give place to other kinds of differentiation as the physiological conditions change.

THE BASIS OF SENESCENCE AND REJUVENESCENCE

The association of a colloid substratum with a chemical reaction-system and the occurrence of growth and reduction and of differentiation and dedifferentiation lead us to a conception of senescence and rejuvenescence which, as will appear in following chapters, seems to be the only one which is in full agreement with the facts of experiment and observation According to this view, senescence is primarily a decrease in rate of dynamic processes conditioned by the accumulation, differentiation, and other associated changes of the material of the colloid substratum. Rejuvenescence is an increase in rate of dynamic processes conditioned by the changes in the colloid substratum in reduction and dedifferentiation

Senescence is then a necessary and inevitable feature of growth and differentiation, while rejuvenescence is associated with reduction and with the various reproductive processes in which more or less differentiated parts of the organism undergo dedifferentiation. Even as regards gametic or sexual reproduction, the facts indicate that the gametes or sex cells are very highly specialized and differentiated cells and that early embryonic development is essentially a period of dedifferentiation and rejuvenescence

Viewed from this standpoint, life is then really a cyclical process as it appears to be. The organism grows, differentiates, and ages, and these processes lead, usually in nature through reproduction of one kind or another, to reduction, dedifferentiation, and rejuvenescence. No part of the organism remains perpetually undifferentiated and perpetually young. The young organism arises from the old, not from a self-perpetuating source of youth, which is itself always young, and the young becomes old again.

REFERENCES

BABCOCK, S. M
    1912. "Metabolic Water: Its Production and Rôle in Vital Phenomena," *Univ. of Wisconsin Agric. Expt. Sta. Research Bull No. 22.*

CHILD, C. M.
    1911. "Experimental Control of Morphogenesis in the Regulation of *Planaria*," *Biol. Bull*, XX

DAVENPORT, C. B
    1897. *Experimental Morphology.* New York

HUXLEY, T. H
    1853. "Review of the Cell Theory," *British and Foreign Med. Chir Rev.*, XII.

KASSOWITZ, M.
    1899 *Allgemeine Biologie.* Wien.

LEPESCHKIN, W W
    1912. "Zur Kenntnis der Einwirkung suppramaximaler Temperaturen auf die Pflanze," *Berichte d. deutsch. bot Ges.*, XXX.

LOEB, J, and WASTENEYS, H.
    1911 "Sind die Oxydationsvorgange die unabhangige Variable in den Lebenserscheinungen?" *Biochem Zeitschr*, XXXVI.

Lyon, E. P.

1902. "Effects of Potassium Cyanide and of Lack of Oxygen upon the Fertilized Eggs and the Embryos of the Sea Urchin (*Arbacia punctulata*)," *Am Jour. of Physiol* , VII.

1904 "Rhythms of Susceptibility and of Carbon Dioxide Production in Cleavage," *Am. Jour. of Physiol.*, XI.

Mathews, A P.

1906. "A Note on the Susceptibility of Segmenting *Arbacia* and *Asterias* Eggs to Cyanides," *Biol Bull.*, XI

Pfeffer, W.

1901. *Pflanzenphysiologie*, Band II. Leipzig.

Schultz, E.

1904. "Über Reduktionen: I, Über Hungererscheinungen bei *Planaria lactea*," *Arch f Entwickelungsmech.*, XVIII.

Spaulding, E. G.

1904 "The Rhythm of Immunity and Susceptibility of Fertilized Sea Urchin Eggs to Ether, to HCl and to Some Salts," *Biol. Bull.*, VI.

PART II

AN EXPERIMENTAL STUDY OF PHYSIOLOGICAL SENESCENCE
AND REJUVENESCENCE IN THE LOWER ANIMALS

CHAPTER III

THE PROBLEM AND METHODS OF INVESTIGATION

THE NATURE OF THE PROBLEM

Both morphological and physiological changes are involved in the processes of senescence and rejuvenescence, and we may attack the problems from either the morphological or the physiological side. On the morphological side we may determine the changes in physical properties, form, and structure of the substratum which occur during senescence and rejuvenescence, and on the physiological side we may investigate the changes in functional activity and in metabolism.

Concerning the morphological changes associated with senescence, particularly in the higher animals and man, we already possess a considerable body of facts. As regards the physiological changes, we know that in the higher animals and man the rate of metabolism per unit of substance undergoes in general a decrease with advancing age from very early stages onward, and that sooner or later a decrease in functional activity and a general deterioration of the organism occurs Our knowledge concerning the lower animals is less complete. We are familiar with the general course of development and differentiation in most forms, but the morphological differences between young and old adults have received comparatively little attention Of the physiological aspect of senescence in the lower forms we have little positive knowledge. We know that in most forms growth is more rapid in earlier stages and that in many plants and animals the length of life under the usual conditions is more or less definite, and in some forms we can observe a decrease in functional activity with advancing age. On the other hand, some organisms live and remain active for an indefinite period and apparently do not grow old. Few attempts have been made, however, to determine by analytic investigation the significance of these various facts and to find a common basis for them

As regards rejuvenescence, biologists are not even agreed that it is of general occurrence The belief that the germ plasm, which is assumed not to grow old, except as it gives rise to a soma, is the only source of young organisms has been so general that the possibility of rejuvenescence has received but little consideration. Maupas' classical investigations upon the infusoria (Maupas, '88, '89) seemed to indicate that a process of rejuvenescence leading to a larger size of individuals and a higher rate of division resulted from conjugation in these forms, but the recent work of Jennings ('13) makes it evident that this is certainly not always the case. The work of E Schultz ('04, '08) and others on reduction and dedifferentiation in the lower forms, the suggestions of a number of others that development is "reversible," Minot's view (Minot, '08) that the egg before fertilization is an old cell and undergoes rejuvenescence during the early stages of embryonic development, and the well-known fact that in plants differentiated cells may lose their differentiation and give rise to new plants—these are the chief data and conclusions which we possess concerning rejuvenescence.

The various facts have led to the formulation of various theories and suggestions as to the nature of senescence, but these are mostly based rather upon observational than experimental evidence, and some of them take account only of man and the higher animals and so do not apply to organisms in general, while others are more or less speculative in character and cannot readily be tested. There is at present no generally accepted theory of senescence, and as for rejuvenescence it can scarcely be said that any theory exists.

The real problem before us is then that of finding a general basis for these phenomena which is applicable to all cases, not merely to those in which the organism manifestly grows old, reproduces, and dies, but also to those in which, instead of dying, the whole organism breaks up or divides into new individuals, which repeat the cycle of growth, development, and reproduction, and finally, to those cases in which the whole organism or parts of it appear not to grow old, but live on indefinitely.

The first step toward accomplishing this is to find some means of determining whether an individual organism in a given case is young or old, not merely morphologically but physiologically   We can of course distinguish embryonic, larval, and juvenile forms from adults by their morphological characters, and in many cases by their physiological characters as well, but it is not always easy to distinguish younger and older individuals of the same general stage of the life cycle.   In the higher animals certain morphological changes which are apparently characteristic of senescence have been observed in some cells, but the morphological features of the cells of different organisms are so different and the visible changes so slight in many cases that, though it is usually possible to distinguish embryonic from definitely differentiated cells, it is very often impossible to distinguish old and young individuals of the same general stage by the morphological characters of their cells. Measurements of the metabolism or of the rate of growth in man and the mammals show that the rates of both per unit of weight decrease as age advances, but the methods employed for such forms are not readily applicable in many other cases, because of the conditions of existence, the small size, the low rate of metabolism, etc.   In the course of my investigation of the process of reproduction in the lower invertebrates a method based on the physiological resistance or susceptibility of the animals to certain conditions has been developed, which has proved to be of great value in distinguishing physiologically young from old organisms as well as for various other purposes.

SUSCEPTIBILITY IN RELATION TO RATE OF METABOLISM

It is a familiar fact that the susceptibility or physiological resistance of man and the higher animals to various external factors, and particularly to those which depress, changes with advancing age, and I have found that this is also true for the lower animals, as far as they have been tested.   On the basis of this relation between susceptibility and physiological age, it has been possible to develop a method which not only enables us to distinguish differences in age, but affords a means of comparing in a general way the rates of the metabolic processes, or of certain fundamental metabolic reactions in different animals   This method, which may be called the susceptibility, physiological resistance, or survival-time method, consists essentially in determining the length of life of different individuals or lots under certain standardized conditions which kill by making impossible in one way or another the continuation of metabolism.

The substances used in my determinations of susceptibility include the cyanides, and ethyl alcohol, ethyl ether, chloroform, chloretone, acetone-chloroform, and in some cases various other narcotics. Carbon dioxide and water in which large stocks of the species under examination have been kept and which therefore contain soluble products of metabolism have also been used in a few cases with essentially similar results. Certain conditions, such as lack of oxygen, low temperature, and high temperature, act in much the same way, at least in certain cases and when properly controlled In my experiments the cyanides have proved most convenient and satisfactory, because the concentrations required are very low and osmotic and other complications are negligible, and because in the lower animals, which have been chiefly used, irritability and movement persist to some extent almost to the death point, while in alcohol, ether, and other narcotics they disappear earlier. There is no doubt that a relation exists between the general metabolic condition of organisms, or their parts, and their susceptibility to a very large number of substances which act as poisons, i.e., which in one way or another make metabolism impossible, and that differences n susceptibility may be used with certain precautions and within certain limits as a means of distinguishing differences in metabolic condition and, more specifically, differences in metabolic rate

Concerning the nature of the action of poisons such as hydrocyanic acid, the cyanides, and the great group of substances commonly called narcotics, opinions at present differ widely As regards the cyanides, it has been very generally believed since Geppert's experiments that they decrease or inhibit cell respiration directly or indirectly [1] Recent experiments by Vernon, Warburg,

---

[1] Carlson, '07, Gasser and Loevenhart, '14, Geppert, '89, Grove and Loevenhart, '11, Kastle and Loevenhart, '01, Loeb and Wasteneys, '13a, '13b, Mathews and Walker, '09; Richards and Wallace, '08, Vernon, '06, '09, '10, Warburg, '10c, '14c. Further references will be found in these papers

and Loeb and Wasteneys have demonstrated that oxygen consumption is greatly decreased in animals by cyanides, and it has also been shown experimentally that the cyanides inhibit oxidations and the action of oxidizing enzymes in various cases outside the organism.   To the hypothesis that the cyanides inhibit oxidations in the organism the objection has been made that they affect, not only aerobic or oxybiotic, but anaerobic animals as well, although in the latter, oxidations requiring atmospheric oxygen do not occur. In answer to this, it has been pointed out that even in anaerobic forms oxidations occur, the oxygen being derived from substances in the body instead of from the atmosphere.

The cyanides and other substances containing the cyanogen radical, CN, are in general extremely powerful poisons, but their action resembles in certain respects that of the substances known as narcotics or anesthetics.

The characteristic physiological effect of all these substances is a decrease or complete loss of irritability, which, however, is completely reversible up to a certain limit and so may be followed by complete recovery.   But the narcotics are like the cyanides poisons, and if they act in sufficiently high concentration or for a sufficiently long time they bring about changes of some sort which are not reversible and which lead to death by retardation and final cessation of metabolism.   Scientific investigation has thus far chiefly concerned itself with the narcotic, i e., the reversible, rather than with the poisonous, irreversible, effects of these substances   Many theories of narcosis[1] have been advanced, and most of them are still in the field.   Brief mention must be made of the more important among these theories

Verworn and his school have long maintained that narcotics decrease the oxidation processes and the respiratory activity of the protoplasm, and Verworn has recently suggested that the narcotics, either by adsorption or by loose chemical combination, render the

[1] The following references include some of the more important literature bearing upon the different theories of narcosis Alexander and Cserna, '13; Bernard, '75, Dubois, '94, Hober, '10, Kisch, '13, R. S. Lillie, '12a, '12b, '13a, '13b, '14, Loeb and Wasteneys, '13a, '13b, A. P. Mathews, '10, '13; H. Meyer, '99, '01, Overton, '01; J. Traube, '04a, '04b, '08, '10, '11, '13, etc.; Verworn, '03, '12, '13, Warburg, '10a, '10b, '10c, '11a, '11b, '12a, '12b, '13, '14a, '14b, '14c, Winterstein, '02, '05, '13, '14

oxygen carriers of the cell incapable of activating the molecular oxygen, and that the cell consequently asphyxiates.   A. P. Mathews and some others have maintained that the action of narcotics upon the oxidations is direct and chemical, and Mathews has recently suggested that the residual valences of narcotic substances are responsible for their action   In this connection it may be noted that the temperature coefficient of the susceptibility of *Planaria* to potassium cyanide and alcohol is of the same order of magnitude as the usual temperature coefficient of chemical reactions (Child, '13a).   This fact indicates that the susceptibility increases in the same ratio as the rate of chemical reaction and therefore suggests that the cyanide and alcohol act directly upon the metabolic reactions or some of them.   But this relation between the temperature coefficients of susceptibility and the rate of chemical reaction cannot be made the basis of positive conclusions because it is possibly nothing more than a coincidence, or it may result from a complex of factors which we cannot analyze

Within the last few years various investigators have recorded results at variance with the Verworn theory of narcosis.   Warburg found that certain narcotics produced narcosis without decreasing the oxygen consumption of the organism   Later Loeb and Wasteneys reported very similar results   They found that in some forms of narcosis the decrease in oxygen consumption was very slight, while in others it was much greater.   With the cyanides particularly, narcosis occurs only when oxygen consumption is greatly reduced, while in alcohol narcosis the decrease in oxygen consumption may be very slight   Oxygen consumption is decreased in all cases, however, if sufficiently high concentrations of the narcotic are used   Kisch has concluded from certain experiments on protozoa that while narcosis does decrease certain oxidations it does not affect all.   Winterstein has also found that in alcohol narcosis of the spinal cord of the frog a slight increase rather than a decrease in oxygen consumption may occur even when irritability is completely lost, there is, however, no increase in oxygen consumption with stimulation.

Assuming that these results are correct and not due to unrecognized technical or other sources of error, we are forced to conclude with these authors that decrease in oxidation is an incident or a result of narcosis which may or may not occur, and that the fundamental feature must be sought in some other change. As regards some of these experiments, however, certain possible sources of error exist and further investigation may alter the results. At present it is difficult to conceive how narcosis can occur without decrease in oxidation

Arguing from the observed parallelism between the fat solubility of various substances and their narcotic power, Meyer and Overton advanced the theory that the cell membrane consisted in at least a considerable part of lipoid or fatty substances and that the action of the narcotics was determined by their solubility in these substances   This theory has undergone development and modification at the hands of later investigators, and the question as to the nature of the narcotic action of the substances which enter the cell by dissolving in the lipoids of the membrane has received various answers   Some have held that the lipoids of the membrane were responsible only for the entrance of the narcotics, which once inside the cell acted chemically or otherwise. Others believe that narcosis is the result of the changes in the lipoids of the membrane produced by the narcotic substances. Warburg considers the physical condition of the lipoids to be of great importance in connection with narcosis. According to Hober, narcosis occurs when the narcotics have collected to a certain molecular concentration in the cell lipoids, because the narcotics then inhibit a change in colloid aggregate condition of the lipoids which is characteristic of excitation. R. S. Lillie finds that narcotics decrease the permeability of the cell membrane or its ability to undergo increase in permeability, and so decrease or inhibit the increase in permeability which he believes to be the essential feature of stimulation.

Some forty years ago Claude Bernard suggested that narcotics brought about a partial reversible coagulation of the protoplasm of the nerve cell. Later Dubois advanced the hypothesis that the narcotics bring about loss of water from the protoplasm and so decrease metabolic activity. Recently J Traube has concluded on the basis of extensive experimentation that the narcotic effect is due to changes in the colloid substratum According to Traube the narcotics act by decreasing surface tension and so increasing the degree of aggregation of the cell colloids, and decrease in oxidation or in metabolism in general results from this change in aggregate condition Other factors may play a part in certain cases, but Traube has shown that a relation exists in many cases between the decrease in the surface tension of water by narcotic substances and their narcotic power, and that narcotic concentrations of many different substances are isocapillary, i e., decrease surface tension by the same amount. Warburg has shown that a close interrelation exists between the oxidations in the cell and the fundamental structure and that, at least in many cases, the narcotics decrease oxidation. He concludes, in essential agreement with Traube, that the narcotics act by altering surface tension and so produce capillary changes, particularly in the lipoids.

The lipoid theory of Meyer and Overton and their followers and Traube's surface tension theory differ from Verworn's asphyxiation theory in that they regard the decrease in metabolic activity in narcosis as resulting from or associated with the changes in the colloid substratum of the cell. The unsatisfactory character of purely or pre-eminently chemical theories of the organism has been pointed out in chap. i, and it seems probable that in narcosis as well as in other changes in chemical activity in the organism, the substratum and the changes which occur in it must be taken into account. It seems not improbable, moreover, that narcosis is not always produced in exactly the same way. Irritability, as Winterstein suggests, probably depends upon the maintenance of a complex dynamic equilibrium of some sort, and this equilibrium may be destroyed with a resulting loss of irritability, by changes of various kinds in the cell It is even conceivable that in some cases the change may concern primarily or chiefly the substratum, and in other cases the chemical reactions, or certain of them, and we must admit the further possibility that both the substratal and the chemical changes may differ with different narcotic substances and yet produce much the same general result as regards irritability Various observations show that very considerable differences do exist in different forms of narcosis. It was noted above that the decrease in oxygen consumption may apparently differ widely in different narcoses, and Alexander and Cserna have found that not only is this true, but that the decrease in carbon-dioxide production is not parallel to the decrease in oxidation in different brain narcoses In short, it is possible that the changes in the cell which bring about narcosis may differ in character with different narcotics and perhaps with different cellular conditions Perhaps. as so often in the history of biological theory, all the theories of narcosis are more or less correct.

But, however the narcotic substances act upon the cell, there can be no doubt that within a given species or organism a general relation exists between metabolic condition and susceptibility to a given narcotic. Differences in metabolic condition do not exist independently of differences in condition of the colloid substratum, and whether the narcotic affects primarily the substratum or certain of the chemical reactions, the susceptibility of the organism or part to its action must differ as the conditions which determine or are associated with metabolic activity differ

Narcosis is only one stage in the action of the narcotic substances. When they are present in sufficiently high concentration or act for a sufficiently long time, they bring about changes which are not reversible and which finally end in death by making the continuation of metabolism impossible. The wide range of variation observed in some cases between narcotic and killing concentrations, both with different narcotics and with the same narcotic at different stages of development (Vernon, '13), indicates that the reversible changes involved in pure narcosis are different in some way from those which result in death With the killing concentrations the relation between susceptibility and metabolic condition is more distinct and uniform than with the lower, purely narcotic concentrations, where incidental factors may sometimes mask or reverse the fundamental relation (see pp. 75–76) With the cyanides, however, where narcotic and killing concentrations do not differ very greatly, this relation appears more distinctly and uniformly than with any other agents thus far used

It cannot of course be maintained that the susceptibility to cyanides or other narcotics of an organism or part at a given moment is an exact measure of its total metabolism at that moment   If the cyanides or other narcotics act directly on the oxidation processes, a general relation between susceptibility and oxidation must exist, but while the oxidations are fundamental metabolic reactions, and serve in a general way as a measure of metabolic activity, a considerable range of variation in the different reactions which go to make up the the metabolic complex may undoubtedly exist   If, on the other hand, these substances act on the substratum and affect the metabolic reactions only or primarily through the substratal changes, susceptibility must be related to the general average of metabolic activity, but certain reactions may be more affected than others in the early stages of action, though sooner or later the metabolic process as a whole is retarded or inhibited.

In concentrations of the cyanides or other narcotics, which not only narcotize but gradually kill, a decrease in metabolism, as measured by oxygen consumption, by carbon-dioxide production, by functional activity, or by other means, occurs in all cases, and metabolism finally ceases   In concentrations in which death occurs at times varying from a few minutes to a few hours and when complicating factors are absent, the susceptibility varies directly with the general metabolic rate   Conditions which increase metabolic activity increase susceptibility, and vice versa.   This method of determining susceptibility I have called the direct susceptibility method (Child, '13a).

The capacity of organisms to acclimate themselves to, or acquire a tolerance to, narcotics has long been recognized   this capacity is well illustrated by the high degree of tolerance for alcohol, cocaine, etc., developed in the human organism.   In concentrations of narcotics which are sufficiently low to permit partial, but not complete, acclimation, we find that the relation between susceptibility and metabolic rate undergoes reversal.   In such concentrations the individual or part with the higher metabolic rate becomes more readily and more completely acclimated and therefore lives longer than the individual or part with the lower metabolic rate which is unable to acclimate itself and so dies earlier.   This relation between metabolic rate and capacity for acclimation is to be expected, for the occurrence of acclimation evidently depends on conditions in the organism which are associated with metabolic activity   Thus the metabolic condition of different individuals or parts may also be compared by means of this indirect or acclimation method

These differences in susceptibility to narcotics, particularly those determined directly with relatively high concentrations, afford, when properly controlled, a very delicate method for comparing general metabolic rates in different individuals and parts, at least in many of the lower animals.   In a recent paper (Child, '13a) the technique of the method for flatworms and similar forms, its different modifications and its limitations have been considered at length.   As regards the relation between susceptibility or resistance to cyanide and rate of metabolism, it was shown in that paper that susceptibility is altered by motor activity, that the temperature coefficient of susceptibility is of the same order of magnitude as that of most chemical reactions, and that differences in carbon-dioxide production correspond to differences in susceptibility.

The estimations of carbon-dioxide production were made by Dr S. Tashiro with the "biometer" devised and recently described by him (Tashiro, '13b).   The sensitiveness and great value of this apparatus are shown by the fact that Tashiro has been able to demonstrate the production of carbon dioxide in the resting nerve, its increase by stimulation, and its decrease by narcotics, and has also shown that living seeds resemble the nerve in most respects as regards irritability (Tashiro, '13a)   In the comparison between the results of the susceptibility method and the carbon-dioxide production the flatworm *Planaria dorotocephala* (see Fig. 6, p 93) was used in most cases.   The susceptibility method shows that the rate of metabolism is higher in young than in old animals, in starved than in fed, and in animals stimulated to movement than in resting animals.   In distilled water the rate of metabolism as measured by the susceptibility method is higher and in 5 per cent sea-water lower than in tap-water   In pieces isolated by cutting, the rate of metabolism is higher in long anterior pieces than in posterior pieces of the same length (cf. Child, '14b).   In each of these cases the animal or piece which possessed the higher rate of metabolism according to the susceptibility method produced more carbon dioxide than the other. The complete agreement between the two methods indicates very clearly that both are concerned in one way or another with fundamental metabolic reactions and that both afford a very delicate means of comparing in a general way the rates of these reactions.

It is evident that accuracy in the use of susceptibility as a method of investigation depends to a considerable extent upon the exactness with which it is possible to determine the quantitative effect of the cyanide or other agent used upon the organism   In the lower invertebrates, particularly the protozoa, coelenterates, and flatworms, which have formed the material for most of my experiments, and in the early stages of development of many other animals where hard skeletal structures are absent and supporting tissues do not possess a high degree of firmness and coherence, or are entirely absent, death is followed in a short time, often at once, by more or less complete disintegration   The body loses its form, swells, breaks down into a shapeless mass, and may finally disappear completely, except for a slight turbidity in the water, which results from the minute particles in suspension   In such cases, however, movement may continue to some extent, particularly in the cyanides, until a short time before disintegration begins, or in some forms up to the very instant of disintegration   In these forms then it is possible to determine with considerable exactness the time when death occurs and so to compare the length of life of different individuals under certain specific conditions, e g , a certain concentration of cyanide, alcohol, etc., or under low temperature or lack of oxygen   In many of my experiments changes of this kind have been taken as the criterion of death, but essentially the same results are obtained with the lower animals if the times of complete cessation of movement in response to stimulation are determined instead of the times of disintegration.

Where such disintegration does not occur, or is retarded by the physical consistency of the organism or part concerned, it is often possible to determine the occurrence of death in small animals under the microscope by other changes in appearance, such as an increase in opacity, a change in color, etc   Moreover, all these methods of determining the death point can be checked and the time of death

determined in cases where such methods are not available by
determining the limits of recovery, i e., at stated intervals a certain
number of the organisms are removed from the narcotic solution to
water. the length of time in the narcotic at which recovery ceases
to occur is at least approximately the survival time

With the flatworms and other simple naked forms the susceptibility method can usually be employed independently of differences
in size, for in such cases the death changes at the surface of the body
may be used as a basis for comparison. Moreover, in such elongated flattened forms as the flatworms, surface increases almost
as rapidly as volume. But in forms where the permeable surfaces
are limited to certain regions of the body or are internal, as in air-
breathing forms, or where the body is covered by an exoskeleton,
the certain elimination of the factor of size often presents a difficult
problem

While most of my determinations of susceptibility have been
made upon the lower invertebrates, some experiments with the
higher invertebrates and the lower vertebrates have demonstrated
that the relation between susceptibility to cyanide and general
metabolic rate is the same in these as in the lower forms   But at
least as regards the vertebrates this is not true for all narcotics.
Vernon ('13) has found, for example, that the susceptibility of tadpoles to some narcotics increases and to others decreases with advancing age, and suggests that these differences are due to changes
in the constitution of the cell lipoids   This is probably not the only
factor concerned· differences in the lipoid solubility of the different
narcotics and differences in the amount as well as the constitution
of lipoids in the nervous system and still other factors are probably
also involved, but further investigation is necessary before the subject is cleared up. In the lower invertebrates I have as yet found
no indication of such differences in the action of different narcotics
as Vernon describes. With some narcotics the age changes in susceptibility are greater than with others, but in all cases thus far
the changes during a given developmental period, as determined by
different narcotics, proceed in the same direction. It seems probable that the differences in the direction of change in susceptibility
observed by Vernon result, at least in part, from differences in the

relation between the narcotics and the cell lipoids In the vertebrates the accumulation and differentiation of lipoids, particularly
in the nervous system, is very much greater than in the lower invertebrates, and it is probable that with some narcotics which are
highly fat soluble, the fundamental relation between susceptibility
and general metabolic condition is completely masked, or even
reversed, by their higher concentration in the cells of the nervous
system with a given external concentration, and consequently by
their greater narcotic effect on these cells. In the lower animals
and in early stages of development the action of narcotics is general,
but with the advance in differentiation the susceptibility of the
nervous system as compared with other organs increases very
greatly. In general it appears that the differences in susceptibility
to all narcotics are much more nearly alike in the lower forms and
the early stages of all, while in the later stages of the higher forms
those substances which are highly water soluble act in much the
same way as in the lower forms, but the action of the highly fat-
soluble narcotics is modified because of the increasing development
and differentiation of lipoids in the nervous system, and very
probably other modifications also occur. Nevertheless, and in
spite of these complicating factors which appear in certain cases,
differences in susceptibility to various agents can, with proper
precautions and checks, be used to a certain extent as a means of
comparing general metabolic condition, even in the vertebrates
The use of the cyanides seems to be freer from complicating factors than that of other agents.

Undoubtedly, however, the chief value of the susceptibility
method lies in its applicability to small simple organisms and to
different regions of a single, intact, not too highly differentiated
individual. By means of it we are able to gain some idea of differences in metabolic rate in many cases to which other methods are
not applicable.

Thus far susceptibility to narcotics, cyanides, and other substances in its relation to metabolism has received but little attention. Lyon ('02, '04) and A. P Mathews ('06) have used
susceptibility to cyanides and to various other substances and conditions as a method for showing differences in rate of metabolism

in the cleavage stages of eggs, and Loeb[1] and others have made use of the cyanides to decrease or inhibit the oxidation processes in eggs, and Drzewina and Bohn ('13) have observed parallel differences in susceptibility to cyanides and lack of oxygen along the longitudinal body-axis of certain flatworms. Some other incidental observations also exist, but the general significance of differences in susceptibility has been either ignored or not recognized

THE DIRECT METHOD

By this method the resistance or susceptibility is determined directly by concentrations of cyanide or other agents which kill the animals within a few hours   For a particular species a concentration must be determined which kills without acclimation, but which does not kill so rapidly that the differences in susceptibility do not appear clearly.   For *Planaria dorotocephala* (see p. 93) and other related species a concentration of one one-thousandth gram-molecular solution (o oo1 mol., 65 milligrams per liter, o oo65 per cent) of potassium cyanide has been found most satisfactory at temperatures about 20° C. and for most purposes.   This kills the animals in from two to twelve hours according to their condition   But a range of concentrations from o oo02 mol. up to o oo5 mol , or even higher, may be used, except where the metabolic rate is very high, as in young animals, without altering anything but the time factor.   Essentially the same results are obtained from 4 per cent alcohol or from 2 per cent ether as from o oo1 mol potassium cyanide.

Since the death and disintegration of different parts of the body usually follow a regular sequence (Child, '13b), it is possible to determine the time, not merely of disintegration of the whole animal, but of the various regions of the body.   The body of *Planaria* consists of two or more zooids (see p. 123) of which only the anterior one is morphologically developed   In this anterior zooid death and disintegration usually begin at the head-region and proceed posteriorly, and the lateral margins of the body usually die and disintegrate before the median region   The most satisfactory method

[1] Loeb, '09, '10, Loeb and Lewis, '02, Loeb and Wasteneys, '10, and various other papers.

of recording the course of death and disintegration has proved to be that of examining the lots of animals at stated intervals, e g., every half-hour, and recording the condition of each individual. In order to accomplish this most readily five stages of disintegration have been more or less arbitrarily distinguished as follows:

Stage I. Intact, not showing any appreciable disintegration Such animals or pieces are always alive and show movement

Stage II In whole animals from the first appearance of disintegration, which is practically always in the head-region, to the first appearance of disintegration of the lateral margins of the body. In pieces, from the beginning of disintegration at one or both ends to the first appearance of disintegration on the lateral margins. Considerable motor activity may still be present.

Stage III. In both whole animals and pieces from the appearance of disintegration on the lateral margins until it has extended over the whole length of the margins Movement may still occur in the parts least affected.

Stage IV. From the end of Stage III to the time when the surface of the body in the median regions disintegrates Motor activity ceases.

Stage V. Disintegration has extended to all parts of the surface and the progress of death over the body is completed. The remaining parts representing the internal organs gradually swell and break up, but the process is not followed beyond the completion of surface changes.

Attention must be called to the fact that these stages represent primarily the progress of the surface changes over the body from one region to another rather than the progress of disintegration through the internal organs. In these and other naked animals differences in size of the animal do not affect the progress of the surface changes, while they may be an important factor in the rate of penetration of the reagent and consequently in the disintegration of the internal organs. But since the surface changes in any region are practically coincident with the death of that region, it is not necessary to follow the internal changes, and in naked-bodied animals the method becomes for all practical purposes independent of size.

There is no difficulty in distinguishing between these five stages with sufficient exactness for all purposes. Where the differences in rate of metabolism between two animals or lots are great, they are clearly shown by the times of the beginning and completion of disintegration in each lot, but by following the different stages of the process it is possible to distinguish slight differences. As regards length of time, the different stages are not strictly comparable in all cases; in large animals, for example, Stage III extends over a somewhat longer time than the other stages, because the progress of disintegration along the margins in the posterior direction requires a longer time than in small animals and pieces where the length of the margins is much less.

In comparing susceptibilities determined at different times with different solutions, great care is necessary, for slight differences in alkalinity of the water alter the susceptibility very considerably, and susceptibility also varies with the temperature. In order to avoid these and other complications, whenever possible susceptibilities to be compared should be determined at the same time, with the same solution, and under the same conditions of temperature and light, etc.

Table I will serve as an example of the method of recording the observations and of the results obtained. In this table, the first

TABLE I

Length of Time in KCN	Lots	Stages of Disintegration				
		I	II	III	IV	V
0.30	1	6	3	1		
	2	10				
1.00	1	2	3	4	1	
	2	9	1			
1.30	1			2	3	5
	2	8	2			
2.00	1				1	9
	2	3	7			
2.30	1					10
	2		8	2		
3.00	2			10		
3.30	2			7	3	
4.00	2			1	6	3
4.30	2				5	5
5.00	2				3	7
5.30	2					10

vertical column gives in hours and minutes the length of time in cyanide at each examination; the second gives the serial number of each lot, and the five columns headed by Roman numerals under "Stages" give the number of animals of each lot in each stage of disintegration at each examination   In this case Lot 1 consists of ten young worms, four to five millimeters in length, and Lot 2

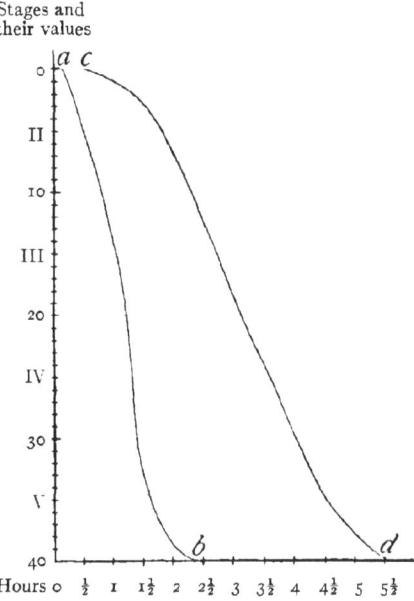

FIG 3 —*Planaria dorotocephala·* susceptibility curves of young (*ab*) and old (*cd*) animals in KCN o oo1 mol   Graphic presentation of the data of Table I   The vertical intervals represent the arbitrary numerical values of the average disintegration stages, the horizontal intervals half-hour periods

of ten old worms fifteen to sixteen millimeters in length, both from the same stock.

The table shows that in the young worms of Lot 1 disintegration begins earlier and proceeds more rapidly than in the old worms of Lot 2.   The young worms have all reached Stage V after two and one-half hours in cyanide, while none of the old worms have reached this stage at this time and all of them reach it only after five and one-half hours. Essentially the same differences appear in 4 per cent alcohol, in 2 per cent ether, and in solutions of various other depressing agents.

These data may be presented more clearly and briefly in graphic form, as in Fig. 3, which is a graphic presentation of Table 1   In Fig. 3 the curve ab is the death curve or susceptibility curve of the ten young worms of Lot 1, the curve cd the susceptibility curve of the ten old worms of Lot 2.[1] Each curve is a descending curve. the distance of its starting-point $(a, c,$ Fig 3) to the right of the vertical line, the axis of ordinates, indicates the length of time between placing the animals in cyanide and the beginning of death and disintegration; its slope indicates the average rate of disintegration; the distance of its lower end $(b, d,$ Fig 3) from the axis of ordinates indicates the length of time between placing the animals

[1] The transformation of the tabulated data into graphic form is accomplished by giving a numerical value to each stage of disintegration and determining the average stage of disintegration in any lot at any given time by multiplying the number of worms in each stage at that time by the value of that stage, adding the products for all stages, and dividing by ten. By marking off vertical intervals from above downward, corresponding to the numerical values assigned to the different stages, as in Fig 3, the average stage of disintegration can be plotted at once by counting downward from the zero point the number of spaces equal to its numerical value, or, in other words, the ordinate of the susceptibility curve for any average stage of disintegration is equal to 40 minus the value of that stage.

The determination of the average stages of disintegration and of the disintegration ordinates for the time 1 30 in Table I will serve to illustrate the method of procedure   The values assigned to the different stages are   Stage I, 0, Stage II. 10, Stage III, 20, Stage IV, 30; Stage V, 40.

Condition of Lot 1   2 animals in Stage III: $2 \times 20 =$ 40
                       3   "   "   "   IV $3 \times 30 =$ 90   Average Stage of Disintegration
                       5   "   "   "   V $5 \times 40 = 200$
                                                    —
                                                    $330 \div 10 = 33$

Condition of Lot 2·   8   "   "   "   I $8 \times 0 =$ 0
                       2   "   "   "   II. $2 \times 10 =$ 20
                                                    $20 \div 10 = 2$

Ordinate for Lot 1 at $1\frac{1}{2}$ hours $= 40 - 33 = 7$
Ordinate "   "   2 "   "   " $= 40 - 2 = 38$

The horizontal distances of the points of the curve from the zero point at the left (abscissae) in Fig. 3 represent lengths of time in the cyanide, half-hour intervals, the intervals at which the condition of the animals was recorded being indicated on the axis of abscissae.

in cyanide and the death of the last part of the body in the animals
of each lot   Thus the differences in susceptibility of two or more lots
of worms are evident at a glance, for the farther to the right the
curve lies, the less the susceptibility, and vice versa.   In Fig 3, for
example, the susceptibility of the young worms, as indicated by
the curve *ab*, is very much greater than that of the old worms, as
indicated by the curve *cd*.

The susceptibility curves in the following chapters are all drawn
in the same way as those in Fig 3 and from data similar to those in
Table I   In general this method is more convenient than the
indirect method described below, and the results are less likely to
be affected by complicating factors

THE INDIRECT METHOD

By this method the susceptibility or physiological resistance to
the depressing agent is determined indirectly, through the ability
of the animals to become acclimated to a given concentration   In
general, but with certain exceptions, the ability of an animal to
acclimate to the cyanides or other depressing agents varies with the
rate of metabolism, that is, animals with the higher rate live longer
than those with a lower rate   In experiments by this method a
concentration of the agent used is determined which does not kill
the animals directly, but allows more or less acclimation   The
concentration to be used depends to some extent upon the condition
of the animals to be tested   For those with a high rate of metabolism higher concentrations are necessary than for those with a
low rate.   With different temperatures also different concentrations
must be used.   For *Planaria dorotocephala* at temperatures near
20° C., potassium cyanide. o 00002–o 00004 mol. (o 00013–0.00026
per cent) serves in most cases and 1–$1\frac{1}{2}$ per cent alcohol or o 2–
o.3 per cent ether gives essentially the same results.   The details
of technique and certain complicating and limiting factors have
been considered elsewhere (Child, '11, '13a, '14a).

The results of such experiments are best presented in graphic
form.   Fig 4 shows the different ability of old and young individuals of *Planaria dorotocephala* to acclimate to $1\frac{1}{2}$ per cent alcohol.   Each small interval represents 2 per cent of the total number

of worms in each lot compared, and each horizontal interval rep
sents one day. Each point of the curve represents the percenta
of worms intact at a given time during the experiment. Ea
curve is plotted from fifty worms and from examinations two d
apart. The curve *ab* shows the survival time of old, large in
viduals, the curve *ac*, that of fifty younger individuals of medi
size.

It will be noted that the relation between survival time and r
of metabolism is the opposite of that observed by the direct meth

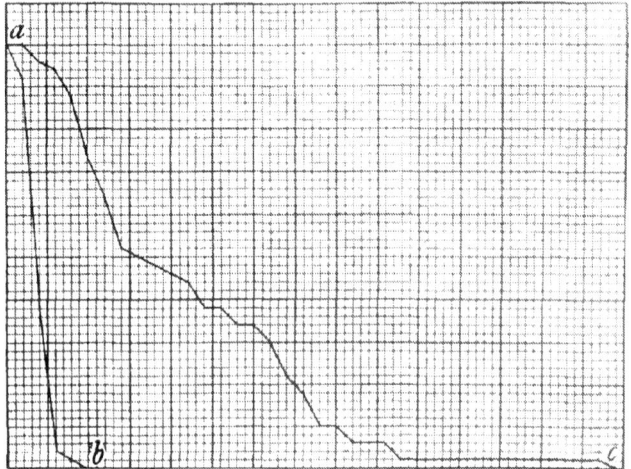

FIG. 4.—*Planaria dorotocephala:* death curves of young and old animals in 1.5
cent alcohol; *ab*, curve of fifty old worms; *ac*, curve of fifty young worms.

Here the younger animals with the higher rate live much lon
than the older with the lower rate. It is also evident that the re
tion between surface and volume in animals of different size pla
no part in the result, for the smaller animals live longer than t
larger. The results obtained with cyanide and other depressi
agents, and even with low temperatures, are essentially the sam
The difference in the ability of the animals to become acclimat
to low concentrations of depressing agents is apparent, not mere
in the length of life, but in the motor activity. The primary effe
of the depressing agent is greater upon the young than upon t

old animals, but the young animals recover more rapidly and more completely under the depressing conditions, and within a few days are very evidently more active than the old.

The relation between the capacity for acclimation and rate of metabolism can be demonstrated very clearly by combining the effect of depressing agents with that of different temperatures. Animals in low concentration of cyanide or alcohol are less capable of acclimation and die earlier at lower than at higher temperatures. Fig. 5 shows the results in an experiment of this sort. The curves

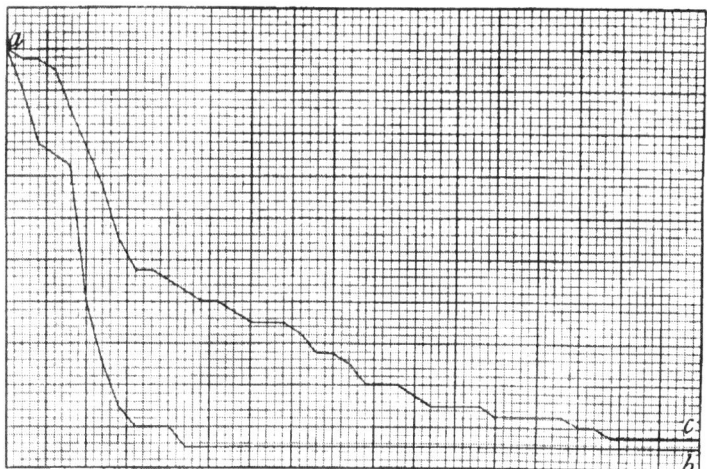

Fig. 5.—*Planaria dorotocephala:* death curves of full-grown animals in 1.5 per cent alcohol at 8°-10° C. (*ab*) and at 20° C. (*ac*).

are plotted in the same way as in Fig. 4. The curve *ab* is the death curve of forty animals in $1\frac{1}{2}$ per cent alcohol at a temperature of 8°–10° C., the curve *ac* that of forty animals of the same size and from the same stock in $1\frac{1}{2}$ per cent alcohol at 20° C. The greater resistance of the animals at the higher temperature is clearly apparent.

But that the rate of metabolism is not the only factor involved in acclimation to depressing agents is evident from the comparison of starved with well-fed animals. In experiments to be described in following chapters it will be shown that in animals undergoing reduction from starvation the rate of metabolism gradually rises, so that a starved animal, reduced to, let us say, one-half its size at the beginning of the experiment, has a much higher rate of metabolism than well-fed animals of its original size and about the same rate as well-fed animals of its reduced size. But the reduced animal has to a large extent lost its ability to become acclimated to depressing agents and conditions, and in spite of its high rate of metabolism is more susceptible to low concentrations of cyanide, alcohol, etc., and also to low temperatures, than well-fed animals of the same size as itself, and shows about the same susceptibility as well-fed animals of its original size, although these possess a much lower rate of metabolism. In other words, the animal which is using its own structural substance as a source of energy is much less able to acclimate itself to depressing conditions than an animal with the same rate of metabolic reaction but with abundant nutritive material. Consequently, it is impossible to determine the differences in rate of metabolism between well-fed and starved animals by the indirect method.[1]

In some cases also, where the differences of size between animals compared are very great, the smaller animals die of starvation before the larger animals undergo sufficient reduction to reach the death point, but this occurs only where the differences are extreme.

In general the indirect method is of value as a means of confirming the results of the direct method, and it can be applied to certain forms where the direct method may be complicated by the relation between surface and volume. The concentration to be used for either method must of course be determined for each species.

OTHER METHODS

There are other physiological differences between young and old organisms besides the rate of metabolism. In many cases marked differences in motor activity exist between young and old

---

[1] Since I was unaware of this relation between the capacity for acclimation and the nutritive condition at the time of my earlier experiments on rejuvenescence by starvation, the use of the indirect method in those experiments led to incorrect conclusions concerning the changes in rate during starvation (Child, '11. pp 547–55), but correction has been made in a later paper (Child, '14a) The reader is also referred to chapter vii below

animals, and the capacity of an individual for growth and development must be regarded as to some extent a criterion of its youth or age. If we can induce an animal to pass through an indefinite number of agamic generations, each of which shows the same vigor and the same cycle of growth and development, we must conclude, either that senescence does not occur in such cases, or else that there is a periodic rejuvenescence associated in some way with the reproductive process or other processes, and we may use the susceptibility methods to determine which of these two alternatives is correct In at least many organisms, probably in all, if the nutritive and other conditions are controlled with sufficient care, the percentage increment of growth decreases with advancing age and serves as a more or less exact indication of physiological condition, though subject to periodic or irregular variation In those forms which attain or approach a more or less definite limit of size, size itself under the normal or usual conditions of existence may serve as a criterion of age, since the size of the organism indicates approximately its position in the life cycle.

The morphological characters, whether those of the cells or of the organism as a whole, may serve as an indication of the youth or age of the individual, but it must be remembered that senescence and rejuvenescence are primarily physiological rather than morphological changes, and that morphological characters are available as criteria only so far as we have learned by experience that certain of them are characteristic of organisms which we can distinguish by other means as physiologically young or old In man and the higher animals the morphological differences between youth and age are clearly evident, but for many of the lower forms this is not the case, although sufficiently minute anatomical or histological investigation would probably disclose some characteristic differences. If these various criteria of youth and age are all valid, we should find that. so far as they can be applied to any particular case, they lead to essentially the same conclusion as regards that case As a matter of fact, they are very generally in agreement, but there are various cases in which one or another of these criteria leads to conclusions different from the others. Some of these cases will be considered in later chapters.

We are accustomed, and experience justifies the custom, to measure age in man and the higher vertebrates by the time elapsed since birth. We say that the individual is a certain number of years old, and from the age in years we can reach fairly definite conclusions as to physiological condition, i e , physiological age In many of the lower forms, however, senescence does not necessarily proceed at an approximately definite rate. In such organisms the time elapsed since the beginning of development does not afford any measure of the physiological age attained, for, as the following chapters will show, the organism has not necessarily continued to grow old during all of that time. Thus it is possible that among members of the same brood, beginning development at the same time, some may attain a much greater physiological age in a given length of time than others. In short, we cannot measure age in all organisms in terms of time.

And, finally, we may attempt to modify the processes of senescence and rejuvenescence and so to gain further insight into their nature. The influence of external conditions and of quantity and quality of nutrition may be determined. We may expect to find that factors which influence the fundamental metabolic processes or the structural substratum will affect the course or character of senescence and rejuvenescence in one way or another if their action continues for a sufficiently long time. In many of the lower forms reproduction may be induced experimentally by the isolation of pieces of the body, which undergo a reorganization into complete new individuals. These experimental reproductions, wherever they can be induced to occur, affect the course of senescence and as a matter of fact bring about a greater or less degree of rejuvenescence. The problem is then accessible to analytic investigation in the lower forms, and the results of such investigation afford a firm foundation for the interpretation of the phenomena of senescence and rejuvenescence in the higher organisms, where they are less accessible to experimental methods.

REFERENCES

ALEXANDER, F. G., and CSERNA, S.
   1913. "Einfluss der Narkose auf den Gaswechsel des Gehirns." *Biochem. Zeitschr.*, LIII.

BERNARD, CL.

   1875   *Leçons sur les anesthétiques,* etc

CARLSON, A. J.

   1907   "On the Action of Cyanides on the Heart," *Am Jour. of Physiol ,*
          XIX

CHILD, C. M.

   1911.   "A Study of Senescence and Rejuvenescence Based on Experiments
           with Planarians," *Arch. f Entwickelungsmech ,* XXXI

   1913a "Studies on the Dynamics of Morphogenesis and Inheritance in
          Experimental Reproduction. V. The Relation between Resist-
          ance to Depressing Agents and Rate of Reaction in *Planaria
          dorotocephala* and Its Value as a Method of Investigation," *Jour.
          of Exp. Zool.,* XIV.

   1913b. "Studies on the Dynamics, etc.: VI   The Nature of the Axial
          Gradients in *Planaria* and Their Relation to Antero-posterior
          Dominance, Polarity and Symmetry," *Arch f. Entwickelungs-
          mech ,* XXXVII.

   1914a. "Starvation, Rejuvenescence and Acclimation in *Planaria doro-
          tocephala," Arch f. Entwickelungsmech.,* XXXVIII

   1914b. "Studies, etc.: VII. The Stimulation of Pieces by Section in
          Planaria dorotocephala," Jour. of Exp Zool., XVI

DRZEWINA, ANNA, et BOHN, G.

   1913   "Anoxybiose et polarité," *Comp rend. Acad Sci Paris,* CXXXVI.

DUBOIS, R.

   1894.   *Anesthésie physiologique.*

GASSER, H. S., and LOEVENHART, A S.

   1914.   "The Mechanism of Stimulation of the Medullary Centers by
           Decreased Oxidation." *Jour. of Pharm. and Exp Therap ,* V.

GEPPERT, J.

   1889.   "Über das Wesen der Blausaurevergiftung," *Zeitschr. f. klin.
           Med ,* XV

GROVE, W. E , and LOEVENHART, A S

   1911.   "The Action of Hydrocyanic Acid on the Respiration and the
           Antagonistic Action of Sodium Iodosobenzoate," *Jour. of Pharm
           and Exp Therap.,* III.

HOBER, R.

   1910.   "Die physikalisch-chemischen Vorgänge bei der Erregung: Sam-
           melreferat," *Zeitschr. f. allgem. Physiol.,* X.

JENNINGS, H. S.

   1913.   "The Effect of Conjugation in *Paramecium," Jour. of Exp Zool.,*
           XIV.

KASTLE, J. H , and LOEVENHART, A. S.

   1901.   "On the Nature of Certain of the Oxidizing Ferments," *Am
           Chem. Jour.,* XXVI.

KISCH, B.

    1913. "Untersuchungen uber Narkose," *Zeitschr. f Biol*, LX.

LILLIE, R. S.

    1912a. "Antagonism between Salts and Anesthetics I. On the Conditions of the Antistimulating Action of Anesthetics, with Observations on Their Protective or Antitoxic Action," *Am. Jour. of Physiol*, XXIX

    1912b. "Antagonism, etc. II. Decrease by Anesthetics in the Rate of Toxic Action of Pure Isotonic Salt Solution on Unfertilized Starfish and Sea Urchin Eggs," *Am Jour of Physiol*, XXX.

    1913a. "Antagonism, etc : III. Further Observations, Showing Parallel Decrease in the Stimulating, Permeability-increasing and Toxic Actions of Salt Solutions in the Presence of Anesthetics," *Am. Jour of Physiol*, XXXI.

    1913b. "The Physico-chemical Conditions of Anesthetic Action," *Science*, XXXVII.

    1914 "Antagonism, etc.: IV. Inactivation of Hypertonic Sea-Water by Anesthetics," *Jour. of Exp Zool*, XVI.

LOEB, J

    1909 *Die chemische Entwicklungserregung des tierischen Eies.* Berlin.

    1910. "Die Hemmung verschiedener Giftwirkungen auf das befruchtete Seeigelei durch Hemmung der Oxydationen in demselben," *Biochem. Zeitchr.*, XXIX.

LOEB, J., and LEWIS, W. H.

    1902 "On the Prolongation of the Life of the Unfertilized Eggs of the Sea Urchin by Potassium Cyanide," *Am Jour. of Physiol.*, VI.

LOEB, J., und WASTENEYS, H.

    1910 "Warum hemmt Natriumcyanide die Giftwirkung einer Chlornatriunlosung fur das Seeigelei?" *Biochem. Zeitschr*, XXVIII

    1913a. "Is Narcosis Due to Asphyxiation?" *Jour. of Biol. Chem.*, XIV.

    1913b. "Narkose und Sauerstoffverbrauch," *Biochem Zeitschr.*, LVI.

LYON, E. P.

    1902. "Effects of Potassium Cyanide and of Lack of Oxygen upon the Fertilized Eggs and the Embryos of the Sea Urchin (*Arbacia punctulata*)," *Am Jour. of Physiol*, VII

    1904. "Rhythms of Susceptibility and of Carbon Dioxide Production in Cleavage," *Am. Jour. of Physiol.*, XI.

MATHEWS, A. P

    1906. "A Note on the Susceptibility of Segmenting *Arbacia* and *Asterias* Eggs to Cyanides," *Biol Bull*, XI.

    1910 "The Action of Ether on Anaerobic Animal Tissue," *Jour. of Pharm. and Exp Therap.*, II

    1913. "The Nature of Irritability and the Action of Anesthetics," *Science*, XXXVII (Proc. Am. Chem Soc)

MATHEWS, A. P., and WALKER, S.
  1909. "The Action of Cyanides and Nitriles on the Spontaneous Oxidation of Cystein," *Jour of Biol Chem.*, VI.
MAUPAS, E.
  1888. "Recherches expérimentales sur la multiplication des infusories ciliés," *Arch de zool exp.*, (2), VI.
  1889. "La rajeunissement karyogamique chez les ciliés," *Arch. de zool. exp.*, (2), VII
MEYER, H.
  1899. "Zur Theorie der Alkoholnarkose· Erste Mitteilung Welche Eigenschaft der Anasthetica bedingt ihre narkotische Wirkung ?" *Arch. f exp. Pathol u. Pharm* , XLII
  1901. "Zur Theorie, etc.: Dritte Mitteilung Einfluss wechselnder Temperatur auf Wirkungstärke und Teilungscoefficient der Narcotica," *Arch. f. exp. Pathol. u. Pharm.*, XLVI.
MINOT, C. S.
  1908. *The Problem of Age, Growth and Death.* New York.
OVERTON, E.
  1901. *Studien über die Narkose.* Jena.
RICHARDS, A N., and WALLACE, G B.
  1908. "The Influence of Potassium Cyanide upon Proteid Metabolism," *Jour. of Biol. Chem* , IV
SCHULTZ, E
  1904. "Uber Reduktionen I Uber Hungererscheinungen bei *Planaria lactea,*" *Arch f Entwickelungsmech.*, XVIII.
  1908. "Uber umkehrbare Entwicklungsprozesse und ihre Bedeutung fur eine Theorie der Vererbung," *Vortr. und Aufs. u. Entwickelungsmech* , IV.
TASHIRO, S
  1913a. "Carbon Dioxide Production from Nerve Fibers When Resting and When Stimulated, A Contribution to the Chemical Basis of Irritability," *Am. Jour of Physiol.*, XXXII.
  1913b. "A New Method and Apparatus for the Estimation of Exceedingly Minute Quantities of Carbon Dioxide," *Am. Jour. of Physiol.*, XXXII.
TRAUBE, J.
  1904a. "Theorie der Osmose und Narkose," *Arch. f. d. ges. Physiol.*, CV.
  1904b "Der Oberflachendruck und seine Bedeutung im Organismus," *Arch. f. d. ges Physiol* , CV
  1908. "Die osmotische Kraft," *Arch f d. ges Physiol* , CXXIII.
  1910. "Die Theorie des Haftdruckes (Oberflachendrucks) und ihre Bedeutung fur die Physiologie," *Arch. f. d ges. Physiol.*, CXXXII
  1911. "Die Theorie des Haftdruckes (Oberflachendrucks), V," *Arch f. d. ges. Physiol* , CXL.
  1913 "Theorie der Narkose," *Arch. f. d. ges. Physiol.*, CLIII

VERNON, H. M.

  1906   "The Conditions of Tissue Respiration," *Jour of Physiol*, XXXV.
  1909   "The Conditions of Tissue Respiration. Part III. The Action of Poison," *Jour. of Physiol*, XXXIX.
  1910   "The Respiration of the Tortoise Heart in Relation to Functional Activity," *Jour of Physiol*, XL.
  1913.   "The Changes in the Reactions of Growing Organisms to Narcotics," *Jour of Physiol.*, XLVII.

VERWORN, M.

  1903.   *Die Biogenhypothese*   Jena.
  1912   *Narkose*. Jena.
  1913.   *Irritability*. New Haven, Conn

WARBURG, O.

  1910a. "Über die Oxydationen in lebenden Zellen nach Versuchen am Seeigelei," *Zeitschr. f. physiol. Chem.*, LXVI.
  1910b. "Über Beeinflussung der Oxydationen in lebenden Zellen nach Versuchen an roten Blutkörperchen," *Zeitschr. f. physiol. Chem.*, LXIX.
  1910c. "Über Beeinflussung der Sauerstoffatmung," *Zeitschr f. physiol. Chem*, LXX
  1911a. "Über Beeinflussung, etc.: II. Mitteilung   Eine Beziehung zur Constitution," *Zeitschr. f. physiol. Chem*, LXXI.
  1911b. "Untersuchungen über die Oxydationsprozesse in Zellen," *Munchener med Wochenschr*, LVII
  1912a. "Untersuchungen, etc., II," *Munchener med. Wochenschr*, LVIII.
  1912b. "Über Beziehungen zwischen Zellstruktur und biochemischen Reaktionen," *Arch f. d ges Physiol.*, CXLV.
  1913.   "Über die Wirkung der Struktur auf chemische Vorgange in Zellen." Jena.
  1914a   "Über Verbrennung der Oxalsaure an Blutkohle und Hemmung dieser Reaktion durch indifferente Narkotika," *Arch. f. d. ges Physiol*, CLIV
  1914b. "Über die Empfindlichkeit der Sauerstoffatmung gegenuber indifferenten Narkotika," *Arch f d. ges Physiol.*, CLVIII
  1914c. "Beiträge zur Physiologie der Zelle, insbesondere uber die Oxydationsgeschwindigkeit in Zellen," *Ergebn d Physiol*, XIV.

WINTERSTEIN, H.

  1902.   "Zur Kenntnis der Narkose," *Zeitschr. f allgem Physiol*, I
  1905.   "Warmelahmung und Narkose," *Zeitschr f. allgem. Physiol*, V.
  1913.   "Beitrage zur Kenntnis der Narkose   I   Mitteilung. Kritische Übersicht uber die Beziehungen zwischen Narkose und Sauerstoffatmung," *Biochem. Zeitschr*, LI
  1914   "Beitrage, etc.: II. Mitteilung. Der Einfluss der Narkose auf den Gaswechsel des Froschruckenmarks," *Biochem. Zeitschr*, LXI

CHAPTER IV

AGE DIFFERENCES IN SUSCEPTIBILITY IN THE LOWER ANIMALS

THE EXPERIMENTAL MATERIAL

Three species of fresh-water planarians, *Planaria dorotocephala,* *P maculata,* and *P. velata,* have constituted the chief material for the more extended investigations. *P. dorotocephala* is found in great abundance in various parts of the United States, chiefly in springs and the streams issuing from them. In nature the animals usually attain a length of twenty to twenty-five millimeters, but in the laboratory with abundant food may reach double that length.

The body, like that of most turbellaria, is dorso-ventrally flattened; the body-wall consists of a one-layered ciliated ectoderm beneath which lie longitudinal and transverse muscle layers and in the spaces between the internal organs a parenchymal tissue. A pigment layer beneath the dorsal ectoderm gives the dorsal surface a deep-brown color, the ventral surface being much less deeply pigmented. The chief features of the internal anatomy are indicated in Fig. 6. The central nervous system consists of a pair of cephalic ganglia beneath the eyes and two longitudinal cords (*ns*) which give off branches and are connected by commissures. The chief sense-organs are the eyes, consisting of pigment cups containing sensory cells and the lateral pointed cephalic lobes, which are organs of chemical sense The margins of the head and body are also sensitive tactile organs.

The mouth (*m*) lies ventrally in the middle of the body and opens into a pharyngeal pouch containing a tubular pharynx (*ph*). At its anterior end the pharynx opens into the alimentary tract which consists of three main branches (*al*) and many secondary branches. A diffuse branching excretory system is also present, but not shown in the figure Under the usual conditions the animals do not become sexually mature, and sexual organs if present at all do not develop beyond very early stages.

The general plan of internal structure of other related species is much the same, but they differ in shape and general appearance. *Planaria maculata* (Fig. 7) does not attain as large a size as *P. dorotocephala* and is less active. The head differs in shape from that of *P. dorotocephala* and the pigment is distributed in large spots. *P. velata* (Fig. 8) is more slender, somewhat less flattened, and without the pointed cephalic lobes. The younger worms are almost black, but become light gray with advancing age.

Various other flatworms, protozoa, the fresh-water hydra, and several marine hydroids have been used in comparative experiments.

AGE DIFFERENCES IN SUSCEPTIBILITY IN
Planaria maculata

Animals of this species kept in the laboratory and fed become sexually mature and deposit egg capsules containing fertilized eggs, and from these capsules the young worms emerge in about four weeks at ordinary temperatures. When first hatched the young worms possess the form of the adult, but are only about two millimeters in length, while in my stock the old, sexually mature worms, which were laying eggs, were about twelve millimeters long.

Fig. 9 shows the susceptibility curves (see pp. 80–82) of young and old animals of this species to potassium cyanide, 0.001 mol. The curve *ab* gives the susceptibility for ten newly hatched worms, the curve *cd*, that for ten full-grown sexually mature worms about twelve millimeters in length. The

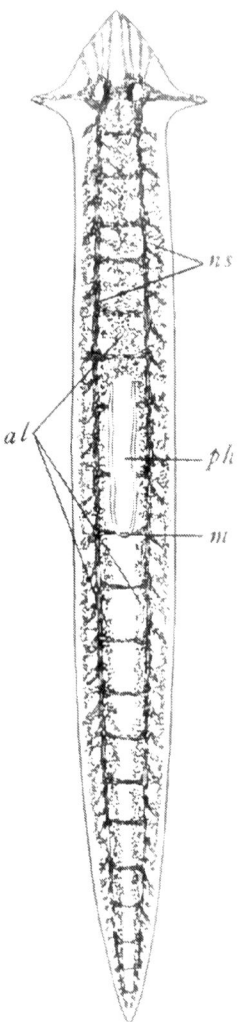

FIG. 6. *Planaria dorotocephala: m*, mouth; *ph*, pharynx; *al*, alimentary tract; *ns*, nervous system.

susceptibility of the newly hatched worms is much greater than that of the full-grown animals, disintegration of the former being

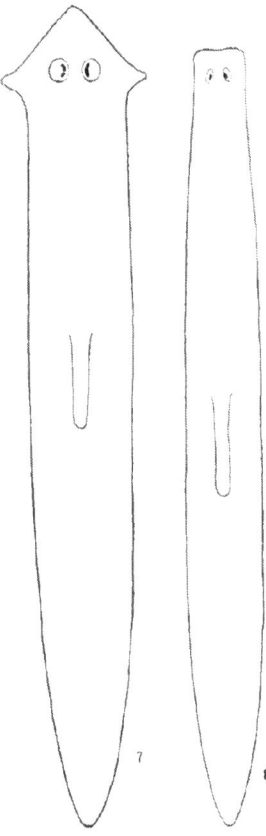

far advanced before it begins in the latter. Since susceptibility measured by the higher concentrations of the direct method varies with rate of metabolism, the young animals must have a much higher rate than the old.

But the method enables us to distinguish age differences in rate of metabolism which are very much less than these. In Fig. 10 the curve *ab* shows the susceptibility of ten worms hatched within the twenty-four hours preceding the beginning of the experiment, and the curve *cd* the susceptibility of ten animals four days after hatching and without food. Here the difference in size between the animals of the two lots is much less than in the preceding case, the younger worms being two millimeters, the older three and one-half millimeters long. The figure shows that the susceptibility of the newly hatched animals is considerably greater, i.e., their rate of metabolism is higher than that of the animals four days after hatching. Since the differences in susceptibility as shown in Fig. 10 are considerable

FIGS. 7, 8.—*Planaria maculata* and *P. velata.*

for four days' time, it is evident that the rate of metabolism must decrease rapidly after hatching.

The young worms are capable of movement before they emerge from the egg capsules, and by opening the capsules with fine needles it is possible to obtain young worms of various stages before hatching. A comparison of the resistance to cyanide of unhatched worms capable of movement with that of worms just hatched shows, as in Fig. 10, that the younger worms have the higher rate of metabolism, although in this case also the difference in age measured by time is no more than a few days.

But it is only during these earlier stages of the life cycle that the rate of metabolism changes appreciably during such short intervals of time. The rate of metabolism decreases most rapidly during the earlier stages, and as development advances the decrease in rate for a given time interval becomes always less. In animals eight or nine millimeters in length, for example, the differences in rate of metabolism for an interval of two or three weeks, under ordinary conditions of nutrition and temperature, and in many cases for a much longer interval, are no greater than the differences shown in Fig. 10 for an interval of four days immediately after hatching. In still older animals the decrease in rate of metabolism under constant conditions is even slower.

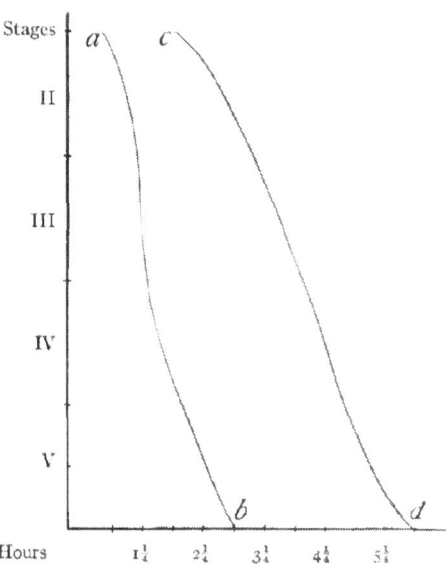

Fig. 9.—Susceptibility of *Planaria maculata* to KCN 0.001 mol.: *ab*, recently hatched worms; *cd* full-grown, sexually mature worms.

In Fig. 11 the susceptibilities of two lots of large old worms are compared. The curve *ab* is from ten worms twelve millimeters in length, and *cd* from ten worms sixteen to eighteen millimeters in length. These worms were collected from their natural habitat

at this size and it is impossible to say whether the larger worms are
older in point of time than the smaller. They have, however,
attained a stage of growth and development which under anything
approaching natural conditions could be reached by the smaller
worms only after at least some weeks.

The larger, physiologically older worms begin to disintegrate
two hours later and also complete their disintegration one and one-
half hours later than the smaller ones.
In other words, their survival time is
about one-fifth greater than that of
the smaller worms   But in Fig. 10
above, the survival time of worms
four days after hatching is almost
one-half greater than that of worms
newly hatched, that is, the difference
in rate of metabolism between the
two lots of Fig 10, which are only
four days apart, is much greater than
that between the two lots of Fig. 11,
which represent physiological conditions several weeks apart in terms of
time   Clearly the rate of metabolism
decreases very much more slowly in
the larger, older worms than in the
stages immediately following hatching   A comparison of Figs 10 and
11 also shows, as does Fig. 9, the
great difference in susceptibility between very young and full-grown
animals.

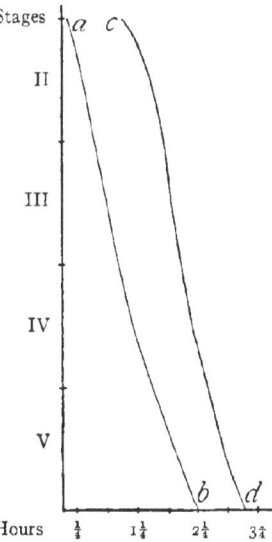

Fig 10 —Susceptibility of *Planaria maculata* to KCN 0 001
mol. *ab*, worms hatched within
24 hours, *cd*, worms four days
after hatching

These results are in complete agreement with the observations
of Minot ('08) and others on the rate of growth in mammals and
birds   The rate of growth as measured by the percentage increment is highest in the youngest animals and decreases with advancing age   As Minot says, "the period of youth is the period of most
rapid decline"   And now we find this to be true, not only for the
rate of growth in the higher animals, but for the rate of metabolism

in such simple forms as the planarian worms. But as will
more clearly in following chapters, time is not a correct m
of physiological age in these lower forms. The animal whic
lived longer is not necessarily the older: the older animal is t
which has undergone more growth and development, bu
amount of growth and development is dependent upon nut
temperature, and other external conditions. It is possil

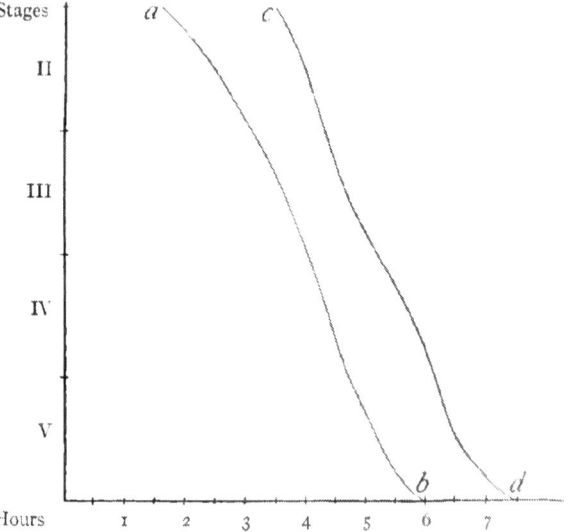

FIG. 11.—Susceptibility of *Planaria maculata* to KCN 0.001 mol.: *ab*,
12 mm. in length; *cd*, worms 16–18 mm. in length.

measure the physiological age of these animals in terms of
only when the conditions of existence are controlled.

Fig. 12 will serve to illustrate this point. In this figur
curve *ab* shows the susceptibility of ten worms nine millin
long from a stock raised in the laboratory from eggs and only
ten weeks "old," while the curve *cb* is plotted from worms ten
meters long, but which had lived at least a year. The temper
was somewhat higher in this series than in those preceding, an
survival times are therefore shorter than they would be for an
of this age at the temperature of the other series.

The worms which are so much "older" in point of time show only a slightly greater resistance, i.e., a slightly lower rate of metabolism than the worms of the "younger" lot. As a matter of fact, the worms of the curve *cb* had been considerably older physiologically at an earlier period than they were at the time when the comparison was made and had been undergoing rejuvenescence in consequence of reduction. We cannot measure the age of such organisms in terms of time unless we know that they have been growing old without interruption, and even then the rate of senescence may vary with conditions.

On the other hand, size, or, more strictly, length—for in the later stages the growth is largely a growth in length—is under the usual conditions and within certain limits, a fairly good criterion of physiological age. Barring individual size differences, which are slight, the length of the animal is an index of

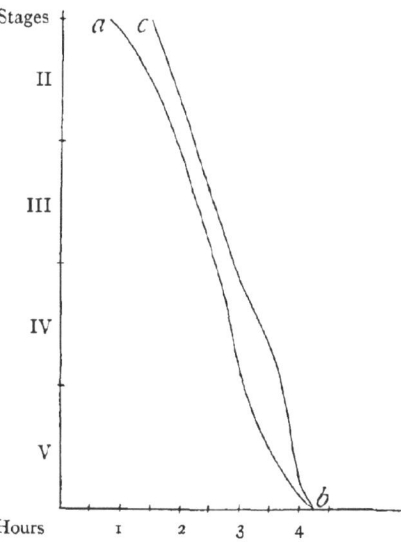

Fig 12 —Susceptibility of *Planaria maculata* to KCN o ooi mol.· *ab*, worms 9 mm. in length and ten weeks after hatching; *cb*, worms 10 mm. in length and at least one year after hatching

the amount of growth and development which has occurred, and we find in general, as the preceding figures show, that the longer animal has a lower rate of metabolism than the shorter. But it does not follow that individuals of the same length always possess the same rate of metabolism. A given size may be attained either by growth from a smaller or reduction from a larger size, and the physiological condition of the animal is not the same in the two cases. But in a single stock, where all individuals have been under essentially the same conditions for a considerable period and where the animals are not undergoing fission, the length of the worm is a real criterion of its physiological condition, the rate of metabolism being lower in the longer than in the shorter worms.

Results obtained by the direct method, such as those presented above, can be confirmed by the indirect or acclimation method, which was described on pp. 82-85. Except where the differences of size are extreme, the animals which have the higher rate of metabolism and die earlier in the concentrations of the direct method live longer than those with the lower rate in the low concentrations used for the acclimation method. In other words, the animals which are larger and therefore physiologically older become less readily and less completely acclimated to the depressing reagent, and so die earlier than the younger animals. Since the results obtained by this method in the present case merely confirm the results of the direct method, it is unnecessary to consider them in detail.

AGE DIFFERENCES IN SUSCEPTIBILITY IN *Planaria dorotocephala*

In a stock of *Planaria dorotocephala* collected from the natural habitat of this species, animals are found ranging in length from four or five millimeters up to twenty millimeters or more. Since there is reason to believe that sexual reproduction does not occur, or at most occurs very rarely in this species under natural conditions in the localities which have come under my observation, it is certain that at least most of the animals collected have arisen by fission (see pp. 125, 384-86). But, ignoring for the present the question of their origin, we should naturally regard the smaller worms in such a stock as the younger and the larger as the older, and we find as a matter of fact that the same differences in susceptibility exist between the larger and the smaller worms as in *P maculata*. This difference is shown in Fig. 3 and in Fig. 13. Fig. 13 gives the susceptibility curves of four lots of ten worms each from a stock which had been in the laboratory only one day. Curve *ab* shows the susceptibility of worms five millimeters in length, curve *ac* of worms seven millimeters, curve *ad* of worms ten to twelve millimeters, and curve *ef* of worms eighteen to twenty millimeters in length. The survival times are considerably longer than those in Fig. 3 because of lower alkalinity of the water used.

A marked difference in the susceptibility of the worms of different size appears in the figure. The smallest worms (curve *ab*) begin to die and disintegrate earlier and disintegrate more rapidly than the others, and the susceptibility in the other lots decreases as the size increases. In short, the larger worms possess a lower

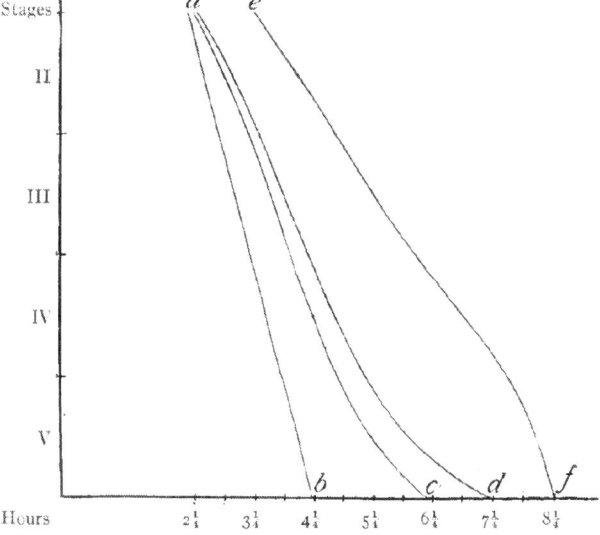

FIG. 13.—Susceptibility of *Planaria dorotocephala* to KCN 0.001 mol.: *ab*, worms 5 mm. in length; *ac*, worms 7 mm. in length; *ad*, worms 10–12 mm. in length; *ef*, worms 18–20 mm. in length.

rate of metabolism than the smaller, and in general the rate of metabolism decreases with increasing size.

Hundreds of animals of this species have been compared in this way, with cyanide, alcohol, ether, etc., as reagents, and the result has been in all cases essentially the same. Tested by the acclimation method, the smaller worms show a greater capacity to acclimate to the reagent, i.e., a higher rate of metabolism, than the larger, so that the results of the two methods check and confirm each other. Moreover, the smaller animals grow more rapidly than the larger under like conditions and are more active.

The only possible conclusion is that in this species individuals resulting from the asexual process of fission show age differences similar in character to those in the sexually produced individuals of *Planaria maculata*. In both cases the rate of metabolism is highest in the young worms and decreases with advancing age Later chapters will confirm this conclusion (see chaps v, vii).

AGE DIFFERENCES IN SUSCEPTIBILITY IN OTHER FORMS

In order to determine whether age differences in susceptibility are of general occurrence and of the same sort, the susceptibility of young and old individuals of a considerable number of species from different groups has been compared by direct method. The general results of these investigations are briefly stated without the data of experiment

The age differences in susceptibility have been determined for various other species of flatworms. In *Dendrocoelum lacteum*, *Phagocata gracilis*, and certain unnamed species of the *Mesostomidae*, all of which reproduce only sexually, the susceptibility by the direct method of the young animals to the cyanides is much greater than that of the old   In *Planaria velata*, the old worms break up into fragments which encyst and undergo reconstitution into new individuals in the cysts and later emerge as young worms capable of repeating the life cycle   In this species also the susceptibility, as determined by the direct method, is greatest in the young worms after they emerge from the cysts, and decreases from this stage on until the next fragmentation (Child, '13).

Differences in susceptibility which are undoubtedly connected with physiological age have been found in certain protozoa (see pp. 141–42).   Among the coelenterates the fresh-water hydra and two species of hydroids, *Pennaria tiarella* (see Fig 50, p 148) and *Corymorpha palma*, have been tested   In the two hydroids the sexually produced young at any stage after attaining the form of the adult show a much greater susceptibility than the full-grown mature animals.   In hydra, sexually produced young have not as yet been obtained, but the young animals asexually produced show a higher susceptibility than the parent.   In the ctenophore, *Mnemiopsis leidyi*, the susceptibility decreases with advancing physiological age, i e , as growth and development proceed.   Here the earliest stages tested were young of about five millimeters in diameter. Their susceptibility is greater than that of later stages and very much greater than that of full-grown animals   In the course of investigations not yet published on several species of oligochete annelids, Miss Hyman has found that the young animals show a greater susceptibility to cyanide than the old   The young in these cases arose by the asexual process of fission and not from fertilized eggs.   Various species of entomostracean crustacea which have been examined show in every case a greater susceptibility in the young than in the old animals, but it is possible that differences in size may be a factor in the result in these forms   In the larvae of amphibia the susceptibility is greater in newly hatched animals than in later stages.

CONCLUSION

The uniform results obtained from widely different groups show very clearly that age differences in susceptibility to cyanides and other narcotics are of general occurrence.   Moreover, in all cases the young animals, at least beyond a certain stage, show the highest susceptibility, and susceptibility decreases with advancing development.   In other words, the rate of metabolism is highest in the young animals and decreases with advancing age.   This conclusion is in full agreement with what we know of the physiological aspects of senescence in the higher animals, and it forces us to the further conclusion that a decrease in rate of metabolism is at least very generally associated with growth and differentiation.

REFERENCES

CHILD, C. M
   1913.   "The Asexual Cycle in *Planaria velata* in Relation to Senescence and Rejuvenescence," *Biol Bull* , XXV.

MINOT, C. S
   1908.   *The Problem of Age, Growth and Death*   New York.

CHAPTER V

THE RECONSTITUTION OF ISOLATED PIECES IN RELATION TO REJUVENESCENCE IN *PLANARIA* AND OTHER FORMS

THE RECONSTITUTION OF PIECES IN *Planaria*

In consequence of the ability of isolated pieces cut from the body to develop into complete individuals, the various species of *Planaria* have served to a very large extent as material for the study of "form-regulation," "regeneration," "restitution," as the changes which occur in such pieces have been variously called The morphological and histological features of the reconstitution of such pieces into new wholes have been repeatedly discussed by various authors and for various species Since the essential features of the process do not differ widely in the different species, a brief description of reconstitution as it occurs in *P. dorotocephala* will serve the present purpose The reconstitution of such a piece as *a* in Fig 14 is shown in Figs 15-17 The cut surfaces of the piece contract after its isolation, and in the course of two or three days outgrowths of new embryonic tissue appear on these surfaces, these outgrowths being readily distinguishable from other parts of the piece by the absence of the dark-brown pigment characteristic of the species. In Fig 15 and following figures these outgrowths of new tissue are marked off from other parts by lines which indicate the boundaries between new and old tissue. During the next two or three days the anterior outgrowth develops into a head with eyes, cephalic lobes and, as the section shows, a new cephalic ganglion, and the posterior outgrowth develops into a posterior end (Fig. 16). At about the same time the new pharynx becomes visible, near the posterior end of the old tissue of the piece, and the intestinal branches present in the piece begin the changes which end in the formation of an alimentary tract like that of a whole animal. The developing animal also elongates and decreases in width, the postpharyngeal region grows at the expense of the prepharyngeal, and finally an individual results (Fig 17) which is in all respects, so far as can be determined, a whole animal of small

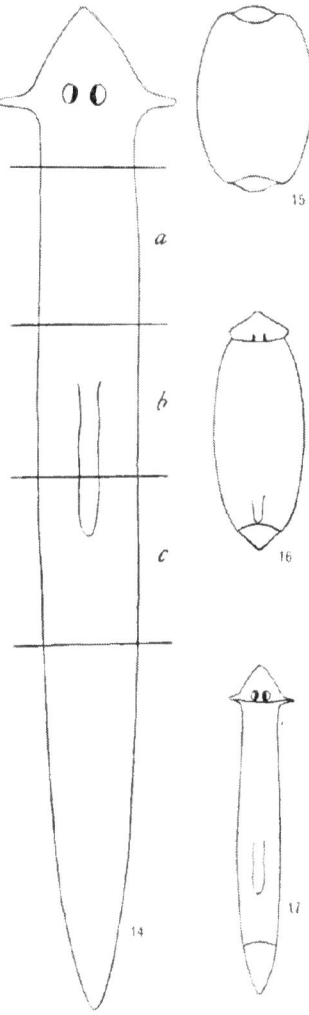

FIGS. 14-17.—Reconstitution of pieces of *Planaria dorotocephala:* Fig. 14, body-outline indicating levels of section; Figs. 15-17, three stages in the reconstitution of an isolated piece.

size. Various details of the process differ according to the size of the piece, the level of the body from which it is taken, the physiological condition of the animal, and the environmental conditions, and a limit of size exists which also varies with all these factors; pieces below this limit of size do not reproduce complete normal animals. The influence of these various factors is evident chiefly in the character of the head, which may range from the normal through a series of teratological forms with a headless condition as the extreme term of the series (Child, '11*b*, '11*c*; see also Figs. 20-23, pp. 111-12). In other species of planarians the process of reconstitution is in general much the same, but with differences in details and in the relation to the various factors mentioned above.

The process of reconstitution in these cases differs somewhat from the replacement of a missing part in higher animals. The isolated piece of *Planaria* does not replace the missing parts in their original condition and size, but develops merely a new head and posterior end and then undergoes an extensive reorganization into a new individual of small size, the size being dependent upon the size of the isolated piece   In the course of the process some parts of the piece atrophy and disappear, new parts arise and differentiate, and a large amount of cell division and growth occur   The piece does not, in many cases cannot, feed until the development of the new individual has reached a certain stage, consequently the energy for the changes which occur must be derived from the nutritive reserves and the tissues of the piece itself.   In this connection it may be noted that the volume of the new animal is always considerably less than that of the piece from which it arose; in other words, the piece undergoes a considerable amount of reduction in producing a new individual.

The development of the new animal in this process of reconstitution is not fundamentally different from embryonic development (Child, '12a, '13)—it merely occurs under rather different conditions; nor is it essentially different from the process of agamic reproduction in nature; it is, in short, an experimental reproduction Moreover, the new animal thus produced resembles a young animal in its morphological features and is capable, when fed, of growth and development, in fact, of going through all stages of the life history beyond that which it apparently represents.   All these facts raise the question whether such an animal is or may be younger physiologically as well as morphologically than the animal from which the piece was taken.   This question is considered in the following section.

CHANGES IN SUSCEPTIBILITY DURING THE RECONSTITUTION OF PIECES

An extensive investigation of the changes during reconstitution in the susceptibility of isolated pieces to cyanide has been made by the direct susceptibility method.   It should be borne in mind that changes in susceptibility as indicated by this method indicate change in the same direction of rate of metabolism.   The results of these experiments are given here only in general terms   The complete data have appeared elsewhere (Child, '14a)

The first change follows immediately upon the act of isolation The susceptibility of the piece immediately after isolation is greater, i e., its rate of metabolism is higher, than that of the same region

of the body in uninjured animals which are as nearly as possible
in the same physiological condition as that from which the piece
was taken.

This is of course to be expected, for the operation of cutting
the piece out of the body undoubtedly stimulates it and so increases
its rate of metabolism, and the presence of the wounds at the two
ends of the piece undoubtedly serves to continue this stimulation
It is an interesting fact that short pieces show a greater increase
in rate of metabolism than long, as the result of section   This
again is only to be expected, for the nearer the cut is to a given
region of the body, the more directly the nervous structures inner-
vating that region are affected by it. When the piece includes a
half or a third of the body, the stimulation following section, as
indicated by an increase in rate in the piece as a whole, is slight,
but the degree of stimulation increases as the length of the piece
decreases, and in short pieces, including one-eighth or less of the
body-length, the increase in rate is great

But this increase in rate following section is only temporary,
as we should expect, if it is due to the stimulation resulting from
section   The rate of metabolism in the isolated piece, as measured
by its susceptibility to cyanide, decreases during the first few hours
after section   In long pieces, including a half or a third of the
body-length, the rate falls to about the same level as that in the
corresponding region of the parent body, or somewhat lower.   But
in shorter pieces the rate does not fall as low, and in very short
pieces it may remain considerably higher than in the same region
of the uninjured animal, probably because in such cases the wound
stimulus involves the whole piece to a greater or less extent.   The
decrease in metabolic rate following the increase after isolation is
evidently due to the gradual recovery from the condition of excitation following the act of section.

But this condition, like the initial condition of stimulation, is
only temporary in cases where the piece undergoes reconstitution.
Within three or four days after section the processes of reconstitution are well under way, and they are accompanied by an increase
in susceptibility, i e., an increase in rate of metabolism in the pieces
This continues as reconstitution goes on, and when the develop-

ment of the new animal from the piece is completed, the susceptibility is greater than that in the corresponding region of the parent animal This means that during reconstitution the rate of metabolism increases until it is higher than before section. This increase in rate is not the result of a stimulation which soon disappears, but is connected with the process of reconstitution and is relatively permanent The rate after reconstitution is the rate characteristic of a physiologically young animal, and it undergoes a gradual decrease as the animal grows and becomes physiologically older Here also size is a factor in the result: the smaller the piece which undergoes reconstitution into a new whole, the greater the increase in rate of reaction during reconstitution. This increase in metabolic activity during reconstitution was first discovered by means of the acclimation method with alcohol as a reagent (Child, '11). In these earlier experiments a marked increase in rate was found in small pieces, but in very large pieces a decrease in rate apparently occurred. As a matter of fact, the rate does not decrease in large pieces during reconstitution, but increases slightly. My error on this point was due to failure to keep the normal animals under the same conditions as the experimental pieces In the case of the large pieces the effect of the conditions more than compensated the slight increase in rate due to reconstitution, but in the small pieces, where the increase was much greater, it appeared in spite of the external conditions.

More recent and extended investigation by the direct method with cyanide as reagent has demonstrated beyond a doubt that reconstitution is accompanied by an increase in rate, the amount of increase varying with the size of the piece, the amount of reconstitutional change, and various other factors.

The partial record of one series of experiments will serve to show both the increase in susceptibility, i e., of rate of metabolism resulting from reconstitution, and the relation between the amount of increase and the size of the piece In this experiment large, physiologically old worms eighteen to twenty millimeters in length constituted the material From a part of these worms pieces including the region ac in Fig 18, from another part pieces including the region ab, i e., just half the length of the preceding lot, were

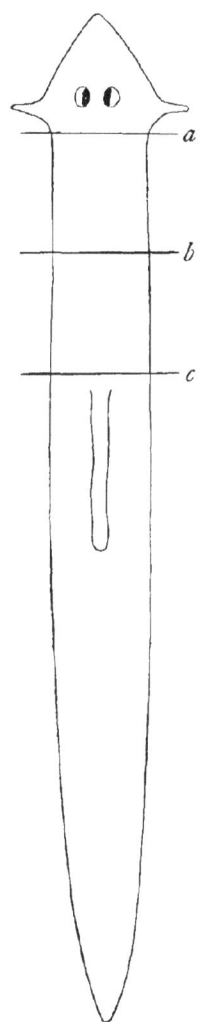

FIG. 18.—Body-outline of *Planaria dorotocephala*, indicating levels of section

cut These two lots of pieces were allowed to develop into new animals A third part of the stock consisting of uninjured worms was kept under the same conditions as a control and since the pieces do not feed during the process of reconstitution, this third lot was not fed. During the reconstitution of the pieces several comparative tests were made of their susceptibility, and of that of the uninjured animals, to cyanide. The results of one of these tests made sixteen days after the pieces were cut from the parent bodies is given in Fig 19 Both the pieces and the whole animals had been without food during this time, but the effects of sixteen days' starvation are not very great as regards susceptibility. During these sixteen days the pieces had become fully developed animals, the longer being seven to eight millimeters, the shorter, five millimeters in length. In Fig 19 the curve *ab* shows the susceptibility of ten animals developed from the shorter pieces, the curve *cd* the susceptibility of ten animals from the longer pieces, and the curve *ef* the susceptibility of uninjured animals the same size as those from which the pieces were taken. It is evident at once from the figure that the susceptibility of the pieces which have undergone reconstitution to whole animals is very considerably greater than that of the uninjured animals like those from which these pieces came, and that further the susceptibility of the animals which develop from the shorter pieces is greater than that of those from the longer. The results of all other similar tests of susceptibility

have been essentially the same. When the pieces are ve
and include a considerable portion of the body, the inc
susceptibility is slight or inappreciable, but with decrease i
piece increase in susceptibility becomes greater, provided th
are not so small that they fail to undergo complete reconst

Recalling the age differences in susceptibility shown
preceding chapter to exist, it is evident that the animals r
from the reconstitution of pieces are, at least as regard

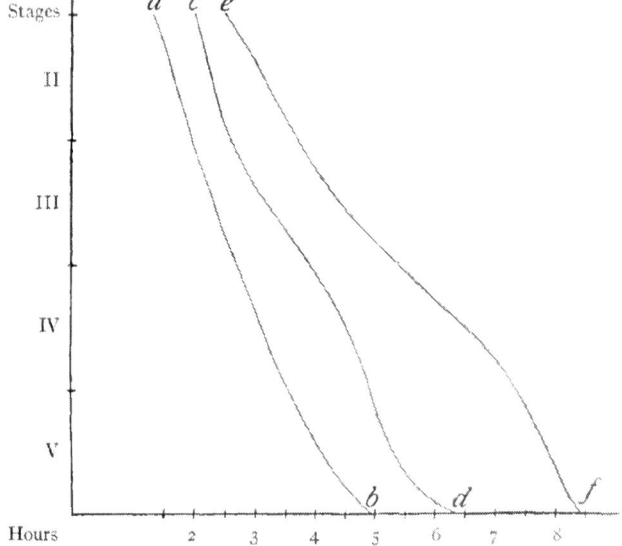

FIG. 19.—Susceptibility of *Planaria dorotocephala* to KCN 0.001 mol.:
pieces; *cd*, long pieces; *ef*, uninjured worms like those from which pieces we

susceptibility, younger than the animals from which the piec
taken. Apparently the process of reconstitution brings al
some way a greater or less degree of rejuvenescence as rega
susceptibility to cyanide, i.e., the rate of metabolism. The
the piece, the greater the amount of reorganization in the
tion of a whole animal and the greater the degree of rejuvene

In this connection it is of interest to note that the new
formed at the cut ends of the piece is for a considerable tim
its formation distinctly more susceptible to cyanide, i.e., y

physiologically, than the old tissues of the rest of the piece. As the new tissue differentiates, however, this difference in susceptibility between it and the old parts gradually disappears, for the new tissue gradually grows old and its rate of metabolism decreases, while the old tissue gradually undergoes reconstitutional changes which involve the atrophy and disappearance of some parts and the formation of others by cell division and growth, and besides this the tissues of the piece, particularly the old tissues with their lower rate of metabolism, are being used up as a source of nutrition for the developing organism In other words, the new embryonic tissue formed at the cut surfaces gradually becomes old after its formation, while other parts of the piece gradually become young by reduction and reorganization, until a dynamic equilibrium is established in the rate of metabolism in the different parts, after which the animal, if fed, undergoes senescence as a whole.

With various other organisms which show a high capacity for reconstitution similar results have been obtained In various other species of flatworms, so far as tested, in *Hydra* and in the hydroid *Corymorpha*, the animals resulting from the reconstitution of pieces show a higher rate of metabolism than the animals from which the pieces were taken. Miss Hyman has found that this is also true for animals developed from pieces of *Lumbriculus* and other fresh-water oligochete annelids.

Animals produced in this way are also younger in other respects than those from which the pieces came. They grow more rapidly and are capable of repeating the developmental history from the stage which they represent onward. There can be no doubt that the process of reconstitution brings about in some way a greater or less degree of rejuvenescence in these relatively simple animals, and that the degree of rejuvenescence is in general proportional to the degree of reorganization in the process of reconstitution of the piece into a whole.

THE INCREASE IN SUSCEPTIBILITY IN RELATION TO THE DEGREE OF RECONSTITUTION

The reconstitutional capacity of pieces of *Planaria dorotocephala*, as of other species, is limited Pieces below a certain size limit, which varies with the condition of the animal, with the level of the body from which the piece is taken, and with various external factors which influence the rate of metabolism, do not produce complete normal animals, although they may undergo a greater or less degree of reconstitution and approach more or less closely to the normal form.   Such pieces show all gradations between the normal animal at one extreme and a completely headless form at the other (Child, '11b, '11c, '12b)   It has been found convenient to distinguish in this graded series of forms five different types, as follows:

Normal —The head is like that of animals found in nature with two completely separated eyes and cephalic lobes at lateral margins (Fig. 17).

FIG 20 —Various degrees of teratophthalmia in *Planaria dorotocephala*

Teratophthalmic.—The head is of the usual form, but the eye spots show differences in size, asymmetry in position, approach to the median line, or various degrees of fusion   Some of the eye forms are shown in Fig 20.   In all teratophthalmic animals the cephalic ganglia show various degrees of fusion or asymmetry, the condition of the eyes being to a considerable extent indicative of that of the ganglia.

Teratomorphic.—Here the preocular region of the head fails to attain its full size or does not appear at all   Consequently the cephalic lobes arise on the anterior margin of the head as in Fig 21 *A*, or in extreme cases are fused together in the median line at the front of the head (Fig 21 *B*).

Anophthalmic.—The anterior outgrowth of new tissue is variable in form and without eyes, but contains a small, single, ganglionic mass, i e., it is a rudimentary head (Figs. 22 *A*, 22 *B*).

Headless —The anterior outgrowth merely fills in the contracted cut surface and does not extend beyond the contours of the margin; the posterior outgrowth, however, is usually even longer than in other pieces, but its differentiation proceeds very slowly and is never completed as long as it is attached to the headless piece (Fig 23).

The difference between the extremes of this series, the normal and headless forms, in the degree of reorganization is very great,

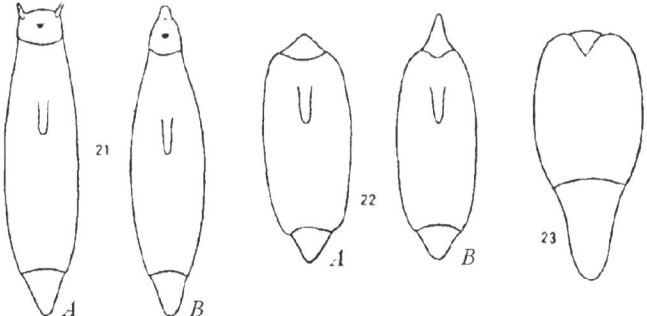

Figs 21–23.—Different degrees of reconstitution in *Planaria dorotocephala*. Fig 21 *A*, *B*, teratomorphic forms, Fig. 22 *A*, *B*, anophthalmic forms, Fig. 23, headless form

particularly in pieces from the postoral region (eg., *a*, Fig 24).   In the development of a normal animal the anterior half or more of such a piece undergoes extensive changes in giving rise to a pharyngeal and prepharyngeal region, and outgrowths of new tissue appear at both ends.   In the piece from this region which remains headless no prepharyngeal or pharyngeal region arises, and changes are limited to the longer outgrowth at the posterior end and the smaller amount of new tissue at the anterior end.

In the teratophthalmic, teratomorphic, and anophthalmic forms the degree of reconstitutional change ranges from a little less than in the normal animal to somewhat more than in the headless form. Moreover the degree of reconstitution decreases somewhat as the character of the head departs from normal. In pieces of the same length and from the same region the size of the head and the length of the pharyngeal and prepharyngeal region are less in teratophthalmic and teratomorphic than in normal animals and less in anophthalmic than in teratomorphic or teratophthalmic forms. Between the teratophthalmic and teratomorphic forms the differences in this respect are not very great except when opposite extremes of the two types are compared.

That the production of a normal or nearly normal animal from a piece requires more energy than the production of a headless form is indicated by the fact that a much greater amount of reduction occurs in the former than in the latter case. Moreover, in a given lot of pieces it is possible by means of external conditions such as temperature, low concentrations of narcotics, etc., whose effect is primarily quantitative rather than qualitative, to determine experimentally within wide limits which of the five forms shall be produced (Child, '11b, '12b). Experiments of this kind have demonstrated that all four forms. from the teratophthalmic to the headless are what might be called subnormal, i.e., they are due to various degrees of retardation or inhibition of the dynamic processes (Child, '11b, '14a, '14b). And, finally, after their development is completed, the normal head shows in general a higher susceptibility than the teratophthalmic and teratomorphic, and these a higher susceptibility tha the anophthalmic.

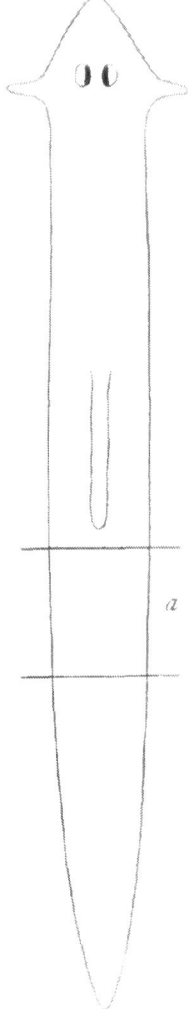

Fig. 24.—Body-outli of *Planaria dorotocepha* indicating levels of section

It is evident, then, from all points of view, that these different forms represent different degrees of reconstitution. If the degree of rejuvenescence, as indicated by the increase in susceptibility, is associated with the degree of reconstitution, then these different forms, when produced under comparable conditions, should show the highest susceptibility in the normal, the lowest in the headless animals, with intermediate conditions in the intermediate forms The following experiment shows to what extent this is the case.

The stock for the experiment consisted of a hundred or more pieces like a in Fig 24, cut from animals of equal size and similar physiological condition and allowed to undergo reconstitution under uniform external conditions   Even under such conditions pieces of this size and from this region may produce anything from normal to headless forms, although the great majority are headless or anophthalmic

Eleven days after section reconstitution was practically complete, and the susceptibilities of lots of ten each of the different forms and at the same time of a lot of ten intact worms like those from which the pieces had been taken were determined. The control animals had been kept under the same conditions as the pieces, and, like them, without food during the eleven days of the experiment, and the difference in susceptibility between the pieces and these whole animals should show how much rejuvenescence had occurred in connection with reconstitution

The results appear in the susceptibility curves of Fig 25   The curve of the whole animal is drawn in an unbroken line, that of the normal animals developed from pieces in short dashes, that of the teratophthalmic forms in long dashes, that of the anophthalmic forms in alternate long and short dashes, and that of headless forms in dots   The susceptibility is highest in the normal animals developed from pieces, slightly lower in the teratophthalmic forms, considerably lower in the anophthalmic forms, and again still lower in the headless forms   In all except the headless forms the susceptibility is higher than in the whole animals, i e , it has increased during reconstitution.

The susceptibility curve of the headless pieces shows an interesting relation to that of the whole animals   In earlier stages the susceptibility of the headless forms falls below that of the whole animals, but later rises considerably above it. This is simply an expression of the fact that there is no part of the headless piece which has as high a rate of metabolism as the head-region of the whole animal, but that the rate in the headless piece is considerably higher than that of the regions of lowest rate in the whole animal. It is also evident from Fig. 25 that the difference between normal

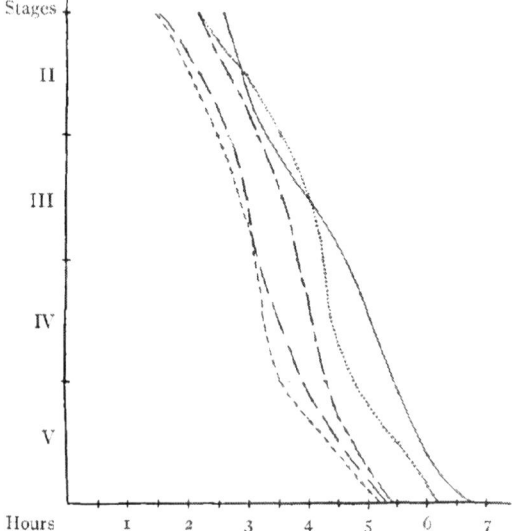

FIG. 25.—Susceptibility of *Planaria dorotocephala* to KCN 0.001 mol. after different degrees of reconstitution: unbroken line, uninjured animals like those from which pieces were taken; short dashes, normal forms after reconstitution; long dashes, teratophthalmic forms; alternate long and short dashes, anophthalmic forms; dots, headless forms.

and teratophthalmic forms is slight and much less than that between teratophthalmic and anophthalmic forms.

These curves are a graphic presentation in dynamic terms of the degree of rejuvenescence in its relation to the degree of reconstitution. Similar tests of the susceptibility of the different reconstitutional forms have been made repeatedly with pieces of different size and from different regions of the body and always with essentially the same result.

THE SUSCEPTIBILITY OF ANIMALS RESULTING FROM EXPERIMENTAL
REPRODUCTION AND SEXUALLY PRODUCED ANIMALS

The belief that the germ cell is the source of youth and that the
old organism cannot become young has been so widely current

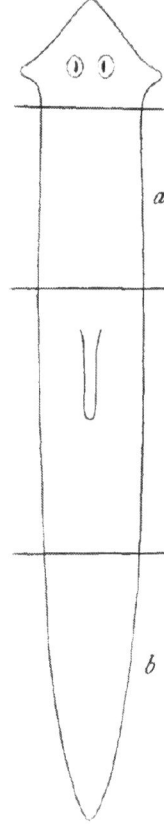

among biologists that it is of some interest to
determine whether the physiological condition
of the animal resulting from reconstitution
approaches that of the sexually produced young
animal. *Planaria dorotocephala* is not available
for such experiments, since it does not reproduce sexually under ordinary conditions, consequently another species. *P. maculata*, has been
used in which the young produced from eggs
can readily be obtained.

In experiments of this kind pieces were cut
from old, sexually mature animals and allowed
to undergo reconstitution; after reconstitution
their susceptibility was compared with that of
sexually produced young of the same size. In
the particular experiment of which the results
are given in Fig. 27 below, two lots of pieces
(*a* and *b*, Fig. 26) were cut from old, sexually
mature worms twelve millimeters in length.
These pieces were left for ten days under uniform conditions, at the end of which time they
had become normal animals five to six millimeters long. They were then fed, and two days
later their susceptibility was compared both
with that of old, sexually mature worms like
those from which the pieces were taken and also
with that of young, growing worms five to six

Fig. 26.—Body-
outline of *Planaria*
maculata, indicating
levels of section.

millimeters long, which had been hatched from
eggs in the laboratory.

Fig. 27 shows the susceptibilities to KCN
0.001 mol. of ten old, sexually mature worms
(*cd*), ten young, growing worms hatched from eggs (*ab*, long
dashes), ten animals developed from the *a*-pieces (*ab*, short

dashes), and ten animals developed from the b-pieces (ab, unbroken line). The figure shows that the susceptibility of animals resulting from the reconstitution of pieces is practically the same as that of the young, growing, sexually produced animals of the same size and much greater than that of the old, sexually mature animals. In other words, the animals resulting from experimental reproduction possess about the same rate of metabolism as sexually produced growing animals of the same size, and a much higher rate than the animals from which the pieces were taken. The process of reconstitution has made the experimentally produced animals as young as the sexually produced animals of the same size.

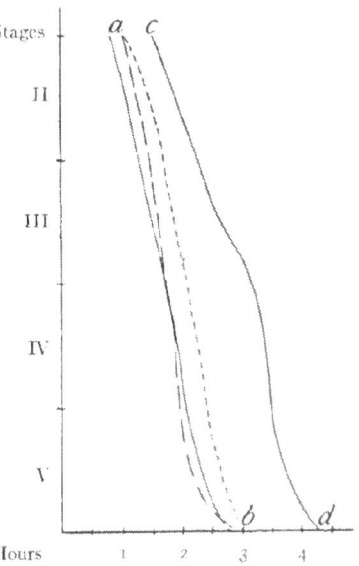

FIG. 27.—Susceptibility of *Planaria maculata* to KCN 0.001 mol.: ab, long dashes, sexually produced young; ab, short dashes and unbroken line, animals resulting from reconstitution of pieces; cd, animals like those from which the pieces were taken.

It is of interest, however, to note that the b-pieces from the posterior end of the animal (Fig. 26) show a somewhat greater susceptibility than the a-pieces from the anterior body region. This difference in susceptibility corresponds to a real difference in the process of reconstitution in pieces from these two regions. In the reconstitution of the b-pieces there is less outgrowth of new tissue and more reorganization of the old than in the a-pieces, so that the old tissue becomes somewhat younger in the former than in the latter; consequently, as the new tissue becomes older and the old tissue younger, they finally attain the same physiological age at a stage somewhat younger in the b-pieces than in the a-pieces. Slight differences of this kind are characteristic of pieces from different body levels and are correlated with differences in the process of reconstitution.

If pieces smaller than these are taken, the increase in susceptibility is greater and the animals attain the condition of still younger sexually produced forms Evidently these experimental reproductions, while they do not carry the organism back to the beginning of development, do carry it back to the physiological condition characteristic of the sexually produced, growing animal of the same size. Experimental reproduction is apparently in this species just as efficient a means of producing physiologically young animals as sexual reproduction

REPEATED RECONSTITUTION

It has been shown in preceding sections that the animals produced by reconstitution are physiologically younger than the animals from which the pieces are taken, and moreover that they are about as young as sexually produced animals of the same size. If this is the case, it should be possible to breed animals indefinitely by means of this process of experimental reproduction. On the other hand, the animal rejuvenated by reconstitution may differ in some way from the sexually produced animal, but so slightly that the difference does not become apparent in a single generation, but requires several or many generations of breeding by experimental reproduction to become distinguishable. Thus far two attempts at reconstitutional breeding have been made, both of which were terminated by accident, but one of them continued long enough to throw at least some light on the question.

The breeding stock for these experiments was obtained as follows: Large individuals of the same size, which had been kept under uniform conditions, were selected, and from each of these a piece of a certain size and from a certain region of the body was taken. These pieces were allowed to undergo reconstitution and after this was completed were fed until they attained approximately the original size. Then from each a piece, including the same region of the body, was taken; these were again allowed to develop, were fed, and so on. In one of these breeding experiments the piece used in each generation was the anterior fifth of the body, including the old head.   In such pieces the old head remains from one generation to another and new tissue appears only at the posterior end; consequently the amount of reorganization is less than in pieces which form a new head or in pieces from the posterior region of the body.   Moreover, the head-region is less capable of reorganization than other parts of the body   If a progressive senescence occurs from generation to generation in spite of reconstitution in each generation, it should become more distinct or appear earlier in such pieces than in those where the reconstitutional changes are more extensive.

In the course of a year and a half the animals passed through thirteen experimental generations without any indications of senescence or depression of any sort.   During the growth of the thirteenth generation, however, most of the stock was killed by high temperature and the remaining animals never regained good condition, but died in the course of the next few generations.   The worms that remained alive in each generation grew more or less normally, and the breeding was continued with these.   In the sixteenth generation only eight worms remained alive, and in order to determine whether more extensive reconstitutional change would bring the animals back to their original condition, the old heads were removed and each animal was cut into several pieces.   Some of these pieces produced complete animals, but deaths continued to occur among these, and some of the pieces died without reconstitution.   The living animals were again cut into pieces after growth, and this was repeated to the nineteenth generation in which the last of the stock died without recovery.

In another stock pieces from the middle region of the body were used for each generation   In the fifth generation this stock was subjected to high temperature at the same time as the preceding, and most of the animals died.   Those that remained alive gradually died during the following generations, until in the tenth generation all were dead.

The results of these two breeding experiments are of value only as far as they go   The first does show, however, that the animals can be bred by experimental reproduction without loss of vigor for at least thirteen generations, even when the old head is continuously present. The first stock was subjected to high temperature in the thirteenth generation, the second in the fifth generation, but in both the result was the same, in that most of the stock was killed and the survivors failed to recover after several months. There can be little doubt that the high temperature rather than the physiological condition of the animals was responsible in one way or another for the death of both stocks.

As a matter of fact, however, the question which these experiments attempted to answer is answered by reproduction in nature in *Planaria dorotocephala* and *P. velata*. It will be shown in the following chapter that the process of agamic reproduction in these forms is not essentially different in any way from the process of reconstitution of pieces, and this is the only method of reproduction which has been observed in these two species under natural conditions.

The results obtained by another method of experiment are of interest in this connection. This is essentially breeding by experimental reproduction without food Pieces from large, old animals are allowed to undergo reconstitution, then, without feeding, pieces are taken from these animals, and so on Here of course each generation is smaller than the preceding, and the experiment is finally brought to an end by the advancing starvation of the animals and the failure of the minute pieces to undergo reconstitution. But susceptibility tests show that the susceptibility increases with such reconstitutions, and in *Planaria maculata*, where sexually produced animals are available for comparison, the animals after a few generations of reconstitution without food show a susceptibility equal to that of animals just hatched from the egg capsule. Their rate of metabolism has increased in consequence of the successive reconstitutions and the absence of food until it equals that of very young sexually produced animals. If fed after such a series of reconstitutions, they grow and are indistinguishable from the animals hatched from eggs.

In short, by successive reconstitutions alternating with feeding and growth, the animals may be brought back to essentially the same stage in the age cycle in each successive generation, and by successive reconstitutions without feeding and growth they may be made progressively younger physiologically in each successive generation, until further reconstitution becomes impossible.

REFERENCES

CHILD, C. M.

1911a "A Study of Senescence and Rejuvenescence Based on Experiments with Planarians," *Arch f Entwickelungsmech*, XXXI

1911b. "Experimental Control of Morphogenesis in the Regulation of *Planaria*," *Biol Bull*, XX.

1911c. "Studies on the Dynamics of Morphogenesis and Inheritance in Experimental Reproduction: I, The Axial Gradient in *Planaria dorotocephala* as a Limiting Factor in Regulation," *Jour of Exp. Zool*, X

1912a "The Process of Reproduction in Organisms," *Biol. Bull.*, XXIII.

1912b "Studies on the Dynamics, etc : IV, Certain Dynamic Factors in the Regulatory Morphogenesis of *Planaria dorotocephala* in Relation to the Axial Gradient," *Jour of Exp. Zool.*, XIII.

1913. "Certain Dynamic Factors in Experimental Reproduction and Their Significance for the Problems of Reproduction and Development," *Arch f Entwickelungsmech.*, XXXV

1914a. "Studies on the Dynamics, etc · VII, The Stimulation of Pieces by Section in *Planaria dorotocephala*," *Jour. of Exp Zool*, XVI.

1914b. "Studies on the Dynamics, etc.: VIII, Dynamic Factors in Head-Determination in *Planaria*," *Jour of Exp Zool.*, XVII.

CHAPTER VI

THE RELATION BETWEEN AGAMIC REPRODUCTION AND RE-JUVENESCENCE IN THE LOWER ANIMALS

THE PROCESS OF AGAMIC REPRODUCTION IN *Planaria dorotocephala* AND RELATED FORMS

Planaria dorotocephala, like many other species of flatworms, undergoes from time to time a process of agamic or asexual reproduction, which consists in the separation by fission of the posterior third or fourth of the body from the rest and its development into a new animal The posterior region which separates is not morphologically distinguishable in any way from adjoining regions of the body, yet the separation occurs at a more or less definite level of the body.

In the course of an extended study of experimental reproduction in *Planaria* I have found that the posterior body region in all except very young animals, while not morphologically distinguishable as a new individual, is nevertheless clearly marked off physiologically from the region anterior to it. Along the main axis of the planarian body a gradient in the rate of metabolism exists (Child, '12, '13a), the rate being highest in the head-region and decreasing posteriorly to the region where separation occurs in fission: here a sudden rise in rate occurs, and posterior to this point another gradient similar to that in the anterior region. That is, the posterior region of the body, which is separated from the rest by the act of fission, possesses an axial gradient in rate of metabolism similar to that of the anterior region In long worms, two, three, or even more of these metabolic gradients may appear, one posterior to the other. These metabolic gradients in the body of *Planaria* appear, not only in the susceptibility of different regions, but also in the differences in the capacity for reconstitution of pieces from different levels (Child, '11b, '11c).

The existence of these metabolic gradients in the posterior region of *Planaria* indicates, as chap. ix will show more clearly, that this region has undergone the first step in the process of individuation. Each one of the gradients is the dynamic expression of this individuation. In fact, the body of *Planaria*, after a certain stage of development, is physiologically a chain of two or more zooids, i.e., of individuals organically connected. In young animals four or five millimeters long only two zooids are distinguishable, the longer, anterior zooid making up the greater part of the body and bearing the head, and the shorter, posterior zooid indicated only dynamically by a second metabolic gradient in the posterior region. The boundary between the two zooids in these small animals is indicated by the dotted line across the body in Fig. 28. As the animal becomes longer, other zooids arise in the posterior region by further physiological division of the original posterior zooid, and when it has reached a length of

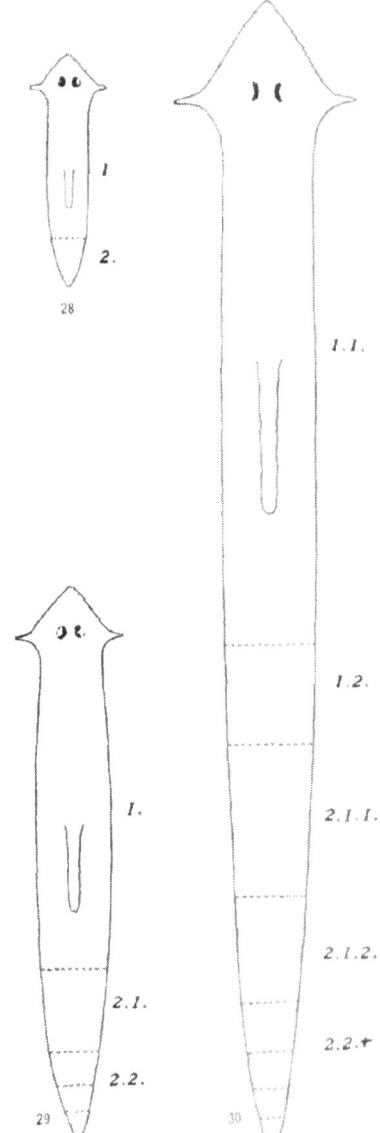

FIGS. 28–30.—Development of zooids in *Planaria dorotocephala:* Fig. 28, a young animal with two zooids, *1* and *2*; Fig. 29, a half-grown animal in which the original posterior zooid has divided into zooids *2.1.* and *2.2.*, and *2.2.* has undergone further division; Fig. 30, a full-grown animal in which still further zooids have appeared.

ten or twelve millimeters the posterior region is more or less clearly marked off by metabolic gradients into two or more zooids (Fig. 29), and the extreme posterior end appears to be a growing tip in which new zooids are arising   In nature, separation at the

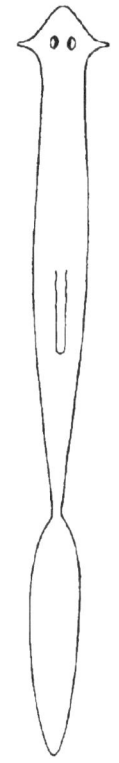

boundary between the first and second zooids very commonly occurs at about this stage, but if the animals are prevented from dividing, which may be accomplished in various ways, they may grow to a length of twenty-five to thirty millimeters and the posterior region may consist of four to five zooids and a growing tip (Fig 30)

The dynamic demarkation of these posterior zooids results, as has been shown elsewhere,[1] from a physiological isolation of the regions concerned in forming the dominant head-region of the animal   The consequence of this physiological isolation is the beginning of a new individuation in the isolated region. in essentially the same manner as in the physically isolated piece which begins to undergo reconstitution, and for the same reason   But the physiological isolation of the posterior region of the planarian body is less complete than in the piece isolated by section, consequently the development of new individuation beyond a very early stage, which is only dynamically distinguishable, is inhibited.   In *Planaria maculata* and various other species of *Planaria* new zooids arise in the same way and exist dynamically as axial gradients, but their morphological development is similarly inhibited until after their physical separation from more anterior regions

FIG   31.—*Planaria dorotocephala* in process of division.

The act of fission in these animals results from an independent motor reaction of posterior and anterior zooids   If the animal is

[1] Child, '10, '11a, '11c, see also chap iv

slightly stimulated when creeping about, or in some cases without any stimulation from external sources being apparent, the posterior region suddenly attaches itself tightly to the underlying surface by its margins, using the ventral surface as a sucking disk, while the anterior zooid continues to creep, and when it feels the resistance to forward movement it exerts itself violently to pull away. The consequence of this lack of co-ordination between the two regions is that the body just anterior to the attached region becomes more and more stretched and finally ruptures, and the posterior region is left behind   Fig 31 shows an animal in the act of fission. The anterior zooid bearing the head is endeavoring to move forward, and the posterior zooid has attached itself firmly to the surface on which the animal was creeping.   In many cases the posterior region of the first zooid becomes stretched into a long, slender band, and even then, particularly in large old animals where the tissues seem to be tougher and rupture less readily, the anterior zooid often apparently becomes exhausted and ceases to exert itself, or else the posterior zooid is torn from its attachment to the substratum or releases itself before the connecting parts are ruptured.   Such failures of fission are very common in the larger, older animals   Fission can also be prevented by keeping the animals on surfaces to which they cannot attach themselves firmly, e g., in vaseline-lined dishes

After separation the smaller posterior piece undergoes reconstitution into a new animal of small size in exactly the same manner as do pieces cut from the body, and the anterior zooid develops a new posterior end in which one or more new zooids may arise.   In *Planaria dorotocephala* this is the only form of reproduction which has been observed in nature during a period of observation covering some ten years, but in the laboratory, animals which have been prevented from undergoing fission have become sexually mature in a few cases.

THE OCCURRENCE OF REJUVENESCENCE IN AGAMIC REPRODUCTION IN *Planaria dorotocephala* AND *P maculata*

Since a greater or less degree of rejuvenescence occurs in the reconstitution of pieces of *Planaria* (see chap. v) and since the

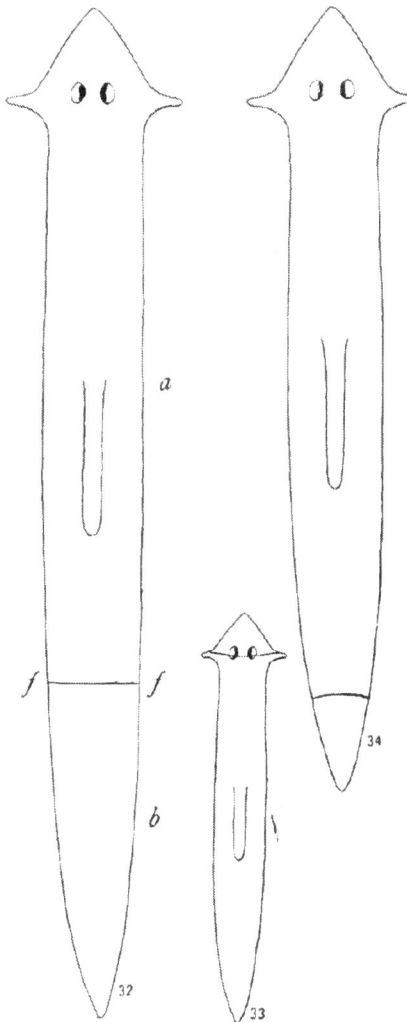

natural process of agamic reproduction resembles so closely the process of reconstitution the occurrence of some degree of rejuvenescence is to be expected in agamic reproduction.

It has already been shown in Fig. 3 (p. 80) and in Fig. 13 (p. 100) that individuals of *P. dorotocephala* of small size and young in appearance, but which supposedly arose agamically, are physiologically much younger as regards their susceptibility than the large, apparently old animals. But in order to obtain conclusive evidence upon this point it is necessary to compare animals which are known to have arisen by fission under controlled conditions with animals like those in which the fission occurred.

This comparison has been made repeatedly and the result confirms expectation. The small animal which develops from the separated posterior region of the parent animal is physiologically much

Figs. 32–34.—Reconstitution after fission in *Planaria dorotocephala:* Fig. 32, animal before fission; *ff*, fission-plane, *a*, anterior, *b*, posterior zooid; Fig. 33, reconstitution of posterior zooid; Fig. 34, reconstitution of anterior zooid.

younger than the latter. Since the results of these experiments
are in all respects essentially identical with those obtained with
pieces artificially isolated by section, it is unnecessary to present
them in detailed form.

In the process of fission the separated posterior zooid undergoes
much more extensive reorganization than the anterior zooid. In
an animal of medium size fission usually occurs at about the level
indicated by the line *ff* in Fig 32. The posterior piece *b* (Fig 32)
is much smaller than the anterior *a*, and it develops a new head and
a new pharynx, and extensive changes in the alimentary tract
occur in the formation of the prepharyngeal region Moreover,
it cannot take food until the new mouth and pharynx have reached
a certain stage of development, consequently the energy for development is derived from its own tissues and it undergoes more or
less reduction during the process. In Fig 33 the animal developed
from the posterior fission-piece is drawn to the same scale as Fig. 32.
This animal is physiologically much younger than the parent from
which it came   Its susceptibility is much higher and it is capable
of more rapid growth than the original animal

In the anterior fission-piece (*a*, Fig. 32), on the other hand, the
original head and the mouth and pharynx persist, the only outgrowth of new tissue formed is at the posterior end, and the only
other change in form is the growth of the postpharyngeal at the
expense of the prepharyngeal region, in consequence of which the
pharynx seems to migrate forward (Fig. 34). When food is present,
this piece may feed and increase in size during the whole process
of reconstitution, but even when it is not fed, the degree of reduction
during reconstitution is slight, because the developing regions have
a relatively large mass to draw upon as a source of energy.   The
relation which was shown in the preceding chapter to exist between
the size of the piece, the amount of reconstitutional change, and the
amount of increase in susceptibility would lead us to expect that
the increase in susceptibility resulting from the reconstitutional
changes in the anterior fission-piece would be much less than in the
posterior piece, and this is in fact the case

The increase in susceptibility in the posterior piece is the same
as that in artificially isolated pieces of the same size. In *Planaria*

maculata the animals developed from these pieces are about as
young physiologically as sexually produced animals of the same
size. In *P. dorotocephala*, where sexually produced animals are
not available for comparison, the degree of increase in susceptibility over that of the parent animals is about the same as in *P.
maculata*. Since these results are so completely in agreement,
both with expectation and with the results obtained from artificially isolated pieces, experimental records are unnecessary.

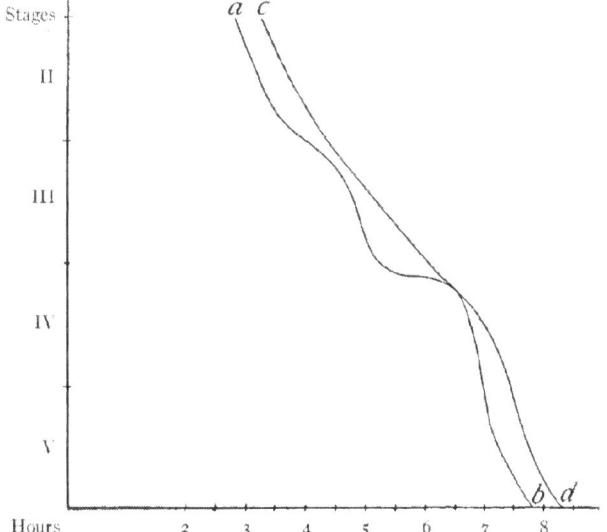

FIG. 35.—Susceptibility of *Planaria dorotocephala* to KCN 0.001 mol.: *ab*,
anterior fission-pieces after reconstitution; *cd*, entire animals before fission.

With respect to the anterior fission-piece, however, it is a matter
of some interest to demonstrate that the reconstitutional changes
occurring in the posterior region of so large a piece as this do alter
the physiological condition of the whole piece, including even the
head-region. For this reason the record of one susceptibility test
of these anterior pieces is given in Fig. 35. For this experiment
worms ten to twelve millimeters in length were induced to undergo
fission and the anterior fission-pieces were kept without food for
twelve days. Another lot of worms of the same size and in the

same physiological condition, but undivided, was kept without food during the same period as a control. In Fig 35, curve *ab* shows the susceptibility of the anterior fission-pieces, curve *cd* that of ten of the undivided animals, also without food. At this time the animals had attained the stage of development shown in Fig 34

The susceptibility of the fission-pieces is distinctly greater than that of the undivided animals, and as a matter of fact the differences are greater than the curves show   At the points in the curve where the two lots appear to be in the same or nearly the same stage of disintegration, examination of the pieces showed that even though the two lots might fall within the same one of the five arbitrarily distinguished stages, the fission-pieces were always more advanced in that stage   The fission-pieces are evidently younger physiologically than whole worms, and this is true, not only for the posterior region where the reconstitutional changes are localized, but for the whole body, including the head. Undoubtedly the anterior regions have served to some slight extent as a source of energy for the developmental changes in the posterior region

Similar results have been obtained repeatedly in other similar experiments   If the anterior fission-pieces are fed during reconstitution and their susceptibility compared with that of whole animals fed at the same time, the increase in susceptibility is found to be less marked or inappreciable   In such cases the food taken, rather than the tissues, provides the energy for the development of the new posterior end. Similarly the larger the animal when division occurs, the less the increase in susceptibility   In the very large, heavily fed animals, in which the anterior fission-piece may be fifteen millimeters or more in length, there is usually no appreciable increase in susceptibility in this piece after fission   Here the amount of reconstitutional change is so slight in relation to the size, and the amount of nutritive reserve is so great, that the body as a whole is not appreciably affected by the development of the posterior end.

The relation between agamic reproduction and susceptibility is the same in *Planaria dorotocephala* and in *P. maculata*   In both species the posterior fission-piece undergoes a considerable increase, the anterior, except when very large or heavily fed, exhibits a slight increase in susceptibility. In other words, agamic reproduction brings about a greater or less degree of rejuvenescence.

AGAMIC REPRODUCTION AND REJUVENESCENCE IN *Planaria velata*

Planaria velata (Fig. 8), a flatworm found very commonly in temporary pools and ditches as well as sometimes in permanent bodies of water, is another species in which only agamic or asexual reproduction has been observed during some thirteen years. The asexual cycle of this species and its relation to senescence and rejuvenescence have been considered at length elsewhere (Child, '13b, '14), and only the more important points need be reviewed here.

Agamic reproduction in this species is a process of fragmentation which occurs only at the end of the growth period The animals appear early in spring, chiefly in temporary pools and ditches in which dead leaves have accumulated. When they first appear they are only two or three millimeters in length, very active, and to all appearances young in every respect They grow rapidly and become deeply pigmented, but the rate of growth gradually decreases, and at the end of three or four weeks, when they have attained a length of about fifteen millimeters, they cease to feed, become lighter in color, their motor activity undergoes a distinct and progressive decrease, and the pharynx undergoes complete disintegration. Within a few days after these changes fragmentation begins at the posterior end of the body. The process of fragmentation resembles in certain respects the process of fission in *P dorotocephala*, described in the first section of this chapter As in that species, the act of separation is accomplished by attachment of the posterior end to the substratum while the animal is creeping, with the result that a small piece tears off and is left behind. But in *P velata* the process may be repeated frequently in the course of a few hours and the fragments vary widely in size. In *P. velata*, as in *P. dorotocephala*, fragmentation is undoubtedly the result of physiological isolation and independent motor reaction of the posterior end of the body, but, instead of occurring periodically during the life of the animal, it does not occur until senescence is

far advanced and the rate of metabolism is very low. Posterior
zooids are not distinctly marked off dynamically, as in *P. dorotocephala*, but the portions which separate are merely small bits of
the body at the posterior end which, as the animal becomes progressively weaker, finally cease to be controlled and co-ordinated
with other parts by the dominant head-region, and so, sooner or
later, react independently and are torn off. In some cases the
animal may leave a trail of such fragments behind it as it creeps
slowly along. The stimulation resulting from the rupture of the
tissues leads to the secretion of slime on the surface of the separated
pieces, and this slime hardens and forms a cyst within which the
pieces gradually undergo reconstitution to whole animals of small
size which sooner or later emerge.

Fragmentation may continue until only the head and a short
piece of the body two or three millimeters in length remain, or it
may be confined to the posterior third or half of the body. After
fragmentation is completed, the anterior piece, whether large or
small, may encyst, or it may remain more or less active and gradually undergo reduction in size in consequence of starvation.
Finally, after considerable reduction has occurred, it develops a
new pharynx and mouth and a new posterior end, and begins to
feed and grow again. Cases of this sort will be considered in
chap vii.

The encysted fragments do not withstand complete desiccation,
but the bottoms of the ditches and pools in which they live retain
sufficient moisture to keep them alive. In the autumn the ditches
do not usually fill again before cold weather, although they may do
so, in which case the worms may emerge from the cysts at that
time, but their growth is soon stopped by low temperature. Commonly, however, they appear only in spring, as soon as the ditches
thaw out. This cycle is repeated year after year, and thus far
neither sexually mature animals nor animals with any part of the
sexual ducts or copulatory organs have ever been found, though
ovaries and testes in early stages of development may sometimes
be present

In the laboratory the animals may pass through the whole life
cycle in two or three months, for the encysted fragments when

kept in water often emerge as young worms within two or three
weeks after encystment.   There is therefore no difficulty in obtaining small animals which are known to have developed from
encysted pieces for comparison with the larger animals at various
stages of the life cycle

Fig. 36 shows the susceptibility of ten animals about two millimeters in length newly emerged from cysts (curve *ab*) compared
with that of ten full-grown animals raised from cysts in the labora-

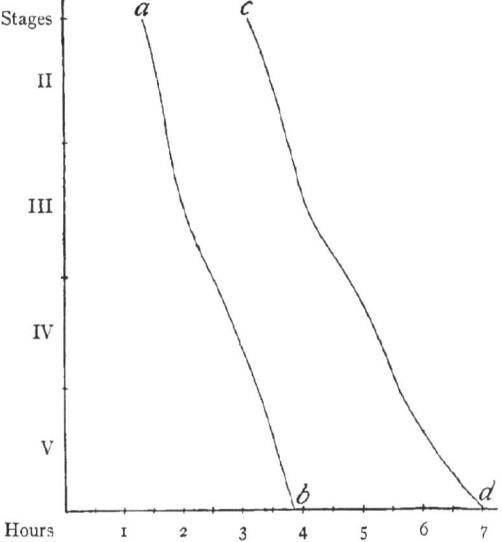

FIG. 36 —Susceptibility of *Planaria velata* to KCN o oo1 mol.   *ab*, animals
newly emerged from cysts, *cd*, full-grown animals.

tory (curve *cd*)   The susceptibility of the small, newly emerged
animals is very much greater than that of the full-grown animals.
In other words, the newly emerged worms are young as regards
rate of metabolism, as they appear to be in every other respect, and
the full-grown animals which are about to undergo fragmentation
are old.   In this species, as in *P. dorotocephala*, agamic reproduction
is simply a separation and reconstitution of pieces, and rejuvenescence is associated with the reconstitutional changes in the piece.

Since the pieces are usually very small, the reorganization is extensive and the degree of rejuvenescence is very much greater than in the larger pieces separated in agamic reproduction in *P. dorotocephala* and *P. maculata*. In cases where large instead of small fragments are formed the animals which develop from them are of course longer than those from the small fragments, the reconstitutional changes are less extensive, and the degree of rejuvenescence is less than in the small fragments.

Apparently the degree of rejuvenescence is essentially the same in successive generations, for this method of reproduction is adequate for the maintenance of the species without visible decrease in vigor or advance in senescence, at least for a considerable number of generations. In the laboratory a stock of these worms has been bred asexually over three years and has passed through fifteen generations without any apparent progressive change in the physiological condition of the animals in successive generations. In each generation the rate of metabolism decreases and the process of senescence ends in fragmentation and encystment, and young animals emerge from the cysts and repeat the life cycle.

This case is of particular interest because the process of senescence, as it occurs under the usual conditions of existence, does not end in death but leads directly to reproduction and rejuvenescence. The occurrence of fragmentation in these animals is very clearly associated with the decrease in rate of metabolism which is the characteristic dynamic feature of senescence (Child, '13b). As the animal grows old its decreasing rate of metabolism makes impossible the maintenance of physiological individuality. Physiological isolation of parts (see chap. ix) occurs and is followed by physical isolation, and the isolated parts of the old individual undergo reconstitution into new, young individuals. Senescence itself is the physiological factor inducing reproduction and rejuvenescence.

AGAMIC REPRODUCTION AND REJUVENESCENCE IN *Stenostomum* AND CERTAIN ANNELIDS

In certain flatworms, among which is the genus *Stenostomum*, the morphological development of the new zooids reaches an advanced stage before they separate from the parent body. In such forms the body consists visibly of a chain of zooids in various

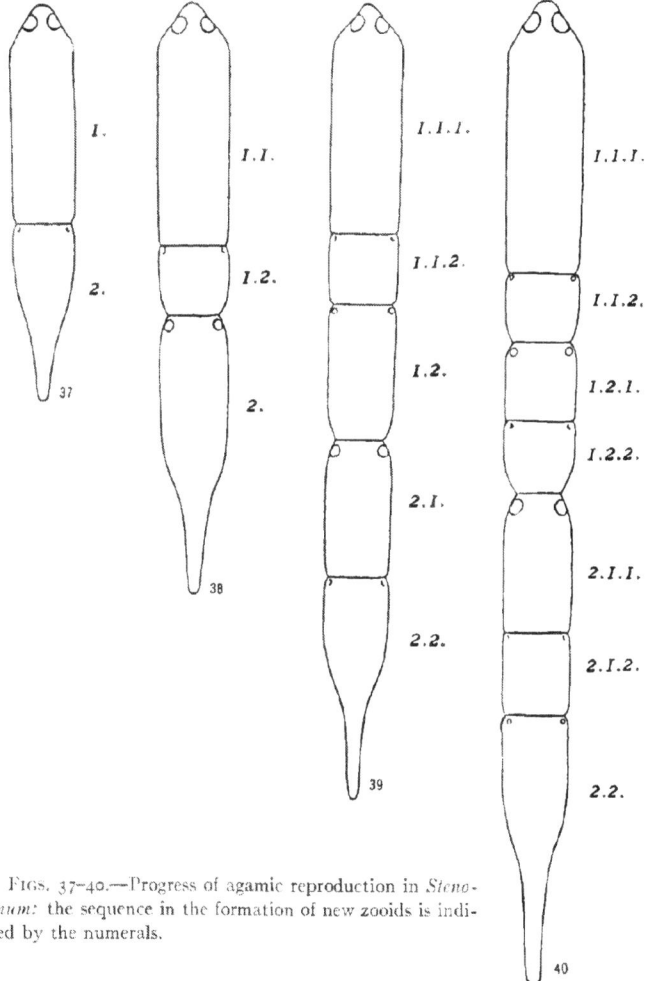

FIGS. 37–40.—Progress of agamic reproduction in *Steno-stomum*: the sequence in the formation of new zooids is indicated by the numerals.

stages of development. The development of such a chain of zooids in *Stenostomum* is shown in Figs. 37–40. In Fig. 37 only the zooids 1 and 2 are present; in Fig. 38 zooid 1 has divided into

1 1 and 1 2., but zooid 2 has not yet divided. In Fig. 39 zooid
1.1 has divided again into 1 1.1. and 1 1.2., zooid 1 2. has not
yet divided, and zooid 2. has divided into 2 1 and 2 2. In Fig 39
still further divisions have occurred, and the relations of the different zooids are indicated by the numbers designating each   Here
morphological development of each zooid is almost completed
before separation occurs. The first separation takes place at the
most advanced fission-plane and as other zooids reach a corresponding stage other separations occur, but meanwhile new zooids have
begun to develop. Thus the breaking up of the old chains and the
formation of new go hand in hand.

Such processes of agamic reproduction do not differ essentially
in any way from the process of reconstitution of pieces isolated by
section in the same species. In both cases a certain region of the
body gradually transforms itself into a whole animal   In both
cases certain parts atrophy and disappear, cell division and localized
growth occur, and new parts develop   In *Stenostomum*, however,
the new zooid receives food during its development, for the alimentary tract common to the whole chain passes through it; consequently it is not dependent upon its own tissues for the energy
necessary for its development as is a physically isolated piece, and
therefore it does not undergo the reduction in size characteristic
of such pieces. In fact it usually increases in size during development.

In *Stenostomum* as in *Planaria* the susceptibility method
demonstrates the existence of a longitudinal axial gradient in rate
of metabolism. Before agamic reproduction begins this gradient
extends the length of the individual, but as new zooids arise the
anterior region of each shows a higher rate of metabolism than the
region immediately anterior to it, and each zooid develops its own
axial gradient like that of the original animal. In the earlier stages
of zooid development the susceptibility of the new zooid is less,
i e., its rate of metabolism is lower, than that of the fully developed
zooid which heads the chain, but as development proceeds the susceptibility increases, until at the time of separation, or soon after,
it is higher than that of the anterior zooid   Separation of the
zooids at an earlier stage of development than that at which it

naturally occurs may be induced by strong stimulation, and in such cases development and the increase in susceptibility are usually somewhat accelerated.

From these facts we must conclude that in *Stenostomum* as in *Planaria* the reconstitution of a given region of the body into a new individual is accompanied by some degree of physiological rejuvenescence. Without doubt the age differences in susceptibility between the developing young zooids and the fully developed, relatively, old anterior zooid of the chain are obscured to some extent by the much greater motor activity of the latter, but the fact that sooner or later the young zooids become more susceptible than this older zooid indicates that rejuvenescence does occur.

In various species of aquatic oligochete annelids agamic reproduction occurs in much the same manner as in *Stenostomum*. In the course of investigations as yet unpublished Miss Hyman has found that these animals, like the flatworms, undergo a greater or less degree of physiological rejuvenescence in connection with agamic reproduction.

THE RELATION BETWEEN AGAMIC REPRODUCTION AND REJUVENESCENCE IN PROTOZOA

The question whether the protozoa undergo senescence or not is of considerable interest at present. The generally accepted view based on the researches of Maupas ('88, '89) that conjugation in the ciliate infusoria terminates an invariable process of race senescence and brings about rejuvenescence requires some modification in the light of recent researches. Woodruff has bred a race of *Paramecium* through nearly five thousand generations without conjugation and without loss of vigor [1] This number of generations is so large that we are justified in maintaining that for the race of *Paramecium* used, and under the conditions of experiment, conjugation is not an essential feature of the life cycle. On the other hand, various investigators [2] have shown

[1] Woodruff, '08, '09, '11a, '13a, '13b, '14, Woodruff and Erdmann, '14. In these and other papers the author records the progress of the agamic breeding

[2] Among these may be mentioned Calkins, '02a, '02b, '04, Enriques, '03, '07, '08; Woodruff (see note 1), Jennings, '10, '13; Baitsell, '12, '14, Zweibaum, '12; Calkins and Gregory, '13.

during the last few years that the occurrence of conjugation is dependent, at least in a large measure, upon external factors. Woodruff has experimentally induced conjugation in members of his culture which has been agamically bred through thousands of generations   Jennings concludes from extended experimentation that conjugation does not bring about rejuvenescence, but merely increases variability, while Calkins and Gregory believe that rejuvenescence does occur, at least in some cases

If conjugation is not a necessary feature of the life cycle, or if it fails to accomplish rejuvenescence, two alternative conclusions present themselves   either these animals do not necessarily undergo senescence or else rejuvenescence is accomplished in some other way than by conjugation.   The relation found to exist between agamic reproduction and rejuvenescence in the flatworms suggests at once the possibility that a similar relation may exist in the protozoa.

Since the protozoa are unicellular animals, agamic reproduction is essentially a process of cell division, but since it is also true that at least many protozoa possess a more or less complex morphological structure, agamic reproduction, as in multicellular forms, resembles the process of reconstitution in that it involves various morphological changes, consisting in the dedifferentiation and disappearance of certain structures and the formation and development of others   In *Paramecium*, for example, agamic reproduction does not consist merely in nuclear and cytoplasmic division, but extensive reorganization also occurs.   In Figs 41–43 the most important changes are diagrammatically represented   Fig. 41 shows the animal before division, the oral groove, *og*, the pharynx, *p*, and the two vacuoles, *v*, being indicated in the figure, as well as the meganucleus, *mg*, and the micronucleus, *mc*   The first indications of division are cytoplasmic, not nuclear, and consist in the formation of a new contractile vacuole in what is to become the anterior region of each individual, the two vacuoles of the parent individual becoming the posterior vacuoles in the daughter animals and new vacuoles, *v'v'*, appearing in the anterior region of each.   The mouth and pharynx and the posterior portion of the oral groove undergo more or less change and become parts of the posterior daughter animal,

while in the anterior daughter animal a new mouth and pharynx
and probably a new oral groove arise (Fig. 42), while both meganucleus and micronucleus[1] undergo division (Fig. 42), the process
in the former being apparently a direct or amitotic division, while
in the latter it resembles the process of mitosis in certain respects.
Before these divisions are completed a transverse constriction
appears at about the middle of the parent body (Fig. 42), and this

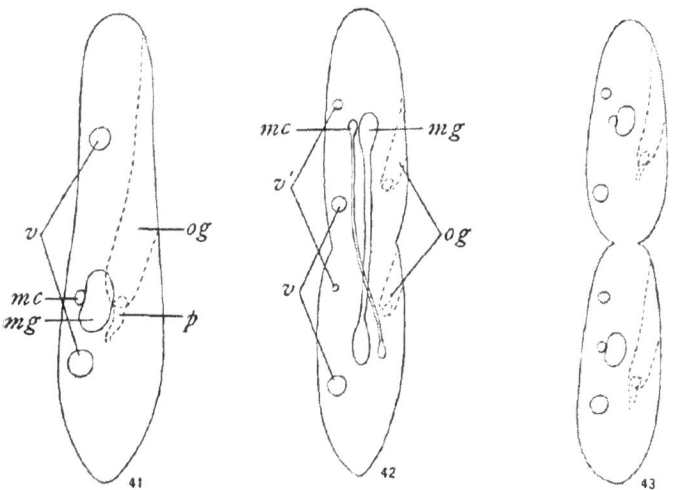

FIGS. 41–43.—Three stages in the division of *Paramecium: mc*, micronucleus;
mg, meganucleus; *og*, oral groove; *p*, pharynx; *v*, vacuoles of original individual;
v', new vacuoles.

deepens (Fig. 43), until finally separation of the two daughter
individuals occurs at this level. Before division occurs the cytoplasmic reorganization has reached an advanced stage (Fig. 42),
but the development of the oral groove and the attainment of the
characteristic proportions are not completed until after separation.

In *Stentor coeruleus* the process of agamic reproduction differs
in certain respects from that in *Paramecium*. In *Stentor* the first
visible stages in division are cytoplasmic, as in *Paramecium*, and

[1] In the *caudatum* group of *Paramecium* only one micronucleus is present, while
in the *aurelia* group there are two. See Jennings and Hargitt ('10). Woodruff ('11b),
for the characteristics of these groups or species of *Paramecium*.

consist in the appearance of a new vacuole near the middle of the body and the development of a band of peristomial cilia (Fig. 44).

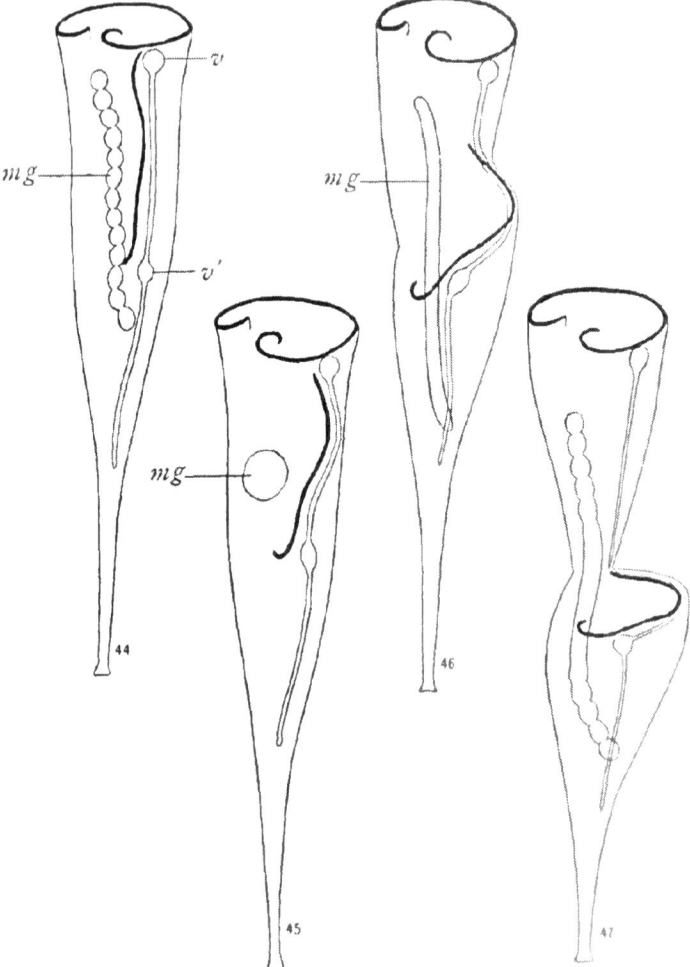

FIGS. 44–47.—Four stages of division in *Stentor:* the margin of both old and new peristomes is indicated by a heavy line; the separation of the new vacuole, *v'*, from the old, *v*, and the changes in shape of the meganucleus, *mg*, are also indicated. After Johnson, '93.

which at first extends almost longitudinally. After these changes have occurred the elongated moniliform meganucleus, *mg*, undergoes concentration to a spherical form, as in Fig. 45, and the new peristomial band of cilia gradually assumes a curved outline   Then a transverse constriction appears in the meganucleus, which defines two approximately equal halves, and this is followed by elongation of the meganucleus (*mg*, Fig 46), but separation of the two halves does not occur until later   As regards the micronuclei, of which there are usually a large number in *Stentor* (Johnson, '93), it is not known whether all or only a part of them divide in each fission.   The new peristomial band of cilia changes its position, becoming more nearly transverse and semicircular in outline (Fig 46), and a mouth begins to develop at its posterior end   This change in shape is accomplished by a lateral outgrowth on one side of the body near the middle which represents the anterior end and the peristome of the posterior daughter individual   Just anterior to this developing peristome the level at which separation will occur is now indicated by a constriction, as in Fig. 46.   Other changes, indicated in Figs 46 and 47, consist in the further development of the new peristome and its continued approach to the transverse position, the deepening of the constriction between the two individuals, and the breaking up of the meganucleus into the characteristic segments, beginning at the two ends   Still later the meganucleus separates at the level of the cytoplasmic constriction, which continues to become deeper, until the anterior member of the pair is attached to the peristome of the posterior member only by a slender peduncle. This finally separates and the process of fission is completed   As regards the essential features of the process of fission, other species of ciliates resemble *Paramecium* and *Stentor*, but the details of reconstitution differ for each species

The process of fission in these forms has been described at some length because it is evident that it is a much more complex process than ordinary cell division in the metazoa.   So far as the cytoplasmic structures are concerned it is manifestly a process of reconstitution resembling that which occurs in agamic reproduction in nature and in isolated pieces in the flatworms and many other metazoa   Moreover, the process differs in the two forms.   In

Paramecium, the original mouth becomes, with more or less reorganization, the mouth of the posterior daughter individual and a new mouth arises in the anterior individual, while in *Stentor* the original mouth and peristome remain as a part of the anterior individual and the new peristome is that of the posterior individual. And, finally, extensive developmental changes occur in the cytoplasm before any visible nuclear changes. Evidently the process is more than ordinary cell division   It is in fact an agamic reproduction comparable to this form of reproduction in the multicellular forms, and as such it exhibits characteristic features for each species and involves much more extensive reconstitutional changes than cell division.

The data presented in chap. v and in the preceding sections of the present chapter demonstrate that in at least many of the metazoa a relation exists between reconstitution and rejuvenescence. That being the case, the extensive reconstitutional changes involved in fission in the ciliates make it at least probable that fission brings about a greater or less degree of rejuvenescence. With this idea in mind, the attempt has been made to determine whether appreciable changes in susceptibility occur in connection with fission in the ciliates   The forms tested thus far are *Paramecium*, *Stentor coeruleus*, a small form of *Colpidium*, and *Urocentrum turbo*, and the results are essentially the same for all. The tests were made upon actively dividing cultures reared from sterile infusions inoculated with a few individuals. The rearing of pure line cultures was not attempted, because definite results were obtained without this procedure

In the early stages of fission no appreciable increase in susceptibility to cyanide has been observed   If any exists, it is not sufficiently great to appear clearly in comparison with individual differences in susceptibility   In pure line cultures some increase in susceptibility in the earlier stages of fission might perhaps be demonstrated. In the later stages of fission, however, when the two daughter individuals are approaching separation and the reconstitutional changes are advanced, the susceptibility is distinctly greater than in the single animals of approximately the same size as the two members of the pair together. The possibility that the dividing pairs and the single animals belong to different races which differ in susceptibility cannot of course be excluded in individual cases except in pure line cultures, but the uniformity of the results obtained with large numbers of individuals and in repeated tests render this possibility negligible.

But the susceptibility is highest after fission is completed. In all cases the smaller individuals are in general very clearly more susceptible than the larger. This difference is not a matter of size or of the relation between surface and volume, for the cilia and the whole body-surface show it. The cilia and ectoplasm of the larger animals are in general much less susceptible to a given concentration of cyanide than those of the smaller animals. As death and disintegration proceed in a lot consisting of hundreds or thousands of individuals, it soon becomes very evident that the smaller animals are dying earlier than the larger. In a culture of *Colpidium*, for example, where division was proceeding very rapidly, animals below a certain size were more than twice as numerous as those above this size, but after deaths began to occur in cyanide, the smaller animals became less than half as numerous as the larger, and still later only about one small to five large was found alive Similar results were obtained with the other species. In a *Stentor* culture where divisions were occurring only in the animals of medium size or above, the susceptibility of the animals below medium size was much greater than that of the larger animals. Some of the smaller animals in these cultures may conceivably have belonged to small races possessing a greater susceptibility at all stages than the large, but as the culture was increasing rapidly in numbers, most of them were certainly the products of recent fission

These data are in complete agreement with those obtained from the study of the flatworms and indicate very clearly that an increase in rate of metabolism is associated with the process of fission in the ciliate infusoria and that the rate of metabolism is highest soon after fission. In other words, after fission the animals are physiologically younger than before fission, and in the interval between two fissions they undergo some degree of senescence

These changes, however, are apparently not the only factors concerned in preventing progressive race senescence   In a recent paper Woodruff and Erdmann ('14) have described periodic changes of another sort which they call "endomixis" and which they believe to be the essential factors in preventing race senescence   These changes consist in the gradual fragmentation, degeneration, and disappearance of the meganucleus, at least two divisions of the micronuclei, degeneration of some of the micronuclei thus produced, and the formation of new meganuclei from others.   This process of endomixis resembles the nuclear changes in conjugation, except that the third micronuclear division of conjugation which gives rise to the migratory and stationary micronuclei apparently does not occur here, and there is no union of micronuclei at any time.   Woodruff and Erdmann point out that endomixis is in certain respects similar to parthenogenesis, but not directly comparable with the usual forms of it.   The occurrence of rhythms of growth and rate of division in protozoan cultures has been recognized by Calkins, Woodruff, and various other investigators.   Periods of more rapid and less rapid growth and division alternate more or less regularly in the history of cultures   Woodruff and Erdmann find that the process of endomixis which extends over some nine cell generations is coincident with the period of lowest rate of growth and division in the rhythms, that at the climax of the process division is greatly delayed, and that with the beginning of differentiation of the new meganuclei recovery is rapid.   They conclude that a causal relation exists between the reorganization process and the rhythms

This process of endomixis occurs in different races of *Paramecium aurelia* and in *P caudatum* also, and probably in other ciliate infusoria.   Many of the observations of earlier authors on degenerative changes and abnormal nuclear conditions undoubtedly concern stages of endomixis

While further investigation is necessary to determine how generally this process occurs and to what extent its occurrence may be experimentally controlled, it is evident that the rhythms and the process of endomixis represent a senescence-rejuvenescence period, and we must inquire what factors are primarily or chiefly concerned in this periodicity   I believe that we must look to the meganucleus

for the answer to this inquiry   The meganucleus of the infusoria
is apparently a specialized vegetative organ of the cell not found in
the same form in other cells, although Goldschmidt ('05) has
attempted to show that all animal cells are physiologically if not
morphologically binucleate and that a distinction between vegetative or somatic and reproductive nuclear substance must be made.
Whether or not we accept this view, the meganucleus is evidently
a specialized organ, and all the facts indicate that it plays an important rôle in the metabolic activity of the cell.   In the process of
division it apparently undergoes no great degree of reorganization,
but is merely separated into two parts and continues to grow   If
the successive divisions of the meganucleus do not balance the
progressive changes between divisions, it will necessarily undergo
progressive senescence, and if no other method of rejuvenescence
occurs, death from old age must finally result.

   This, I believe, is what actually occurs   The period from the
low point of one rhythm to the low point of the next represents the
length of life of the meganucleus under the existing conditions
As the meganucleus undergoes senescence after its differentiation
as a meganucleus, the rate of growth and division decreases, sooner
or later the meganucleus begins to degenerate, and a physiological
relation of some sort undoubtedly exists between these changes
and the micronuclear divisions which occur.   In other words, the
process of endomixis is apparently the periodic replacement of a
part which has grown old by a new, young part and is therefore
analogous in certain respects to the replacement of differentiated
old cells by young in the multicellular organism.   Like such cells,
the meganucleus apparently does not undergo rejuvenescence but
dies of old age and is replaced by a new one.

   Further investigation will probably show that the length of
time between two successive endomixes may, like many other
senescence periods, be altered and controlled experimentally to a
greater or less extent   It is in fact possible that under certain conditions the degree of rejuvenescence occurring in the ordinary
divisions may be sufficient to maintain the race without progressive
senescence of the meganucleus and so without endomixis, although
it may be that the rejuvenescence in division is rather cyto-

plasmic than nuclear   That the age cycle of certain flatworms may be altered to a very considerable extent by experimental nutritive and other conditions will be shown in chap. vii   Moreover, the different behavior of different races as regards conjugation[1] suggests that internal as well as external factors will be found to play a part in determining the periodicity.

But whatever the differences resulting from race or environmental conditions, the occurrence in the ciliates of some degree of senescence in each generation and some degree of rejuvenescence in each agamic reproduction and the occurrence of progressive senescence in the meganucleus ending in its death and replacement by a new, young organ demonstrate that these unicellular animals are not fundamentally different from multicellular forms.   They are not, as Weismann ('82) believed, immortal because they do not grow old, but simply as other organisms are, because they reproduce and undergo reconstitution during reproduction and because old organs die and are replaced by young.

AGAMIC REPRODUCTION AND REJUVENESCENCE IN COELENTERATES

Among the coelenterates only the fresh-water hydra and one species of the colonial hydroids have been tested by the susceptibility method.   In hydra agamic reproduction is a process of budding.   In *Hydra fusca* the bud arises near the junction of the thicker body with the more slender stalk, and in its earlier stages is merely a rounded outgrowth including both ectodermal and entodermal layers of the body-wall (Fig 48).   Cell division and growth occur rapidly in it, it elongates, and in the course of a few days tentacles and a mouth begin to develop at its distal end (Fig 49). Meanwhile the region of attachment to the parent body gradually undergoes constriction, until finally the new, small animal separates from the parent, falls to the bottom, attaches itself, and begins to lead an active life   In this process a portion of the body-wall of the parent has undergone reconstitution into a new, independent individual

A comparison of the susceptibility to cyanide of small animals newly developed in this way with the larger parent shows that the

[1] Jennings, '10, '13, Calkins and Gregory, '13.

newly developed individuals are distinctly more susceptible than
the parents, i.e., they are physiologically younger. In the earlier
stages of the bud, however, while it is still attached to the parent
body and before it has developed the capacity for motor activity,
its susceptibility is not appreciably different from that of adjoining
regions of the parent body, or it may be even less susceptible than
these regions.

The fact that the increased susceptibility appears only after
the asexually produced individual is separated from the parent

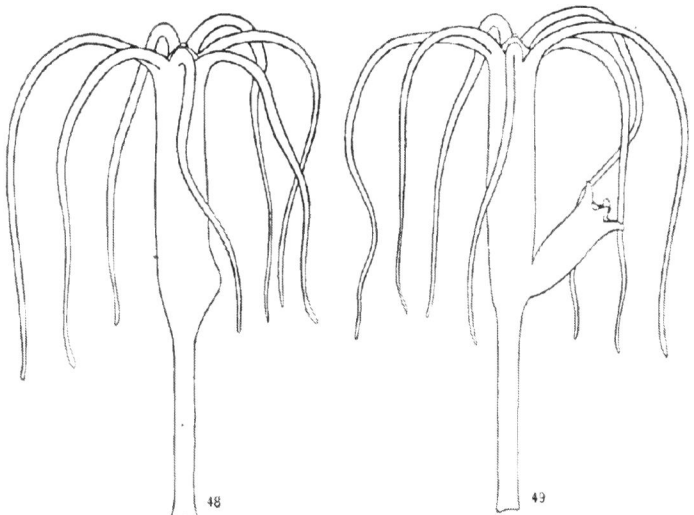

Figs. 48, 49.—Two stages in the development of a bud in *Hydra*

seems at first glance not to agree fully with the data and conclusions
from other forms, but this disagreement is only apparent, and results from the complication of the results by the factors of motor
activity and food. Motor activity of an individual, or even of a
region of the body in hydra, increases very considerably the susceptibility of that individual or region to cyanide. It is very
generally the case that the animals which show the greater motor
activity after being placed in cyanide die and disintegrate earlier
than the less active, and it has often been observed that marked

contraction in cyanide of a particular body region is followed by the death and disintegration of that region before other parts Evidently motor activity, although slow, increases the rate of metabolism in hydra to a very marked degree. This is perhaps to be expected from the fact that the motor mechanism in this organism is not highly developed, but is merely a part of the ectoderm cell. Motor activity undoubtedly involves the whole cell and at least all the cells of the ectoderm in the region where it occurs. To all appearances it is a very laborious process, and even after the strongest stimulation it is relatively slow and inefficient. In short, the observations made by the susceptibility method indicate that the increased metabolism associated with motor activity is relatively very great.

The bud in the early stages of development exhibits very little motor activity, and movement does not attain its maximum until separation from the parent takes place   The result of this difference in motor activity between bud and parent is that, even though growth and development are proceeding more rapidly in the bud than in the parent, the rate of metabolism is not greater in the bud where motor activity is slight than in the parent where it is much greater   But as soon as the bud becomes independent, its motor activity is comparable with, perhaps even greater than, that of the parent, and then its susceptibility to cyanide is distinctly greater, i e., its rate of metabolism is higher than that of the parent.

Moreover, the young bud while still attached to the parent grows at the expense of food ingested by the parent body, rather than at the expense of its own tissues. It does not undergo reduction, but grows during its reconstitution from a part of the parent body into a new individual. Since rejuvenescence is undoubtedly associated with reduction, as the following chapter will show, the bud, which receives food and grows rapidly throughout its development, does not become as young physiologically at any stage as if its development occurred at the expense of its own tissues

In the marine hydroid *Pennaria tiarella*, agamic buds are produced as in hydra but remain permanently in connection with the parent stem or branch, so that a branching tree-like colony with the

zooids or hydranths at the tips of the branches results.   Fig. 50
shows a portion of such a *Pennaria* colony.   In this species the new

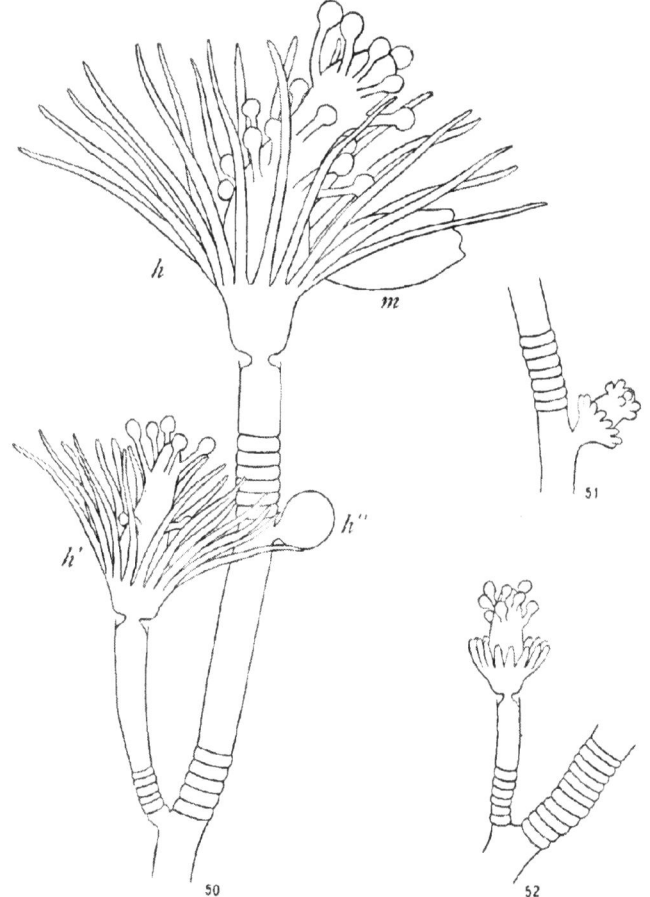

FIGS. 50–52.—*Pennaria tiarella:* Fig. 50, part of a colony, including a large,
old hydranth, *h*, bearing a medusa bud, *m*, a younger hydranth, *h'*, and a hydranth
bud, *h''*; Figs. 51, 52, developmental stages of hydranth.

hydranth bud arises laterally a short distance below the terminal
hydranth of a stem or branch (Fig. 50, *h''*).   It is an outgrowth

including both layers of the body-wall, as in hydra, and in its earlier stages is rounded in form and inclosed in the chitinous perisarc which covers the stem.   As development proceeds, it emerges from the perisarc, undergoes elongation, and the tentacles begin to appear, as indicated in Fig. 51   A later stage of development is shown in Fig. 52, a fully developed hydranth in Fig. 50, h', and an old hydranth bearing a medusa bud, m, in Fig 50, h.   The agamic production of hydranths in this form is then a reconstitution of a portion of the stem into a new hydranth.

As regards the susceptibility of the different stages, both motor activity, as in hydra, and the presence of the chitinous perisarc contribute to obscure the changes in susceptibility associated with the reconstitution of stem into hydranth.   The susceptibility of the early stages of hydranth development, such as h'' in Fig 50, cannot be compared directly with that of stages like Figs 51 and 52, because these early stages are inclosed like the stem in the chitinous perisarc, while in the later stages the hydranth is naked Neither are these early stages directly comparable with such stages as Fig 50, h or h', for in the former motor activity is absent, while in the latter it is fully developed.   It is possible, however, to compare the susceptibility of such a stage as Fig. 50, h'', with that of adjoining regions of the stem, for both are inclosed in perisarc, and a comparison of this sort shows that the early bud is in general distinctly more susceptible, i.e., it possesses a higher rate of metabolism and is physiologically younger than the stem adjoining it But in this case, as in hydra, the increase in rate connected with the formation of a new individual is less than it would be if the region were physiologically isolated and underwent development at the expense of its own tissues rather than of nutritive material As it is, the bud has abundant food and grows during development, while the isolated piece undergoes reduction

In the later stages of development the perisarc no longer enters as a factor, but differences in motor activity still exist between different stages   At the stage shown in Fig. 51 motor activity is absent or inappreciable, but the susceptibility of this stage is nevertheless usually somewhat greater than that of an old hydranth, like h in Fig 50, and less than that of a younger hydranth, like

h' in Fig 50. At the stage of Fig. 52 motor activity is present to some extent, though much less than in still later stages   This stage is distinctly more susceptible than such hydranths as h in Fig. 50. Here, where motor activity has begun to appear, even though it is still slight, the difference in physiological condition between morphologically young and old hydranths becomes distinctly evident. From this stage on the susceptibility decreases as development proceeds, but it does not attain a constant level even after the morphological form of the hydranth is fully developed   On a stem like that shown in Fig 50, for example, the hydranth h', which is younger in point of time than the terminal hydranth h, shows in general a higher susceptibility, i e., is physiologically younger than the latter.   In spite then of the presence of the perisarc in certain stages and the differences in motor activity in other stages, the differences in susceptibility indicate that a certain degree of rejuvenescence is associated with the agamic reproduction of hydranths in *Pennaria*. It is still a question, however, to what extent new parts which arise by budding in hydroids are formed by dedifferentiation and redifferentiation of old cells and to what extent by the interstitial cells which are small cells lying in groups between the other cells of the body-wall and which are commonly regarded as embryonic reserve cells.   From this point of view the apparent rejuvenescence which occurs in connection with budding might be regarded as simply a replacement of the older differentiated cells by the younger, undifferentiated   Doubtless the interstitial cells are less highly specialized than various other cells and so react more readily to the change in conditions, but the very fact that they were inactive before and became active in the development of the bud indicates a change in their physiological condition in the direction of a higher rate of metabolism.   Moreover, there is every indication that at least many of the specialized cells of the body-wall do take part in bud-formation and actually undergo more or less dedifferentiation

In addition to the asexual production of hydranths, *Pennaria* also gives rise asexually to medusa buds, which do not usually, however, develop into free-swimming medusae but remain attached to the parent body   These appear on the body of the hydranth im-

mediately distal to the circle of proximal tentacles (*m*, Fig. 50).
Three stages of development of the medusa bud drawn to the
same scale are shown in Figs 53–55   In the early stages the
medusa bud is always more susceptible to cyanide than the adjoining regions of the hydranth from which it arose, and its susceptibility decreases as development proceeds, the large, fully developed
bud being much less susceptible than the adjoining regions of the
parent hydranth.   These differences in susceptibility are not
dependent upon differences in size, for they concern primarily
the surface of the body.   Differences in motor activity may be
concerned in the difference in susceptibility between the fully
developed medusa bud and the hydranth, but the greater susceptibility of the bud in early stages as compared with the hydranth
cannot be accounted for in this way, for motor activity is present

FIGS. 53–55 —*Pennaria tiarella*. three stages in the development of a medusa bud

in the hydranth but not in the medusa bud.   Evidently the
medusa bud in early stages is physiologically younger than the
region of the hydranth from which it arises.

But the susceptibility of young medusa buds is in general
distinctly less than that of young hydranths of the stage of Figs
51 and 52, after emergence from the perisarc   That is, the young
medusa bud is not as young as the young hydranth   The medusa
bud arises from a more highly specialized region of the colony than
the hydranth bud and develops into a more highly specialized
zooid or individual   Apparently the reconstitution of a portion
of the hydranth body into a medusa bud does not carry the region
concerned back to so early a physiological stage as that attained
in the reconstitution of a region of the stem into a young hydranth.
This difference in physiological condition between hydranth bud
and medusa bud is probably the dynamic basis, or at least the

dynamic correlate, of the difference in morphological development. In this connection it is also of interest to note that in *Pennaria* medusa buds appear only upon hydranths which are physiologically relatively old, while the hydranth buds usually arise on the physiologically younger regions of the stem   In other species of hydroids, where the growth form is different, the physiological relations may also prove to be more or less widely different although medusa buds in general arise in connection with a fully developed hydranth, or a highly specialized reproductive zooid or from an apparently specialized region of the stem just proximal to a hydranth, while hydranth buds arise from less highly specialized regions.   It is probable that where such complicating factors as presence of the perisarc or differences in motor activity do not obscure the differences in susceptibility associated with physiological age, similar differences between the different forms of agamic reproduction will be found in other species.

To sum up, the susceptibility method indicates not only that a considerable degree of rejuvenescence is associated with agamic reproduction in *Pennaria* but also that different stages of rejuvenescence are represented in the different forms of agamic reproduction in this species.   In the more specialized reproductive process the young stages are apparently somewhat older physiologically than in the less specialized process.

REFERENCES

BAITSELL, G A.

   1912. "Experiments on the Reproduction of Hypotrichous Infusoria·   I, Conjugation between Closely Related Individuals in *Stylonychia pustulata*," *Jour. of Exp Zool* , XIII

   1914. "Experiments, etc   II, A Study of the So-called Life Cycle in *Oxytricha fallax* and *Pleurotricha lanceolata*," *Jour. of Exp Zool.*, XVI

CALKINS, G N.

   1902a. "Studies on the Life-History of Protozoa: I, The Life Cycle of *Paramecium caudatum*," *Arch. f. Entwickelungsmech* , XV

   1902b "Studies, etc : III, The Six Hundred and Twentieth Generation of *Paramecium*," *Biol Bull* , III.

   1904. "Studies, etc. IV, Death of the A-Series. Conclusions," *Jour of Exp. Zool.*, I.

CALKINS, G. N , and GREGORY, L. H

    1913.   "Variations in the Progeny of a Single Ex-Conjugant of *Paramecium caudatum,*" *Jour. of Exp Zool.*, XV.

CHILD, C. M.

    1910   "Physiological Isolation of Parts and Fission in *Planaria,*" *Arch f. Entwickelungsmech* , XXX (Festbd f Roux), II Teil

    1911a. "Die physiologische Isolation von Teilen des Organismus," *Vortr und Aufs u Entwickelungsmech* , XI.

    1911b. "Studies on the Dynamics of Morphogenesis and Inheritance in Experimental Reproduction: I, The Axial Gradient in *Planaria dorotocephala* as a Limiting Factor in Regulation," *Jour of Exp Zool* , X

    1911c. "Studies, etc.: III, The Formation of New Zooids in *Planaria* and Other Forms," *Jour of Exp Zool* , XI

    1912   "Studies, etc   IV, Certain Dynamic Factors in the Regulatory Morphogenesis of *Planaria dorotocephala* in Relation to the Axial Gradient," *Jour. of Exp. Zool* , XIII.

    1913a. "Studies, etc.: VI, The Nature of the Axial Gradients in *Planaria* and Their Relation to Antero-posterior Dominance, Polarity and Symmetry," *Arch. f. Entwickelungsmech.*, XXXVII.

    1913b "The Asexual Cycle in *Planaria velata* in Relation to Senescence and Rejuvenescence," *Biol Bull* , XXV.

    1914. Asexual Breeding and Prevention of Senescence in *Planaria velata,*" *Biol Bull* , XXVI

ENRIQUES, P.

    1903   "Sulla cosi detta' degenerazione senile' dei protozoi," *Monitore Zool. Ital.*, XIV

    1907   "La conjugazione e il differenziamento sessuale negli Infusori," *Arch. f. Protistenkunde*, IX.

    1908   "Die Konjugation und sexuelle Differenzierung der Infusorien," *Arch. f Protistenkunde*, XII.

GOLDSCHMIDT, R.

    1905. "Der Chromidialapparat lebhaft funktionierender Gewebszellen," *Zool. Jahrbucher; Abt. f. Anat u Ont.*, XXI.

JENNINGS, H. S.

    1910. "What Conditions Induce Conjugation in *Paramecium?*" *Jour of Exp Zool* , IX

    1913   "The Effect of Conjugation in *Paramecium,*" *Jour. of Exp Zool.*, XIV

JENNINGS, H. S , and HARGITT, G. T.

    1910   "Characteristics of the Diverse Races of *Paramecium,*" *Jour of Morphol* , XXI

JOHNSON, H P.
    1893. "A Contribution to the Morphology and Biology of the Stentors," *Jour of Morphol.*, VIII.

MAUPAS, E.
    1888 "Recherches expérimentales sur la multiplication des Infusories ciliés," *Arch de zool exp* , (2), VI.
    1889. "La rajeunissement karyogamique chez les ciliés," *Arch de zool exp.*, (2), VII

WEISMANN, A.
    1882. *Über die Dauer des Lebens.* Jena.

WOODRUFF, L L.
    1908. "The Life-Cycle of *Paramecium* When Subjected to a Varied Environment," *Am Nat.*, XLII.
    1909. "Further Studies on the Life-Cycle of *Paramecium*," *Biol Bull.*, XVII.
    1911a. "Two Thousand Generations of *Paramecium*," *Arch. f Protistenkunde*, XXI.
    1911b "*Paramecium aurelia* and *Paramecium caudatum*," *Jour. of Morphol.*, XXII
    1913a. "Dreitausand und dreihundert Generationen von *Paramecium* ohne Konjugation oder kunstliche Reizung," *Biol. Centralbl.*, XXXIII.
    1913b. "Cell Size, Nuclear Size and the Nucleo-cytoplasmic Relation during the Life of a Pedigreed Race of *Oxytricha fallax*," *Jour. of Exp Zool* , XV.
    1914. "On So-called Conjugating and Non-conjugating Races of *Paramecium*," *Jour. of Exp. Zool.*, XVI.

WOODRUFF, L. L , and ERDMANN, RHODA
    1914. "A Normal Periodic Reorganization Process without Cell Fusion in *Paramecium*," *Jour. of Exp. Zool.*, XVII.

ZWEIBAUM, J (ENRIQUES et ZWEIBAUM).
    1912 "La conjugaison et la différenciation sexuelle chez les Infusories: V, Les conditions nécessaires et suffisantes pour la conjugaison du *Paramoecium caudatum*," *Arch. f. Protistenkunde*, XXVI

CHAPTER VII

THE RÔLE OF NUTRITION IN SENESCENCE AND REJUVENES-CENCE IN *PLANARIA*

REDUCTION BY STARVATION IN *Planaria*

The various species of *Planaria* are capable of living for months without food from external sources. During such periods of starvation, however, they undergo reduction in size, many cells degenerate, and some organs may completely disappear. Various investigators, among them F R. Lillie, '00; Schultz, '04, Stoppen-brink, '05, have considered one phase or another of this process of reduction, and Lillie and Schultz particularly have called attention to the fact that in its proportions and chief morphological characteristics the animal reduced by starvation resembles the young animal and have pointed out that the changes which occur during reduction indicate that the process of development is reversible. In an earlier chapter (p. 57) I have suggested that it is preferable to use the term "regressibility" rather than reversibility for such changes, since the occurrence of reduction or dedifferentiation in an organism does not necessarily imply a reversal of the reactions concerned in progressive development. Only from the morphological viewpoint are we justified in speaking of a reversal of development.

The reduction in size of *Planaria* during starvation is unquestionably due to the re-entrance of its structural material into metabolism as a source of energy. Schultz finds that reduction in *Planaria* is due to the disappearance of whole cells and organs rather than to decrease in size of the cells in general. This is undoubtedly true to a large extent, but my own unpublished observations indicate that some decrease in size does occur in at least many cells in the starving planarian, and other authors who have investigated the cellular changes in animals during starvation have reached similar conclusions [1]

[1] The following references constitute a partial bibliography of the subject Kasanzeff, '01, and Wallengren, '02, found marked reduction in the size of *Paramecium* during hunger Citron, '02, observed decrease in size of ectoderm cells in a coelenterate

In the course of observations on *Planaria dorotocephala* I have found that the lower limit of reduction differs rather widely according to the original size of the animal   Animals of twenty-five millimeters in length before starvation begin to die when they are reduced to a length of five or six millimeters, while animals which are six or seven millimeters in length before starvation may undergo reduction to a length of one or two millimeters before death. As I have suggested elsewhere, death in these cases is probably not due to lack of available material, for pieces isolated from starving animals are capable of reconstitution to whole animals and may then undergo reduction to a much smaller size before death   Death, at least in the larger animals reduced by starvation, is probably due to altered correlative conditions resulting from changes in the axial gradient in rate of metabolism (Child, '14, p. 443).

In consequence of their ability to undergo extreme reduction before death occurs from starvation the planarians would constitute valuable material for the study of physiological and particularly of metabolic changes connected with inanition if it were not for their small size.   But now with the Tashiro biometer and with the susceptibility method we are able to obtain some light on at least certain features of the metabolism in these starving animals Some of the data bearing upon this problem are presented in the following section.

CHANGES IN SUSCEPTIBILITY DURING STARVATION IN
Planaria dorotocephala AND *P velata*

Since the animals reduced by starvation resemble young animals morphologically, the question whether they are young physiologically at once suggests itself.   If the reduced animals are fed, growth begins again, and the animals are not only indistinguishable from young, growing animals in appearance and behavior, but are able to go through the life history again from the stage at which feeding began.   Moreover, the reduced animals are very active

during starvation   In the higher animals decrease in size of gland cells, muscle cells, and nerve cells during starvation has been recorded by various authors, among whom are Heumann, '50, Rindfleisch, '68; Morpurgo, '88, '89, Downerowitsch, '92, Statkewitsch, '94, Lukjanow, '97, Morgulis, '11

and highly irritable, reacting strongly and rapidly to various kinds
of stimuli. Slight movements of the water or a slight jarring of
the aquarium, to which well-fed, old worms do not respond at all,
will bring them into active movement, and when wounded or when
the body is cut in two they react much more strongly than old
worms. In all these respects they resemble young rather than old
animals. In fact, their general behavior indicates very clearly
that they have become physiologically young during the course of
reduction. But with the aid of the susceptibility method it is
possible to obtain more positive knowledge upon this point.

The comparative susceptibility of starving animals may be
determined in two ways· when temperature and other external
conditions are controlled, the susceptibilities of a uniform stock at
different stages of starvation may be directly compared with each
other. This method of procedure will show directly whether the
susceptibility increases, decreases, or remains constant during
starvation. On the other hand, the susceptibility of animals at
any stage of starvation may be compared with that of fed animals
of the same size or of animals of the original size and condition of
the stock before starvation. In this way also changes in susceptibility may be determined. Records of experiments of both sorts
are given below

In Table II the decrease in length and increase in susceptibility.
determined at intervals of about two weeks during three months of

TABLE II

Length of Starvation Period in Days	Length of Animals in Millimeters	Survival Time of Ten Animals in KCN 0 001 Mol	Mean Survival Time
0	15–18	6^h30^m–9^h00^m	7^h45^m
14	15–17	6^h00^m–7^h00^m	6^h30^m
32	10–12	5^h00^m–6^h30^m	5^h45^m
45	9–10	4^h00^m–5^h00^m	4^h30^m
60	7– 8	2^h00^m–4^h00^m	3^h00^m
77	5	2^h00^m–3^h30^m	2^h45^m
91	3 5–4	1^h30^m–2^h30^m	2^h00^m

starvation, are recorded The first two columns of the table are
self-explanatory; in the third column the times given are the times
of complete disintegration of the first and last of the worms of each

lot of ten worms. i.e., this column gives the extremes of the survival times and the fourth column the means. The table shows at a glance that the susceptibility of the animals increases very greatly during the course of starvation, the mean survival time decreasing from seven hours and forty-five minutes in the large, well-fed animals at the beginning of the starvation period to two hours in the reduced animals after ninety-one days of starvation

The changes in susceptibility have been determined in the same way for several other starvation stocks, some made up from larger animals than these, others from smaller, and still others from animals of the same size   Different stocks were kept during starvation under various conditions of temperature, light, aeration, and change of water, but in all essentially the same result was obtained, viz., a great and, except for slight irregularities in a few cases which were evidently due to incidental uncontrolled factors, a continuous increase in susceptibility during starvation.

According to the second method of procedure mentioned above, the susceptibility of the starved animals may be compared directly with that of fed animals. The records of two tests of this sort are presented

In the first of these several hundred worms fifteen to eighteen millimeters long were selected from freshly collected material as a starvation stock. After eighty-one days of starvation the animals were reduced to a length of seven to eight millimeters, and the susceptibility of ten of the reduced worms is shown in the curve *cd* of Fig 56   For comparison the susceptibility curves of ten animals of the same size and condition as the members of the starvation stock before reduction (*ef*, Fig 56) and of ten well-fed, young animals of the same size as the animals reduced by starvation (*ab*, Fig 56) are given. The young, fed animals are most, the old, fed animals the least, susceptible, but the susceptibility of the animals reduced by starvation is much nearer that of the young animals than that of the old and therefore must have undergone marked increase during reduction

In another case the starvation stock was composed of animals twenty to twenty-four millimeters long, and the determination of susceptibilities recorded in Fig. 57 was made after ninety days of complete starvation in filtered water. The curve *ab*, drawn as unbroken line in Fig. 57, is the susceptibility curve of ten star animals which have undergone reduction to a length of seven eight millimeters. The second curve *ab*, drawn as a broken l shows the susceptibility of ten newly collected, young, grow animals of the same size as the reduced worms. A part of original stock was fed, while the others were starved, and the cu

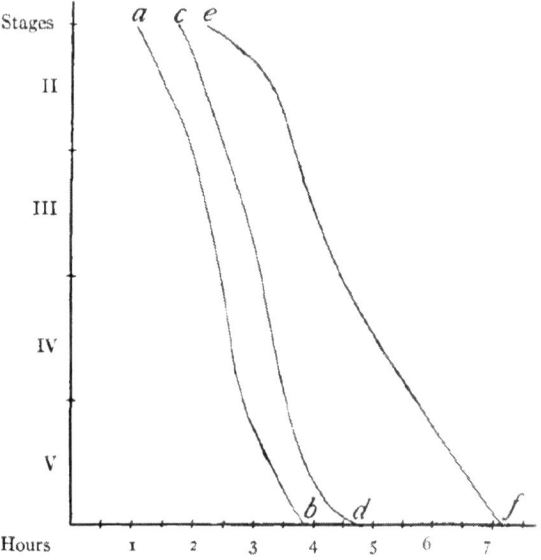

FIG. 56.—Susceptibility of *Planaria dorotocephala* to KCN o.oo1 mol. in rela to nutritive condition and age: *ab*, susceptibility of well-fed, growing animals mm. in length; *cd*, susceptibility of animals reduced by starvation from 15–18 r to 7–8 mm.; *ef*, susceptibility of well-fed animals 15–18 mm. in length.

cd shows the susceptibility of these animals. During the th months of feeding these worms have of course grown somewl older, but in full-grown animals like these the change in th months is slight. But the susceptibility of the starving anim has increased until it is about the same as that of young, growi animals of the same size.

Determinations of susceptibility by the direct method w cyanide, alcohol, and ether as reagent have been made on seve hundred individuals of *Planaria dorotocephala* in various stages of starvation, and in all cases the susceptibility has been found to increase during starvation. In *P. velata* also the susceptibility to cyanide has been found to increase during starvation. This species does not undergo reduction in size as rapidly as *P. doroto-cephala*, but the effect of starvation is essentially the same in both. If the susceptibility of these animals is in any degree a measure of

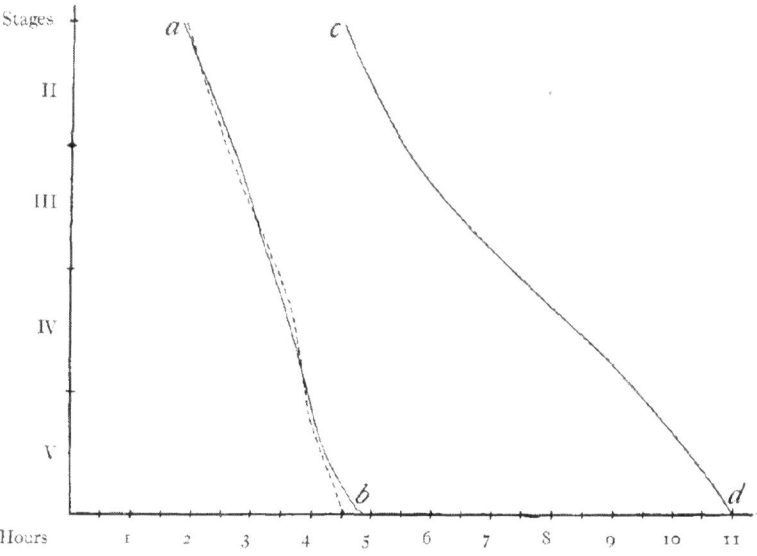

FIG. 57.—Susceptibility of *Planaria dorotocephala* to KCN 0.001 mol. in relation to nutritive condition and age: *ab*, dashes, well-fed, growing animals; *ab*, unbroken line, animals reduced by starvation from 20–24 mm. to 7–8 mm.; *cd*, animals from the same stock and of the same size at the beginning of the experiment as the starved animals, but which have been fed while others were starving.

physiological age, the starving animals certainly undergo rejuvenescence, the degree of rejuvenescence varying with the degree of starvation and reduction.

THE PRODUCTION OF CARBON DIOXIDE BY STARVED ANIMALS

The invention of the Tashiro biometer (Tashiro, '13) has made possible a direct estimation and comparison of carbon-dioxide production in different individuals and pieces or tissues of small animals. The agreement between the results obtained with this apparatus and those of the susceptibility method has already been mentioned (pp 73 74).

A number of estimations of carbon-dioxide production in starved, reduced animals, as compared with well-fed, growing animals of the same size, have been made with the aid of this apparatus.[1] The worms used for the estimation of carbon-dioxide production were taken from a starvation stock after ninety-four days of starvation. The animals were twenty to twenty-four millimeters long at the beginning of the starvation period, and after ninety-four days without food had undergone reduction to a length of seven millimeters In each estimation the carbon-dioxide production of one of these starved animals was compared with that of a young, well-fed animal of the same size

Two estimations were made with normal uninjured animals and in both cases the carbon-dioxide production of the starved animal in a given length of time was slightly greater than that of the fed animal. But since the animals moved about to some extent, and since the apparatus is so sensitive that differences in carbon-dioxide production resulting from differences in motor activity might be a serious source of error, it was thought desirable to eliminate movement as far as possible. This was accomplished by removing the heads of the two animals to be compared and making the estimation after they had become quiet. These headless animals remained quiet in the chambers of the biometer, but gave essentially the same result as those with heads In the two estimations made with such animals the carbon-dioxide production of the starved animal was practically the same as that of the fed animal. In other words, the rate of production of carbon dioxide in the starved, reduced animal is practically equal to that in the young, growing animal of the same size, and this rate is much higher per unit of body weight than that in large, old animals The results obtained by the direct susceptibility method are thus fully

[1] These estimates were made at my request by Dr. Tashiro before the biometer was available for general use, and I take this opportunity of acknowledging my obligation to him, both for conducting the experiments and for permitting me to use the results

confirmed by the estimations of carbon-dioxide production.   In
rate of carbon-dioxide production the starved, reduced animals
resemble young rather than old animals, such as they were before
starvation.

THE RATE OF DECREASE IN SIZE DURING STARVATION

When the animals are kept entirely without food the rate of
decrease in size shows in general an increase, at least during the
later stages of starvation.   Thus far only incidental observations
have been made concerning this point, the approximate lengths of
lots of animals being noted as they were removed from time to
time for determination of the susceptibility.   But even in these
measurements the differences in rate of decrease in size appear,
though with some irregularities, and in most cases the increase in
rate in the later stages of starvation is evident without measure-
ment.   Table III, for which the data are given in Table II (p. 157),
gives the average length of the animals in a starvation stock at
monthly intervals, and Table IV gives similar information, but

TABLE III

Length of Starvation Period in Days	Length of Animals in Millimeters	Percentage of Decrease in Length
0...............	15 – 18	....
32...............	10 – 12	30
60...............	7 – 8	31
91...............	3.5– 4	51

TABLE IV

Length of Starvation Period in Days	Length of Animals in Millimeters	Percentage of Decrease in Length
0...............	6–7	....
32...............	4–5	30
60...............	2–2.5	50

from a stock of animals of smaller size before starvation.   In
Table III the average decrease in length during the first month is
about 30 per cent, during the second about the same, and during

the third about 50 per cent Similarly, in the much smaller worms
of Table IV the average decrease in length during the first month
is 30 per cent, and during the second, 50 per cent In these cases
the measurements for each month were made on different lots of
worms from the same stock Doubtless a continuous series of
measurements of the same individuals would bring out the differences in rate of decrease still more clearly. When the animals are
not kept entirely without food the rate of reduction does not increase, but may even decrease in later stages, for the smaller the
animals, the more completely does a small amount of food retard
or inhibit reduction. This increase in rate of reduction during
starvation confirms the observations on susceptibility and on
carbon-dioxide production, for it indicates that the rate of metabolic processes increases as reduction proceeds.

In this connection the study by Mayer ('14) of loss of weight
in a jelly-fish, *Cassiopea*, is of interest From his data Mayer concludes that the relative loss of weight for each day or other period
is in general the same throughout the course of starvation Moreover, the nitrogen-content and water-content of the body do not
show any change in relation to starvation. At first glance it
appears that the course of starvation in this medusa differs from
that in *Planaria*. While the metabolic condition of the animals
during starvation has not been determined, the constancy in the
percentage of loss of weight indicates that the metabolic rate does
not increase as starvation and reduction proceed As a matter of
fact, however, Mayer's data, and particularly the curves of loss
of weight, show that in most cases the loss of weight in uninjured
animals during the first two or three weeks of starvation is slightly
less than the calculated loss according to the formula which Mayer
has adopted, while during the later period of starvation the observed
loss of weight equals or in many cases exceeds the calculated loss.
In mutilated animals, which are undergoing regeneration as well
as starvation, the observed loss of weight during the earlier stages
of starvation is in most cases more rapid than the calculated loss,
but the two coincide more nearly in later stages

It is probable then that Mayer's law of loss of weight is only an
approximation based on averages, and that some slight increase

in the percentage of loss in a given time interval does occur in uninjured animals   In regenerating animals, on the other hand, the
loss is more rapid in earlier stages because of the use of body substance in the formation of new parts as well as for function.   As
regeneration proceeds, the growth of the new parts becomes less
rapid and requires less material, and the loss of weight becomes
slightly less rapid   If these suggestions are correct, starvation in
Cassiopea follows essentially the same course as in *Planaria* and
is accompanied by increase in metabolic rate and some degree of
rejuvenescence   For the study of this aspect of starvation, however, the medusa is a particularly unfavorable form because the
volume of cellular substance is exceedingly small, as compared
with the volume of gelatinous material which, according to Mayer,
constitutes the chief source of nutrition during starvation, and since
this is extra-cellular, its disappearance does not alter the cellular
condition   For the same reason changes in chemical constitution
and water-content of the protoplasm, so far as they occur, are
inappreciable, though in an animal with so little differentiation as
the medusa the changes are probably not very great.   There is
also the possibility that, as Pütter believes, substances in solution
in the water serve as a source of nutrition to some extent   If this
is the case, the influence of such substances on the rate of loss of
weight must be greater in the later stages of starvation when the
animal is smaller and the absolute loss less than in the earlier
stages, and will therefore contribute to mask the increasing rate of
loss in these stages   Taking all these facts into account, it appears
highly probable that the changes in the cellular substance of the
medusae are very similar to, though probably less extensive than,
those in *Planaria*   Mayer notes that the cells decrease in size,
their boundaries become indistinct, and some cells die   Determinations of the changes in susceptibility of the cellular portions of the
body of the medusa during starvation would be of interest.

THE CAPACITY OF STARVED ANIMALS FOR ACCLIMATION

In general the ability of planarians to become acclimated to
depressing agents or conditions varies with the rate of metabolism
Young animals, for example, become much more readily and more

completely acclimated to cyanide or alcohol, low temperature, etc., than old, and acclimation occurs more readily at higher than at lower temperatures (Child, '11). In the low concentrations of reagents used in the acclimation susceptibility method (pp. 82–84), starved animals show very little capacity for acclimation as compared with well-fed animals of the same size; in most cases even less than large, old animals. In my earlier studies of susceptibility only this acclimation method was used, and since in general the capacity for acclimation had been found to vary with the rate of metabolism, the very slight capacity of starved animals for acclimation was regarded as indicating that their rate of metabolism was low. But the results obtained in later investigation by the direct susceptibility method which have been briefly presented above, and the confirmation of these by the estimations of carbon-dioxide production, force us to the conclusion that the rate of metabolism increases during starvation. This being the case, the decrease in capacity for acclimation in starved animals cannot be due to a low rate of metabolism, but must be associated with the nutritive condition in some way independent of metabolic rate (Child, '14). When feeding is begun after a long period of starvation, the capacity for acclimation rises almost at once (Child, '11) and continues to increase as feeding continues and growth replaces reduction.

Since the nature of the process of acclimation is at present unknown, this relation between nutritive condition and capacity for acclimation cannot at present be analyzed, but must simply be recorded as a fact. But whether acclimation results primarily from a change in the metabolic substratum, or in the character and relation of the metabolic reactions, the fact that the individual with a supply of nutritive material from external sources has a greater capacity for acclimation than the starving animal which is undergoing reduction is at least suggestive, as indicating the greater possibility of change under changed external conditions in the well-fed animal

Whatever may be the nature of the relation between nutrition and capacity for acclimation, the facts demonstrate that, although the starved, reduced animals are practically identical with young, growing animals of the same size as regards rate of metabolism, they differ widely from these in their capacity for acclimation. This difference raises the question whether capacity for acclimation is a fundamental or only an incidental feature of the age cycle. If it is a fundamental feature, then the reduced animals have undergone rejuvenescence only in certain respects and have actually become older physiologically in certain other respects If, on the other hand, it is merely incidental, then the reduced animals have undergone what is essentially rejuvenescence and merely require food in order to make them identical with young, growing individuals. The latter alternative seems to be the correct one If the decrease in capacity for acclimation during starvation is regarded as a process of senescence, it becomes necessary to admit that an animal which is old in this respect may become young within a few hours when it is fed. The susceptibility as measured by the direct method and the rate of carbon-dioxide production are certainly much more adequate criteria of physiological age and condition than the capacity for acclimation. In other words, reduction by starvation is essentially a process of rejuvenescence in these animals, and the difference between them and young, growing animals as regards capacity for acclimation is an incidental rather than a fundamental difference.

When the animal reduced by starvation is again fed, its physiological condition very soon becomes indistinguishable from that of growing animals of about the same size. In the advanced stages of reduction the susceptibility of the reduced animal is almost always somewhat greater than that of fed animals of the same size, and the effect of renewed feeding is a decrease in susceptibility to about the same level as that of the fed animal. The capacity for acclimation, as already noted, increases even after a single feeding, but in advanced stages of reduction by starvation several feedings are usually necessary, i e , the animal must attain a well-fed condition before the capacity for acclimation is equal to that of growing animals The effect of a single feeding may appear within an hour or two, but lasts at most only a few days, the animal rapidly returning to the completely starved condition But if other feedings follow at sufficiently short intervals, growth soon begins, and both susceptibility and capacity for acclimation undergo a gradual decrease as the animal once more becomes physiologically older After at most a few feedings, then, the reduced animal is indistinguishable from the young animal in nature, and, as regards susceptibility, carbon-dioxide production, and capacity for acclimation, is capable of undergoing senescence again   That a real rejuvenescence has occurred during starvation cannot be doubted

PARTIAL STARVATION IN RELATION TO SENESCENCE

The asexual life history of *Planaria velata* was described in chap. vi and it was pointed out that in this species the decrease in rate of metabolism characteristic of the period of growth, differentiation, and senescence apparently leads automatically to fragmentation of the body and so to the reconstitution from the fragments of small, physiologically young animals, which repeat the life history.

If this process of fragmentation is associated with senescence and if starvation and reduction bring about rejuvenescence, it should be possible, not only to prevent the occurrence of fragmentation, but to keep the animals indefinitely at a certain age by giving them a quantity of food just sufficient to prevent reduction but not sufficient to permit growth. This experiment has been performed with a stock of these animals. During almost three years they have been fed at intervals varying from two or three days to two or three weeks, the feeding being regulated according to the condition of the animals   If growth occurred the intervals between feedings were increased, and if the animals decreased in size they were fed with greater frequency   If some animals showed more growth or reduction than others, they were isolated and the feedings regulated as required until all were again of approximately the same size. During the early stages of the experiment growth was twice allowed to proceed too far, and a few of the larger worms of the stock underwent some fragmentation.

During the three years of the experiment the animals have been kept at lengths varying from four to seven millimeters. In all this time no fragmentation has occurred except in the two cases mentioned above, when growth was allowed to go too far   The animals are still in good condition and show the activity of young animals. Susceptibility determinations have not been made, since the stock is not large and is gradually depleted by occasional accidental losses in changing water   However, there is every reason to believe that the animals are as young physiologically as their size would lead one to suspect, and they have shown no indications of the changes in color, cessation of feeding, and decrease in motor activity characteristic of old worms

While the animals of this insufficiently fed stock have remained at essentially the same physiological age during almost three years, another portion of the same original stock which emerged from cysts in the laboratory at the same time, but which has been fed often enough to permit rapid growth, has passed through thirteen asexual generations.   A comparison of these two stocks leaves no doubt as to the effect of partial starvation in inhibiting senescence and the changes accompanying it.   In these animals the length of life or of the developmental period is not measured by time, but by rapidity of growth   With abundant food this species may pass through its whole life history, from the stage of emergence from a cyst to fragmentation and encystment, in three or four weeks, but when growth is prevented by loss of food, it may continue active and young for at least three years, as the foregoing experiment has demonstrated, and doubtless for a much longer period.   It is of course possible that continuation of the experiment during a sufficiently long time might show that a slow process of senescence was occurring in spite of the absence of growth.   Only such continuation can determine whether this will be the case or not.   But the fact remains that senescence can be retarded or inhibited for a length of time, which, compared with the length of the active life in nature, is very long—in the present case about thirty-six times as long, and eighteen times as long as the average length of a generation in the laboratory

Similar experiments with *Planaria dorotocephala* have been carried sufficiently far to show that this species also can be kept in approximately the same physiological condition for some months. As long as the animals do not receive food enough to permit growth, there are no indications of senescence, but when growth occurs the susceptibility begins to decrease.

In these experiments with partial feeding the susceptibility does not of course remain the same at all times   Each feeding is followed by a distinct decrease in susceptibility, and later, as the animals begin to starve, the susceptibility increases again.   Thus the life of such animals actually consists of alternating periods of senescence and rejuvenescence   But if the intervals between feedings are sufficient, the changes in the two opposite directions balance each other and the mean physiological condition remains the same.

THE CHARACTER OF NUTRITION IN RELATION TO THE AGE CYCLE

Up to the present time the problem of the relation between the character of nutrition and the life cycle has received comparatively little attention, although it is evident from the results already obtained that an interesting and important field of investigation is open here.   In the attempt to find a suitable food for the breeding of *Planaria velata* in the laboratory it was soon observed that the size attained before the animals ceased to feed, the character of fragmentation, and even its occurrence and the physiological condition of the small animals which develop from the encysted fragments, were all dependent to some extent upon the character of nutrition   In these experiments the food did not in all cases consist of single tissues or organs, so that it is not possible to correlate the effects produced with the characteristics of particular tissues and still less with particular chemical constitution.   There is no doubt, however, that this species constitutes favorable material for nutrition experiments of this kind, such, for example, as Gudernatsch ('12, '14) and Romeis ('13, '14) have carried out on the tadpole, using various tissues and organs, including thyroid, thymus, adrenals, etc., as nutritive material.

Only certain important points in the feeding experiments on *P. velata* need be mentioned here.   When the animals are fed beef liver the life cycle approaches more closely to that of animals in nature than with any other food thus far used, but cessation of feeding and fragmentation occur at a smaller size than in nature. The liver-fed animals also differ from animals in nature in not losing their pigment before fragmentation and in encysting rather

frequently without fragmentation. The encysted fragments from
liver-fed animals give rise to physiologically young animals which
are able to repeat the life cycle, and asexual breeding may be continued with liver as food through at least many generations.

Animals fed with earthworm have a rather different life history.
They attain a larger size before fragmentation and, when kept at a
low temperature, they continue to grow until very much larger
than any individuals ever seen in nature, and finally die, apparently
of old age, usually without fragmentation and always without
sexual reproduction. At higher temperatures they cease to feed
at a certain stage, and some give rise to two or a few fragments
which are usually larger than under natural conditions. Some
animals encyst whole without fragmentation, and some do not
encyst at all.

The further history of these different groups is of interest. The
encysted fragments give rise to physiologically young worms The
animals which encyst without fragmentation remain in the cysts
until they have used up their reserves and more or less of their own
tissues, and then emerge as smaller, physiologically younger animals
also capable of repeating the life cycle. But the history of the
animals which do not encyst shows the most interesting features
The normal form of a full-grown, well-fed animal is shown in Fig 8
(p 94). At the time these animals cease to feed, the pharynx
disintegrates and no new pharynx develops in its place. In the
course of a few days the posterior end of the body becomes inactive
and assumes a rounded form, as in Fig 58, being dragged about
by the rest of the body as if it were a dead mass or a foreign substance During the next few days this change in form and behavior extends farther anteriorly, so that the rounded mass becomes
larger and the active portion of the body smaller (Fig 59). At
this stage this process may cease in some individuals, but in others
it continues still farther. as in Fig 60, until only a short anterior
portion with the head remains active In this condition the small,
active anterior region is scarcely able to drag the large inert mass
about, although it makes violent attempts to do so

In some cases the rounded mass disintegrates at this stage and
is lost, and the anterior region slowly undergoes reconstitution to a

whole animal of small size by development of a new p<
and a pharynx (Fig. 65), and is once more ready to feed

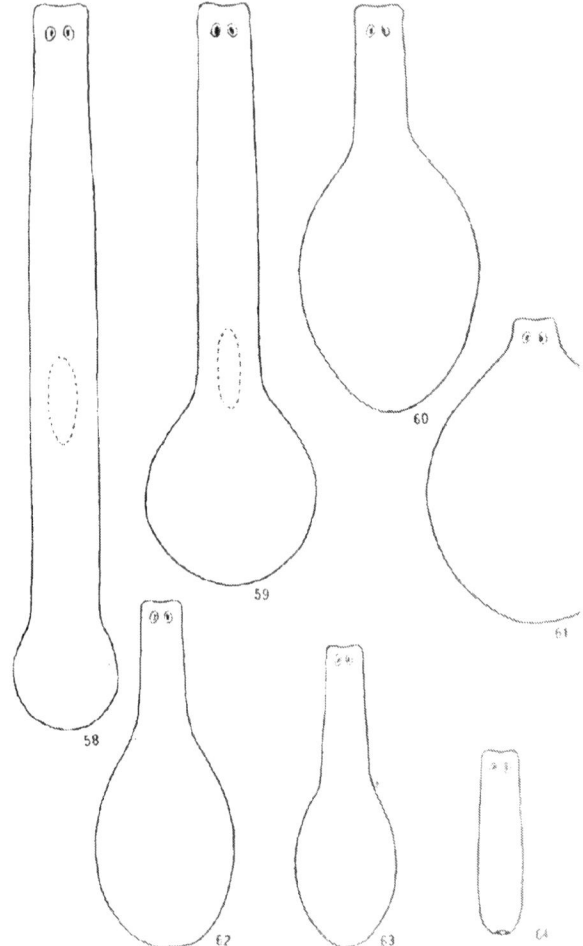

FIGS. 58–65.—*Planaria velata:* a life cycle without reproduction:
the changes of advanced age; Figs. 62–65, the period of rejuvenescence.

the life history. But in other cases the change in form
until nothing but the head remains active, as in Fig. 61.

disintegration begins and the whole animal, including the head,
dies   In the rounded mass the internal structure gradually disappears with extensive necrosis and disintegration of cells, until
little more than a sack remains containing some living tissue and a
large amount of granular substance resulting from the cell disintegration.   In other words, this mass represents to a large extent a
process of involution and death of cells and tissue

In those individuals in which this process of involution ceases
at the stage of Fig. 59 or Fig 60, the mass usually does not undergo
complete disintegration, but remains attached to the body and is
gradually resorbed, the process extending over a month or two
During this time the mass evidently serves as a source of nutrition
for the active region and is in some sense analogous to the yolk
sac of many embryos.   In such individuals the anterior region
remains continuously active and the involution mass gradually
becomes smaller (Figs. 62 and 63), until completely resorbed and
only a longer or shorter anterior region considerably reduced in
size remains.   In cases where the resorption of the posterior mass
begins at a stage like that of Fig. 59, the portion of the body remaining after complete resorption may include the anterior half, but
where resorption does not begin until involution is more advanced,
as in Fig 60, the portion remaining after resorption may be only
the anterior fourth (Fig 64).

After resorption of the posterior mass is completed, the remaining portion slowly undergoes reconstitution, developing a new
posterior end and a new pharynx and mouth (Fig. 65), and thus
finally attaining the same condition as in those cases where the
involution mass disintegrates and is lost without resorption.   At
this stage the small animal is physiologically young, as its high
susceptibility indicates, and is again ready to take food and grow
and repeat the life cycle.

In this remarkable process of senescence and death of a part of
the body and rejuvenescence of the remainder, no reproductive
process is involved except the reconstitution of the anterior region
into a new whole   That portion of the body which under natural
conditions undergoes fragmentation and encystment, the fragments
undergoing reconstitution to new animals, is in these cases appar-

ently too far advanced in senescence to recover, and undergoes complete death and disintegration or gradual degeneration and resorption. That it serves as a source of nutrition for the portion which remains active is indicated by the fact that the reduction in size of this portion is much less rapid than in starving normal animals. Nevertheless, it is evident that the supply of food in the involution mass is not adequate to prevent the occurrence of reduction sooner or later, and since the animal during resorption of the posterior region is without pharynx or mouth, it cannot take food in the usual way; consequently as the source of supply in the involution mass gradually fails, the anterior region gradually starves and undergoes reduction. But when a certain stage of reduction is reached, the new posterior end and pharynx develop at the expense of other regions, and the process of rejuvenescence is completed   In these cases, then, senescence leads to death in certain parts of the body while other parts remain alive and undergo rejuvenescence by starvation, reduction, and reconstitution

The question of the conditions concerned in the localization of death in the posterior region of the body requires some consideration. The facts indicate that fragmentation is usually inhibited by certain internal conditions and that, as the rate of metabolism decreases during senescence, the lower limit for the continued existence of differentiated structure is finally reached and passed in the posterior region, and the processes of involution or disintegration begin. The earthworm diet has been repeatedly used with animals of different stocks and the results are always essentially the same. Continued feeding in successive generations of the same stock has not thus far brought about any further changes, and the animals which do not die show no indications of progressive senescence in successive generations.

Another diet used consists of the bodies of fresh-water mussels The portions used for food are chiefly the reproductive organs and the digestive gland, and the animals apparently eat chiefly the reproductive cells

In the first generation the effect of this diet is to decrease the frequency of fragmentation   In most animals the involution of the posterior region occurs, as in Figs. 58–61, but very commonly

this process ends with the death of the whole animal and no resorption or rejuvenescence occurs   In some animals, however, the
involution mass disintegrates and is lost at the stage of Fig. 60,
and the anterior portion develops a new pharynx and posterior end.
With the mussel diet a few very small fragments arise from some
individuals.   .

The animals which undergo partial involution and disintegration
followed by reconstitution feed a few times on mussel, but cease
to grow at about half the size of the preceding generation, and most
of them undergo involution and die.   Some encyst entire and others
produce one or two fragments and then encyst, but in all cases thus
far the encysted animals or pieces die in the cysts and no third
generation appears, i e , that portion of the second generation which
arises from the non-encysting members of the first generation dies
without giving rise to a third generation

As regards the encysted fragments from the first generation,
about half die in the cysts, the others emerge as small worms;
these feed a few times on mussel, grow slowly to about half the size
of the first generation, and undergo involution or in a few cases
fragmentation, as in the preceding generation.   Most of these
worms die at this time, either as the result of involution or in the
cysts, but a very few emerge from cysts as a third generation
These scarcely react to food at all, show almost no growth, and soon
undergo involution and die with or without fragmentation, or
die in the cysts   In no case has a single animal of the fourth generation been obtained from stocks fed on mussel, and very few live
to the third generation.

These stocks show every indication of a progressive senescence
in successive generations   It is of interest to note that a few of the
animals from encysted fragments reach the third generation, while
the animals developed from the pieces surviving partial involution
or encystment without fragmentation all die in the second generation.   The encysted fragments are smaller than the others and
undergo more extensive reorganization, and consequently a somewhat greater degree of rejuvenescence in the process of reconstitution to whole animals   But the animals after emergence from cysts
or reconstitution following partial involution are not as young

physiologically as those kept on other diets. Their susceptibility is distinctly lower than that of animals at the same stage in nature or in stocks kept on a diet of liver or earthworm. Their motor activity is also less than that of these animals and their rate of growth is slow. There can be no doubt that these animals undergo much less rejuvenescence in the reproductive and reconstitutional processes than do those on the other diets, and it is evident that the degree of rejuvenescence is progressively less in each successive generation

These experiments with different diets have been described at some length because they demonstrate that the course of the life cycle may be very greatly altered by the character of nutrition The effect of the mussel diet is to a certain degree inherited and cumulative from one generation to another and in this respect differs from that of the other diets. The chief value of these experiments lies in their suggestiveness as indicating what may be accomplished with diets carefully limited to particular kinds of cells or tissues or to substances of particular chemical constitution

REFERENCES

CHILD, C M.

1911   "A Study of Senescence and Rejuvenescence Based on Experiments with Planarians," *Arch f. Entwickelungsmech*, XXXI

1914   ' Starvation, Rejuvenescence and Acclimation in *Planaria dorotocephala*," *Arch f Entwickelungsmech.*, XXXVIII.

CITRON, E.

1902.   "Beitrage zur Kenntnis von *Syncoryne sarsii*," *Arch f Naturgeschichte*, Jhg LXVIII

DOWNEROWITSCH.

1892.   "On the Changes in the Spinal Cord during Complete Starvation" (Russian), *Bolnitschnaja Gaseta Botkina*, 1892.

GUDERNATSCH, J. F

1912   "Feeding Experiments on Tadpoles. 1, The Influence of Specific Organs Given as Food on Growth and Differentiation, *Arch. f Entwickelungsmech.*, XXXV

1914   "Feeding Experiments on Tadpoles II, A Further Contribution to the Knowledge of Organs of Internal Secretion," *Am Jour e Anat*, XV.

HEUMANN, G.
   1850. *Mikroskopische Untersuchungen an hungernden und verhungerten
          Tauben.* Giessen. (Referat aus *Canstatt's Jahresberichte u. d.
          Fortschritte d ges Med* , I, 1851)

KASANZEFF, W.
   1901 *Experimentelle Untersuchungen uber "Paramecium caudatum "*
          Dissertation   Zurich

LILLIE, F. R.
   1900. "Some Notes on Regeneration and Regulation in Planarians,"
          Am Nat , XXXIV.

LUKJANOW, S
   1897 "L'Inanition du noyau cellulaire," *Rev. Scient* , 1897.

MAYER, A. G.
   1914 *"The Law Governing the Loss of Weight in Starving* Cassiopea,"
          extract from *Carnegie Instit Publ 183*

MORGULIS, S.
   1911 "Studies of Inanition in Its Bearing upon the Problem of Growth,"
          Arch. f. Entwickelungsmech., XXXII

MORPURGO, B
   1888. "Sull processo fisiologico di neoformazione cellulare durante la
          inanizione acuta dell' organismo," *Arch Sci Med.,* XII
   1889 "Sur la Nature des atrophies par inanition chez les animaux à sang
          chaud," *Arch. Ital. de Biol.,* XII.

RINDFLEISCH.
   1868. *Lehrbuch der pathologischen Gewebe*   Bd III.

ROMEIS, B
   1913 "Der Einfluss verschiedenartiger Ernahrung auf die Regeneration
          bei Kaulquappen (*Rana esculenta*)," I, *Arch f. Entwickelungs-
          mech* , XXXVII.
   1914. ' Experimentelle Untersuchungen uber die Wirkung innersekreto-
          rischer Organe: II, Der Einfuss von Thyreoidea- und Thymusfut-
          terung auf das Wachstum, die Entwicklung und die Regeneration,"
          Arch. f. Entwickelungsmech., XL, XLI.

SCHULIZ, E.
   1904. "Uber Reduktionen· I, Uber Hungererscheinungen bei *Planaria
          lactea,"* *Arch f. Entwickelungsmech* , XVIII

SIATKEWITSCH, P.
   1894. "Uber Veranderungen des Muskel- und Drusengewebes, sowie
          des Herzganglien beim Hungern," *Arch f. exp Pathol. u Pharm* ,
          XXXIII.

STOPPENBRINK, F

    1905. "Der Einfluss herabgesetzter Ernahrung auf den histologischen Bau der Susswassertricladen," *Zeitschr f wiss. Zool*, LXXIX

TASHIRO, S

    1913 "A New Method and Apparatus for the Estimation of Exceedingly Minute Quantities of Carbon Dioxide," *Am Jour. of Physiol*, XXXII.

WALLENGREN, H.

    1902. "Inanitionserscheinungen der Zelle Untersuchungen an Protozoen," *Zeitschr. f. allgem. Physiol*, I.

CHAPTER VIII

SENESCENCE AND REJUVENESCENCE IN THE LIGHT OF THE PRECEDING EXPERIMENTS

REVIEW AND ANALYSIS OF THE EXPERIMENTAL DATA

In addition to the differences in size, structure, and behavior which constitute more or less definite criteria of age in the lower organisms, characteristic differences in rate of metabolism have been shown to exist, the rate being highest in the youngest animals and decreasing with advancing age. These age differences in rate of metabolism are sufficiently well marked as compared with such individual and incidental differences as occur under ordinary conditions, to make possible their use as criteria of physiological age, and so to compare the physiological ages of different individuals

In this way it has been shown that, in general, physiological senescence accompanies the productive and progressive processes, i e, growth, specialization, morphogenesis, and differentiation, and that physiological rejuvenescence is a feature of reduction and of processes associated with the reconstitution and agamic development in nature of new individuals from parts of a pre-existing individual

There can, I think, be little question that among the experiments described the reduction experiments are most significant. Here the possible complications connected with reproduction and reconstitution are absent, and only loss of substance with the changes conditioned by it occurs The association, on the one hand, of physiological rejuvenescence with reduction, and, on the other, of senescence with growth and differentiation, not only demonstrates that rejuvenescence is not necessarily associated with reproduction, but also constitutes a positive experimental foundation for a physiological conception of the age changes It is evident that in the organism in which differentiation has begun and is progressing the addition of substance brings about in some way a decrease in metabolic rate and so a decrease in the capacity for further growth and development, while the removal of substance by starvation increases the rate of metabolism and so the capacity for growth and development From an advanced physiological age it is possible to bring the animals back practically to the beginning of post-embryonic life by forcing them to use up and eliminate the substance which they have accumulated during post-embryonic growth and development. Here no reproductive process, asexual or sexual, is involved, but, to return to the analogy between the organism and the flowing stream, the metabolic current is forced to erode its channel instead of depositing material along its course

These experiments leave no basis for the contention that the organism or the cell cannot become young after it has once undergone senescence, and that the only source of youth is an undifferentiated germ plasm The planarian reduced by starvation consists entirely or almost entirely of cells which formed functional differentiated parts of the original, physiologically and morphologically old animal, but after renewed feeding it is younger in every respect and in all parts of the body, so far as can be determined, than before starvation, and is again capable of growth and senescence. In short, these experiments demonstrate that the differentiated somatic cells can return to a physiological condition which at least approaches that of embryonic or undifferentiated cells, and there is no reason for believing that a hypothetical parcel of germ plasm in the nucleus of these cells is in any way responsible for this regression The results of these physiological experiments are in complete agreement with the conclusions reached by E. Schultz ('04, '08), on the basis of morphological data.

The few experiments on the influence of the kind of nutrition upon the course of the life cycle indicate clearly that the course and results of senescence may differ widely with the character of the food. The experiments do not throw any light on the question of the factors concerned in the differences produced, but with more complete control of the kind of nutrition more definite results on this point will doubtless be possible Even these experiments show, however, that the age cycle in these lower animals is by no means independent of nutritional factors Perhaps the most important point is that with certain foods a progressive senescence from generation to generation occurs, while with other foods senescence and rejuvenescence apparently balance each other in each cycle   Evidently certain physiological characteristics of the organism, which are associated either with its metabolic processes or with its structural substratum, or more probably with both, are dependent upon the character of its nutrition, to such an extent at least as to modify the age cycle very essentially.

In the light of the starvation experiments the occurrence of rejuvenescence in connection with the reconstitution of pieces and with agamic reproduction in nature is not difficult to understand   In the reconstitution of pieces some cells undergo dedifferentiation to a greater or less extent and take part in the development of new structures, or the new parts arise from cells which have remained relatively young and less specialized than others, some cells may undergo degeneration and disappear completely, and, except where the isolated piece takes food, the energy for the various changes is derived from reserves and from the tissues themselves which undergo more or less reduction.

The degeneration of differentiated cells does not contribute directly to the rejuvenescence of the piece, but if cells undergo dedifferentiation or if the new structures arise from cells which have retained a more or less "embryonic" condition, the result is of course a younger organism.   And if in addition any appreciable amount of reduction occurs, rejuvenescence, particularly in the old parts which constitute the chief source of nutritive supply in such cases, proceeds still farther.

We have seen that the degree of rejuvenescence varies with the size of the piece and with the degree of reconstitution, i e., the degree of approach to wholeness in the piece.   The reason for these relations is clear.   Provided reconstitution occurs, the smaller the piece the greater the loss of old structure and the development of new, and the greater the reduction of the whole piece in furnishing energy for the process.   Moreover, the greater the degree of reconstitution, the greater the reorganization, and the greater the supply of nutritive material required from the piece

Thus in the piece undergoing reconstitution a new metabolic equilibrium is attained   The parts formed anew are young and have a higher rate of metabolism than the others, but they become older and their rate decreases as they grow and differentiate. At the same time, the remaining parts of the piece are drawn upon as a source of energy for the growth of the new parts, and in consequence they undergo reduction and their rate of metabolism rises· in fact, they become younger Sooner or later a condition is attained in which the young, new parts can no longer grow at the expense of the old parts because the rate of metabolism in the former is declining while that in the latter is increasing When this stage is attained reconstitutional changes can proceed no farther. If the animal is fed at this stage it grows essentially like any other animal, and if not fed it undergoes reduction like any other starved animal. At the time equilibrium is attained the rate of metabolism in general will vary with the size of the piece and the degree of reconstitution. The smaller the piece and the greater the amount of reconstitutional change, the higher the rate at which this equilibrium is reached, and so the younger the animal becomes during reconstitution.

As already noted, the cases of agamic reproduction examined in chap. vi do not differ fundamentally from the experimental reproductions or reconstitutions following the physical isolation of pieces, and we should expect that if rejuvenescence occurs in the one case it would in the other. Whether a piece develops into a new whole as the result of artificial isolation by section or other means, or of physiological isolation by conditions arising in the organism in nature, the result is essentially the same In one respect, however, there is a difference of degree: in many cases of budding, fission, etc., the new developing individual remains in organic continuity with the parent until its development is advanced or completed and so is supplied with nutritive material In such cases, as for example, in hydra, the new individual, instead of undergoing reduction, grows throughout its development, and the degree of rejuvenescence is much less marked than in those cases where the tissues of the developing piece or region are the source of energy Here the dedifferentiation of cells, or the substitution of less differentiated younger cells for those previously existing, are the chief factors in rejuvenescence, although apparently some degree of metabolic equilibration does occur in the old parts, i e., these parts become somewhat younger, even though nutrition is present.

The results of the experiments together with the results of observation in nature constitute an adequate foundation for the conclusion that a greater or less degree of rejuvenescence must be associated with agamic reproduction As we have seen in the case of *Pennaria* (pp. 148–51), it may be less in the more specialized than in the less specialized types of reproduction and it must differ in degree with various other conditions, but wherever reconstitutional or reductional changes are involved we must expect to find some degree of rejuvenescence.

The persistence of the embryonic condition in the growing tip and meristematic tissues of the higher plants and in the growing regions of many of the lower animals shows, however, that under certain conditions growth may continue over long periods of time without any very great degree of, and in many cases perhaps without any, senescence. So far as we know, the long-continued persistence of the embryonic condition in rapidly growing tissues is always associated with a high frequency of cell or nuclear division, and the experiments on the infusoria (see pp. 137–42) indicate that at least in these forms some degree of rejuvenescence occurs in connection with cell division There is every reason to believe that in nuclear and cell division in general, as in other forms of reproduction, some degree of change in the direction of rejuvenescence occurs Whether this balances the changes which occur between successive cell divisions depends upon the frequency of division, the rate of growth, and various other conditions. Where a balance is attained or approached, differentiation and senescence do not occur, or proceed slowly; otherwise they proceed more or less rapidly, according to conditions

The only possible conclusion in view of all the facts seems to be that senescence is associated with the productive and progressive phases, and rejuvenescence with the reductive and regressive phases, of the life cycle.

THE NATURE OF SENESCENCE AND REJUVENESCENCE

The theories of senescence that have been advanced fall mainly into two groups. Those of the one group regard the phenomena of senescence as in some sense secondary or incidental, and not as a necessary and inevitable consequence or a part of the cycle of development. According to such theories senescence is due to incomplete excretion of toxic products of metabolism of one kind or another, or to a wearing out of certain organs for one reason or another, to evolutionary adaptation, or to some other incidental factor The theories of the other group regard senescence as a result of the same processes which determine growth, differentiation, and what we call development in general. These theories attempt to find the conditions and processes which determine senescence in the conditions and processes which underlie development From this point of view senescence is a feature of development The experimental data presented in the preceding chapters leave little room for doubt that both senescence and rejuvenescence are necessary and inevitable features of the life cycle. Certainly the worn-out organs of old animals cannot be repaired by an extended period of starvation, nor is the elimination of toxic metabolic products likely to be assisted by the structural degeneration of parts which occurs in various cases of reconstitution Senescence and development are simply two aspects of the same complex dynamic activities

Since our knowledge of the metabolic reactions, on the one hand, and of the colloid substratum of the organism, on the other, is not very far advanced, we cannot at present determine the exact nature of the relation between growth, differentiation, and senescence, and reduction, dedifferentiation, and rejuvenescence. Nevertheless we can point with considerable confidence to certain features of growth and development as affording a basis for the changes of the age cycle.

It was pointed out in Part I that during development the general metabolic substratum of the organism, the unspecialized or embryonic cell, undergoes a progressive change in the direction of greater physiological stability in consequence of changes in the substratum and additions to it in the course of growth and differentiation The general result of these changes is a decrease in the metabolic activity of each unit of weight or volume of the organism because the proportion of the relatively stable constituents in the substratum increases.

Such changes are most conspicuous in those cells which become loaded with non-protoplasmic inclosures, such as granules or droplets, or in which the cytoplasm is largely transformed into the inactive substance of skeletal or supporting tissues, but it is evident that similar changes occur to a greater or less extent in all cells during differentiation Development must then be accompanied by a progressive decrease in the rate of metabolism per unit of weight or volume of the substance of the organism.

But other factors are probably more or less generally concerned in bringing about the decrease in metabolic rate which occurs during development. It is a familiar fact that emulsoid colloid sols and gels outside the organism undergo changes in aggregate condition with time. The degree of aggregation increases, the water-content decreases, and shrinkage occurs To what extent such changes occur in the colloids of the living organism is a question, but that there is more or less change of this sort in the more stable portions of the colloid substratum is highly probable, and in any case the continued accumulation of colloids in the cell as a product of metabolism probably brings about an increase in concentration and of aggregation in the colloid. The rate of chemical reaction in a colloid substratum is more or less intimately associated with the condition of the colloid and very generally decreases with increasing aggregation. The increasing density and aggregation of the colloid substratum may lead, then, to an actual decrease in the rate of chemical reactions. Moreover, the increase in density and thickness and the decrease in the permeability of membranes may retard the exchange through them The retardation of enzyme activity by accumulation of the products may also play a part in decreasing metabolic rate, though it is probable that such decreases in metabolic activity are usually less permanent than the age changes and are associated with other shorter periods in the life of the organism. Various other factors, as yet unrecognized, may also be concerned, but it is evident in any case that the decrease in rate of metabolism is a part of development itself and not an accidental or incidental feature of life. The decrease in metabolic rate during development is in fact a necessary and inevitable consequence of the association of the chemical reactions which constitute metabolism with a colloid substratum produced by the reactions

The development of metabolic mechanisms, such as the striated muscles, which are capable when stimulated of a very high rate of metabolism, is in no sense an exception to or a contradiction of the general law that a decrease in rate of metabolism is associated with development. In the early stages of development correlative functional stimulation of the cells of the organism certainly occurs only to a very slight degree, so far as it occurs at all and cannot be compared to the degree of functional stimulation which occurs in later stages after development of the stimulating mechanism — in the case of striated muscle, the nervous system   This being the case, we must compare the rate of metabolism in the unstimulated or very slightly stimulated differentiated cell—not the rate of the cell under strong stimulation—with the rate of the embryonic cell, if we are to attain a correct conception of the difference   Bearing this point in mind, it is easy to see how great the difference in rate is   In the case of striated muscle, for example, the rate of metabolism in the earlier stages of development is sufficiently high to bring about the morphogenesis of the muscle without the accelerating influence of nerve impulses, but later the muscle atrophies unless its rate is frequently accelerated by nervous stimulation.

From this point of view senescence in its dynamic aspect consists in a decrease in the rate of metabolism determined by the changes in the substratum during development, and, in its morphological aspect, in the changes themselves.   The idea that senescence is in one way or another simply an aspect or result of development itself has been more or less clearly expressed by various authors, and various features of the developmental process have been regarded as the essential factors,[1] but discussion of the different theories is postponed to a later chapter.

Attention has already been called to the fact that growth may give place to reduction and progressive development to regressive

----

[1] Among more recent writers who have advanced this view in one form or another are the following   Cholodkowsky, '82, Enriques, '07, '09, Jickeli, '02, Kassowitz, '99, Minot, '08, '13, and several papers of earlier date, Muhlmann, '00, 10

In reduction, substance previously accumulated in the cell is broken down as a source of energy and eliminated or serves for new syntheses, and the cell undergoes regression toward the embryonic condition   Such a change means the removal to a greater or less extent of the conditions which have brought about a decrease in rate of metabolism. the proportion of less stable to more stable substance increases, the aggregation of the substratum decreases, and the rate of metabolism increases   These changes constitute rejuvenescence   Dynamically rejuvenescence consists in increase in rate of metabolism and morphologically in the changes in the substratum which permit increase in rate

If this definition of rejuvenescence is correct, it follows that there is no necessary relation between rejuvenescence and gametic or any other kind of reproduction   The changes in the substratum may result from reduction connected with starvation, or from some change in the character of metabolism which brings about the removal of certain substances previously accumulated, as well as from the reductional and reconstitutional changes connected with the reproduction of cells, parts of a complex organism, or new whole organisms   And earlier chapters have demonstrated that not only agamic reproduction in nature and experimental reproduction, but also reduction by starvation may bring about rejuvenescence to such an extent that the animals thus produced are as young physiologically as sexually produced animals in the same morphological stage.   And, finally, as will appear in chaps. xiii–xv, the facts indicate that in the cycle of gametic reproduction the period of gamete formation is a period of senescence and that of early embryonic development a period of rejuvenescence.

As regards the conception of the nature of senescence, this theory does not differ fundamentally from others which have been advanced at various times, but in its emphasis upon the occurrence and significance of rejuvenescence it departs from commonly accepted views   The idea that life proceeds only in one direction from youth to age and death must be abandoned.   Rejuvenescence is as essential a feature of life as senescence   Senescence often leads inevitably and automatically through reproduction or reduction and dedifferentiation to rejuvenescence.

PERIODICITY IN ORGANISMS IN RELATION TO THE AGE CYCLE

Before leaving the question of the nature of senescence and rejuvenescence it is necessary to call attention to their relation to other periodic or cyclical changes in the organisms. According to the conception developed here, there is nothing unique in the processes of senescence and rejuvenescence; they are, on the contrary, of the same general character as many other changes in rate of metabolism in the organism, the chief difference being that the factors concerned in the age changes are the more stable and less rapidly changing features of the substratum, while other shorter cycles may result from changes in less stable features. In fact, it is not possible to make any sharp distinction between the age changes and many other periodicities. The differences are differences of degree rather than of kind. Recognition of this fact is important, because senescence has often been regarded as a rather mysterious process, quite different from anything else in the life cycle, but the experimental evidence points to a very different conclusion.

The more or less regularly periodic or cyclical changes are among the most conspicuous and characteristic features of living organisms. They range in the individual from momentary, evanescent changes, such as occur in stimulation and the return to the original condition which follows, to the changes of the age cycle which often coincide with the whole life of the individual. Some of these periodic changes are of course directly determined by external conditions, such as temperature, light, etc., while, as regards others, internal factors are more important. Any extended consideration of these various periodicities is quite beyond the present purpose, but the fact that many of them seem to be more or less similar in character to the age cycle, except as regards the time factor, demands some sort of interpretation. According to the physico-chemical conception of the organism, many different periodic changes in rate of metabolism are possible, for different conditions in the substratum which accelerate or retard the rate of metabolism may arise and disappear with very different rapidity, and the variety of more or less definitely periodic phenomena in life is in full agreement with theoretical possibility.

A simple case in point is the accumulation of carbon dioxide which decreases the rate of metabolism in a very short time, while recovery occurs as rapidly when it is eliminated. According to the theory of stimulation by R. S Lillie ('09a, '09b), the concentration of carbon dioxide in the cell is the chief factor in decreasing the rate of reaction after stimulation. Lillie suggests that in the absence of excitation the plasma membrane of cells is impermeable or only slightly permeable to carbon dioxide, consequently the carbon dioxide resulting from metabolism accumulates in the cell and decreases the rate of metabolism   A stimulus is any external factor which increases the permeability of the membrane to carbon dioxide and so permits its escape from the cell and consequently brings about an increase in rate of metabolism, which is followed by a decrease in rate as the temporary increase in permeability of the membrane disappears

Fatigue, i.e , the decrease in rate of metabolism which follows continued stimulation, is generally believed to be due to the accumulation of toxic products of metabolism (see p. 297).   During rest these products are eliminated and recovery occurs   Various metabolic intoxications are probably very similar in character, although in many of these cases the toxic substances are the products of metabolism of micro-organisms and not of the affected organism itself. The decreased metabolic activity which occurs after feeding in many animals is undoubtedly due to accumulation of some substance or substances which decrease the rate of reaction   As the accumulated substance disappears, activity increases until feeding again takes place.

In these and many other cases the changes in metabolism are readily and rapidly reversible, because the substances or conditions which determine them are readily eliminated or are themselves reversible. Moreover, except where the activity of the cell is largely accumulatory or secretory, these changes are not ordinarily accompanied by any very marked morphological changes. When extreme or long continued, however, stimulation may bring about very considerable structural changes, even in cells where functional activity is largely dynamic rather than structural, such, for example, as the nerve cells, in which the morphology of function has been described by various authors.[1] As might be expected such changes, if they do not proceed beyond a certain limit, are reversible, and recovery occurs rapidly

In cells where function is accompanied by extensive accumulation and discharge of substances, such, for example, as the gland cells, storage cells, etc., the cycles of activity and morphological change are essentially age cycles, that is to say, the period of loading of the cell is a period of decreasing metabolic activity, of "senescence," and the period of discharge one of increasing activity, of "rejuvenescence," which makes possible a repetition of the cycle In such cells the structural changes are often very marked   In the pancreas, for example, the cell which is loaded with the granules which give rise to the secretion presents a very different appearance from the cell after continued stimulation and discharge.

Figs 66-68 show different stages in the cyclical changes of the pancreas cells of the toad.   Fig 66 shows the loaded cells ready to secrete when stimulated   The whole outer portion of the cell, i.e., the part next to the duct, is filled with large granules, and cytoplasm appears only near the base about the nucleus. This condition is analogous to that of advanced differentiation in which the cytoplasm has been largely transformed into substances which are inactive or less active.   In this loaded condition the pancreas cell is only very slightly active metabolically, and its activity is probably due in large measure to the fact that it does secrete slightly, and so the substance of the granules is being changed and eliminated to some extent, more or less continuously.

But when stimulated to secretion, the oxygen consumption of the cell increases greatly (Barcroft, '08), the granules rapidly disappear, and the cytoplasmic zone extends from the base of the cells out toward the periphery   Fig 67 shows four cells in various stages of discharge and Fig. 68, cells after long-continued stimulation.   In this condition the cell is again capable of a high rate of metabolic activity, if nutrition is present the process of loading occurs once more, and the cell approaches quiescence

[1] See, for example, Dolley, '13, '14, Hodge, '92, '94, Lugaro, '95 Mann, '95, Pick, '98, Pugnat, '01, Valenza, '96 Further references concerning periodic and other functional changes in structure will be found in these papers

This cycle of changes, which may occur within a few hours and which may be repeated in a single cell, is, I believe, not fundamentally different from the age cycle in organisms. All the essential features of both senescence and rejuvenescence up to a certain

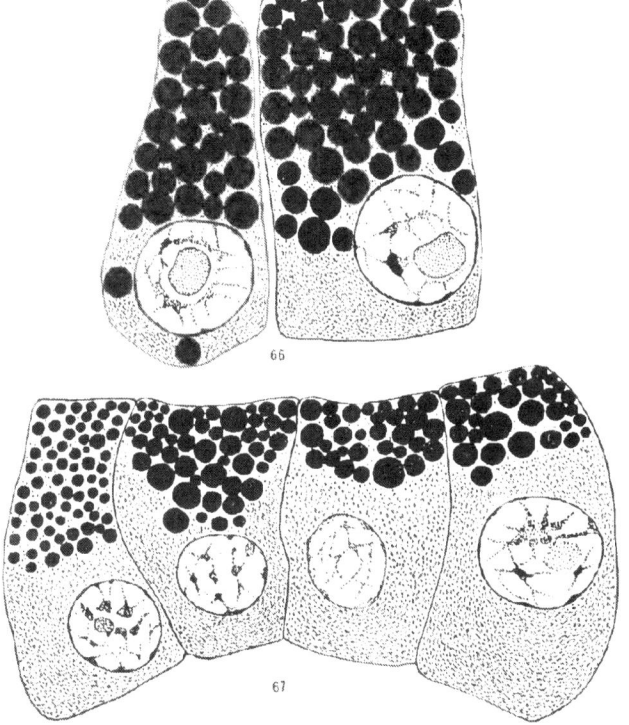

FIGS. 66, 67.—Pancreas cells of toad: Fig. 66, fully loaded and almost quiescent; Fig. 67, partially discharged after stimulation. From preparations loaned by R. R. Bensley.

point are present. The cell probably does not return to the embryonic condition at any point in the cycle, but it certainly does undergo changes similar in character to those of the age cycle, though their period is short. At the same time the gland cell may be undergoing senescence in the stricter sense, that is, more

stable components of the protoplasm may be accumul
undergoing changes which are not, or not wholly, comp
by the functional cycle.

Other gland cells undergo very similar periodic ch
structure, the whole peripheral region being discharged b
some cases and the cell regenerating from a small basal
Many other cells in the organism not regarded as gland c
through somewhat similar cycles. Various cells, for c
accumulate reserves, such as starch in plants and fat in
and various other substances. As the loading of such c

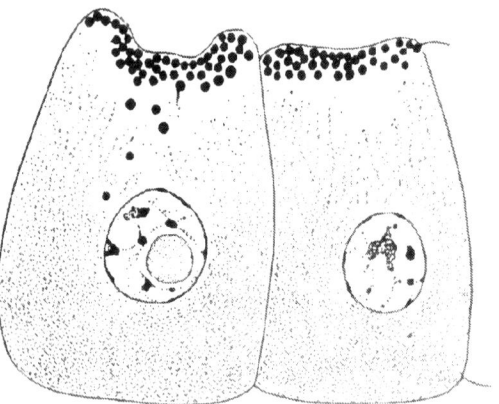

Fig. 68.—Pancreas cells of toad almost completely discharged after
stimulation. From preparations loaned by R. R. Bensley.

ceeds, they approach quiescence, but when conditions ch
that the previously accumulated substances are removed, th
undergo a rejuvenescence. Although we have at preser
positive knowledge along this line, it seems probable that
periodic changes in organisms or parts are of this general ch
Quiescent periods following periods of abundant nutriti
accumulation of substance occur in the protozoa and othe
animals as well as in many plants, particularly in parts spe
as storage organs, such as bulbs, tubers, etc. It is a famil
that in certain tropical species of trees the loss of leaves, f
by a quiescent period, occurs at different times on different b

of the same tree[1] In such cases the periodicity may perhaps be associated with the alternate accumulation and removal of substance It is also possible that periods which appear superficially to be seasonal may be at least often of this character Schimper believed that an internally determined periodicity might occur independently of climatic and other conditions Klebs, however, denies the existence of such periodicity, yet at the same time he regards the accumulation of organic substances, which as products of enzyme activity inhibit or retard further activity, as a factor in bringing about quiescent periods. If such substances are produced more rapidly than they are used, they must accumulate, and it seems probable that, at least sometimes, an internally determined periodicity may result.

The view that the formation of the gametes or sex cells is essentially a process of differentiation and senescence and the early stages of embryonic development a process of rejuvenescence has already been mentioned and will be discussed more fully in later chapters The cycle of changes in the egg is somewhat similar to that in the gland cell, with the difference that in the egg the yolk becomes a source of energy and substance for growth.

If the point of view advanced here is correct, then the age cycle in the strictest sense is merely one of many periodicities or cycles in organisms, some longer, some shorter, which result from the relations existing between the chemical reactions of metabolism and the substratum in which they occur The distinction between an age cycle and other cycles is but little more than a matter of convenience or custom. The changes which fall into the category of what we are accustomed to call age changes are merely those in which the more stable and less rapidly changing features of the organism are involved Various other cycles of different length differ mainly in that less stable and more rapidly changing conditions in the substratum are concerned. Whether we call one cycle an age cycle and another something else is of little importance, except as regards convenience. From the cycle of fatigue and recovery at one extreme, to the cycle of senescence and rejuvenescence in the stricter sense at the other, there are many intermedi-

[1] See, for example, Schimper, '98, pp. 260-81, Klebs, '11, Volkens, '12; Simon, '14

ate cycles In some of these the products of metabolism accumulate only temporarily, and the period may cover only a few moments or a few hours, while in others the fundamental features of organic structure are concerned, and the period coincides with the life cycle.

SENESCENCE AND REJUVENESCENCE IN EVOLUTION

It is pertinent, at this time, at least to raise the question whether the point of view and the conclusions reached from the study of individuals have any value beyond the individual life cycle Is there any indication of the progressive senescence of species or groups, and, if such senescence occurs, does it always lead to death, i e , extinction, or is rejuvenescence possible ? On the other hand, is continued existence of a species without senescence possible ?

Any answers to these questions must at the present time be little more than guesses. It is possible, however, that the metabolic substratum of the species may undergo very gradual progressive changes of the same general character as those concerned in individual senescence, but which are not entirely eliminated or compensated during the periods of individual rejuvenescence, and it is conceivable that under altered conditions regression might occur as in individual rejuvenescence. It is also possible that the union of two gametes from different lines of descent in gametic reproduction may be an important factor in retarding or accelerating such changes, if they occur.

The records of paleontology are so fragmentary and our ignorance of the factors involved in the extinction or persistence of species is so great that positive answers to these questions cannot be looked for in that direction Certainly many species have become extinct in the course of geological time, but whether their extinction has in any case been the result of a senescence we cannot determine. Decreasing numbers or decreasing size preceding extinction may be due entirely to external conditions But certain forms, such for example as *Limulus*, the horseshoe crab, and the brachiopod *Lingula*, have persisted practically unchanged from exceedingly remote geological periods Have such species not undergone senescence, or has a rejuvenescence occurred somewhere, or perhaps periodically, in the course of their descent ?

That a process similar to senescence has occurred in the evolution of the higher organisms from the lower is suggested by various lines of evidence. The protoplasmic substratum of the higher forms is certainly more stable and undergoes structural alteration less readily and less extensively than in the lower. The higher forms undergo a greater degree of differentiation during development than the lower, and in the higher animals the capacity for agamic and experimental reproduction is absent and growth is limited. Moreover, the metabolic activity for each unit of weight is probably less under similar conditions of temperature, oxygen supply, nutrition, etc , in the higher than in the lower forms, even in early stages of development   In short, there are various resemblances between the course of evolution and that of individual development, and the latter is a period of senescence   And as in the individual altered conditions may bring about rejuvenescence, so in the course of evolution the occurrence of rejuvenescence is conceivable.   If a secular senescence of protoplasm has constituted a factor in evolution, the protoplasm of the higher forms must have undergone this change more rapidly than that of those which remained as lower forms   Moreover, such a senescence might proceed more or less independently of the environment, though the course and rate of the change would doubtless be influenced by environmental conditions.   In other words, protoplasmic senescence, if it plays any part in evolution, is to some extent an internal factor, and evolution itself is in some degree a progressive change from less to more stable equilibrium, rather than in the opposite direction

The purpose of the present section is to suggest possibilities, rather than to develop theories   Since there is continuity of protoplasmic substance from generation to generation, there may be internally determined progressive change in that substance similar in some degree to the change during individual life (see pp. 464–65).

REFERENCES

BARCROFT, J.

    1908   "Zur Lehre vom Blutgaswechsel in den verschiedenen Organen," *Ergebn d Physiol.*, VII.

CHOLODKOWSKY, N

    1882   "Tod und Unsterblichkeit in der Tierwelt," *Zool. Anzeiger*, V.

CONKLIN, E. G.

    1912. "Cell Size and Nuclear Size," *Jour of Exp Zool*, XII

    1913. "The Size of Organisms and of Their Constituent Parts in Relation to Longevity, Senescence and Rejuvenescence," *Pop Sci Monthly*, August, 1913.

DOLLEY, D H.

    1913 "The Morphology of Functional Activity in the Ganglion Cells of the Crayfish, *Cambarus virilis*," *Arch. f Zellforsch*, IX

    1914. "On a Law of Species Identity of the Nucleus-Plasma Norm for Nerve Cell Bodies of Corresponding Type," *Jour. of Comp Neurol*, XXIV.

ENRIQUES, P.

    1907. "La morte," *Riv di Sci.*, Ann. I.

    1909. "Wachstum und seine analytische Darstellung," *Biol Centralbl*, XXIX.

HODGE, C F.

    1892 "A Microscopical Study of Changes Due to Functional Activity in Nerve Cells," *Jour. of Morphol*, VII

    1894. "A Microscopical Study of the Nerve Cell during Electrical Stimulation," *Jour of Morphol*, IX.

JICKELI, C. F.

    1902. *Die Unvollkommenheit des Stoffwechsels*, etc Berlin

KASSOWITZ, M

    1899. *Allgemeine Biologie* Wien.

KLEBS, G

    1911 "Über die Rhythmik in der Entwicklung der Pflanzen," *Sitzungsber. d. Heidelberger Akad d Wiss.· Math naturwiss Kl*

LILLIE, R. S.

    1909a. "On the Connection between Changes of Permeability and Stimulation and on the Significance of Changes in Permeability to Carbon Dioxide," *Am Jour of Physiol*, XXIV.

    1909b "The General Biological Significance of Changes in the Permeability of the Surface Layer or Plasma Membrane of Living Cells," *Biol. Bull.*, XVII.

LUGARO, E.

    1895. "Sur les modifications des cellules nerveuses dans les divers états fonctionnels," *Arch Ital de Biol*, XXIV

MANN, G.

    1895 "Histological Change Induced in Sympathetic, Motor and Sensory Nerve Cells by Functional Activity," *Jour of Anat and Physiol*, XXIX

MINOT, C. S.

 1908 *The Problem of Age, Growth and Death* New York

 1913 *Moderne Probleme der Biologie* Jena

MUHLMANN, M

 1900 *Uber die Ursache des Alters.* Wiesbaden

 1910 "Das Altern und der physiologische Tod," *Sammlung anat u. physiol Vortr.*, H XI

PICK, F

 1898. "Uber morphologische Differenzen zwischen ruhenden und erregten Ganglienzellen," *Deutsche med Wochenschr* XXII

PUGNAT, C A.

 1901 "Modifications histologiques des cellules nerveuses dans la fatigue," *Jour. de Physiol. et de Pathol. gén*, III

SCHIMPER, A F W.

 1898. *Pflanzen-Geographie auf physiologischer Grundlage* Jena.

SCHULTZ, E

 1904 "Über Reduktionen· I, Uber Hungererscheinungen bei *Planaria lactea,*" *Arch. f. Entwickelungsmech*, XVIII

 1908 "Uber umkehrbare Entwickelungsprozesse und ihre Bedeutung fur eine Theorie der Vererbung," *Vortr und Aufs. u Entwickelungsmech*, IV.

SIMON, S V.

 1914 "Studien uber die Periodicitat der Lebensprozesse der in dauernd feuchten Tropengebieten heimischen Baume," *Jahrbucher f wiss Bot*, LIV.

VALENZA, G. B.

 1896. "I cambiamenti microscopici della cellula nervosa nell' attivita funzionale e sotto l'azione di agenti stimolanti e distruttori," *Atti R Acad Scienze fisiche e nat di Napoli*, VII.

VOLKENS, G

 1912 *Laubfall und Lauberneuerung in den Tropen.* Berlin

PART III

INDIVIDUATION AND REPRODUCTION IN RELATION TO THE
AGE CYCLE

CHAPTER IX

INDIVIDUATION AND REPRODUCTION IN ORGANISMS

THE PROBLEM

Living organisms exist as more or less definite individuals   An individual may be provisionally defined as a more or less complex entity which acts to some extent as a unit or whole   Such a definition emphasizes the unity of the individual, but affords no clue to the integrating factor or factors, i.e , to that which makes a unity, a whole out of the complex.

Two very conspicuous characteristics of the organic individual, particularly in its more highly developed forms, are its orderly behavior and the definiteness of form and structure which is one feature of this behavior   Nowhere do these characteristics appear more clearly than in the remarkable sequence of events which constitutes what we call the development, the ontogeny of the individual.   In the simpler organisms the morphological definiteness is often less conspicuous, both the structure and the behavior being more susceptible of modification by external factors, but the modifications are themselves definite and orderly and are manifestly not a direct and specific effect of the external factors which are acting, but rather a reaction of an individual of some sort to an external change.

In short, although we may attempt to ignore or deny it, as various biologists have done, the fact remains that an ordering, controlling principle of some sort exists in the organic individual   The existence of such a principle does not, however, as has so often been asserted, distinguish the living from the non-living inorganic individual.   In an electrical or a magnetic field or in a planetary system, for example, we have individuations of a definite, orderly character, though it is evident that such individuations are not very similar to living organisms   The crystal also is an individuation of a highly orderly and definite character, and the attempt has often been made to find some fundamental similarity between living organisms and crystals, but without any great success. The crystal is fundamentally a physical individuation among molecules of like chemical constitution, although in certain cases some heterogeneity of composition occurs. In the organism, as the facts show, individuation is evidently associated with chemical activity, and widely different substances may enter into the constitution of the individual. The mere existence of axes in both the organism and the crystal, which is one of the grounds for comparison, is no criterion of essential similarity, for axes may be the expression of very different conditions in different cases. No adequate evidence for the identity or similarity of the axes of the organism and those of the crystal has ever been presented, and there is much evidence to show that they are very widely different.

Apparently two distinct types of individuation exist in the organic world. In the one, which may be called the centered or radiate type, the parts are arranged and their behavior is integrated with reference to a central region; in the other, which we may call the axiate type, with reference to one or more axes The radiate type of individuation appears most clearly in the simple cell and in the radiate structures which arise within it in connection with division, while the axiate type is found both in cells and in organisms. Moreover, the two types of individuation often appear in combination· in the starfish, for example, the body as a whole possesses an oral aboral axis in the direction between the two surfaces, and the arms are axiate structures with longitudinal and transverse axes, but they are arranged radially about a central region Most unicellular organisms and most cells which form parts of multicellular organisms show indications of a more or less definite and permanent axis or axes superimposed upon the centered activities of the cell. In the organism, as contrasted with the cell, the axiate type of individuation is predominant, and the axiate organization becomes increasingly definite, conspicuous, and permanent as individuation advances. In fact, the very general occurrence of an axiation of some sort, or of physiological polarity as it is commonly called, is the foundation of the belief widely current among zoologists that polarity is a fundamental characteristic of protoplasm. While most cells undoubtedly do possess at least temporary polarity, there are many facts which indicate that their polarity is not self-determined, but is either acquired during the course of their existence as a reaction to external conditions, or is merely the polarity of the parent cell persisting in the products of division Moreover, there are various activities in the cell which are manifestly not axiate but radiate, and, finally, no one has been able to discover the slightest indication of polarity in the fundamental physical structure or optical properties of protoplasm

But the fact remains that most organisms possess one or more axes, the axes of polarity and symmetry, so called, and that these axes are manifestly of fundamental importance in individuation The degree of physiological coherence and unity in the individual is associated with the definiteness and fixity of its axes, and development always proceeds in a definite and orderly way with reference to whatever axes may exist. Evidently the axes of the organism are not simply geometrical fictions, but rather the expression of some fundamental factor in the axiate type of individuation, a factor which influences the rate and character of the metabolic reactions and so plays an essential part in both morphogenesis and functional activity.

In the more complex organisms a polarity and symmetry of the whole organism often exist at the same time with a multitude of polarities and symmetries of various parts, organs, and cells which do not coincide with the general axes, but make all possible angles with them and may be widely variable. This fact makes it evident at once that the axiation of the organism as a whole is not simply the general expression of the axiation of its parts Many different polarities and symmetries coexist and persist independently of each other, and yet the whole course of development is an orderly process with a definite result.

These characteristics of organic individuals are not satisfactorily accounted for by the current theories of the organism. Whether we regard the organism from the viewpoint of the corpuscular theories as an aggregation of distinct, self-perpetuating entities, or as a chemical or physico-chemical system, we cannot escape the necessity of accounting in some way for its definite and orderly behavior and for the very evident relation in axiate forms between this behavior and the axes of polarity and symmetry.   Here lies the problem of organic individuation.

From time to time parts of the individual give rise to new individuals, in which either the original axiation may persist or a new axiation arise   This is reproduction   In the case of gametic or sexual reproduction the process is further complicated by the union of two nuclei, usually the nuclei of two highly specialized cells, preceding the development of the new individual.   The problem of how and why these new individuals arise is the problem of reproduction.   And, finally, it is at once evident that the problems of senescence and rejuvenescence are closely associated with these problems of individuation and reproduction.

During some fifteen years' study of reproductive processes in the lower animals under experimental conditions I have been brought face to face with these problems and have attempted to gain some insight into the nature of the factors concerned in individuation and reproduction.   In the remainder of the present chapter the theory of individuation and reproduction which has grown out of this investigation is outlined, and some of the more important experimental evidence upon which it is based is briefly stated

THE AXIAL GRADIENT

By means of the susceptibility method described in chap. iii, controlled in certain cases by estimations of carbon-dioxide production by means of the Tashiro biometer (Tashiro, '13b), it has been possible to demonstrate the existence of a distinct gradient in rate of metabolic reactions along the chief or so-called polar axis of axiate animals, so far as they have been investigated [1]   In its simple, primary form this axial gradient consists in a more or less uniform decrease in rate of metabolism from the apical or anterior region along the main axis   The point of importance is that the apical region, or the head-region in cases where a head is formed, is primarily the region of highest rate of metabolism and that in general regions nearer to it have a higher rate than regions farther away.   In some animals, as for example in *Planaria*, this gradient persists throughout life in the single individual, except

[1] Child, '12, '13a, '13b, '14a, '14b, '14c

for some temporary changes during growth, but when new zooids arise in the posterior region of the body (see pp. 122 25) each zooid develops its own axial gradient. In other cases, such as the segmented worms, where the body increases in length for a time or indefinitely by the addition of new segments arising from a growing region just in front of the posterior end, the gradient appears in its simple form during the early stages of development, but undergoes some secondary changes in the posterior regions of the body as the new segments are formed

Up to the present time axial gradients have been found in all forms examined, which include among unicellular forms some ten species of ciliate infusoria, and among multicellular forms hydra and several species of hydroids and sea anemones, eight species of turbellaria, the developmental stages of the sea-urchin and starfish and of the polychete annelids *Nereis* and *Chaetopterus*, several species of oligochete annelids examined by Miss Hyman, the developmental stages of two species of fishes, and the cleavage and early larval stages of salamanders and frogs   The variety of forms examined with positive results leaves no doubt that the axial metabolic gradient occurs at least very widely among axiate animals.

Where definite axes of symmetry exist there are indications that metabolic gradients are also present along these axes, and these gradients show a definite and constant relation to the course of development with reference to these axes.

These metabolic gradients are of course merely the expression of a general condition and may undergo more or less variation in steepness, i.e., in the amount of change in rate of metabolism from level to level, or may even disappear temporarily, or in later life permanently. But the fact that in each species gradients exist which are characteristic and constant within certain limits, at least during the earlier stages of development, is of the greatest significance.

In addition to these results, obtained chiefly by means of the susceptibility method, there are many other data of observation and experiment which point unmistakably to the existence of axial metabolic gradients as a characteristic feature of axiate organisms in both plants and animals At present, however, it is possible to call attention only very briefly to some of these It is, for example, a well-known fact that in those plants which possess a definite physiological and morphological axis or axes the apical region of the axis is the region of highest rate of metabolism, and a more or less definite downward gradient in rate exists along the axis, at least for a certain distance from the apical region This gradient appears in the rate of growth at various levels of the axis, in the precedence in development of the lateral buds near the apical end when the chief growing tip has been removed, and in many other features of plant life, but the question of its significance has received little attention

As regards animals, the so-called law of antero-posterior development indicates the existence of a metabolic gradient along the main axis of the organism during embryonic development. This "law" is merely the statement of the observed fact of embryology that in general the first parts to become morphologically visible are the apical or anterior regions, and these are followed in sequence by successively more posterior or basal parts. In other words, that region of the egg or early embryo which has the highest rate of metabolism gives rise to the apical or head-region, which, in consequence of the higher rate, becomes differentiated in advance of other parts, and these follow in sequence along the axis. This fact of embryology is familiar to every zoologist, and its significance as the expression of a gradient in dynamic activity along the axis cannot be doubted, although, so far as I am aware, no one has called attention to it.

Moreover, other facts of animal embryology indicate very clearly the existence of symmetry gradients In the bilaterally symmetrical invertebrates, with ventral nerve cord, including most worms and the arthropods, and particularly in those forms where the egg contains much yolk so that the embryo is more or less spread out upon it, the ventral and median regions of the embryo at any given level of the body develop more or less in advance of the dorsal and lateral regions. In such forms the regions which give rise to ventral and median parts must have a higher rate of metabolism than those which give rise to dorsal and lateral parts.

Fig. 69, a longitudinal section near the median plane of the embryo of a turbellarian worm, *Plagiostomum girardi*, shows very clearly both the antero-posterior and the ventro-dorsal gradients. At this stage only the head and ventral region of the animal are represented by cell masses, the regions where the more dorsal structures will later develop consisting chiefly of yolk. Moreover, the anterior region is more advanced in development than any other part. Fig. 70 is the embryo of the earthworm. In the anterior region the body has attained its final form, but posteriorly the segmentation is more and more limited to the ventral region, the dorsal region being little more than a yolk sac, and in the extreme posterior region segments have not yet become visible. In the arthropods the relations are in general similar. The embryology of other invertebrate groups indicates more or less clearly the existence of symmetry gradients, but

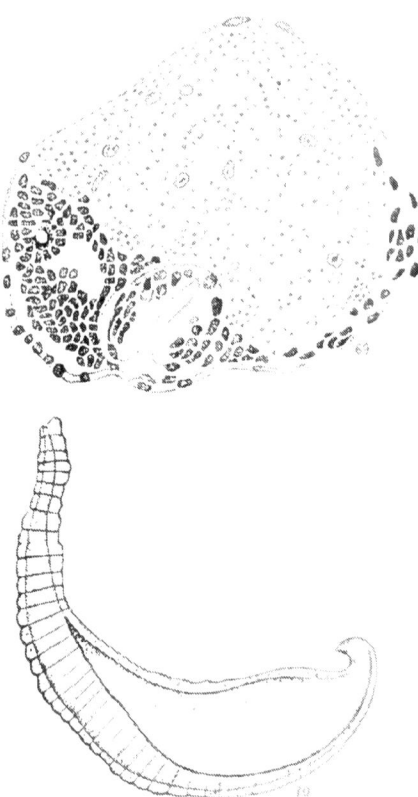

FIGS. 69, 70.—Axial developmental gradients in embryonic stages of invertebrates: Fig. 69, a somewhat oblique, longitudinal (sagittal) section of the embryo of a turbellarian worm, *Plagiostomum girardi*; the cephalic ganglia and eye—at the left—are advanced in development, as is also the pharynx, but farther posteriorly fewer cells are present, the ventral (lower) region is also much farther advanced than the dorsal (from Bresslau, '04). Fig. 70, advanced embryo of the earthworm *Lumbricus agricola*; development is more advanced anteriorly and ventrally than posteriorly and dorsally (from Kowalewsky, '71).

the axes of symmetry differ in different groups. and it is impossible to consider the various details here.

In the vertebrates the developmental gradients of the longitudinal and transverse axes like those of most bilaterally symmetrical invertebrates, show a decrease in rate from the anterior region posteriorly and from the median region laterally, but the gradient along the dorso-ventral axis is the reverse of that in the invertebrates, the dorsal region preceding instead of the ventral   Fig 71

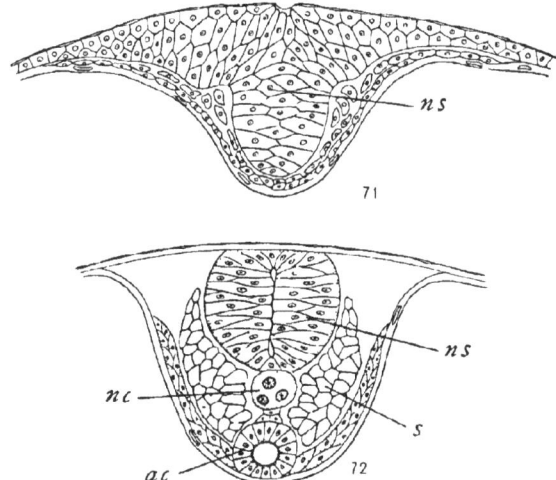

FIGS 71, 72 —Axial developmental gradients in the fish embryo· in Fig. 71 the embryo consists chiefly of the median dorsal region, in which the nervous system, *ns*, is developing, in Fig 72 development has proceeded laterally and ventrally, the somites *s*, the notochord *nc*, and the alimentary canal *ac* being present   From H V. Wilson, '89.

represents a transverse section of a fish embryo at an early stage of development   At this stage the embryo consists chiefly of the embryonic nervous system (*ns*), the other parts being represented by only a few cells.   Ventral to the embryo is a very large mass of yolk, not shown in the figure.   Here the median dorsal region precedes lateral and ventral regions in morphogenesis   Fig. 72 shows a later stage in which morphogenesis has advanced both laterally and ventrally from the median dorsal region.   The development of the chick is essentially similar. Fig 73 is from a transverse section of a very early stage in which cells from what will later become the median dorsal region are separating from the outer ectodermal layer to form the mesoderm Somewhat later the central nervous system arises by an infolding of the ectoderm. beginning at the anterior end and proceeding posteriorly in this same region. In Fig. 74, a more advanced stage, the embryonic nervous system is already present in the form of the neural tube, and it is evident that morphogenesis is proceeding both laterally and ventrally from the median dorsal region The developmental gradient along the longitudinal axis is also indicated by Figs 73 and 74, for both are from the same embryo. the latter from a more anterior, the former from a more posterior, level of the body. The more posterior level has only attained the stage of Fig 73. while the more anterior level has passed far beyond this stage.

Particular parts and organs of the individual very often possess an axis or axes of their own and without any uniform relation to the axis of the body as a whole. Although but little attention has been paid to this point, there are many facts which indicate that metabolic gradients exist along these axes, at least in the earlier stages of development.

In many animals the chief axial gradient along the longitudinal axis and often also the symmetry gradients persist throughout life or disappear only in advanced stages of development In fact as will appear below, the continued existence of the individual in the lower organisms is dependent upon the persistence of the gradients In higher forms where agamic reproduction from pieces of the body does not occur it is possible that in the adult the gradients may be altered or eliminated without altering the individuation to any marked degree.

The axial gradients arise in various ways which cannot be considered in detail here, but the different lines of evidence indicate that in the final analysis they result from the differential action of factors external to the protoplasm, cell, or cell mass concerned We see gradients arising in nature in this way, and it is possible to produce them experimentally by these means. In many cases of the reconstitution of pieces into new individuals the stimulation of the

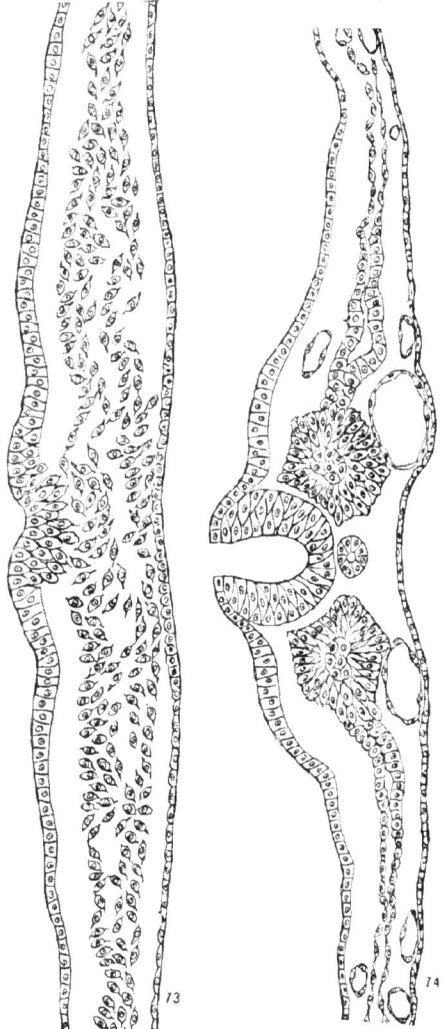

Figs. 73, 74.—Axial developmental gradients in the chick embryo: Fig. 73, showing the formation of the mesoderm, is from the posterior region of the same embryo as Fig. 74, from a more anterior region, in which morphogenesis has extended both laterally and ventrally from the mid-dorsal region. From embryological preparations of the University of Chicago.

region adjoining the wound determines the origin and direction of a new gradient and so the axis of a new individual In many cases also the origin and direction of the new gradient may be controlled and determined experimentally in other ways Undoubtedly, after it is once established a gradient may often persist from one individual to another through the process of reproduction, but there are no adequate grounds for believing that such gradients are fundamental properties of protoplasm, although, on the other hand, it is probable that no cell or cell mass can exist for any great length of time in any natural environment without acquiring, at least temporarily, one or more gradients, because external conditions at different points of its surface can never remain uniform. In general it may be said that the axial gradients of an organism are either the parental gradients persisting in the organism, as in many cases of fission, or that they are produced *de novo* by conditions which determine different rates of metabolism in different parts of the cell or cell mass at some stage of its existence.

The essential feature in the establishment of a gradient in metabolic rate in living protoplasm is the establishment of the region of highest rate. If such a region is established in an undifferentiated cell or cell mass, a more or less definite gradient in rate, extending to a greater or less distance from this region, arises because the changes in the primary region spread or are transmitted, but with a decrement in intensity or energy, so that at a greater or less distance they become inappreciable. In this way the region of highest rate becomes the chief factor in determining the rate of other regions, and since the rate thus determined is higher in regions nearer to it and lower in those farther away, a gradient in rate results In its simplest form, then, the gradient may arise merely from the spreading or transmission of metabolic changes from the region of highest rate

If metabolic gradients are characteristic features of the axes in living organisms, the question at once arises whether the axis in its simplest terms is anything more than such a gradient In other words, are not physiological and morphological polarity and symmetry primarily the expression of gradients in rate of metabolism? At present it can only be said in answer to this question

that there is much evidence in favor of this view and none which
seriously conflicts with it   But whatever their relation to polarity
and symmetry, the metabolic gradients are fundamental factors
in individuation, as the following sections will show

The process of experimental reproduction in the lower animals,
that is, the development of new individuals or parts of individuals
from pieces cut from the bodies of other individuals, affords an
insight into the problem of individuation which cannot be obtained
in any other way   In many of these cases of experimental reproduction a new individuation takes place under such conditions that
it is possible to learn something of the manner in which it occurs
A few of the more important points which have been established
are briefly considered here

Apical regions or heads may arise and develop in complete
independence of any other part of the body, but other levels along
the main axis can arise only in connection with an apical or head
region, or in its absence with some region representing a more
apical or anterior level   A few examples will make the point clear

In its simple, unbranched form the hydroid *Tubularia* consists
of the parts indicated in Fig 75, at the apical end the hydranth
with its two sets of tentacles and the reproductive organs between
them, below this a long stem, and in contact with the substratum
a stolon   Isolated pieces of the stem more than two or three
millimeters in length produce a hydranth at the distal end and a
second hydranth may arise later at the proximal end (Fig. 76), this
second hydranth being the result of a reproductive process similar
to that occurring in this species in nature (see p 220).   But when
the pieces are below a certain length, which varies with different
regions of the body and different animals and also with different
external conditions, they give rise to hydranths or apical regions of
hydranths at one or both ends with more or less complete absence
of other parts.   In the longer pieces of this sort a short stem may
be formed (Figs 77, 78), in slightly shorter pieces single or double,
or more properly biaxial hydranths both complete in all respects
(Figs 79, 80), or a biaxial structure like Fig 81 with one complete

hydranth and another consisting of only the more apical (Fig. 81). In still shorter pieces the proboscis with the so

short tentacles, and mouth may appear in single or biaxial form without any vestiges of other parts (Figs. 82, 83). And, finally, very short pieces give rise only to single biaxial apical portions of the proboscis with mouth and short tentacles (Figs. 84, 85).

Whether the short pieces produce single or biaxial structures, it is at once evident that the more apical regions of the tubularian body, i.e., the hydranth, or the apical regions of the hydranth, can develop from any piece of the stem quite independently of the presence of any other part of the body. The conditions necessary for the development of these parts are present in each piece, and the absence of the stem or even the basal portion of the hydranth makes no essential difference in the result. The occurrence of the biaxial structures is as a matter of fact an incidental result of the shortness of the pieces. In such pieces the rate of metabolism at

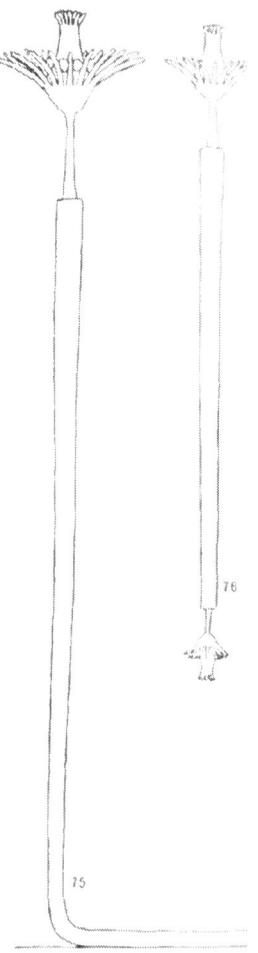

FIGS. 75, 76.—*Tubularia:* Fig. individual; Fig. 76, reconstituti piece of stem.

the two ends is often practically the same because th sent only a very small fraction of the whole axial

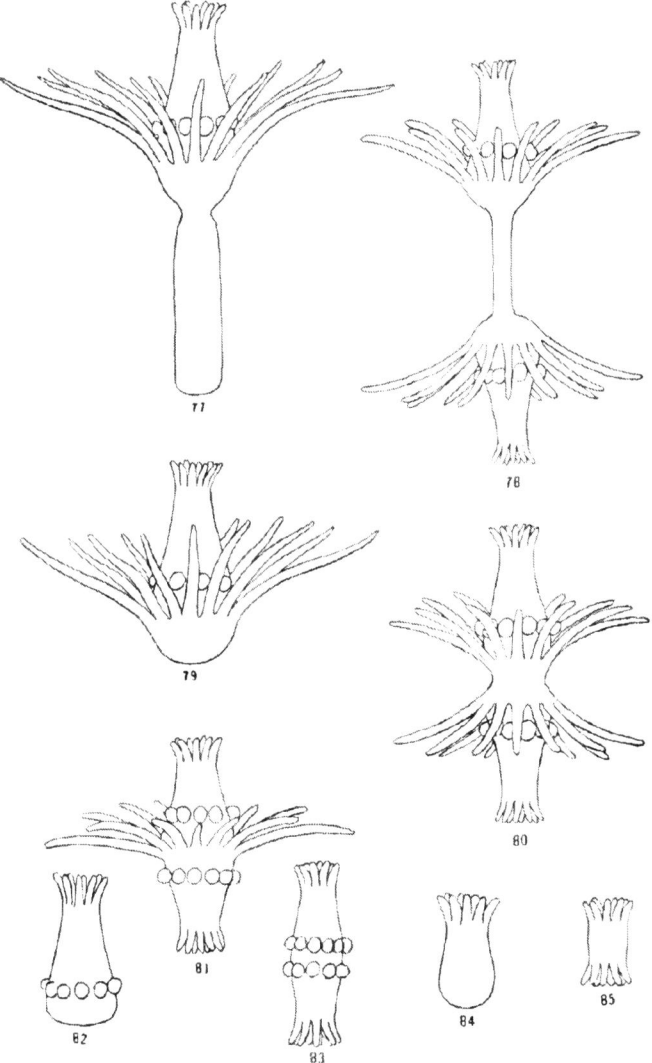

Figs. 77–85.—Different results of reconstitution in short pieces of the stem of *Tubularia*, showing that the formation of the apical region is independent of other parts.

Consequently the two ends react with equal rapidity, and begin development at the same time, and neither becomes dominant over the other.[1]

Short pieces of this character have never been known to undergo transformation into stolons or stems without hydranths. A stolon or a stem develops only in connection with a hydranth, or with a piece of stem or stolon, and as an outgrowth from it   In other hydroids and in coelenterates in general, as far as they have been examined, the same relations obtain   The apical region can arise independently of other parts, but stems and stolons arise only in connection with other parts and more specifically with parts which represent physiological regions nearer the apical end, rather than with those to which they give rise

In the flatworms we find similar relations of parts   Short pieces from the body of *Planaria*, for example, may develop into single or biaxial heads without any other part of the body.   The head of *Planaria* when separated from the body by a cut at the level *a* in Fig. 86 may develop a head on its cut surface, as in Fig 87, and short pieces from other regions, such as the piece *bc* in Fig. 86, may give rise to single heads like Figs 88 and 89, or sometimes to biaxial heads with a short anterior body region between them, like Fig. 90.   Evidently development of a head from a piece is possible, even in the complete absence of other parts (Child, '11*b*)

In *Planaria*, as in *Tubularia*, posterior regions do not arise independently of other parts, but always in connection with regions which are more anterior   Any piece of the planarian body is capable of giving rise to all parts posterior to its own level, whether a head is present or not (Fig. 91), but no piece is capable of producing any part characteristic of more anterior levels than itself, unless a head begins to form first.   This point is illustrated by Figs. 91 and 92.   These pieces represent the region *bd* in Fig. 86   When such pieces remain headless, as in Fig 91, no changes occur at the anterior end except the slight growth of new tissue, the piece does not give rise to a new pharynx, nor does the more anterior region undergo transformation into a prepharyngeal region   At the posterior end, however, a large outgrowth occurs which slowly attains the

[1] See Child, '07*a*, *b*, *c*, '11*a*, pp 101–19

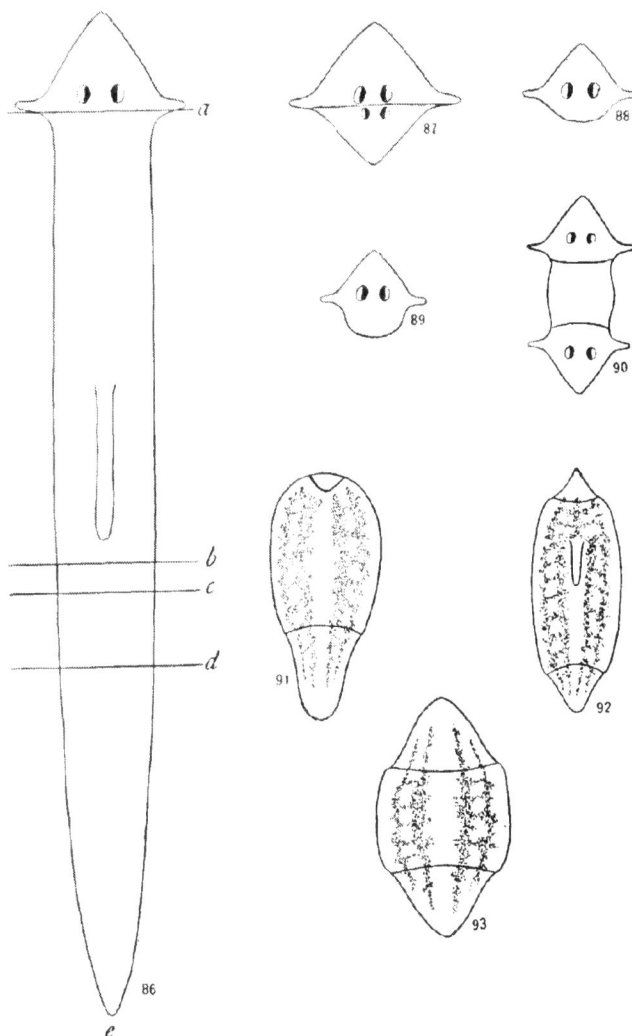

FIGS. 86–93.—Reconstitution in short pieces of *Planaria dorotocephala*: Fig. 86, body-outline, indicating levels of section; Figs. 87–89. biaxial and single heads formed independently of other parts; 90, biaxial form with partial body; Fig. 91, headless piece without reconstitutional changes in the anterior region; Fig. 92, anophthalmic form in which anterior region has undergone reconstitution into the anterior and middle body-region of a whole worm; Fig. 93, biaxial tails.

characteristic structure of a posterior end   Under certain conditions short pieces give rise to biaxial posterior ends, as in Fig. 93. Morgan ('04) has also described biaxial posterior ends from *Planaria simplicissima*.   But when such pieces give rise to a head, even though it is of the rudimentary, anophthalmic type of Fig. 92, a new pharynx and mouth arise and the anterior region becomes structurally and functionally a prepharyngeal region, as the change in the intestinal branches in Fig 92 indicates.   In some way all the changes in the piece which concern the development of parts anterior to its own level are dependent upon the presence of a head, or, more correctly, of a head-forming region.

It has also been shown (Child, '13a, '14b, '14c) that the development of a head on a piece of the planarian body is not the replacement of a missing part under the influence of other parts of the piece, but that head formation takes place, if it takes place at all, in spite of the remainder of the piece.   The more vigorous the other regions of the piece, i.e., the higher their rate of metabolism, the less likely is the piece to give rise to a new head, and vice versa On the other hand, the higher the rate in a piece, the more likely it is to produce a posterior end.   In short, the development of a new individual from such pieces of *Planaria* is essentially the same process as the development of an individual from the egg.   It begins with the formation of a head, and the head-region in some way determines the reconstitution of certain parts of the piece into more anterior parts, while other parts persist with more or less change in size and proportion as corresponding parts of the new animal.   In the absence of a head-region any level of the body controls and determines the development of all more posterior levels.   Much evidence, largely as yet unpublished, indicates that similar relations exist in other forms where the development of whole animals from headless pieces occurs.

These facts force us to the conclusion that in such experimental reproductions there is a relation of dominance and subordination of parts.   The apical or head-region develops independently of other parts but controls or dominates their development, and in general any level of the body dominates more posterior or basal levels and is dominated by more anterior or apical levels.

It is a well-known fact that a similar relation of dominance and subordination exists in plants, the apical region or growing tip of an axis being the dominant or controlling region of that axis   The "law" of antero-posterior development in animals suggests that the relations are at least primarily the same in embryonic development as in experimental reproduction.   The cases of apparent mutual independence of different regions or parts of the embryo represent beyond question a secondary condition, so far as the independence shall prove to be real

As regards the longitudinal axis of the organism, then, the region of highest rate of metabolism dominates other regions in the earlier stages of development, and in general any region of higher rate dominates regions of lower rate.   The developmental gradients along the axes of symmetry mentioned above (pp 204-7) suggest the existence of a dominance and subordination along these axes also.

The remarkable parallelism between the relations of dominance and subordination and the relations of metabolic rate along the axis suggests that dominance and subordination may depend primarily on rate of metabolism   As regards the plants, it is evident that dominance depends on metabolic activity, for the effect on other parts of decreasing or inhibiting the metabolism of the growing tip without killing it, for example, by inclosure in plaster or in an atmosphere of hydrogen, is the same as that of killing it, or removing it completely.   In other words, the reproduction or development of other growing tips which was previously inhibited now proceeds.   McCallum ('05) has demonstrated very clearly that this relation of dominance and subordination in plants is not dependent upon nutrition, water-content, or other more or less incidental and widely varying conditions, but that it is a physiological correlation of some sort apparently dependent upon fundamental factors in the plant constitution   As regards animals also, there are many facts, some of which will be considered below, which indicate clearly that dominance and subordination of parts in the individual are primarily dependent upon rate of metabolism, although with the development of a highly irritable conducting system between dominant and subordinate parts, such as the nervous system, it is conceivable that other factors may play a part.

THE NATURE AND LIMITS OF DOMINANCE

As regards the nature of the influence of the dominant region upon other parts, the physico-chemical theory of the organism affords two alternatives   Physiological correlation in the organism, the influence of one part upon another, so far as it is not directly mechanical, is accomplished in two ways: by the production and transportation of substances, commonly known as chemical correlation, and by the transmission through the protoplasm in general, or along specialized conducting paths, of excitations which have often been regarded as electrical in nature, but which now appear to be associated with chemical changes (Tashiro, '13a).   If chemical correlation is the basis of the influence of the dominant region on other parts, then we must suppose that metabolism in the dominant region gives rise to certain chemical substances which are transported in some way through the body, but are gradually used up or transformed so that their effects cease at a certain distance from the region of origin.   We may assume, further, that different substances are transported at different rates or are completely used up at different distances from the point of origin.   On the other hand, the dominance and subordination of parts may conceivably be accomplished by transmitted impulses   On the basis of this alternative the metabolic activity of the dominant region must produce certain changes or excitations which are transmitted through the protoplasm, but which decrease in energy or effectiveness as they are transmitted, so that finally a limit is reached beyond which they are ineffective.

Many facts favor the second alternative   In the first place, chemical substances may be transported to any distance in the fluids of an organism, and it is difficult to see how any definite and characteristic limit of effectiveness of such substances could exist, unless we could assume that they were diffusing through a homogeneous medium or being transported at a definite rate and undergoing destruction also at a definite rate during transportation. But it is certain that neither of these possibilities is realized in all organisms in which a limit of effectiveness of dominance appears, and it is a fact that the existence of a decrement and a limit of effectiveness in transmission has been observed in many cases among both plants and animals, and for excitations transmitted through the general protoplasm, as well as those transmitted through muscle and nerve [1] In some of the lower animals the gradual fading out, with increasing distance from the point of origin, of the muscular contractions following a slight local stimulation, affords a visible demonstration of the decrease in effectiveness with transmission, and the relation between the distance from the point of stimulation at which the contraction ceases to occur and the strength of stimulation indicates further that the more intense excitation is transmitted to a greater distance than the less intense.   And, finally, there can be no doubt that impulses may be transmitted to greater distances over specialized conducting paths, of which nerves are the most highly developed form, than through the general protoplasm, and apparently some nerves conduct with less decrement per unit of distance than others.

Certain physiologists maintain that the medullated nerves of vertebrates conduct impulses without any decrement   If this is true, an impulse might be transmitted in such a nerve to an infinite distance from its point of origin.   There are, however, certain facts which indicate that even in these nerves a decrement does occur in the course of transmission, although it is often so slight as to be inappreciable under ordinary conditions in the relatively short pieces of nerves usually available for experiment.   In the first place, the electrical change, the negative variation accompanying the passage of a nerve impulse, has been shown to undergo decrease with increasing distance from the point of stimulation, and the effectiveness of the impulse in producing muscular contraction decreases in the same way   Moreover, various investigators have recorded the existence of a decrement in the intensity of the impulse in partially anaesthetized nerves, and there is no reason to believe that the partial anaesthesia alters the fundamental nature of the nerve as conductor. in all probability it merely makes the nerve a less efficient conductor, so that the decrement becomes apparent

[1] For general consideration of the whole subject of conduction see Fitting, '07, for plants, especially pp 91–93 and 122–24, Biedermann, '03, especially pp 204–8, and Verworn, '13, chap vi for animals See also Boruttau, '01, Ducceschi, '01, A. Fischer, '11, Kretzschmar,'04, Lodholz, '13

within a shorter distance than in the normal nerve. It is impossible to consider the literature of this much-discussed problem here, but it may be said that there is considerable evidence which indicates that a decrease in energy or effectiveness occurs in the course of transmission, even in the most highly developed nerve fibers, while, up to the present time, no one has actually demonstrated that conduction without decrement over any considerable distance occurs. It appears, then, that transmitted excitations in organisms do in general show a more or less rapid decrement and consequently a limit of effectiveness at a greater or less distance from the point of origin. In other words, such excitations gradually die out like a wave or an electric impulse, but the more intense the excitations or the better the conducting path, the greater the distance between point of origin and limit of effectiveness. From our knowledge of conduction of excitations in non-living substances this is what we should expect in conduction in living substance.

If the dominance of one region over another in the organism depends upon such transmitted excitations, there must be a spatial limit to such dominance. And since the excitations which proceed from the dominant region must result from metabolic changes occurring there, we should expect to find them varying in intensity with the rate of metabolism in the dominant part. Moreover, the more intense the excitation and the better the conductor through which the excitation is transmitted, the greater its effective range i e, the distance to which it can travel before becoming ineffective. Consequently the spatial limit of dominance must vary with the rate of metabolism in the dominant part and the efficiency of the conducting path between that and other parts. In the plants and lower animals and in early stages of embryonic development of all forms the efficiency of conduction is low and dominance is in general effective over rather limited distances. In the later stages of development of those forms which possess a nervous system the efficiency of conduction increases very greatly as the nerves develop, and the spatial limit of dominance likewise increases very greatly.

In the plants and lower animals the limit of dominance is indicated very clearly by the size of the individual or part concerned.

and growth beyond this size results in the formation of a new individual or individuals from some part of the old, that is, in some form

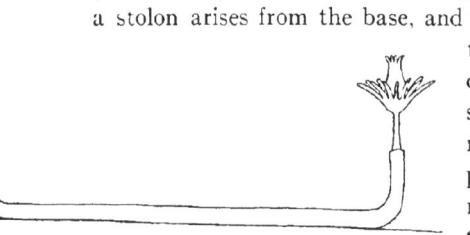

of reproduction   The repetitive development in series of parts, such as node and internode, in the stem of the plant, of segments in segmented animals, and many other cases, are examples of similar relations between parts.   The organic individual in fact exhibits a more or less definite sequence of events in space as well as in time, and it is impossible to doubt that a physiological spatial factor of some sort is concerned.   This problem has been considered at some length in an earlier paper (Child, 'IIa), and only brief mention of some of the important points is possible here.

   In the simpler cases of reproduction the spatial factor in dominance is clearly evident in the position of the part concerned in reproduction with respect to the original dominant region. In *Tubularia* (Fig 75, p 211), for example, the stem and stolon increase in length, and when a certain length, varying with conditions which affect rate of metabolism, is attained, the tip of the stolon turns upward away from the substratum and gives rise to a hydranth, as in Fig. 94   This hydranth and its stem grow in turn, a stolon arises from the base, and when a certain length of stem plus stolon is reached, the process of reproduction is then repeated.

Fig 94 —The primary form of agamic reproduction in *Tubularia*

Evidently the stolon tip gives rise to a hydranth only when it has attained a certain distance from the original hydranth   The formation of a hydranth at the basal end of pieces of the stem of *Tubularia* under experimental conditions (Fig. 76, p. 211) is simply the same reproductive process which occurs in nature, except that under the experimental conditions it occurs in a shorter length of stem because the rate of metabolism is lower. In *Planaria* and other flatworms which undergo fission the body attains a certain length and then the posterior region becomes a new zooid, as described in chap. vi. The length which the individual attains can be widely varied and controlled by experimental conditions which affect the rate of metabolism (Child, '11c).

FIG. 95.—Reproduction of new plants from runners in the strawberry. From Seubert, '66.

In plants similar relations are of very general occurrence. In the strawberry plant, for example (see Fig. 95), the runner attains a certain length before the growing tip gives rise to a new plant, but by cutting off or inhibiting the metabolism of the growing tip of the parent plant the development of a new plant at the tip of the runner can be induced at any time. These few cases will serve to call to mind many others among both plants and animals in which a spatial factor and a limit of effectiveness of the dominance of the apical or head-region is evident.

Within the limits of the individual organism the same factor appears in the length and position of various parts, and it has been shown elsewhere (Child, 11b) that in *Planaria* the spatial relations of parts can be altered experimentally by altering the rate of metabolism in the dominant head-region. For example, a piece of *Planaria* including any considerable portion of the postpharyngeal region such as *bc*, Fig. 86 (p. 214), when allowed to undergo reconstitution in water at room temperature, forms an animal which in

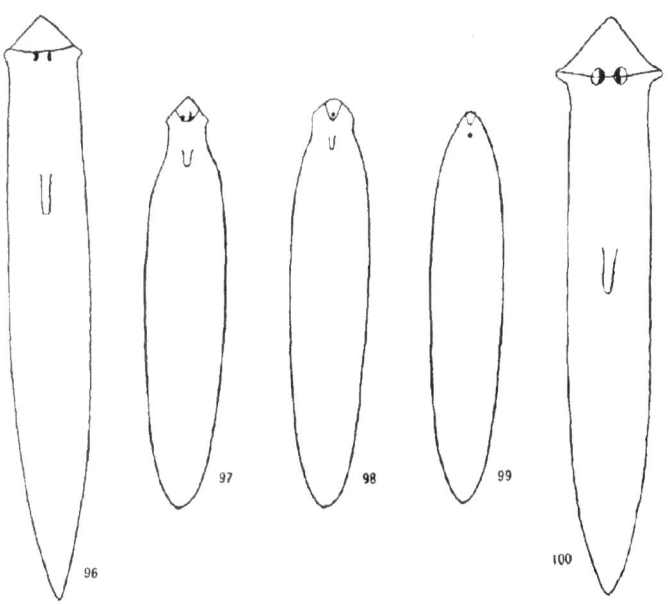

FIGS. 96-100.—Reconstitution of similar pieces of *Planaria dorotocephala* under different conditions, to show different positions of pharynx and lengths of prepharyngeal region: Fig. 96, reconstitution in well-aerated water at 20° C.; Figs. 97-99, different degrees of reconstitution in weak solutions of narcotics; Fig. 100, reconstitution in well-aerated water at 28° C.

its earlier stages is like Fig. 96. The new pharynx and mouth appear anterior to the middle of the piece at a certain characteristic distance from the head, and in the region between the pharynx and head the characteristic structure of the prepharyngeal region develops. But if such pieces undergo reconstitution in weak solutions of alcohol, ether, chloretone, or other anaesthetics, or under other conditions which decrease the rate of metabolism, the head is smaller and develops more slowly, the pharynx appears much nearer the head, and the new prepharyngeal region is correspondingly shorter (Figs 97, 98). In extreme cases the head may be teratomorphic (Fig. 99), or even anophthalmic (see pp 111–12), and no reconstitution occurs posterior to it In similar pieces, under conditions which increase the rate of metabolism, such as high temperature, the prepharyngeal region is longer and the pharynx appears farther from the head (Fig 100). Evidently the distance from the anterior end at which certain conditions arise in the piece under its influence varies with the rate of metabolism in the dominant anterior region. When the rate is very low the anterior region does not bring about any visible change in regions posterior to itself, and the higher the rate the greater the distance at which particular changes occur.

In the higher animals, such as the vertebrates, as well as in the higher invertebrates, the size of the adult individual is limited by other factors than the limit of dominance, so that such animals never attain anything like what might be called the physiological maximum of size The chief limiting factor in these cases is apparently the higher degree of differentiation of the cells which results in the retardation and sooner or later in the almost complete or complete cessation of growth. Only in those forms in which agamic reproduction occurs can we be certain that the individual attains the physiological maximum, i.e., the size determined by the limit of dominance. In the adult stages of the higher animals dominance may extend to almost indefinite distances, but individual size is limited by differentiation and lack of capacity for indefinite or long-continued growth. Even in these forms, however, the size of parts and their repetitive reproduction during development may be determined by the limits of dominance in the early stages

When we consider all these facts and many others, some of which have been mentioned elsewhere[1] but cannot be discussed here, we are forced to conclude that a relation of dominance and subordination of parts in the organism really exists, that it is effective only within a certain spatial limit, varying with conditions in the

[1] Child, '11a, '11b, '11c, '13a, '14b, '14c.

organism, and that it seems to depend primarily upon impulses or changes of some sort transmitted from the dominant region, rather than upon the transportation of chemical substances. Chemical substances arising in the course of metabolism are undoubtedly important factors in determining the constitution and character of particular organs and parts, but it is difficult to understand how they can account for the definite and orderly spatial characteristics of living things. Hormones, internal secretions, and other chemical substances unquestionably play a very essential rôle in physiological correlation, particularly in the higher animals where different organs are highly differentiated, but for the production of such different specific substances different organs are necessary. At present we are concerned with the question of the primary origin of these organs, with the appearance and localization of differences which make possible the production of different specific substances in different parts of the individual, and it is evident that these primary specializations and differentiations, their localization and orderly and definite spatial arrangement, cannot be accounted for by the action or interaction of such substances.

According to the conception developed above, the dominance of a region depends primarily upon its rate of metabolism as compared with that of other regions within the range of its influence. Where the region of high rate is the primary factor in maintaining the gradient, as it undoubtedly is in the lower organisms and in the early stages of development of many higher forms, it is of course the chief factor in determining the metabolic rate in other regions and so maintains its original dominance. But in more highly differentiated forms, or in later developmental stages, where relatively permanent structural differentiations have arisen along the course of the gradient, so that it has become structurally fixed, the region of highest rate still remains dominant because it gives rise to more powerful impulses than do other regions and consequently influences them more than they do it. Lastly, in the higher animals, where, in all except early embryonic stages, transmission through nerves is the chief factor in physiological integration (see Sherrington, '06), the original gradient in metabolic rate may persist chiefly, or perhaps in some cases only, in the efferent conducting paths of the nervous system, while in other parts of the body the metabolic rate has been altered by various factors.

At present there seems to be no good reason for believing that the changes or impulses transmitted from the dominant region affect the metabolic processes in regions which they reach in any other than a quantitative way. The dominant region is not to be conceived as giving rise to a variety of different kinds of impulses which produce different, specific, formative effects, but rather merely as a region of high metabolic rate, from which changes connected with its metabolic activity spread or are transmitted to other regions and increase their metabolic activity. Since these transmitted changes decrease in energy or effectiveness with transmission, they must determine a higher rate in the regions nearer the dominant region than in those farther away. In this way the determination of a high rate of metabolism in one region may result in the establishment of a metabolic gradient in one or more directions from that region. Each point along an axis is then characterized by a more or less definite rate of metabolism, and if more than one axis is present each point in the organism has a rate determined by its position in each of the axial gradients.

From this point of view the axiate individual, whether it is a whole organism or a part, when reduced to its simplest terms consists of one or more gradients in rate of metabolism in a cell or cell mass of specific constitution. Of course this condition represents only the first step in individuation. Whether every individual organism in every generation has its beginning in a condition as simple as this can be determined only by extensive investigation. Certainly other factors, such as difference of conditions at the surface and in the interior, the presence of reserve substance such as yolk in certain cells, etc, play a part sooner or later in many cases. But that the simplest axiate individuals among organisms consist essentially of metabolic gradients in a specific protoplasm is a conclusion supported by a large body of evidence. The axes of the organism or its parts are, according to this view, in their simplest terms nothing but such gradients, and the structure of the apical region or head of the organism represents merely the developmental result of a high rate of metabolism and independence of other parts.   With a sufficiently high rate of metabolism and when not subordinated to other parts, any part of the simpler organisms is capable of developing into an apical region or head.

The objection may be raised that even if such a metabolic gradient is established, there is nothing to maintain it with the necessary degree of constancy to produce definite results.   As a matter of fact, regional differences in metabolism do maintain themselves to a remarkable degree and may even be accentuated Certain muscles frequently or strongly stimulated become capable of greater activity, and little-used parts gradually lose their capacity for activity.   There is good reason to believe that within certain limits an increase in rate of metabolism in a protoplasmic substratum changes the condition of the substratum so that a still higher rate is possible, and vice versa   The analogy between the organism and the stream referred to in chap. i is perhaps of service here.   An increase in rate of flow of the stream alters the channel so that a still higher rate is possible, and a decrease in rate of flow produces conditions which bring about further decrease.   Moreover, the region of high rate of metabolism in the organism once established is more susceptible because of its high rate to the action of external conditions· in animals, particularly in motile forms, this region becomes the seat of the special sense-organs and is therefore the most important part of the body as regards relations between the organism and the external world.   These conditions result from the original high metabolic rate of the region, but they also contribute toward maintenance of a relatively high rate of metabolism.

And, finally, the question whether purely quantitative differences along an axis are sufficient to account for the morphological differences which arise along that axis is one which can be answered only after the most extended and painstaking investigation   At present we know that morphological characters can be altered very widely by conditions whose effect upon the organism is primarily quantitative.   The different types of anterior end in pieces of *Planaria* (see pp 111–12) are cases in point   The very general belief that qualitatively different substances or entities of some kind are necessary as a basis for morphological development does not rest upon direct or experimental evidence, but is an inference from the morphological characters themselves As a matter of fact we know that even in relatively simple chemical reactions quantitative differences may very often give rise to qualitatively different results. And when we recognize the very great complexity of metabolism in even the simplest organism, we cannot but admit that there must be many possibilities in the metabolic complex for the origin of qualitative differences in characters, organs, etc , from quantitative differences in metabolism Manifestly, quality and quantity in organisms are not and cannot at present be clearly distinguished That qualitative differences in the chemical constitution and metabolism of different organs exist is evident, but there is at present no valid evidence that such differences cannot be reduced to a quantitative basis

DEGREES OF INDIVIDUATION

If the organic individual consists fundamentally of one or more gradients in rate of metabolism with a relation of dominance and subordination between regions of higher and those of lower rate, it is at once apparent that the degree of integration of such an individual into a physiological unit, the degree of physiological coherence and of orderly behavior, must vary widely with various factors of its constitution. Since it will often be necessary in following chapters to call attention to differences in the degree of individuation, some of these factors must be briefly considered here

The efficiency of conduction is a most important factor in individuation In the lower organisms and in the embryonic stages of even the higher animals where the decrement in conduction is great, the degree of individuation is much lower than in those forms or stages which possess a well-developed nervous system, where the decrement is much less or almost inappreciable. In the lower forms and in embryonic stages a higher metabolic rate is necessary for permanent individuation; in other words, in order to become or remain dominant, a given level must have a higher rate of metabolism in relation to other levels than when a nervous system is present.

Another factor in individuation is the physiological stability of the structural substratum The greater the stability of the substratum, the greater the possibilities of specialization and differentiation along the axis in relation to the gradient and therefore the more intimate and complex the correlation between parts and the higher the degree of unity in the whole. In the lower forms, where structures once formed may disappear in a few hours or a few days under altered physiological conditions, there is no possibility of such minute and delicate interrelation and adjustment of parts to each other as in the higher forms, where regressive changes are much less extensive. In fact, the advance in development of the nervous system itself from the lower to the higher forms is in part dependent upon the increase in stability of the structural substratum.

The degree of individuation is dependent upon the rate of metabolism. At any given stage of development the higher the rate of metabolism, the higher the degree of individuation. But we cannot properly compare earlier and later stages of development in this way, for, although the rate of metabolism decreases during development, the degree of individuation increases in most cases up to the adult stage, because of the increasing efficiency of conduction and the specialization and interrelation of parts It is only after the adult stage is attained that the further decrease in metabolic rate with advancing senescence determines a gradual decrease in the degree of individuation, a physiological disintegration.

Many other incidental and external factors may alter the degree of individuation in organisms. In general, depressing factors decrease and stimulating factors, at least up to a certain limit, increase it. The point of chief importance is, however, the possibility of distinguishing different degrees of individuation and of interpreting them to some extent, however incompletely, in physicochemical terms

PHYSIOLOGICAL ISOLATION AND AGAMIC REPRODUCTION

If the axiate individual consists of a dominant and of subordinate parts, the structure, differentiation, and special function of the subordinate parts are dependent, at least to a considerable degree, upon their relation to the dominant part. Isolation of such parts from the influence of the dominant part must result, if the isolated parts are capable of reacting to the change, first, in a loss of their characteristics as parts, and, secondly, if conditions permit, in a new individuation which may bring about the development of a complete new individual from the isolated part. In short the isolation of a subordinate part from the influence of the dominant part is a necessary condition for reproduction. In experiment pieces are physically isolated from the body of the animal by section, and in the lower simpler forms reproduction follows such isolation, and the piece becomes a new whole, or at least undergoes changes in that direction.

There are certain features of the simpler reproductive processes in nature which suggest that in these cases, as in the experimental reproduction of artificially isolated pieces, an isolation from the influence of the dominant part is the essential condition for reproduction. In many forms, both plants and animals, growth beyond a certain length or size, which is dependent upon rate of metabolism, degree of differentiation, etc., results in the transformation of that portion of the individual most distant from the dominant part into a new individual. The case of *Tubularia* mentioned above (Fig. 94, p 220) is a good illustration, and in many plants similar vegetative reproductions occur. It is impossible to doubt that in such cases growth to a certain size brings the region in question into a condition where it is able to behave as if it were physically isolated, like a piece cut from the body.

It is also a fact, however, that reproduction may occur in consequence of the weakening or removal of the dominant part and without any preceding increase in size of the individual. Such cases are very common among the plants, where the removal or inhibition of metabolism of the growing tip of the main axis or stem is followed by development of a new axis from a lateral branch or bud. Very commonly also the removal of all growing tips is followed by the development of "adventitious" growing tips, which often arise from differentiated cells by a process of dedifferentiation and growth. Among the lower animals similar cases occur Increase in size is not then a necessary condition for reproduction. Decrease in rate of metabolism or inhibition of metabolism in the dominant region may bring about reproduction as readily as growth.

The analysis of the simple forms of agamic reproduction in connection with the experimental reproductions in artificially isolated pieces leaves no room for doubt that the formation of a new individual from a part of a pre-existing individual results from the removal of an inhibiting factor rather than from a positive stimulation. According to the conception of the individual developed above, a more or less complete physiological isolation of the region or part concerned is a necessary condition for reproduction, or, more specifically, this part must in some way escape from the control of the dominant region before it can lose its characteristics as a part and so serve as the basis for a new individuation.[1]

In the simpler organisms, where isolated parts are capable of reconstitution into new individuals, the effect of physiological isolation of a part is essentially the same as that of physical isolation by section, except that physiological isolation is a less violent and injurious procedure. The isolated part undergoes dedifferentiation to a greater or less extent and begins a new development, an agamic reproduction occurs. But in the higher forms, where isolated parts are incapable of reconstitution, physiological isolation may lead to death of the part isolated, or if nutrition is available the part may continue to exist in its original form or to grow and differentiate along the lines previously determined by its relations with other parts.

It is evident that the final size of the individual is determined by the limit of dominance only in the lower, simpler organisms. It was pointed out above that in the higher animals other factors—such as the rapid differentiation and loss of capacity for growth and division of cells and perhaps the increasing disproportion between surface and volume—limit the individual to a size far below that which the limit of dominance alone would determine. If, for example, the size of man and mammals were limited only by the limit of effective transmission of nerve impulses in fully developed nerve fibers, they would certainly be very much larger than they are. In early embryonic stages, however, the limit of dominance is

[1] For experimental data see Child, '07a, '07b, '10, '11c, and for a general consideration of physiological isolation of parts, the ways in which it is brought about, and its significance, see Child, '11a

undoubtedly a factor in determining the limits of the individual in at least some mammals, for Patterson ('13) has shown that the four embryos of the nine-banded armadillo are the result of agamic reproduction, of a process of budding of the primarily single embryo, and suggests that duplicate twins and double monsters may arise in the same manner.

There can be no doubt that during the course of individual development a greater or less degree of extension of dominance occurs as the paths of transmission develop. In the early embryonic stages the influence of the dominant region extends only a short distance, but, particularly in organisms where a nervous system develops, transmission of impulses to greater distances becomes possible as development proceeds. Consequently the size of the individual may increase during development, in many cases very greatly, without physiological isolation of any part and so without agamic reproduction

If the control of the dominant over the subordinate parts in the individual is accomplished by means of transmitted impulses or changes which show a decrement with transmission and a limit of effectiveness, then physiological isolation of a part may be brought about in four different ways (Child, '11a). First, physiological isolation may result from increase in size to or beyond the limit of dominance Many of the phenomena of budding, fission, etc, which occur in consequence of growth, both in plants and in animals, are examples.

Secondly, physiological isolation may result from a decrease in the limit of dominance, which in turn is the consequence of a decrease in rate of metabolism in the dominant part It is a well-known fact that many plants give rise to buds or other reproductive bodies under conditions unfavorable to metabolic activity, and while this form of reproduction has often been regarded teleologically as in some sense an attempt of the plant to save its own life, it is undoubtedly to be interpreted as the result of a decrease in the limit of dominance. The formation of new buds in plants in consequence of the removal or inhibition of metabolism of the dominant region, the vegetative tip, are likewise reproductive processes which belong to this category In the lower animals also many cases are known where conditions which decrease metabolism bring about budding or fission. A comparison of these two methods of physiological isolation makes it evident that the same result, viz , the physiological isolation of parts and their development into new individuals, may be attained by subjecting the organism to conditions which act in very different ways, producing in the one case an increase in rate of metabolism, growth, and increase in size, in the other a decrease in rate of metabolism (Child, '10). It is possible that both of these factors are concerned in many cases of budding and fission, that is, if an organism has attained a size at which some part is approaching physiological isolation, a slight physiological depression may bring about a sufficient isolation to initiate dedifferentiation and reproduction.

Thirdly, physiological isolation of a part may conceivably result from a decrease in the conductivity of the path over which the correlative factors from the dominant region are transmitted In many organisms the conductivity of the paths apparently increases as the morphological differentiation of conducting structures proceeds during development, so that in spite of a decrease in rate of general metabolism the general physiological limits of the individual are extended and physiological isolation of parts is delayed or prevented   In many of the flowering plants, for example, new growing tips arise and pass through the early stages of their development at very short distances from each other and from the axial growing tip (Fig 101), but in later stages, when the conducting structures are fully developed, the dominance of the growing tip extends over a much greater distance.   In the flatworms likewise the length which the individual attains before formation of a new zooid at the posterior end increases up to a certain point with advancing development (Child, '11c), while any considerable changes in conductivity in the opposite direction may bring about reproduction in many cases.

And, finally, it is possible that physiological isolation of a part may result from the direct action of external factors upon it, increasing its rate of metabolism, or otherwise altering it, so that it is less receptive, or no longer subordinate to the correlative factors, and so becomes independent in spite of them.   In various plants the development of buds can be induced, in spite of the presence and activity of the chief growing tip, by subjecting the part concerned to external conditions especially favorable for growth and develop ment. To what extent this process of physiological isolation occur in nature is as yet a question, though it probably occurs very fre quently.

Many cases of agamic reproduction have not as yet been ana lyzed from this point of view, but it appears probable that all are the result of either physiological or physical isolation. In some cases, where the degree of individuation is slight, physical isolation is probably the primary factor, that is, some internal or external con- dition operates to isolate a part physically from other parts and reproduction re- sults. This may occur in va- rious cases of spore formation among the lower plants, although even here it is prob- able that physical isolation is possible only because the parts are normally but slightly subordinated to a dominant region.

We may conclude, then, that the first step in agamic reproduction is the isolation

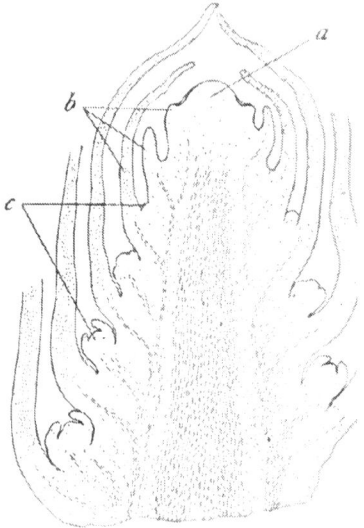

FIG. 101.—Longitudinal section of th apical region of a seed plant: a, growing tip b, developing leaves; c, axillary buds. From Strasburger, etc., '98.

of a part from the correlative conditions in the individual which determine its existence and persistence as a part. In at leas many cases this isolation is primarily physiological, rather than physical. In consequence of this isolation the part undergoe more or less dedifferentiation, a new individuation arises in i in various ways, some of which have been analyzed in certain cases (Child, '14b, '14c), but which cannot be discussed here

Such reproduction is possible only where the isolated part is capable of reacting to the isolation by dedifferentiation and reconstitution According to this conception, agamic reproduction in organisms results in one way or another from the physiological or physical isolation of a subordinate part from the influence of the dominant part. At first glance gametic or sexual reproduction appears to be a totally different kind of reproduction but, except for the occurrence of fertilization, it is in reality very similar to the agamic process Before taking up the problem of sexual reproduction, however, it is necessary to consider the relation between individuation, agamic reproduction, and the age cycle

REFERENCES

BIEDERMANN, W.

    1903 "Elektrophysiologie," *Ergebn. d Physiol* , Jhg II, Abt II.

BORUTTAU, H

    1901 "Die Aktionsstrome und die Theorie der Nervenleitung," *Arch f. d ges. Physiol* , LXXXIV

BRESSLAU, E

    1904 "Beitrage zur Entwicklungsgeschichte der Turbellarien: I, Die Entwicklung der Rhabdocolen und Alloiocolen," *Zeitschi f wiss Zool* , LXXVI.

CHILD, C. M.

    1907*a* "An Analysis of Form Regulation in *Tubularia*· I, Stolon-Formation and Polarity," *Arch. f. Entwickelungsmech* , XXIII

    1907*b* "An Analysis, etc.   IV, Regional and Polar Differences in the Time of Hydranth-Formation as a Special Case of Regulation in a Complex System," *Arch f Entwickelungsmech* , XXIV.

    1907*c* "An Analysis, etc   V, Regulation in Short Pieces," *Arch f Entwickelungsmech* , XXIV.

    1910 "Physiological Isolation of Parts and Fission in *Planaria*," *Arch f. Entwickelungsmech.*, XXX (Festband f Roux), II Teil.

    1911*a* "Die physiologische Isolation von Teilen des Organismus," *Vortr und Aufs u. Entwickelungsmech.*, XI.

    1911*b* "Studies on the Dynamics of Morphogenesis and Inheritance in Experimental Reproduction   II, Physiological Dominance of Anterior over Posterior Regions in the Regulation of *Planaria dorotocephala*," *Jour of Exp. Zool* , XI.

    1911*c*. "Studies, etc : III, The Formation of New Zooids in *Planaria* and Other Forms," *Jour of Exp Zool* , XI

CHILD, C. M

1912 "Studies, etc · IV, Certain Dynamic Factors in the Regulation of *Planaria dorotocephala* in Relation to the Axial Gradient," *Jour of Exp Zool.*, XIII

1913a. "Certain Dynamic Factors in Experimental Reproduction and Their Significance for the Problems of Reproduction and Development," *Arch f. Entwickelungsmech*, XXXV

1913b. "Studies, etc.: VI, The Nature of the Axial Gradients in *Planaria* and Their Relation to Antero-posterior Dominance, Polarity and Symmetry," *Arch f. Entwickelungsmech*, XXXVII

1914a "Susceptibility Gradients in Animals," *Science*, XXXIX.

1914b. "Studies, etc : VII, The Stimulation of Pieces by Section in *Planaria dorotocephala*," *Jour. of Exp. Zool*, XVI.

1914c "Studies, etc : VIII, Dynamic Factors in Head-Determination in *Planaria*," *Jour. of Exp Zool.*, XVII.

DUCCESCHI, V

1901. "Uber die Wirkung engbegrenzter Nervencompression," *Arch. f. d. ges. Physiol.*, LXXXIII.

FISCHER, A

1911 "Ein Beitrag zur Kenntnis des Ablaufes des Erregungsvorgangs im marklosen Warmbluternerven," *Zeitschr. f. Biol.*, LVI.

FITTING, H

1907. "Die Reizleitungsvorgange bei den Pflanzen," Sonderabdr aus *Ergebn d. Physiol*, Jhg. IV u. V. Wiesbaden.

KOWALEWSKY, A

1871. "Embryologische Studien an Wurmern und Arthropoden," *Mém. Acad St Pétersbourg*, (7) XVI.

KRETZSCHMAR, P

1904 "Uber Entstehung und Ausbreitung der Plasmastromung in Folge von Wundreiz," *Jahrbucher f wiss Bot*, XXXIX

LODHOLZ, E.

1913. "Das Dekrement der Erregungswelle im erstickenden Nerven," *Zeitschr. f allgem. Physiol*, XV.

McCALLUM, W. B

1905. "Regeneration in Plants," *Bot Gazette*, XL.

MORGAN, T H

1904. "Regeneration of Heteromorphic Tails in Posterior Pieces of *Planaria simplicissima*," *Jour of Exp Zool*, 1

PATTERSON, J. T.

1913 "Polyembryonic Development in *Tatusia novemcincta*," *Jour of Morphol*, XXIV.

SEUBERT, M.

    1866   *Lehrbuch der gesammten Pflanzenkunde* IV Auflage

SHERRINGTON, C S.

    1906   *The Integrative Action of the Nervous System.* New York

STRASBURGER, E , NOLL, F., SCHENCK, H , und KARSTEN, G.

    1908   *Lehrbuch der Botanik* IX Auflage Jena

TASHIRO, S.

    1913*a* "Carbon Dioxide Production from Nerve Fibers When Resting and When Stimulated, a Contribution to the Chemical Basis of Irritability," *Am Jour of Physiol.*, XXXII.

    1913*b* "A New Method and Apparatus for the Estimation of Exceedingly Minute Quantities of Carbon Dioxide, ' *Am Jour of Physiol ,* XXXII

VERWORN, M

    1913   *Irritability.* New Haven, Conn

WILSON, H V

    1889. "The Embryology of the Sea Bass," *Bull of the U S Fish Commission,* IX.

CHAPTER X

THE AGE CYCLE IN PLANTS AND THE LOWER ANIMALS

Any consideration of the age cycle and particularly of rejuvenescence in plants would be incomplete without reference to a remarkable book, *Considerations on the Phenomenon of Rejuvenescence in Nature*,[1] by the German botanist Alexander Braun, published in 1851. The book is remarkable, not only as a consideration of rejuvenescence, but as one of the pre-Darwinian statements of a theory of evolution. This work became known to me only after I had attained definite conclusions on the basis of experiment, and it has been a matter of very great interest to discover to how great an extent Braun had anticipated in his views the results of experiment. He regards reproduction in the broadest sense and primarily cell reproduction as the basis of rejuvenescence, describes and discusses dedifferentiation, and recognizes clearly the important fact that the vegetative life of plants is in most cases a series of reproductions. In fact, the conclusions reached in the present chapter are in many respects essentially those of Braun, but modified and brought into relation with modern physiological conceptions and with my own experimental results on the lower animals

INDIVIDUATION AND AGAMIC REPRODUCTION IN THE LIFE CYCLE OF PLANTS

According to the conception of individuation discussed in the preceding chapter, every growing tip, together with the region which it dominates, is in greater or less degree a plant individual All except the simplest plants therefore are in reality, as botanists have repeatedly pointed out, asexual colonies consisting of a larger or smaller number of individuals which are not completely isolated from each other. In animal colonies such individuals are commonly known as zooids, and for convenience the individuals in a plant colony may be termed phytoids In most plants there is evidently also some degree of individuation of the colony as a whole, for new

[1] *Betrachtungen uber die Erscheinung der Verjungung in der Natur*

buds arise in a definite sequence and space relation to each other, and numerous experiments have demonstrated that the growing tip of the main axis which is often itself a complex of young buds dominates to a greater or less extent the whole stem. In the root system somewhat similar relations exist between the growing region of the main axis and the lateral branches. In such plants also the relation between the spatial boundaries of the individual and the development of conducting paths is clearly apparent. Various facts indicate that in vascular plants transmission of stimuli takes place more rapidly and to greater distances along the vascular bundles than through other tissues (see Fitting, '07), and some botanists have regarded the sieve vessels as the chief conducting elements. In the apical growing region of the main axis, where the tissues are embryonic and vascular bundles have not yet developed, new buds, i e , new phytoids, often arise at very short distances from each other in spite of the high rate of metabolism in this region, while farther down the stem, where the vascular bundles have differentiated, the dominance of a growing tip may extend over much greater distances and the dominance of the whole growing region at the apical end of the main axis may extend over the whole length of the stem.

The prothallia of the liverworts and ferns apparently are single plant individuals, at least during their earlier stages, and some throughout life, with a dominant growing region possessing the highest rate of metabolism and a metabolic gradient along the axis But even these prothallia in many cases show agamic reproduction after a certain stage is reached or under certain conditions.

Many botanists regard the formation of new growing tips in the vegetative life of the plant merely as growth, and reserve the term "reproduction" for the specialized forms of reproduction, such as the formation of spores, gemmae, and other reproductive bodies, including the gametes. Actually, however, each new growing tip represents a new individuation with the potentialities of a whole plant and fails to produce a whole plant only because it is organically connected with other parts. Properly speaking, then, the formation of new growing tips or buds is a reproductive

process as truly as any other more specialized kinds of reproduction
For convenience it may be distinguished from these as vegetative
reproduction.

Agamic reproduction is, then, a characteristic feature of the
vegetative life of plants. The degree of individuation is so low that
growth leads very readily to physiological isolation of parts and
new individuation, and, without doubt, also, conditions which
decrease the metabolic activity of the dominant region accomplish
the same result   Most of what is commonly called growth in plants
involves the formation of new phytoids   The new buds of each
season or active period in perennial plants are new individuals

THE VEGETATIVE LIFE OF PLANTS IN RELATION TO SENESCENCE

It is important at the outset to distinguish clearly between the
occurrence of senescence in the plant as a whole and its occurrence
in single phytoids or parts.   The vegetative propagation of plants
from cuttings, which in the case of some species—such, for example,
as the banana—has continued for hundreds of years and the
capacity of the lower plants for indefinite vegetative growth under
proper nutritive conditions demonstrate clearly enough that the
life of the plant or some part of it may continue indefinitely without
any indication of aging   On the other hand, in many plants the
length of life under natural conditions is more or less definitely
limited, though the life period may range from a few hours to
centuries in different forms   In the higher plants, particularly
in the woody forms, certain of the cells cease sooner or later to
divide, undergo specialization, show all signs of aging, and sooner
or later die, while others apparently remain young indefinitely
Must we then conclude that some plants and not others undergo
senescence? In all except the earlier stages of the life cycle the
old differentiated or dead cells usually constitute by far the larger
proportion of the plant mass, the young cells in which growth and
division occur being often but a minute fraction of the whole   Are
we then to conclude that some plants and not others, and some parts
of a plant and not others, undergo senescence and die of old age?

As regards metabolic condition, it is well known that plants
and plant organs in general show a higher rate of oxidation in

earlier stages of development, when they are physiologically
young, than in later stages Under given external conditions
the rate of oxidation in buds, for example, is higher than in
fully developed stems and leaves, and in germinating seeds it is
higher than in later stages of development. Evidently in plants,
as in animals, a decrease in rate of oxidation, a real metabolic
senescence, occurs and is accompanied by a decreasing rate of
growth and by progressive differentiation to a greater or less extent.[1] The case of the flower, which shows a very high rate of
respiration is considered in chap xiv

The metabolic changes of age proceed much more rapidly in
some parts of the plant than in others. The leaf and the stem
undergo differentiation and grow old, at least in large part, while
the growing tip and other meristematic tissues seem to remain
young indefinitely or to undergo senescence relatively slowly.

There can be no doubt that the behavior of the plant and its
parts in relation to senescence depends upon the relation between
individuation and reproduction. In general, the higher the degree
of individuation, or of physiological integration, the more definite
and continuous the process of senescence, because reproduction
is less frequent. In Part II it was shown for various animal species
that the reconstitution of a new individual from a part of a pre-
existing individual is associated with some degree of rejuvenescence
In the case of the plant similar changes undoubtedly occur when the
part concerned in the reconstitution is a differentiated part, as it
often is, but the cells chiefly concerned in reproduction in the higher
plants are commonly regarded as undifferentiated or embryonic,
i e , as physiologically young In general the degree of rejuvenescence associated with the reconstitution of a part into a new whole
depends upon the degree of individuation. In certain of the algae
and fungi the degree of individuation is so slight it is difficult to
determine whether the plant is anything more than a cell or an
aggregate of cells In such plants as these the formation of a new
individual from any part of the old doubtless involves little
change beyond nuclear or cell division, and therefore but little

[1] For references to literature concerning respiration in plants see Pfeffer, '97,
pp. 523-31, Nicolas, '09 See also Nicolas, '10.

dedifferentiation and rejuvenescence occur.   In such cases, however, the slight degree of individuation determines that reproduction shall be almost continuous during vegetative existence; consequently there is but little possibility of differentiation and senescence Under such conditions the plant as a whole may remain physiologically young for an indefinite period, simply because new individuations from parts of pre-existing individuals occur very frequently Even in those algae and fungi which consist of a single multinucleate cell, the localization and development of a new branch unquestionably brings about some degree of reconstitutional change, for it involves a local increase in the rate of growth.   It is the continued reorganization which keeps such plants from growing old under such conditions

In some of these lower plants certain parts, usually those which bear the spores, become more highly individuated than the rest of the plant and consequently undergo a greater degree of differentiation and usually undergo a more or less continuous senescence and die of old age, while the less highly individuated and so less differentiated portions may continue to live and remain young indefinitely.   Many of the fungi, and particularly the mushrooms and related forms, are cases in point   The mushroom itself is the more highly individuated spore-bearing portion of a plant whose vegetative form consists of thread-like branching hyphae, which are merely strings of like cells attached end to end   The mushroom passes through a definite course of development and differentiation, attains maturity, ceases to grow, and finally dies, but the vegetative hyphae may continue to grow indefinitely without any perceptible progressive morphological or physiological change

The course of plant evolution from the lower to the higher forms is characterized by an increasing differentiation in the vegetative plant body and a more and more definite limitation of vegetative reproduction, at least under the usual conditions, to certain parts or tissues of the plant which remain undifferentiated and physiologically young for a long time or indefinitely, while the other parts undergo differentiation, senescence, and, it may be, death.   In the mosses and ferns the regions which retain their youth and

embryonic character are more or less definitely localized as vegetative tips and certain other regions but in these forms vegetative
reproduction often occurs from other more highly differentiated
parts of the plant as well as from these regions   In the seed plants,
however, these embryonic or meristematic tissues, as they are
called, are still more definitely localized, and in the highest forms
other regions of the plant body usually take but little part in
vegetative reproduction, at least as long as the meristematic
tissues are present and active.

The continued existence of this embryonic tissue in plants at
the same time that differentiation and senescence are occurring in
other parts raises at once the question why different parts of the
plant behave differently in these respects.   While it is impossible
to give a complete answer to this question, certain facts indicate
very clearly the direction in which an answer is to be sought.

In the first place, cell division in the plant occurs chiefly in the
embryonic cells and the earlier generations of their descendants.
The susceptibility experiments on the infusoria recorded in Part II
(pp. 141-42) indicate that in those forms cell division is accompanied by some degree of rejuvenescence and in all cases cell division
is a reproductive process, and as such involves more or less rejuvenescence.   Cells which divide rapidly do not undergo any great
degree of differentiation, and cells which resume division after
udergoing differentiation first undergo a greater or less degree of
dedifferentiation.   In short, continued nuclear and cell division
is undoubtedly an important factor in maintaining cells in the
embryonic condition and continued metabolism in the presence of
nutrition and without cell division is a factor in senescence   But
cell division alone is by no means always adequate to maintain cells
in the embryonic condition.   In embryonic development many
cells apparently grow old in spite of division, and sooner or later
division becomes impossible or possible only under altered conditions.

If frequent cell division is a factor in maintaining certain plant
tissues in the embryonic condition, we must inquire why cell
division is more frequent in certain regions than in others   This
question we are unable to answer at present, since our knowledge

of the conditions determining cell division and of the conditions in different parts of the plant is very incomplete   As regards the plant, we can only say that in certain regions progressive and regressive changes balance each other more or less completely, and consequently these regions remain undifferentiated and young or undergo differentiation and senescence very slowly, while in other regions progressive changes are more nearly or quite continuous   The fact that differentiated cells may become embryonic or embryonic cells may differentiate when physiological conditions change, shows that these differences in behavior depend, not upon a fundamental difference in constitution of the cells, but upon the conditions to which they are subjected in the regions of the plant   The solution of the problem undoubtedly lies in the physiological make-up of the plant individual as a whole and the character of its metabolism.

But even in the so-called embryonic tissue of the higher plants the cells are not absolutely alike   Some degree of individuation exists, for the activities of this tissue are orderly, and a relation of dominance and subordination exists in it.   Many facts indicate the existence of an axial gradient in rate of metabolism, the region of the vegetative tip possessing the highest rate and dominating other parts.   Since this is the case, the formation of new vegetative tips, i e , of buds—a characteristic feature of the vegetative life of most of the higher plants—must involve a change of some degree and kind in the embryonic tissue.   This change is probably primarily an increase in rate of metabolism in the part concerned, but such an increase in rate is essentially a rejuvenescence in some degree.   The changes involved in these vegetative reproductions are undoubtedly slight in many cases, but nevertheless they constitute a factor in the maintenance of the embryonic condition. Each new bud formed from a part of a pre-existing plant individual involves to some extent a reconstitutional process, even though it may be merely an increase in rate and the establishment of a new axial gradient   Vegetative reproduction is then another factor concerned in retarding the progressive course of senescence and differentiation in the plant tissues chiefly concerned   Observation confirms this conclusion, for we find that the plants or the phytoids of a plant which show a low degree of individuation, and consequently frequent vegetative reproduction, are capable of continuing their vegetative activity for a long time or even indefinitely, without indications of senescence of the meristematic tissues, while the length of life is usually more or less definitely limited in plants or phytoids with infrequent or no vegetative reproduction. In various plants with subterranean stems, such as the flags and rushes, for example, the stem shows repeated vegetative reproduction, giving rise to the aerial shoots, and its length of life is apparently unlimited The aerial shoots, however, show a much higher degree of individuation with little or no vegetative reproduction, and their length of life is short

In spite of the occurrence of nuclear and cell division and vegetative reproduction, however, the vegetative tips and other meristematic tissues of many plants show indications of progressive changes. The shoots produced from later buds may differ in character from those of earlier origin, the later leaves often differ in form and structure from the earlier and the rate of growth may decrease until growth finally ceases (Diels, '06; H M. Benedict, '12, '15). The relations between vegetative growth and reproduction and the formation of tubers, bulbs, bulbilli, and other individuals or parts which contain nutritive reserves also indicate the occurrence of progressive changes, of a real life history, although Vochting ('87, '00) and others have shown that the formation of reserve-bearing structures, like other features of the life history, can be controlled experimentally by retarding or accelerating the progressive development of the plant with the aid of external conditions. There is much evidence in favor of the view that the change from vegetative reproduction to flowering is connected with advancing senescence and specialization of the meristematic tissues of the plant (see chap xiv)

The conclusion to which the various lines of evidence point is that senescence is a characteristic feature of the vegetative life of plants, but that it is not an uninterrupted, continuous process. The low degree of individuation in plants determines a high frequency of agamic reproduction, which brings about a greater or less degree of rejuvenescence and so balances more or less completely the progressive changes Undoubtedly also the character of metabolism determines a more rapid senescence with less capacity for regression in some plants than in others, and the work of Klebs and many other investigators on the effect of nutritive and other external conditions indicates that these also influence the rate of senescence and the character of differentiation

The process of differentiation of the plant cell is apparently not fundamentally different from that of the animal cell. It consists in the development of relatively stable structural features, the deposition of relatively inactive substances in the cytoplasm or on its surface, in many cases substances, such as starch, which may serve as nutrition under other conditions. The accumulation of fluid in vacuoles is also a very characteristic feature of differentiation in plant cells. In general here, as in animals, the process of differentiation involves a decrease in the proportion of the chemically active "undifferentiated" protoplasm.

THE OCCURRENCE OF DEDIFFERENTIATION AND REJUVENESCENCE IN PLANT CELLS

It was pointed out above that the formation of a new vegetative tip by the embryonic tissue of the plant must involve a new individuation and some slight degree of physiological rejuvenescence. But the occurrence of dedifferentiation, even among the higher plants, is not limited to such changes as this Cells which have clearly lost their embryonic character and have undergone more or less morphological as well as physiological change have been repeatedly observed to undergo dedifferentiation and become embryonic, both in appearance and in behavior. Experiment has demonstrated again and again that among the lower plants every cell, or almost every cell, of the plant body may be capable of giving rise to a new individual with all the capacities of the individual which develops from the egg Among the liverworts and in many of the ferns the cells of the prothallium very generally retain the capacity to give rise to new individuals, either when physically isolated by section, or when physiologically isolated by growth of the prothallium, removal of the growing tip, or other conditions, and this change in behavior in all cases undoubtedly involves a greater or less degree of rejuvenescence

Even in the seed plants new growing tips which are capable of developing into new, complete plants and producing sex cells often arise from cells which have undergone visible differentiation. In *Begonia*, for example, the formation of so-called adventitious buds from epithelial cells of the leaf has been observed, and in many other plants new individuals develop from cells which are far from being embryonic. The cells concerned in such cases lose their differentiated character and return to the embryonic condition, resume growth and division, and enter upon a new developmental cycle. The formation of meristematic, or embryonic, tissue from the parenchyma of the leaf petiole and from other differentiated tissues has also often been noted. The transformation of inflorescence into vegetative shoots has been experimentally induced by Klebs and others in various plants, and its occurrence in nature has been repeatedly observed. One case described by Winkler ('02) in a species of *Chrysanthemum* deserves brief mention. In the disk flowers the style formed the stem and the stigma gave rise to two leaves like normal upper leaves of the species. The embryo sac developed and the pollen was capable of germination. but the embryo died at an early stage. The corolla became green, the vascular system increased and branched, and stomata appeared. In this case the flower evidently underwent a partial transformation into a vegetative structure, and this change must have involved some considerable degree of dedifferentiation and rejuvenescence

In fact. the occurrence of dedifferentiation among plants has been demonstrated beyond question [1] Certainly in the plant, as in the animal, senescence is associated with specialization and differentiation of cells, and it is just as certain that dedifferentiation is accompanied by rejuvenescence. Moreover, the increased activity in growth and division of the cells concerned, as well as their

---

[1] The following references will serve as an introduction to the extensive bibliography of the subject Brefeld, '76, '77, Burns and Heddon, '06, von Faber, '08, Goebel, '08, pp 141–65, Heim, '96, Hildebrand, '10, Jost, '08, Vorlesung 26, Klebs, '03, '06a, '06b, Kohler, '07, Kreh, '09, Magnus, '06, Miehe, '05; Noll, '03, Regel, '76, Riehm, '05; Schostakewitsch, '94, Tobler, '02, '04; Vochting, '85, Winkler, '02, '07

ability to go through a new course of development and differentiation, indicates very clearly that they have become physiologically
younger, and, though I know of no observations bearing directly
upon this point, no one can doubt that when a differentiated cell
dedifferentiates into a growing tip an increase in rate of respiration
and other metabolic processes occurs.

THE RELATION OF THE DIFFERENT FORMS OF AGAMIC REPRODUCTION IN PLANTS TO THE AGE CYCLE

Most plants exhibit more than one form of agamic reproduction,
and in some species, e.g., certain mosses, several different forms
occur. But two forms of agamic reproduction are particularly
characteristic of nearly all plant species, one the vegetative form
of reproduction, often called vegetative growth, in which new vegetative individuals essentially similar to the old arise by the formation of buds, branches, etc ; the other the process of spore formation,
which usually occurs only in certain regions of the plant body and
after a period of vegetative growth. In some cases, as in the rusts,
four or five different kinds of spores are produced by a single species
The spore is in general a cell which becomes isolated from the
plant body and sooner or later gives rise to a new individual. In
some cases this isolation is physiological, in others it is physical.
In the algae and fungi, which must be considered before turning to
the higher plants, the spores usually develop into individuals like
those from which they arose, and the spore may be either a resting
or a motile stage between two vegetative generations   Spore formation in these plants is essentially a process of complete or partial
disintegration of existing individuals into cells, rather than the
addition of new individuals as the result of growth, as in vegetative
reproduction under the usual conditions. In the alga *Ulothrix*, for
example, any cell of the filamentous, unbranched plant body may
break up into zoospores (Figs. 102, 103), in the branching form
Vaucheria the terminal region of the branch separates as a multinucleate zoospore (Fig 104). Among the brown algae the spores
arise by separation into single small cells of the contents of special
organs, the sporangia (Fig 105). In the fungus *Saprolegnia* (Fig
106) the sporangium is the terminal region of the vegetative body,

while in *Mucor* (Fig. 107, *A–C*) the sporangium arises at the end of
a specialized stalk, the sporophore, which grows out of the nutritive substratum into the air, and in *Penicillium* still another type of
sporophore appears (Fig. 108). In other forms still other methods
of spore formation occur with various degrees of specialization in
the spore-forming organs, but everywhere the process consists in a

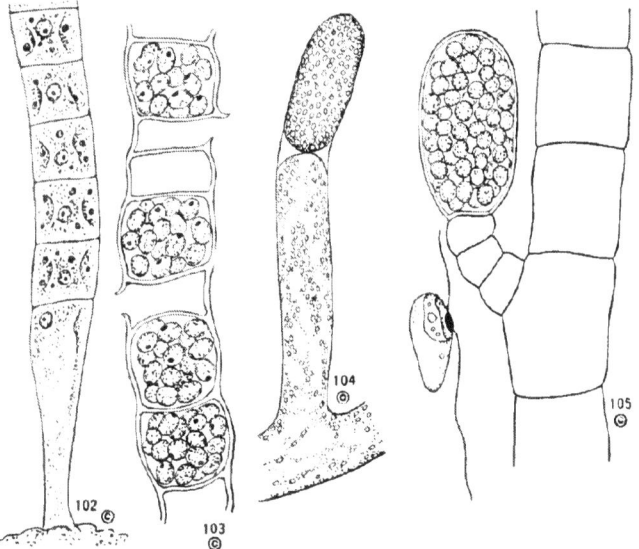

FIGS. 102–105.—Formation of spores in various algae: Figs. 102, 103, *Ulothrix;*
Fig. 104, a stage in the development of the zoöspore in *Vaucheria;* Fig. 105, a filament
of *Ectocarpus* bearing a sporangium and at the left a more highly magnified zoöspore.
From Coulter, etc., '10.

disintegration of the plant body or some part of it into independent
cells.

According to the conception of individuation presented in the
preceding chapter, return to the condition of the free-living, independent cell must mean a decrease in the physiological coherence of
the plant individual, and it might be expected to result from conditions which decrease the metabolism of the plant and so allow it,
or a part of it, to separate into its constituent units, the cell indi-

viduals. Various investigators, prominent among whom is Kleb
have investigated and analyzed the external conditions whi
determine spore formation in the algae and fungi, and the results
their work agree well with this idea.

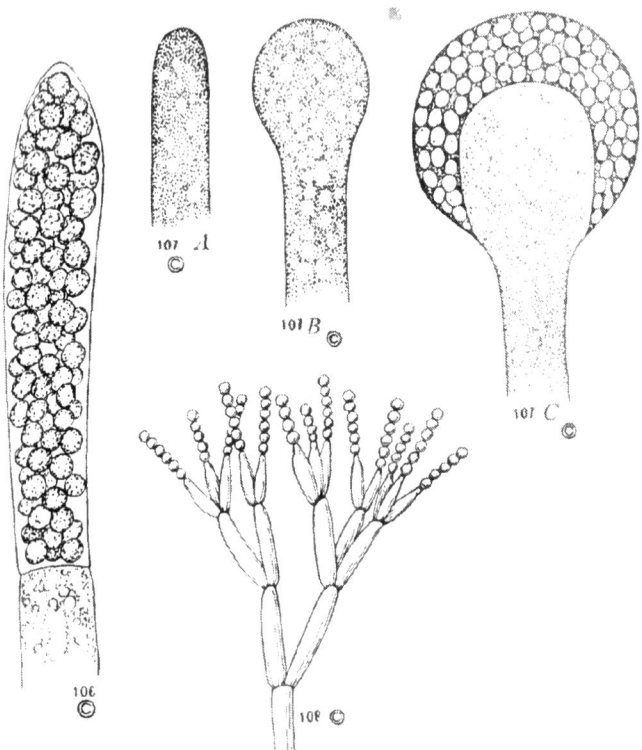

FIGS. 106–108.—Formation of spores in lower fungi: Fig. 106, a terminal cell
Saprolegnia producing zoöspores; Fig. 107, *A–C*, three stages in the development
the sporangium in *Mucor;* Fig. 108, branches of the sporophore of *Penicillium*, pr
ducing series of conidia. From Coulter, etc., '10.

While these forms in nature usually go through a more or le
definite life history in which vegetative growth or growth wit
reproduction of new vegetative phytoids occurs for a time, and
followed by the formation of spores and in many cases still late

<hr />

[1] See Klebs, '93, '96a, '96b, '98, '99, '00a, '00b, '03, '04.

by the formation of gametes, experiment has demonstrated that this life history is by no means fixed in its course. In the fungus *Saprolegnia mixta*, for example, which occurs on the bodies of dead insects in water, Klebs ('03, p. 41) has found that uninterrupted vegetative growth may occur for an indefinite period in all good nutritive solutions, provided they are kept fresh and do not undergo alteration. On the other hand, a rapid and complete transformation of the vegetative form, the mycelium, into sporangia occurs when a well-nourished mycelium is transferred from the nutritive solution to pure water. Growth and vegetative reproduction, together with continuous spore formation, occur in cultures nourished on agar-albumin in flowing water. When mycelium grown on gelatin-meat extract is transferred to water and allowed to continue its growth on dead insects, growth and vegetative reproduction are followed, first, by formation of spores, and later by gamete formation. In water containing fibrin or syntonin growth and vegetative reproduction, formation of spores and of gametes occur together on different parts of the plant. In a weak solution of haemoglobin, growth and vegetative reproduction are followed by formation of gametes and later by formation of spores

Another example is the alga *Vaucheria repens*. According to Klebs ('04, p. 497), the following conditions induce zoöspore formation: decrease of the salt-content of the medium to a point near the minimum by transference from more to less concentrated solutions, or to water; increase of moisture by transference from air to water; decrease of the oxygen content of the medium by transference from flowing to standing water; decrease of light intensity, even to darkness, lowering of temperature to near the minimum; increase of the salt-content to near the maximum

Klebs believes that external conditions produce their effects on organisms by acting upon a complex of internal conditions, and he attempts to interpret his experimental results on this basis, pointing out that many of the conditions which induce spore formation decrease or inhibit growth, i e , vegetative reproduction   In this way, as he believes, a higher concentration of organic substance is attained in the plant, and this favors spore formation and a still higher concentration, gametic reproduction. Apparently, for Klebs, there is no question either of individuation or of possible age changes involved, the reproductive changes being due primarily to the action of the external conditions.

As a matter of fact, however, these data when considered in their proper relations to individuation and the age cycle are readily interpreted and are directly in line with what we know of other forms.   Spore formation is, at least in most cases, a more specialized reproductive process than vegetative reproduction, and therefore might be expected to occur in later stages of development than the latter.   Moreover, since spore formation usually consists in the disintegration into single, independent cells of a parent body or part already formed rather than in the growth of a new individual or part, we should expect it to occur when the rate of metabolism in the plant is low as compared with the rate in vegetative growth and reproduction.   Such a low rate of metabolism may result, either from aging of the individual or part, or from the action of external conditions.   If the conclusions reached from the study of the lower animals are applicable to the algae and fungi, and the facts seem to indicate that they are, the plant under certain conditions may remain indefinitely in the vegetative condition, because the differentiation and senescence in each individual is balanced by the rejuvenescence occurring in each vegetative reproduction.   Under other conditions senescence may overbalance rejuvenescence, and the plant individuals undergo progressive development and senescence, their rate of metabolism undoubtedly decreases, and sooner or later the disintegration of the plant or parts of it into spores occurs.   The results of Klebs's experiments indicate that this condition may be induced in the plant either by lowering the rate of metabolism directly by low temperature lack of oxygen, lack of nutritive salts, etc., or by loading the cells with organic material. While it is impossible from the data at hand to furnish a complete demonstration, it appears highly probable that the effect of the various conditions used by Klebs in his experiments in inducing spore formation is either to bring about a natural senescence in the plant by the accumulation of inactive substances or to decrease its rate of metabolism so that a physiological condition like that attained in natural senescence is brought about.   In short, by controlling the rate of vegetative reproduction, the rate of metabolism, or the accumulation of inactive material, it is possible to determine whether the plant or the phytoid shall remain indefinitely in the vegetative stage and physiologically young, or whether it shall attain the physiological condition characteristic of an older plant and produce spores There are, however, certain cases which apparently cannot be accounted for in this way for example, Klebs finds that when the alga *Oedogonium* is cultivated at a low temperature a rise of a few degrees induces spore formation, but when cultivated at a higher temperature a rise in temperature has no such effect As regards this case, it is probable that the degree of individuation at the low temperature is so slight that when an increase in metabolic activity occurs with a rise in temperature the cells become independent before their activity is subordinated or controlled by the increased degree of individuation

To sum up, there is good reason to believe that algae and fungi may undergo senescence and rejuvenescence like the lower animals, and that the different forms of reproduction are characteristic of different stages in the life cycle. But since reproduction and consequently rejuvenescence are characteristic of younger as well as older stages, it is possible to control and modify the course of the life history in a great variety of ways This possibility of control does not prove that these plants have no definite life cycle it indicates merely that progressive and regressive development can be determined experimentally in the plant, as in the animal

As regards the spores themselves, there can be no doubt that extensive reconstitution and rejuvenescence occur in their formation. In the case of the motile zoospores characteristic of many forms (Figs 104, 105, 106), this is conspicuously the case, for the zoospore is a free-living, unicellular organism and bears little resemblance to the plant from which it arises. This new individuation of the zoospore from the physiologically old vegetative stage involves reconstitutional changes which result in a simpler and more primitive kind of individual than the vegetative form This change must be associated in some way with the change from the multicellular or multinucleate to the unicellular or uninucleate condition In the development of the vegetative form from the spore, reconstitutional changes are again involved, at least in the case of zoospores, which show more or less morphological differentiation, and here again some degree of rejuvenescence must occur. Bearing all the facts in mind, it is not difficult to understand how it is that, under proper conditions, spore formation may continue through an indefinite number of generations without any appreciable progressive senescence of the stock

In the mosses, ferns, and seed plants where alternation of generations occurs, the fertilized egg gives rise to the asexual generation or sporophyte which may show extensive and long-continued vegetative reproduction, but sooner or later gives rise to spores. The spore in turn gives rise to the sexual generation or gametophyte, which also may show vegetative reproduction, but which finally produces gametes; that is, sexual reproductive cells.

In the mosses and ferns spore formation is very evidently a process belonging to the later stages of development of the sporophyte and it is, as in the algae and fungi, a process of disintegration of an individual or part into independent cells   In the fern, for example, the spores are formed only when the frond has completed or largely completed its growth.   In the seed plants the gametophyte generation is so reduced that spore formation is closely connected with the formation of gametes, and there is much evidence to be considered in later chapters which indicates that gamete formation belongs to a more advanced stage of the life cycle than the various agamic processes   In these plants, as in the algae and fungi, spore formation is, then, in general a process belonging to more advanced stages than vegetative reproduction.

Among algae and fungi there is apparently complete rejuvenescence between the formation of the spore and the development of a new plant from it, for it usually gives rise to a new plant like that from which it arose, while in the plants with alternation of generations the spore gives rise to an individual of different character from that which produced it. Evidently it has become different in its developmental capacity from the egg   The simplest conception of this change is that the spore is in these forms a specialized cell which does not entirely lose its specialization in reproduction In the seed plants, where the gametophytes do not lead an independent vegetative life, but are usually so much reduced that only a few cell divisions occur between the spore and the formation of gametes, the specialization of this reproductive process is evident, but in the mosses where the sporophyte is merely a sporogonium—a spore case without an independent vegetative life—and the gametophyte is the vegetative form, it is not so clear. If, however, we consider the whole cycle from the fertilized egg of one generation to that of the next, it is at once evident that in the mosses the process of spore formation comes relatively early in this cycle, in the ferns at a more advanced stage, and in the seed plants at a still more advanced stage. In this connection it is of considerable interest to note that the amount of agamic reproduction in the gametophyte varies according to the point in the life cycle at which the gametophyte appears In the mosses, where the sporophyte shows almost no vegetative activity before spore formation, the gametophyte, which is the moss plant, usually shows extensive, often indefinite, vegetative reproduction, and in many cases various, more or less specialized, forms of agamic reproduction occur. In the ferns where the sporophyte—the fern plant—shows extensive vegetative growth and reproduction there is usually but little and in many cases no agamic reproduction in the prothallium which represents the gametophyte. And, finally, in the seed plants, where the whole vegetative life of the plant occurs in the sporophyte stage, the gametophyte does not as a rule reproduce gametophytes asexually. In other words, the earlier in the life cycle the gametophyte appears, the less its specialization and the more conspicuous its vegetative activity and reproduction.

All these facts indicate very clearly that a real life cycle with progressive development and specialization exists in the plants, but this life cycle is complicated by the occurrence of various forms of agamic reproduction, and the regressive and reconstitutional changes involved in the new individuations which occur in these reproductions may balance the progressive changes and so retard or prevent indefinitely the progressive advance of the plant in the life cycle. And since external conditions influence individuation and agamic reproduction, it is often possible to control experimentally the developmental progress of the plant within very wide limits. And, finally, there are certainly very clear indications that a general decrease in rate of metabolism, doubtless interrupted by greater or less increases in rate accompanying the various reproductions, occurs from the early vegetative stages to the stage of gamete formation.   There seems, in short, to be adequate ground for the conclusion that the life cycle of the plant is not fundamentally different from that of the animal and that senescence does occur in the plant, not only in certain cells, organs, or tissues and in the phytoids which make up most plants, but in the plant as a whole The slight degree of individuation in plants makes possible frequent reproduction, so that senescence is not a continuous or nearly continuous process, as in the higher animals, but may be interrupted repeatedly, or may even be compensated for an indefinite length of time by periodic reproduction and rejuvenescence, such as has been shown in Part II to occur in some of the lower animals.

INDIVIDUATION, AGAMIC REPRODUCTION, AND THE AGE CYCLE IN THE LOWER ANIMALS

Experimental evidence on the relation between agamic reproduction and rejuvenescence in various animals was presented in chap vi, and only certain points of more general significance remain to be considered   The occurrence of agamic reproduction in the lower animals, as in the plants, is commonly either the result of growth or decreased dominance, and often the same reproductive process may be brought about in both ways.   The variety of forms of reproduction is less than in the plant, but in various protozoa growth and division occur under the usual conditions, while under others, apparently such as decrease metabolism, the body may break up into small independent cells, which are usually known as spores.   Such fragmentations of the body may apparently result either from a physiological senescence or from a decrease in metabolic activity due to external conditions.   Fragmentation often occurs during encystment and is preceded or accompanied by complete dedifferentiation of the original individual   These cases in fact constitute some of the strongest evidence for the occurrence of dedifferentiation in animals.   Often, particularly in the sporozoa, which are parasitic and show a very low degree of individuation, fragmentation into spores follows the union of the gametes and may probably be regarded as corresponding to the period of cleavage and rejuvenescence in the embryonic development of multicellular forms

In many sponges new zooids arise as the result of growth, but under depressing conditions and probably also in advanced senescence, so far as it occurs, existing individuals may undergo more or less extensive fragmentation into cell masses known as gemmules which are capable of producing new sponge bodies   It was pointed out in chap. vi that the medusa bud of the hydroids apparently results from a decrease in dominance which is associated with a decrease in rate of metabolism, while the hydroid bud usually results from growth beyond the limits of individuation.   In certain of the bryozoa also budding occurs during growth and a partial fragmentation into reproductive bodies, the statoblasts, under depressing external conditions and apparently also in advanced physiological age.   On the other hand, in *Tubularia* (p 220), in *Planaria* (pp. 122–25), and in various other animals the same form of reproduction may result either from growth or from decrease in dominance   The evidence presented in chap. vi justifies the conclusion that the regressive and reconstitutional changes involved in all these reproductive processes bring about a greater or less degree of physiological rejuvenescence.

Reproduction, however, is not the only rejuvenating process in the lower animals.   Many forms undergo encystment or become quiescent under conditions which do not permit active life and become active again after a certain length of time, or when external conditions permit   Usually there is at least some small amount of metabolic activity during these quiescent periods, and a considerable degree of starvation and reduction may occur, as in the case of *Planaria velata* (pp. 130–33), before resumption of active life The effectiveness of reduction as a rejuvenating factor in planarians has been demonstrated in chap vii, and it certainly plays a similar rôle in many other forms.   Moreover, in some cases the increase in number of individuals or the decrease in supply of nutrition with the change of seasons or other environmental changes determines more or less regularly recurring periods of starvation during active life, and these also play a part in rejuvenescence.

And, lastly, the replacement of old by young cells in the body of the animal also delays the senescence of the organism as a whole This process occurs more or less widely in all multicellular animals, and in many of the lower forms it occurs to a very considerable extent and more or less generally throughout the body The old cells or parts die and are either cast off or resorbed and replaced by younger cells. In such cases senescence and even death are occurring at all times, but the replacement may keep pace with the aging and death of cells, so that the organism as a whole does not grow old. Conditions in these forms are somewhat similar to those in the higher plants discussed in an earlier section of this chapter, where certain parts of the plant remain embryonic and give rise more or less continuously or periodically to the various organs which undergo senescence and death. In all cases of this sort cellular reproduction is of course concerned and is unquestionably the essential factor in the maintenance of an age equilibrium or retardation of senescence in the organism as a whole.

The occurrence in animals of morphological rejuvenescence, i e , of dedifferentiation, has often been denied, but such denials are based primarily rather on theoretical considerations than upon observation There can be no doubt that dedifferentiation occurs extensively among the lower animals. The dedifferentiation of protozoan cells has already been mentioned, and concerning those cases there is no room for doubt that the morphological differentiation disappears and reappears in the same cell E Schultz ('08) and J Nusbaum ('12) have brought together many cases of dedifferentiation from the literature of the subject and have discussed their significance in a general way. It is impossible here to do more than refer very briefly to a few of the well-established instances of dedifferentiation As regards the sponges, various authors have described the occurrence of dedifferentiation of at least some of the cells of the body under different conditions, such as absence of lime salts, starvation, and dissociation of cells, and there seems to be no doubt that extensive dedifferentiation may occur in hydroids also.[1] One of the most interesting cases in the

[1] See, for example, on sponges Bidder, '95; Maas, '06, '07, '10, Masterman, '94, K. Muller, '11a, '11b, '11c, H V Wilson, '11a, on hydroids Berninger, '10, H C Muller, '13, '14, H V Wilson, 11b

latter group is that described by H. C. Muller, of the dedifferentiation after isolation and mutilation of the parts which bear the
sexual organs—the so-called gonophores—of certain hydroids into
masses of embryonic cells which give rise to stolons and so may produce new vegetative, asexual colonies   Dedifferentiation occurs
in the reduction by starvation of planarians (E. Schultz, '04).   The
parenchymal cells of *Planaria*, which play the chief part in the
formation of new tissue in regeneration, are certainly to all appearances differentiated cells and undergo dedifferentiation when they
begin their growth as new tissue.   In the tapeworm *Moniezia* the
sex cells may arise by the dedifferentiation of parenchymal cells
(see pp 331–32)   The return of old, flat ectoderm cells to the
embryonic condition has been observed by Romer ('06) in the
regeneration of bryozoa.   Krahelska ('13) has described the
dedifferentiation of the albumen gland in certain snails during
oviposition.   In the remarkable reduction of the branchial region
in isolated pieces of the ascidian *Clavellina*, which represents a
return to the condition of a bud in an early stage of development,
extensive dedifferentiation of cells certainly occurs (Driesch, '02;
E Schultz, '07).   Schaxel ('14), however, maintains that in this
case the differentiated cells are lost and the new parts arise from
undifferentiated cells which remain, but his assumption that the
cells which take part in the new development are undifferentiated
is not proved.   In the regeneration of the lens of the eye in
amphibia the cells of the iris which give rise to the new lens very
evidently undergo dedifferentiation (G Wolff, '95, Fischel, '00).

Numerous other cases of more or less complete dedifferentiation have been more or less closely observed and described and
doubtless many others still remain to be described in connection
with agamic reproduction, reconstitution, and even in the normal
life of organisms   The changes in gland cells during their cycle of
activity (pp. 189–91) and various other periodical changes also
belong in this category.   But the morphological criterion of rejuvenescence is at best unsatisfactory, for it is merely a rather unre-
liable indicator of the physiological condition of the cells.   As is
evident from the experimental study of the developmental stages
of many animals, cells may undergo considerable changes in the

direction of specialization without any characteristic morphological differentiation, and there is every reason to believe that changes in the opposite direction, if not very great, do not necessarily involve changes in the visible morphological features of the cell. Since senescence and rejuvenescence are processes which concern the dynamic activity of the cell, changes in this activity must be the chief criterion for the occurrence of age changes, although morphological changes, when they occur, may be of value as indications of the changes in activity.

SENESCENCE AS A CONDITION OF REPRODUCTION AND REJUVENESCENCE

Agamic reproduction of one kind or another unquestionably occurs in the plants and lower animals in consequence of the decrease or elimination of dominance, i e, the physiological disintegration of the individual may result in the reconstitution of new individuals. Moreover, decrease or elimination of dominance may result from decrease in rate of metabolism as well as from growth, and finally a decrease in rate of metabolism occurs in senescence It is possible, therefore, that agamic reproduction with the accompanying rejuvenescence may occur simply as the result of senescence. The fragmentation of *Planaria velata* (pp. 130–33) is undoubtedly a case of this sort, and it is probable that this relation between senescence and reproduction is very general. In fact, the formation of spores in plants and in the protozoa, of gemmules in the sponges and statoblasts in the bryozoa, and various other reproductive processes, which are not directly connected with growth, are probably very often simply the result of senescence of the individual concerned, although they may of course appear when the rate of metabolism is lowered by external conditions The formation or development of new buds in many perennial plants often results from decrease in activity of the dominant growing tip, and this decrease is probably very frequently due to senescence. The formation of buds or the development of buds already formed on the leaves of various plants may likewise result from senescence of the leaf or plant. During the earlier stages of senescence disintegration of the individual may be prevented by the development and increasing conductivity of the paths of correlation, even though increase in size occurs, but in the lower organisms where the degree of dominance is slight and conduction paths do not attain any high degree of development, the decrease in rate of metabolism in the dominant region which occurs with advancing senescence may sooner or later bring about the physiological isolation of parts of the individual, and reproduction and rejuvenescence result. Extended experimental and analytic investigation is necessary to determine how far a natural physiological senescence and how far incidental or external factors are concerned in particular cases, but it must be borne in mind that the possibility of inducing and controlling these reproductions with the aid of external conditions does not in any way prove that they may not also be induced or controlled by internal conditions quite independently of the environment

Since this relation between senescence and reproduction unquestionably exists, it is evident that in the plants and lower animals senescence must very frequently lead automatically to reproduction and rejuvenescence in at least some parts of the previously existing individual   In such cases senescence does not lead to death of the whole, and often where the individual breaks up into separate cells or fragments, death does not occur in any part.   Instead of leading inevitably to death, senescence in the lower organisms may itself be a condition of reproduction and rejuvenescence and so of indefinite continuation of life.

CONCLUSION

In the plants and lower animals the low degree of stability of the protoplasmic substratum and the consequent low degree of individuation make possible the frequent occurrence of agamic reproduction.   Since a greater or less degree of rejuvenescence is associated with such reproduction, the process of individual senescence may be more or less completely compensated in many cases and the organism may appear not to grow old and may never reach the death point   Often the decrease in metabolic rate with advancing senescence is the primary factor in bringing about physiological isolation of parts, reproduction, and rejuvenescence, and in such cases a certain degree of senescence is followed automatically by reproduction and rejuvenescence   The agamic reproductions of advanced age are often more highly specialized in character than those of earlier periods of the life history.

Senescence may be retarded or compensated in many forms by conditions which induce frequent agamic reproduction, while under other conditions senescence may be accelerated and death may occur   The relation between senescence and rejuvenescence determines whether an organism undergoes progressive senescence and passes through a definite life history or persists indefinitely in a certain physiological condition, apparently without a definite life cycle.

REFERENCES

BENEDICT, H. M
    1912.   "Senility in Meristematic Tissues," *Science*, XXXV
    1915.   "Senile Changes in the Leaves of *Vitis vulpina* and Certain Other Perennial Plants": Proc of Bot Soc. of America, *Science*, XLI.

BERNINGER, J.
    1910.   "Einwirkung von Hunger auf *Hydra*," *Zool. Anzeiger*, XXXVI.

BIDDER, G. P.
    1895.   "The Collar Cells of Heterocoela," *Quart. Jour. of Micr. Sci*, XXXVIII

BREFELD, O.
    1876.   "Die Entwicklungsgeschichte der Basidiomyceten," *Bot Zeitg*, XXXIV.
    1877.   *Botanische Untersuchungen uber Schimmelpilze*, III

BURNS, G P., and HEDDON, MARY E.
    1906   "Conditions Influencing Regeneration of Hypocotyl," *Beihefte z. Bot Centralbl.*, XIX, Abt. I.

COULTER, J. M , BARNES, C. R., and COWLES, H. C.
    1910.   A Textbook of Botany. New York.

DIELS, L
    1906   *Jugendformen und Blutenreife im Pflanzenreich*.   Berlin.

DRIESCH, H
    1902   "Studien uber das Regulationsvermogen der Organismen· VI, Die Restitutionen von *Clavellina lepadiformis*, Über ein neues harmonisch-aquipotentielles System und uber solche Systeme uberhaupt," *Arch. f Entwickelungsmech*, XIV.

FABER, F. C., VON.
    1908   "Über Verlaubung von Cacaobluten," *Berichte d. deutsch. bot. Ges.*, XXV.

FISCHEL, A

1900.   "Uber die Regeneration der Linse," *Anat Hefte*, XLIV

FITTING, H

1907   "Die Reizleitungsvorgange bei den Pflanzen," Sonderabdr aus
Ergebn. d. Physiol., Jhg. IV und V

GOEBEL, K.

1908   *Einleitung in die experimentelle Morphologie der Pflanzen.* Leipzig.

HEIM, C

1896   "Untersuchungen an Farnprothallien," *Flora*, LXXXII

HILDEBRAND, F.

1910   "Umanderung einer Blutenknospe in einen vegetativen Spross
bei einem Phyllocactus," *Berichte d. deutsch. bot Ges*, XXVIII.

JOST, L.

1908   *Vorlesungen uber Pflanzenphysiologie.* II. Auflage. Jena.

KLEBS, G.

1893.   "Uber den Einfluss des Lichtes auf die Fortpflanzung der Gewachse," *Biol. Centralbl*, XIII.

1896*a*. *Die Bedingungen der Fortpflanzung bei einigen Algen und Pilzen.*
Jena

1896*b* *Uber die Fortpflanzungsphysiologie der niederen Organismen.* Jena

1898   "Zur Physiologie der Fortpflanzung einiger Pilze I, *Sporodinia
grandis*," *Jahrbucher f wiss Bot*. XXXII

1899.   "Zur Physiologie, etc. II, *Saprolegnia mixta*," *Jahrbucher f. wiss.
Bot*, XXXIII

1900*a*. "Zur Physiologie, etc : III, Allgemeine Betrachtungen," *Jahrbucher f wiss Bot.*, XXXV.

1900*b*. "Einige Ergebnisse der Fortpflanzungsphysiologie," *Berichte d.
deutsche. bot Ges*, XVIII

1903.   *Willkurliche Entwicklungsanderungen bei Pflanzen.* Jena.

1904   "Uber Probleme der Entwicklung *Biol. Centralbl*, XXIV.

1906*a*. *Uber kunstliche Metamorphosen* Stuttgart.

1906*b*. "Über Variation der Bluten," *Jahrbucher f. wiss Bot*, XLII.

KOHLER, P.

1907.   "Beitrage zur Kenntnis der Reproduktions- und Regenerations-
vorgänge bei Pilzen, etc ," *Flora*, XCVII.

KRAHELSKA, MARIE

1913.   "Drüsenstudien. Histologischer Bau der Schneckeneiweissdruse
und die in ihm durch Einfluss des Hungers, der funktionellen
Erschopfung und der Winterruhe hervorgerufenen Veranderungen," *Arch. f. Zellforsch.*, IX.

KREH, W

1909   "Über die Regeneration der Lebermoose," *Nova Acta; Abh. d.
Kais. Leop. Carol deutschen Akad. d. Naturforscher*, XC

MAAS, O.
    1906. "Über die Einwirking karbonatfreier Salzlosungen auf erwachsene
        Kalkschwamme und auf Entwicklungsstadien derselben," *Arch.
        f Entwickelungsmech.*, XXII.
    1907 "Über die Wirkung des Hungers und Kalkentziehung bei Kalk-
        schwammen und anderen kalkausscheidenden Organismen."
        Sitzungsber d Gesell. f. Morphol u Physiol. Munchen.
    1910 "Über Involutionserscheinungen bei Schwammen und ihre Bedeu-
        tung fur die Auffassung des Spongienkörpers," *Festschr. z 60
        Geburtstag R. Hertwigs*, Bd III.

MAGNUS, W.
    1906. "Über Formbildung der Hutpilze," *Arch f. Biontologie*, I

MASTERMAN, A. J.
    1894. "On the Nutritive and Excretory Processes in Porifera," *Ann
        and Mag. of Nat Hist.*, (6), XIII

MIEHE, H.
    1905. "Waschstum, Regeneration und Polaritat isolierter Zellen,"
        Berichte d. deutsch bot. Ges., XXIII.

MULLER, H C
    1913. "Die Regeneration der Gonophore bei den Hydroiden und an-
        schliessende biologische Beobachtungen I, Athecata," *Arch f
        Entwickelungsmech*, XXXVII.
    1914. "Die Regeneration, etc.: II, Thecata," *Arch f. Entwickelungs-
        mech*, XXXVIII.

MÜLLER, K
    1911a "Beobachtungen uber Reduktionsvorgänge bei Spongilliden,"
        Zool Anzeiger, XXXVII
    1911b. "Das Regenerationsvermogen der Susswasserschwamme, insbeson-
        dere Untersuchungen uber die bei ihnen vorkommende Regenera-
        tion nach Dissociation und Reunition,".*Irch. f. Entwickelungsmech*,
        XXXII.
    1911c "Reduktionserscheinungen bei Susswasserschwammen," *Irch. f.
        Entwickelungsmech.*, XXXII

NICOLAS, G
    1909. "Recherches sur la respiration des organes végétatifs des plantes
        vasculaires," *Ann. des sci. nat Bot*, (9), X.
    1910. "Sur variations de la respiration des végétaux avec l'age," *Bull.
        Soc hist nat. Afrique du Nord*

NOLL, F
    1903. "Beobachtungen und Betrachtungen uber embryonale Substanz,"
        Biol. Centralbl., XXIII.

NUSBAUM, J.
  1912. "Die entwicklungsmechanisch-metaplastischen Potenzen der tieri-
         schen Gewebe," *Vortr. und Aufs. u. Entwickelungsmech.*, XVII.
PFEFFER, W.
  1897. *Pflanzenphysiologie.* II Auflage. I. Bd.
REGEL, F.
  1876. "Die Vermehrung der Begoniaceen aus ihren Blattern," *Jen
         Zeitschr. f. Naturwissenschaften*, X.
RIEHM, E.
  1905. "Beobachtungen an isolierten Blattern," *Zeitschr. f. Naturwis-
         senchaften*, LXXVII.
RÖMER, O.
  1906. "Untersuchungen uber die Knospung, Degeneration und Regenera-
         tion von einigen marinen entoprokten Bryozoen," *Zeitschr f wiss.
         Zool*, LXXXIV
SCHAXEL, J.
  1914   "Reduktion und Wiederauffrischung," *Verhandlungen d deutsch.
         zool. Gesell.*
SCHOSTAKEWITSCH, W.
  1894. "Über die Reproduktions- und Regenerationserscheinungen bei den
         Lebermoosen," *Flora*, LXXIX.
SCHULTZ, E
  1904   "Über Reduktionen: I, Über Hungererscheinungen bei *Planaria
         lactea*," *Arch f. Entwickelungsmech*, XVIII.
  1907   "Über Reduktionen: III, Die Reduktion und Regeneration des
         abgeschnittenen Kiemenkorbes von *Clavellina lepadiformis*,"
         Arch f. Entwickelungsmech, XXIV.
  1908. "Über umkehrbare Entwickelungsprozesse und ihre Bedeutung
         fur eine Theorie der Vererbung," *Vortr. und Aufs. u. Entwickelungs-
         mech*, IV.
TOBLER, F.
  1902. "Zerfall und Reproduktionsvermögen des Thallus einer Rhodo-
         melaceae," *Berichte d. deutsch bot Ges*, XX.
  1904. "Über Eigenwachstum der Zelle und Pflanzenform," *Jahrbucher
         f. wiss Bot*, XXXIX
VOCHTING, H
  1885. "Über die Regeneration der Marchantieen," *Jahrbucher f wiss.
         Bot.*, XVI.
  1887   "Über die Bildung der Knollen," *Bibliotheca bot.*, H 4
  1900   "Zur Physiologie der Knollengewachse," *Jahrbucher f. wiss. Bot.*,
         XXXIV.

WILSON, H V
    1911a "Development of Sponges from Dissociated Tissue Cells," *Bull of the Bureau of Fisheries*, XXX
    1911b. "On the Behavior of Dissociated Cells in the Hydroids, Alcyonaria and *Asterias*," *Jour. of Exp. Zool.*, XI

WINKLER, H
    1902. "Über die nachtragliche Umwandlung von Bluthenblattern und Narben in Laubblatter," *Berichte d deutsch. bot. Ges* , XX
    1907 "Über die Umwandlung des Blattstiels zum Stengel," *Jahrbucher f. wiss. Bot* , XLV.

WOLFF, G.
    1895 "Entwickelungsphysiologische Studien: I, Regeneration der Urodelenlinse," *Arch. f. Entwickelungsmech* , I

CHAPTER XI

SENESCENCE IN THE HIGHER ANIMALS AND MAN

The problem of senescence in man and the higher animals has very naturally claimed the attention of the anatomist, the physiologist, the investigator along medical lines, and the zoologist, and for the layman also it has always possessed a vital interest quite different from that which attaches to many scientific problems. Man's interest in the problem of his own senescence, old age, and death undoubtedly dates from the time when he first began to think and ask himself questions concerning himself From ancient times to the present the problem has been discussed again and again, and from the most various points of view. It has always been an attractive field for speculation, but a large volume of scientific data bearing upon one aspect or another of it has accumulated A considerable portion of the literature of the subject deals with the problem from the point of view of the physician and medical investigator rather than that of the general zoologist or physiologist, and of course the data are very largely descriptive and statistical, rather than experimental and analytic.

It is neither possible nor necessary at this time to attempt any extended review and critique of the literature. My purpose is merely to analyze and interpret the more important facts from the point of view attained through study of the lower animals, and to show how the age cycle in man and the higher animals, so far as it differs from that in the lower organisms, is the necessary and inevitable result of the course of evolution.

INDIVIDUATION AND REPRODUCTION IN THE HIGHER FORMS IN RELATION TO THE AGE CYCLE

The increase in the degree of individuation or physiological integration of the individual, which is a conspicuous feature of evolution, is evident in the higher animals and man in the increasing co-ordination and interrelation of parts, both dynamically and chemically, and in the greater structural and functional specialization and differentiation. The problem of the nature of this change

and the factors concerned in it is of course the problem of the evolution of the individual, but only certain aspects of this problem
need consideration here

The evolution of the individual is evidently closely associated
with an increasing functional and structural stability of protoplasm.
In the higher forms a cell or a group of cells, once started along a
certain course of development, reacts less readily than in the lower
organisms to altered conditions by regression and change in the
course of development.   In the adult vertebrates the capacity for
regression is in most cases so narrowly limited that the cells of one
tissue are under any known conditions incapable of giving rise to
other tissues.   In other words, the ability of the cells, so conspicuous in the lower organisms, to react to altered conditions by a change
in activity which brings about the breakdown and elimination of
previously accumulated structural substance is very slight in the
higher animals   From this point of view evolution appears as a
change from less stable to more stable dynamic equilibrium, in the
course of which the morphogenetic and functional behavior of the
organism has become less directly dependent on external and more
dependent on internal conditions.   This increase in structural and
functional stability results in a greater degree of continuity in
progressive development and so in a greater specialization of parts
and a greater differentiation of structural mechanisms with definite
functions, which in turn provide a basis for a more varied and
intimate correlation of parts and so for a wider range and greater
delicacy of functional adjustment.

Among these changes the most important for the integration of
the individual are the functional and structural evolution of the
nervous system.   The high metabolic rate in the cells of the central nervous system undoubtedly determines that the accumulation
and transformation of substance in the structural substratum
which bring about senescence occur less rapidly here than in other
tissues; because of its high rate of metabolic flow, the nerve cell
deposits structural sediment relatively slowly.   This is particularly
true after the stage of specialized functional activity is attained,
for then stimulation through the sense-organs and other parts of
the body plays a very important part in maintaining the nerve

cell at a very high metabolic level. Consequently the degree of dominance and of individuation may increase up to a certain point as development proceeds. Moreover, the increasing differentiation of the nerve fibers determines a more effective conduction of impulses, and the increasing centralization of the nervous system and complexity of nervous correlation results in a greatly increased unity and co-ordination of the parts of the individual. It was pointed out in chap. ix that the decrement in the conduction of impulses in the nerves of the higher animals is scarcely appreciable within the limits of the individual body. This means that in the adult the limit of dominance, the physiological limit of individuation, is far beyond the actual size attained by the individual Growth in these forms is limited by progressive differentiation, consequently the final size of the individual remains far below the limit of dominance in the differentiated nervous system, and the physiological isolation of parts so frequent among the plants and lower animals does not occur under ordinary conditions in the higher animals after the functional capacity of the nervous system has fully developed.

For the occurrence of agamic reproduction in differentiated organisms the physiological or physical isolation of a part and capacity of the part to react to isolation by regression and reconstitution are necessary   These conditions are not present in the later stages of development of the higher animals, but isolation of parts does occur to a limited extent in early stages of development before the cells have undergone appreciable differentiation and before the individual has attained the degree of integration characteristic of later stages. Consequently agamic reproduction in these forms is limited to these stages   In a few species polyembryony occurs as a normal feature of development, the egg undergoing separation during cleavage or later embryonic stages into two or more individuals   In certain parasitic insects, for example, individuation is apparently almost entirely absent during early stages and, instead of developing in an orderly way as a single embryo, the eggs as they divide separate repeatedly into cells or cell groups, each of which finally gives rise to an embryo (P Marchal, '04; Silvestri, '06).   In these cases a single egg may give rise to a large number of individuals.   In the nine-banded armadillo the embryo begins development as a single embryo, but later undergoes reconstitution into four embryos by a process of budding (Patterson, '13). In other species of armadillo a similar process of embryonic reproduction undoubtedly occurs.   The cases of duplicate twins and various forms of double monsters are probably also cases of embryonic reproduction from a single egg (Wilder, '04), but it is not certainly known at what stage the reproduction occurs.

In addition to the occasional occurrence of polyembryony the process known as segmentation occurs as a characteristic feature of development in all the higher animals, both invertebrates and vertebrates.   Segmentation, however, is rather a repeated individuation of parts from embryonic tissue than a reproduction from differentiated cells, and does not therefore involve any considerable regression and reconstitution   The segment-individuals which arise in succession as morphogenesis proceeds posteriorly along the axis (see Figs. 70, 197, 198) never complete development to whole animals, but remain as segments subordinate to the dominating head-region.   Aside from these cases of polyembryony and repetitive formation of segments, agamic reproduction plays no part in the normal life history of the higher animals, and it is evident that these reproductions, since they occur so early in development, can have but little significance in bringing about rejuvenescence or retarding the progressive course of senescence.

A most important consequence of the stability of structure and the absence of agamic reproduction in these animals is the greater continuity of progressive development and senescence   In the lower forms progressive development may be interrupted repeatedly, or even periodically completely compensated, by agamic reproduction of one kind or another with its accompanying rejuvenescence   Where such reproduction is absent the regressive changes may occur to some extent in tissue regeneration, in the periodic elimination of previously accumulated material in gland cells (see pp. 189–91), or during starvation, and under certain other conditions which bring about excessive structural breakdown, but such changes are either narrowly localized and without appreciable effect upon the body as a whole, or they are so slight that it is a question whether they can properly be called rejuvenescence, or else they bring about death before any great degree of rejuvenescence occurs, so that in such animals life after the early embryonic stages is practically a continuous progression and senescence. Such a continuous progressive development and senescence without counterbalancing regression and rejuvenescence must inevitably and necessarily terminate sooner or later in death in consequence of decrease in rate of metabolism. From this point of view, then, the increasing continuity of senescence and the appearance of death as a natural termination of development in the course of evolution from the lower to the higher animals are to a large degree the consequence of the increasing fixity or stability of the structural substratum of the organism which determines on the one hand the increasing degree of individuation and on the other the limitation of regression and reproduction

But in the course of this life history which ends in death, sexual differentiation appears, and at a certain stage of development the individuals of each sex or the organs of each sex in a hermaphroditic individual give rise to the gametes which are highly specialized, sexually differentiated cells, the egg and the spermatozoon   These cells are cast off from the body which produced them like other cells which have completed their developmental history and grown old, and in most cases they do not react to the isolation by regression, rejuvenescence, and reconstitution of a new individual, but sooner or later die, unless union between two gametes of opposite sexes, that is, fertilization, occurs   This union, when it does occur, initiates in some way the process of regression and rejuvenescence in the resulting cell, the zygote, and the reconstitution of a new individual, or what we call embryonic development, occurs   The gametes are the only cells in the higher animals which undergo complete rejuvenescence and so escape death   This conception of gametic reproduction will be considered more at length in Part IV.

THE PROCESS OF SENESCENCE IN THE HIGHER FORMS

The process of senescence in man and the higher animals is not widely different in its general features from the age changes which occur in the lower forms when agamic reproduction is absent. The rate of metabolism and the rate of growth decrease, the water-content of the body likewise decreases, and the tissues become denser. But the condition known as old age or senility accompanied by atrophy of tissues, which is well marked in man and has also been observed in various mammals, is either less clearly defined in the lower forms or else is not usually reached because advancing senescence induces reproduction and rejuvenescence.

Because of the absence of agamic reproduction and the limited capacity for regression and reduction in these forms, they constitute much less favorable material than the lower forms for study and analysis of age processes, and theories of senescence based only or chiefly on data obtained from the higher forms have in most cases but little general biological value   Much of the literature of the subject belongs primarily to the medical field and throws little light upon the general biological problem of senescence, but various attempts have been made to formulate general theories of senescence from the study of the higher animals and man alone [1]

In the following sections of this chapter the chief characteristics of senescence in the higher forms are briefly considered and the bearing of some of the recent experimental work upon the problem is discussed.

THE RATE OF METABOLISM

Most authorities agree that the rate of metabolism in man and mammals, so far as determined, undergoes in general a decrease with advancing age [2]   Rubner has attempted to show that in warm-blooded animals the rate of metabolism per unit of surface of the

---

[1] The following references are selected from the more recent literature dealing primarily with senescence and old age in man   Bilancioni, '11, with bibliography, Demange, '86, Friedmann, '02, Lorand, '11, with bibliography, Metchnikoff, '03, '10, Ribbert, '08, Rubner, '08   Recent more general considerations of the problem of senescence, but concerned chiefly with man and the higher animals, are Dastre, '03, Muhlmann, '00, '10, Minot, '08, '13

[2] The article by Magnus-Levy on "Metabolism in Old Age" with bibliography in the Anglo-American issue of von Noorden's *Metabolism and Practical Medicine* (1907), is a valuable general survey of our knowledge on the subject   See also Muhlmann, '00 (p 164)   Among special papers dealing with the question of metabolic changes in relation to age in man and mammals may be mentioned V V and V M Hill, 13, von Hosslin, '88, Kovesi, '01, Magnus-Levy and Falk, '90, Rubner, '83, '85, '08, '09, Sonden and Tigerstedt, '95, Speck, '89

body is constant irrespective of age Table V (Rubner, '85) gives
the rate of metabolism in man at different ages, measured in terms
of heat production in calories for periods of twenty-four hours,
and also the heat production per kilogram of body-weight and per
square meter of body-surface

TABLE V

Weight of Persons in Experiment in Kilograms	Calories in 24 Hrs Minus Heat of Combustion of Feces	Calories per Kilo in 24 Hrs	Body-Surface in Square Centimeters	Calories per Square Meter of Body-Surface
Children 4 03 .	368	91 3	3,013	1,221
" 11 8 .	966	81 5	7,191	1,343
" 16 4 .	1,213	73 9	7,681	1,579
" 23 7	1,411	59 5	10,156	1,389
" 30 9	1,784	57 7	12,122	1,472
" 40 4 .	2,106	52 1	14,491	1,452
Man during medium labor 67	2,843	42 4	20,305	1 399

It is evident from this table that the heat production per square
meter of surface does show a considerable degree of constancy in
the individuals of different sizes and weights. In various other
papers Rubner has presented additional evidence for his view that
the rate of metabolism per unit of body-surface remains essentially
the same throughout life According to Rubner then the rate of
metabolism is in some way regulated by the relative amount of
body-surface, i.e , the loss of heat determines the heat production,
and since the surface increases less rapidly than the volume or
weight of the body the rate of metabolism per unit of weight must
decrease, as the third column of Table V shows.

This view has not found general acceptance. Not only has the
method of measuring body-surface been criticized, but it has been
pointed out that during later life in man the rate of metabolism
and therefore of heat production certainly decreases progressively
while the body-surface remains practically unaltered According
to Magnus-Levy the minimum metabolism in old age may be as
low as 20 per cent of the normal, and various authors have shown
that the daily metabolic exchange also decreases. Hill has recently
shown also that the ratio of heat production to body-surface is not
constant in rats of different size In small individuals it is as high

as one hundred and forty calories; in medium-sized, ninety-nine calories per square centimeter of body-surface In other words, the rate of metabolism is determined by age, rather than by surface

According to the data compiled by Magnus-Levy from various authors, the amount of proteid necessary to keep old persons in health is less than that necessary in early life After a certain time old persons in general take less food than is necessary to maintain their weight, and a gradual loss of weight occurs which varies in rate and amount according to various conditions. Moreover, the whole course of the life history from youth to old age with its decrease in bodily activity and in rate of growth, and its advancing differentiation and accumulation of structural substance points very clearly to a decreasing rate of metabolism per unit of weight. It may also be noted that the process of chemical differentiation of the brain of the white rat during growth indicates that the rate of metabolism is decreasing during this period (W. and M. L. Koch, '13), and Dr. S. Tashiro kindly permits the statement from unpublished data that in the horseshoe crab, *Limulus polyphemus*, the production of carbon dioxide per unit of weight in the nervous system decreases as the weight of the nervous system increases; apparently, the larger and older the animal, the lower the rate of carbon-dioxide production in the nervous system.

THE RATE OF GROWTH

The rate of growth also shows, in general, a decrease from early stages of development onward, although in many cases periodic or occasional increases in rate of greater or less magnitude occur. The decrease in the rate of growth during development in man and the higher vertebrates has been demonstrated beyond all question from a great variety of data, and its significance for the problem of senescence has been so ably presented by various authors[1] that only a brief consideration is necessary at this time. It must be remembered that, as Minot ('91) pointed out, absolute increments of weight, volume, length, or any other component of growth during equal successive periods are not measures of the rate of growth, for

[1] See particularly Donaldson, '95, the chapters on growth, Minot, '91, '08, chap iii, "The Rate of Growth"; Muhlmann, '00.

during each period the weight or other growth component of the body increases. The rate of growth is measured by the proportional or percentage increments in given periods, consequently the rate of growth may remain constant or may even decrease, while the absolute increments of growth become successively larger. In

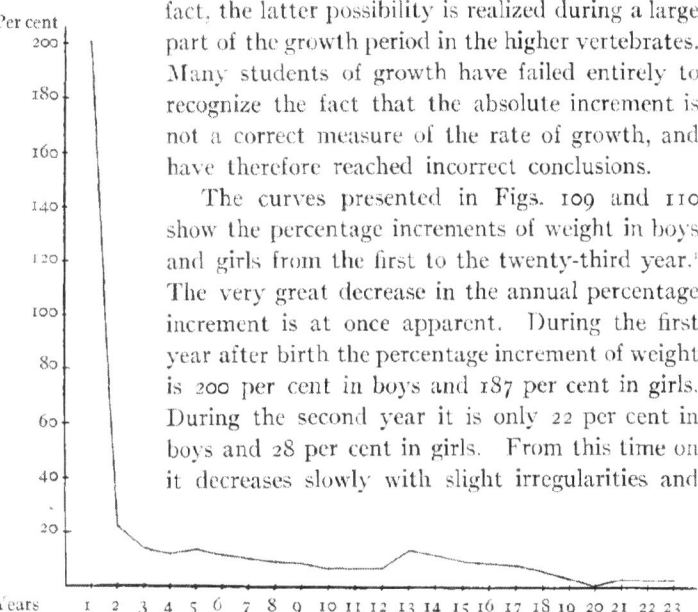

fact, the latter possibility is realized during a large part of the growth period in the higher vertebrates. Many students of growth have failed entirely to recognize the fact that the absolute increment is not a correct measure of the rate of growth, and have therefore reached incorrect conclusions.

The curves presented in Figs. 109 and 110 show the percentage increments of weight in boys and girls from the first to the twenty-third year.[1] The very great decrease in the annual percentage increment is at once apparent. During the first year after birth the percentage increment of weight is 200 per cent in boys and 187 per cent in girls. During the second year it is only 22 per cent in boys and 28 per cent in girls. From this time on it decreases slowly with slight irregularities and

FIG. 109.—Curve showing the decrease in the rate of growth in boys from the first to the twenty-third year: each vertical interval indicated on the axis of ordinates represents 20 per cent increment in weight, each horizontal interval on the axis of abscissae one year. Fom Mühlmann's tables (Mühlmann, '00) calculated from Quetelet's data.

with a distinct but slight increase at the age of puberty, after which it falls again. Various other data from different sources, including statistics on the increment of body-length, monthly increments of weight during the first year, decrease in weight during later life, etc., all show that in man the rate of growth decreases, and that

[1] The curves are based on the percentage increments determined by Mühlmann ('00) from the statistics in Quetelet's L'Anthropométrie (1835 and 1840).

as age advances growth sooner or later gives place to reduction. Data from the population of England[1] give essentially the same results. Minot ('08) also gives data and curves from his own investigations of the growth of guinea-pigs, rabbits, and chicks which likewise show that the rate of growth decreases very greatly, particularly during the early part of postembryonic life. Figs. 111 and 112 are curves from Minot's data showing the average daily percentage increments in weight of male and female rabbits beginning three days after birth. The abscissae represent number of days after birth; the ordinates, percentages. Here again it is evident that the rate of growth decreases with a few interruptions, at first very rapidly and later more slowly. According to Donaldson ('06) the curve of growth of the white rat is very similar to that of man, except that the length of the growth-period is much shorter. If the decrease in the rate of growth is in any degree a measure of the rate of senescence—and

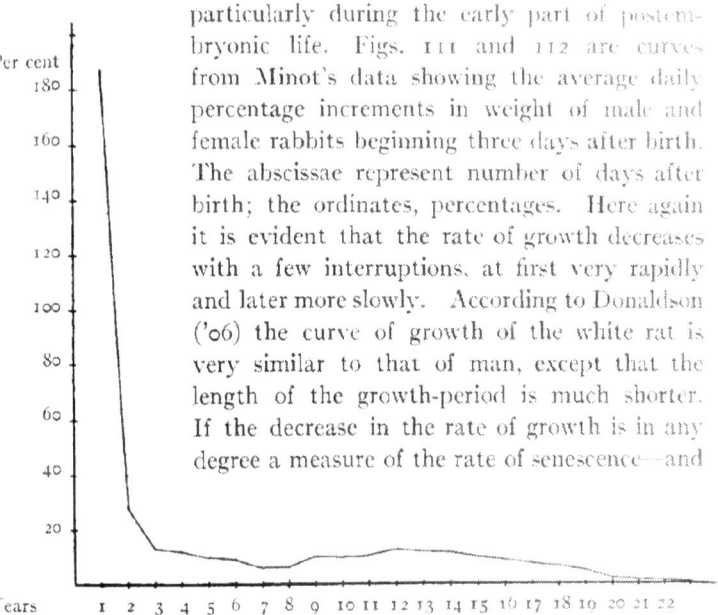

Fig. 110—Curve showing the decrease in the rate of growth in girls from the first to the twenty-third year: similar to Fig. 109. From Mühlmann's tables (Mühlmann, '00), calculated from Quetelet's data.

there can be little doubt that it is one of the features of senescence —Minot is entirely correct in asserting that the rate of senescence is highest in youth and lowest in advanced life.

In most vertebrates, as well as in many invertebrates, the final size of the individual is subject to relatively slight variation, and the amount of growth during development is within certain limits

[1] Figs. 38 and 39 and Tables II and III in Minot's *Age, Growth and Death* give these statistics in graphic and tabular form as revised by Donaldson from Robert's *Manual of Anthropometry* (1878).

a fixed quantity. Among the fishes, amphibia, and reptiles there are, however, some forms in which growth apparently continues during at least most of the life of the animal, although it is very slow in later stages. Growth is apparently periodic rather than continuous in all these cases, and its continuance throughout life or up to a late stage is probably due to the fact that these animals undergo partial rejuvenescence from time to time during periods of quiescence or starvation, a point which is discussed below (pp. 299–300). That the fundamental laws of growth are essentially the same throughout the organic world there is every reason to believe. Everywhere apparently the rate of growth is high in the young organism, or in the young cells and tissues of the organism, and decreases as development proceeds and the rate of metabolism falls. With adequate nutrition and under external conditions which permit growth, the rate of growth appears to be in a general way dependent upon the

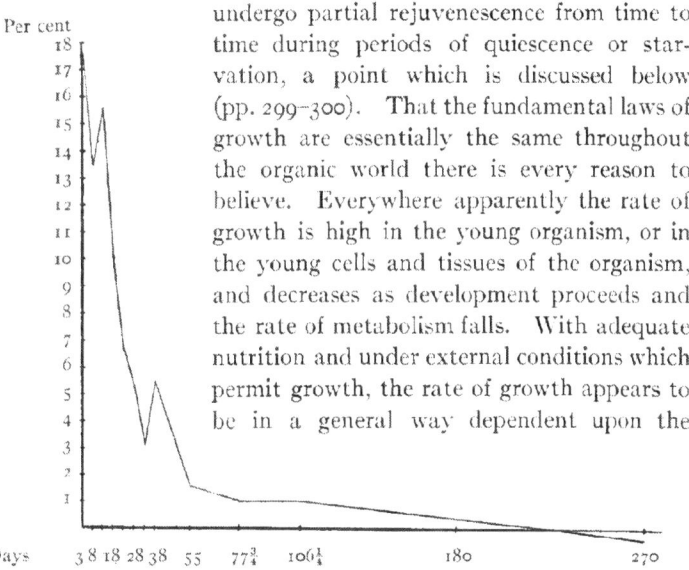

FIG. 111.—Curve showing the decrease in rate of growth in male rabbits from 3 to 270 days after birth; each vertical interval indicated on the axis of ordinates represents 1 per cent increment in weight and each horizontal interval on the axis of abscissae the length of time between successive weighings; during the first 38 days after birth weighings were made every 5 days, after that at increasingly longer intervals. From Minot's tables (Minot, '08).

rate of metabolism. Discussion of the conception of growth as an autocatalytic reaction which undergoes acceleration in rate to a maximum is postponed to chap. xvi.

NUTRITION, GROWTH, AND SENESCENCE

The advance during the last ten years in our knowledge of the chemical constitution of the proteid molecule, in which the work of

Kossel, E. Fischer, and Abderhalden and their students has played a very important part, has opened up new fields of investigation. It is now possible to attack the problem of nutrition and its relation to physiological condition, maintenance, development, and growth, at least in the higher animals, with more exact and more scientific methods than heretofore. Since we have become familiar with the nature of the constituent substances (*Bausteine*, i.e., building stones), the amino-acids and certain other substances, which go to make up the proteid molecule, and know more or less exactly which of these substances are present and in what proportions in various proteids, we are able by feeding animals with different proteins or with one or another of the constituent substances to learn something of the capacities of the animal for building up its own specific proteid molecules and of the relations of each of the various nutritive substances

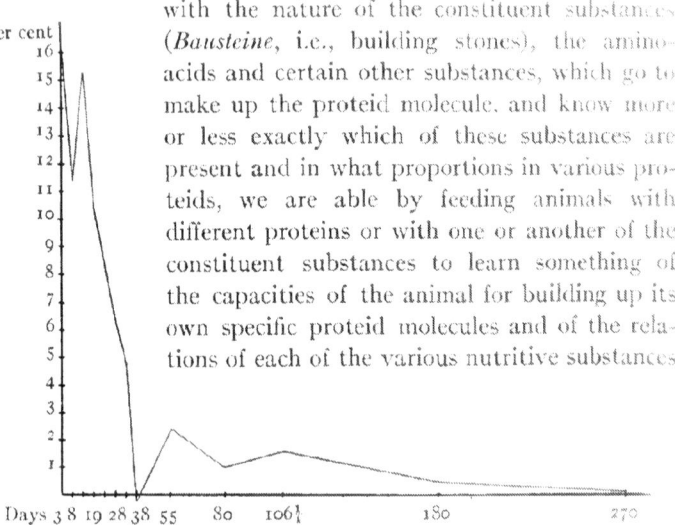

FIG. 112.—Curve showing the decrease in rate of growth in female rabbits from 3 to 270 days after birth: the intervals indicated are the same as in Fig. 111. From Minot's tables (Minot, '08).

to its various activities. Many difficulties still exist in connection with these investigations: the methods of isolating the various substances in pure form for feeding are in many cases far from satisfactory, and it is often difficult to devise a food from the isolated substances which the animal will eat in quantities sufficient to supply the necessary energy. Moreover, the complexity of metabolism and the impossibility of following the various steps within the organism are serious obstacles. Notwithstanding all these difficulties there can be no doubt that this method of investigation will throw light on various features of life heretofore obscure. Any extended discussion of the results already attained in this field is quite beyond the present purpose, and I do not regard myself as qualified to undertake it, but certain points which bear more or less directly upon the problem of senescence demand some consideration

In extensive and carefully controlled feeding experiments with white rats, Osborne and Mendel[1] have been able to show that certain proteins—gliadin from wheat and rye, hordein from barley—are adequate for maintenance of weight and good nutritive condition, but not, or only to a slight degree, for growth under the usual conditions. But after male and female animals had been fed during some five months with gliadin as the only protein, they were mated, and the female gave birth to four normal young which showed normal growth as long as nourished on the milk of the mother, and only later when placed on the gliadin diet showed retarded growth. During gestation there must have been somewhere a synthesis of the specific body-proteins in sufficient quantity to permit the normal embryonic development and growth of the young. The ability of the body to synthesize from a certain diet the substances necessary for growth evidently differs under different physiological conditions McCollum has concluded on the basis of his experiments that "the processes of replacing nitrogen degraded in cellular metabolism are not of the same character as the processes of growth," and suggests further that cellular katabolism and repair do not involve the destruction and reconstruction of an entire protein molecule. Growth, of course, so far as it involves increase in amount of proteid substances, must involve the construction of new molecules

In an earlier chapter it was suggested that growth is fundamentally the accumulation of substances which cannot readily leave the cell without change of constitution and which under the usual conditions are not readily or rapidly changed so as to become eliminable. If this conception is correct, the further possibility suggests itself that tissue breakdown and repair, under ordinary conditions, in the higher animals, may consist largely or wholly, on

---

[1] Osborne and Mendel, '11a, '11b, '12a, '12b, '12c, '13, '14; Mendel, '14 See also Hopkins. '12, McCollum, '11, Ruth Wheeler, '13 Osborne and Mendel give numerous references to the literature of the subject

the one hand, of the separation and breakdown of certain constituent chemical groups, which are less firmly attached to the molecule or less stable than other parts which remain as a more stable
nucleus, and, on the other, of the replacement of the lost parts of
the molecule from nutritive substances In actual protoplasmic
growth, however, the whole molecule, including the more as well
as the less stable portions, must be built up out of the *Bausteine*, or
in some other way. Consequently some proteins whose constituent
substances can supply the losses due to tissue breakdown may not
contain in sufficient quantity or not at all certain components
necessary for the building up of new molecules, but under exceptional conditions, as in the gestation period in Osborne and Mendel's
rats, the organism may be able to synthesize these molecules in
other ways. The general relation between the rate of growth and
the rate of metabolism suggests that the synthesis of the more
stable molecules or molecular groups occurs more readily with a
high than with a low rate of metabolic reaction, and this suggestion
is also in accord with the fact that growth, morphogenesis, and
differentiation occur chiefly in the earlier stages of the life history.

The rats fed on gliadin with maintenance of weight but little or
no growth retain their capacity for growth for at least several
months and, when placed on a mixed diet, or one containing adequate proteins, resume growth at the normal rate. But the experiments do not as yet show whether they will retain indefinitely the
capacity for growth Besides remaining young as regards growth
capacity, these animals also retain the general appearance of
growing animals of the same size. Apparently, progressive development and with it senescence have been inhibited or greatly retarded
Nevertheless, after long periods of such feeding the nervous system
shows the water-content characteristic of old animals and the possibility cannot be ignored that, even in the absence of growth,
progressive changes in the direction of greater stability of the
protoplasmic substratum may have occurred.

The results of experiments on mammals with a diet which is
adequate qualitatively, but sufficient in quantity only for maintenance and not for growth, are quite different from those of
Osborne and Mendel. Waters ('08, '09) found that underfed

cattle might remain for a long period at a constant body-weight but at the same time undergo an increase in height and a decrease in the amount of fat. Evidently the skeleton undergoes growth, at least in length of bones, even under these conditions, and other parts must grow to some extent and in certain dimensions in accordance with the growth of the skeleton, but this growth is in part at the expense of the reserves. After a certain length of time this growth ceases.

Aron ('11), working with growing dogs, succeeded in maintaining a constant body-weight for a long time, in some cases nearly a year, by limiting the quantity of food   He also found that the animals increased in size, the skeleton underwent growth, and the brain retained its weight or increased in weight, while the animals became progressively thinner and their fat reserves and muscular tissue suffered marked losses. If the food was not increased in amount the animals finally died of starvation after three to five months, with a slight loss of weight.   But if the quantity of food was somewhat increased they could still be maintained at a constant weight and in a condition of extreme emaciation, but now no further growth occurred   The results of later experiments on rats (Aron, '12, '13) are essentially similar and these experiments on animals agree well with the observations of various earlier authors on children

Aron concludes from his experiments that the internal growth-impulse exists primarily in the skeleton and that other parts merely follow the growth of the skeleton as far as nutritive conditions permit.   This is probably true for mammals or for vertebrates as regards growth in stature during later stages of development, but it is certainly not true for the early stages of development of vertebrates nor for many invertebrates where no skeleton is present It seems probable that in these animals growth of the more stable substances of the body, in part at the expense of the less stable, has occurred.   The diet in these cases is merely quantitatively, not qualitatively insufficient; it contains the constituents necessary for the construction of the relatively stable structural substances, but not in sufficient quantity for the growth of all parts   Under these conditions it might be expected that growth or maintenance, if it occurs anywhere, would be limited to the more stable tissues or substances of the body, while the less stable would undergo more or less reduction, for in the one case the losses from breakdown are slight and are more than balanced, while in the other they are greater and are not balanced and the products of breakdown of the less stable tissues take part to a greater or less extent in the upbuilding of the more stable   The organic structural substance of the skeleton is scarcely to be regarded as living; it is rather of the nature of a secretion, and after its formation it takes but little part in metabolism, except when altered functional conditions determine a change in bone structure. Consequently in underfed animals there is little loss of skeletal substance, and every addition counts for growth   Skeletal growth may therefore continue while reduction is going on in various other organs, the products of breakdown of the latter serving to build up the more stable substance of the former.

As regards the nervous system, conditions are somewhat similar   The nervous system is certainly one of the most stable, perhaps the most stable living tissue in the body   Its cells persist throughout life, and dedifferentiation of nerve cells is not known to occur in vertebrates. The losses of the nervous system during starvation are relatively slight, and in underfed animals it maintains its weight or grows at the expense of the less stable tissue, as the products of their breakdown are synthesized into more stable forms in the nervous system, and so become more permanent constituents of the structural substratum of the body   This stability of the nervous system is not, however, like that of the skeleton, the stability of a dead secretory substance, but is the stability of a living protoplasm and is undoubtedly associated with the high metabolic rate in the nervous system.

The result of return to a normal diet after a period of insufficient nutrition apparently depends in part on the length of that period   It has been clearly demonstrated that in man as well as in animals the retarding effect upon growth of even a considerable period of insufficient nutrition may be compensated later on a normal diet. But it is also true that a sufficiently long period of underfeeding may result in permanent "stunting," the body apparently being

unable to recover its full capacity for growth   Stunting in man and
the mammals is undoubtedly due in large measure to subnormal
skeletal growth, and while the effect of long-continued underfeeding
on the physiological condition of the skeletal tissues is not known,
the facts suggest that the usual relation between senescence and
growth is altered   In other words, the cells which give rise to the
skeletal substance probably undergo some degree of senescence
during underfeeding without being able to produce as much skeletal
substance as under continuous good nutritive conditions, consequently their rate of metabolism is lower and they are less capable
of producing skeletal substance after such a period than the cells
of an individual of the same size which has been continuously well
fed.   The skeleton of the individual which has been subjected
to underfeeding for a sufficiently long time will therefore cease to
grow, even under good nutritive conditions, at a smaller size than
that of the continuously well-fed individual, and very probably
the same is true to a greater or less extent in other tissues.   In the
underfed animal the proportion of more stable to less stable components of the tissues must increase more rapidly than where nutrition is sufficient for all requirements, for in the former case the less
stable components must break down to a larger extent than in the
latter.   In the absence of sufficient food these substances must
serve to a larger extent as a source of energy or for the synthesis
of the more stable components than where sufficient nutritive substance is available.   Consequently the substitution of more stable
for less stable substances in the tissues goes on during the period
of underfeeding, but with less than the usual amount of growth
because the less stable substances are present as structural components in smaller proportion than under the usual conditions.
After a long period of underfeeding the tissues are physiologically
older and therefore less capable of growth, even when nutrition
is present in excess, than in the continuously well-fed animal of the
same size.   According to this conception, senescence in the higher
animals and man may proceed to some extent even when little or
no growth occurs, because the body substance is gradually transformed to a greater or less extent from more active to more stable
conditions

CHANGES IN WATER-CONTENT AND CHEMICAL CONSTITUTION

From a certain stage of development on, the water-content of the body undergoes in general a decrease with advancing age, as many authors have shown. Davenport ('97) has found that in the frog the percentage of water increases from 56 to 96 per cent during the first two or three weeks after hatching, and then begins to decrease. In the chick embryo and the human fetus the percentage of water decreases from an early stage. Aron ('13) has compiled the data concerning the changes in water-content in man and the higher animals.

The decrease in water-content is not uniform for the different organs, nor is its progress in a given organ entirely uniform in all cases The extensive investigations of Donaldson and Hatai[1] on the water-content of the nervous system of the white rat show that the percentage of water in this tissue changes very regularly with advancing age   At birth it is about 88 per cent, at maturity 78 per cent, and it is altered only very slightly by nutritive conditions and external factors. Donaldson states that it affords the best index known of the age of these animals   It is probable that further investigations on other mammals would give similar results for the nervous system, but for various other tissues, e.g., the muscles, the variation in water-content is much greater.

It is an undoubted fact that after a certain stage the body becomes more and more solid as the structural substance accumulates. The decreasing water-content is in fact probably to some extent merely another aspect of the process of structural accumulation in the cells, although it may be in part the result of changes in the aggregate condition of the colloids, as Bechhold ('12) and others have suggested.

It is impossible to consider at length the changes in chemical constitution which occur with advancing age. Aron's recent compilation of the data on the biochemistry of growth ('13) affords a good survey of our present knowledge on this question. In general an increase in the percentage of proteid and of inorganic substances occurs, and this increase is more rapid during the earlier years of

[1] Hatai, '04; Donaldson, '11a, '11b, Donaldson and Hatai, '11.

life than later. Certain organs also undergo characteristic changes in constitution, but the relation between these changes and the age cycle is in most cases not yet clear

THE MORPHOLOGICAL CHANGES

If senescence is merely one aspect of progressive development the morphology of senescence in man and the higher forms is simply, as elsewhere, the morphology of progressive development. The morphological changes in the cells consist in general of the appearance of more or less definite structural substances, which differ in form and character according to the direction of differentiation in particular cells or organs Morphological differentiation of the cell involves either an accumulation in the cytoplasm of substances different in appearance and constitution from the cytoplasmic substratum of the embryonic cell, or a replacement of the embryonic substratum by such substances. This process of differentiation, or cytomorphosis as Minot prefers to call it, very commonly involves an increase in the volume of the cytoplasmic portions of the cell as compared with the nucleus. In embryonic cells the nucleus is in general, relatively to the cytoplasm, larger than in differentiated cells. Minot has laid particular emphasis on this change in the proportion of nucleus and cytoplasm as a fundamental feature of progressive development and as the determining factor in the decrease in metabolic rate which occurs in senescence. Such a change undoubtedly does occur in at least many cells in the course of differentiation, particularly in the higher animals, but it is by no means universal, as Minot maintains. In certain of the lower animals there is little if any difference between the embryo and the adult in this respect, and the differentiation of plant cells is very generally accompanied by vacuolization rather than by increase of cytoplasm.

Figs 113 and 114 show embryonic and differentiated cells from the spinal cord of the chick. The cells in Fig 113 are from the neural tube soon after its formation, and in Fig. 114, drawn to the same scale, nerve cells from the spinal cord after eleven days of incubation, at which time some of the nerve cells have attained practically their full size Measurements of the volume of nuclei

and cell bodies indicate that there is comparatively little chan
in proportion during the process of differentiation. Of cour
such measurements are not exact, and, besides, the measurements
the cytoplasm do not include the dendrites and the nerve fib
arising from the cell: if the volume of these were added to t
cytoplasmic volume of the cell the total would undoubtedly sh

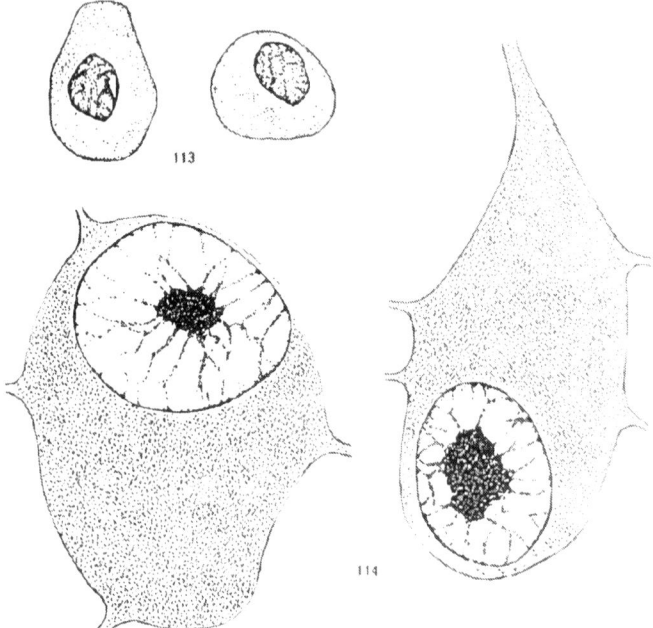

FIGS. 113, 114.—Cells from the nervous system of the chick embryo: Fig. 1
embryonic cells from neural tube at 31 hours; Fig. 114, differentiated mot
cells from spinal cord at 11 days, drawn to the same scale. From embryologi
preparations of the University of Chicago.

an increase in cytoplasmic volume during differentiation. B
how can the dendrites and the nerve fiber contribute to decrease th
rate of metabolism in the cell body, since they are merely slend
outgrowths from it? The cell body has unquestionably undergot
senescence during differentiation, but without any very gre
change in the nucleo-cytoplasmic relation. A marked proportion

increase in the amount of cytoplasm does occur in many cases, but it is an incidental rather than a fundamental feature of senescence. The important change is not the change in amount, but the change in the proportion of chemically active to inactive, or more active to less active substance.

In the higher animals and man morphological differentiation of the cells is much more conspicuous and varied than in the lower forms, but the essential nature of the process is evidently the same in all forms Differentiation consists primarily, not in increase in amount of cytoplasm, but in the accumulation of substances different in some way from the embryonic cytoplasm and giving the cell its characteristic structure. And it is unquestionably the increase in these substances, not the increase in the amount of cytoplasm, which determines the decrease in rate of metabolism and rate of growth. The structural substances produced by different cells differ in character in one way or another because in the course of development different metabolic conditions arise in different regions, and in the higher animals these conditions must be more definite and fixed in character than in the lower organisms, because the degree of individuation is higher, i.e., the correlation between parts is more intimate and definite These factors, together with the limited regressibility in many parts, must also determine that differentiation shall proceed farther than in the lower forms. The structural differences in different cells are more permanent and more conspicuous and in general involve the cell to a greater extent.

So far as they have turned their attention to the phenomena of senescence the anatomists, histologists, and pathologists have often failed to recognize what the study of the lower organisms forces us to admit as a fact, viz., that senescence is merely one aspect of development, and have confined their attention to, and based their theories upon, the morphological changes which occur in later life, and particularly in what we are accustomed to call old age One reason for this attitude among those investigators who have been chiefly concerned with man lies in the fact that old age in man and the higher vertebrates is associated with certain morphological changes in the cells which seem to be different in character and direction from the developmental changes These changes are commonly known as senile atrophy [1] They consist essentially of a decrease in size, with more or less degeneration of cells These changes are often so extensive and so widely distributed that there is considerable decrease in size and weight of the body as a whole

The atrophy may involve to a greater or less extent most or all of the more highly specialized organs of the body, liver, kidneys, alimentary tract, lungs, muscular system, skeleton, and nervous system. The arterial system always shows changes in the direction of decreased elasticity and contractility, and the hardening of the walls known as arteriosclerosis is very commonly present, although some authors maintain that it is not a characteristic feature of old age. The heart often becomes hypertrophied instead of atrophied, but this is believed by many to be a functional reaction to the increased work of the heart in consequence of the changes in the arterial system, rather than a feature of old age. The connective tissue becomes stiffer and harder, but its less highly specialized forms may increase and take the place of more highly specialized organs or tissues which have undergone atrophy In connection with these changes of old age the deposition of fatty substances, evidently products of metabolism, occurs in the cells of muscles, liver, brain, and various other tissues

The difference in appearance of the spinal ganglion cells of man at birth and in a case of death from old age at ninety-two years are shown in Figs. 115 and 116. In the first figure the young cells have not yet attained their full size, but compared with them, the cells on the left of the second figure are seen by the spaces about them to be greatly shrunken and their cytoplasm contains numerous fat granules stained black by the method of preparation   On the right of Fig. 116 the débris of two cells which have undergone degeneration is seen

The atrophy of tissues in old age is manifestly associated with the decrease in rate of metabolism   It is a well-known fact that a decrease or cessation of functional activity in the specialized organs after their development brings about atrophy quite independently

[1] For more recent discussions of senile atrophy see Bilancioni, '11, Demange, '86, Metchnikoff, '03, '10, Minot, '08, chap ii, Muhlmann, '00, '10, Ribbert, '08, articles in medical dictionaries, cyclopedias, etc.

of age   Under such conditions, or where the rate of metabolism
has fallen below a certain level in consequence of age, the breakdown and elimination of the substratum is not compensated by the
synthesis of new substance, consequently a decrease in size and
finally cell death occur.   Atrophy in the higher animals differs
from reduction in the lower forms in that, while decrease in size
occurs, there is little or no dedifferentiation.   The cell has apparently become so highly differentiated that it has lost the capacity
for synthesizing a substratum adequate in quantity or constitution

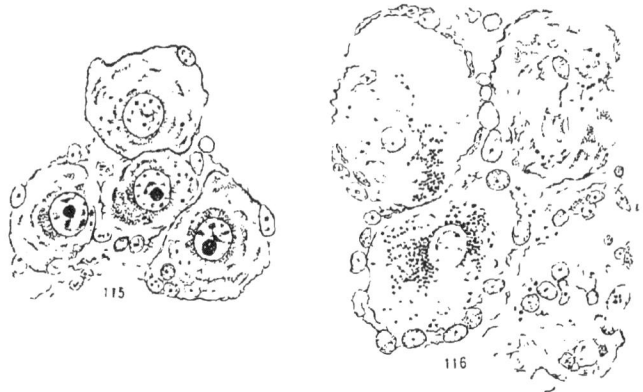

FIGS 115, 116 —Cells from the first cervical ganglion of man at different ages
Fig 115, from fetus killed by accident of birth, Fig 116, from man dying of old age
at ninety-two years, showing on the left two cells shrunken and undergoing atrophy
and on the right the outlines of spaces formerly occupied by cells now degenerated
After Hodge, '94

to carry on metabolism   Consequently the losses from degradation
and breakdown of the existing substratum are not compensated by
the synthesis of new substral substance, and sooner or later the
fundamental mechanism of the cell is destroyed and degeneration
and death occur.   The atrophy of old age in organs of such fundamental importance as the nervous system indicates that there is
some truth in the statement, so often made, that the later stages of
senescence are a "wearing out" of the physiological mechanism or
some essential part of it.   Apparently the nerve cells or some of
them do "wear out" because they are no longer able to synthesize

the substratum necessary for their continued function   But even though the final stage of senescence, which terminates in death, may be regarded as a wearing out and a breaking down of the physiological mechanism at some point, it must not be forgotten that this stage is merely the final stage of progressive development and that the factors which determine it act from the beginning of development on

CONCLUSION

So far as the facts go, the process of senescence appears to be essentially the same in the higher and lower organisms; the chief difference is that with the absence of reproduction and the greater degree of individuation and differentiation the later atrophic stages of senescence are conspicuous and characteristic features of the life history in the higher forms, while in the lower they either do not appear or else occur in only a few cells at any given time.   From the lowest forms to man senescence is simply one aspect of the developmental process, and we may expect to find it occurring wherever the progressive changes are not balanced or overbalanced by regression

The apparent continuity and irregressibility of senescence in man and the higher forms is responsible for the very general belief that the process is irregressible everywhere, but the plants and lower animals show us clearly enough that this is not the case.   Viewed in the light of what we have learned from the lower forms, senescence in the higher animals and man is merely a less frequently interrupted process of the same kind as that which occurs in all progressive stages of the life cycle in the plants and the lower animals.

REFERENCES

ARON, H
    1911   "Wachstum und Ernahrung," *Biochem Zeitschr* , XXX
    1912   "Weitere Untersuchungen uber die Beeinflussung des Wachstums durch die Ernahrung," *Verhandlungen d Gesell f. Kinderheilkunde.*
    1913   *Biochemie des Wachstums.* Erweiterte Sonderausgabe aus dem *Handbuch d. Biochemie* Erganzungsbd   Jena.
BECHHOLD, H
    1912.   *Die Kolloide in Biologie und Medezin*   Dresden.

BILANCIONI, G
    1911. "Il problema della vecchiaia e della morte naturale," *Arch. di Farmacol. sperimentale*, XI

DASTRE, A
    1903. *La vie et la mort* Paris

DAVENPORT, C. B
    1897. "The Rôle of Water in Growth," *Proc. of the Boston Soc. of Nat. Hist.*, XXVIII.

DEMANGE
    1886. *Étude clinique et anatomo-pathologique de la vieillesse*

DONALDSON, H. H
    1895 *The Growth of the Brain.* London.
    1906. "A Comparison of the White Rat with Man in Respect to Growth of the Entire Body," *Boas Memorial Volume* New York.
    1911a. President's Address, Philadelphia Neurological Society. *Jour. of Nerv. and Mental Diseases*, XXXVIII.
    1911b. "The Effect of Underfeeding on the Percentage of Water, on the Ether-Alcohol Extract and on Medullation in the Central Nervous System of the Albino Rat," *Jour. of Comp Neurol.*, XXI.

DONALDSON, H. H , and HATAI, S
    1911. "A Comparison of the Norway Rat with the Albino Rat in Respect to Body Length, Brain Weight and the Percentage of Water in Both the Brain and the Spinal Cord," *Jour. of Comp Neurol.*, XXI

FRIEDMANN, F.
    1902. *Die Altersveranderungen und ihre Behandlung* Wien.

HATAI, S.
    1904 "The Effect of Partial Starvation on the Brain of the White Rat," *Am Jour of Physiol*, XII.

HILL, A V. and A M.
    1913 "Calorimetrical Experiments on Warmblooded Animals," *Jour. of Physiol*, XLVI

HODGE, C F
    1894 "Changes in Ganglion Cells from Birth to Senile Death," *Jour. of Physiol*, XVII

HOPKINS, F. G
    1912. "Feeding Experiments Illustrating the Importance of Accessory Factors in Normal Dietaries," *Jour of Physiol.*, XLIV.

HOSSLIN, H. VON.
    1888 "Über die Ursachen der scheinbaren Abhangigkeit des Umsatzes von der Grosse der Korperoberflache," *Arch. f. Physiol.*, Jhg 1888

KOCH, W and M. L
1913. "Contributions to the Chemical Differentiation of the Central Nervous System III, The Chemical Differentiation of the Brain of the Albino Rat during Growth," *Jour of Biol. Chem*, XV.

KOVESI, G.
1901 "Über den Eiweissumsatz im Greisenalter," *Zentralbl f innere Med.*, XXII.

LORAND, A
1911 *Das Altern, seine Ursachen und seine Behandlung.* Leipzig

McCOLLUM, E V
1911 "The Nature of the Repair Processes in Protein Metabolism," *Am Jour. of Physiol.*, XXIX.

MAGNUS-LEVY, A , and FALK, E
1899. "Der Lungengaswechsel des Menschen in den verschiedenen Altersstufen," *Arch. f. Physiol.* Supplement-Band

MARCHAL, P
1904 Recherches sur la biologie et le développement des Hyménoptères. I, La polyembryonie ou germinogonie," *Arch de zool Exp*, (4) II.

MENDEL, L. B.
1914 "Viewpoints in the Study of Growth," *Biochem. Bull*, III

METSCHNIKOFF, E.
1903. *The Nature of Man* English translation New York and London
1910 *The Prolongation of Life* English translation. New York and London

MINOT, C. S.
1891 "Senescence and Rejuvenation," *Jour. of Physiol*, XII
1908. *The Problem of Age, Growth and Death.* New York.
1913 *Moderne Probleme der Biologie.* Jena

MUHLMANN, M.
1900. *Über die Ursache des Alters.* Wiesbaden.
1910 "Das Altern und der physiologische Tod," *Sammlung anat u physiol Vortr.*, XI.

OSBORNE, T B , and MENDEL, L B.
1911a. "Feeding Experiments with Isolated Food-Substances," Parts I and II. *Carnegie Inst., Publ 156*
1911b "The Rôle of Different Proteins in Nutrition and Growth," *Science*, XXXIV.
1912a "Beobachtungen uber Wachstum bei Futterungsversuchen mit isolierten Nahrungssubstanzen," *Zeitschr f. physiol Chem*, LXXX.
1912b. "The Rôle of Gliadin in Nutrition," *Jour of Biol. Chem*, XII.

OSBORNE, T B , and MENDEL, L B

    1912c "Maintenance Experiments with Isolated Proteins," *Jour of Biol. Chem* , XIII.

    1913 "The Relation of Growth to the Chemical Constituents of the Diet," *Jour of Biol Chem* , XV.

    1914 "Amino-Acids in Nutrition and Growth," *Jour of Biol Chem* , XVII.

PATTERSON, J. T

    1913. "Polyembryonic Development in *Tatusia novemcincta*," *Jour. of Morphol.*, XXIV.

RIBBERT, H

    1908. *Der Tod aus Altersschwache* Bonn.

RUBNER, M.

    1883. "Über den Einfluss der Korpergrösse auf Stoff- und Kraftwechsel," *Zeitschr. f Biol.*, XIX

    1885. "Calorimetrische Untersuchungen," *Zeitschr. f Biol* , XXI.

    1908. *Das Problem der Lebensdauer und seine Beziehungen zu Wachstum und Ernahrung* Munchen.

    1909. *Kraft und Stoff im Haushalte der Natur.* Leipzig.

SILVESTRI, F

    1906 "Contribuzione alla conoscenza biologica degli Imenotteri parasiti: I, Biologia del *Litomastix truncatellus*," *Ann. Scuola Agric. Portici*, VI.

SONDEN, K , und TIGERSTEDT, R

    1895. "Untersuchungen uber die Respiration und den Gesammtstoffwechsel des Menschen," *Skand Arch. f Physiol.*, VI

SPECK, C.

    1889. "Das normale Athmen des Menschen," *Schriften d. Gesell. z Beford d. ges. Wissensch* , XII.

WATERS, H. J

    1908. "The Capacity of Animals to Grow under Adverse Conditions," *Proc. of the Soc. for the Promotion of Agric Sci* , XXIX

    1909 "The Influence of Nutrition upon the Animal Form," *Proc. of the Soc. for the Promotion of Agric Sci* , XXX.

WHEELER, Ruth.

    1913. "Feeding Experiments with Mice," *Jour of Exp. Zool.*, XV.

WILDER, H H

    1904. "Duplicate Twins and Double Monsters," *Am. Jour. of Anat* , III

CHAPTER XII

REJUVENESCENCE AND DEATH IN THE HIGHER ANIMALS AND MAN

REJUVENESCENCE IN THE LIFE HISTORY

While much has been written concerning senescence and death in man and the higher animals, but little attention has been paid to the question of the occurrence of rejuvenescence, and many authorities still maintain that life is always a progressive process and that rejuvenescence does not occur. It is of course true that in the higher animals the progressive features of development are predominant and that development ends in death, and many studies of senescence have been based on these forms alone, without consideration or knowledge of the lower organisms. But if we are to reach a general conception of the age cycle in organisms, the wide occurrence and significance of dedifferentiation and rejuvenescence in the lower animals and the plants must at least raise the question whether similar processes do not occur to some extent in higher forms

Even in man and the other mammals the different tissues do not undergo senescence alike. Certain cells, such as the Malpighian layer of the skin, continue to divide and replace the old dying or dead cells of the epidermis, and remain relatively young in appearance and behavior throughout the life and even after the death of the individual In various other tissues such replacement of old differentiated, or dead cells by younger cells occurs more or less extensively in normal life, and tissue regeneration, following injury or loss of tissue cells, occurs to a greater or less extent in all tissues except the nervous system.

The process of tissue regeneration, whether in normal life or as a reaction to injury, undoubtedly retards the aging of the tissue or organ concerned as a whole, but the question whether it involves an actual dedifferentiation and rejuvenescence of the cells concerned in the regeneration must be briefly considered Minot ('08, '13) has attempted to prove that dedifferentiation does not actually occur in such cases and that the regeneration takes its origin from cells or parts of cells which have never undergone differentiation, so that even in these cases development is progressive, not regressive. His conclusions are based on the histological appearance, not upon the behavior of the cells One of the cases cited by him as an example is the regeneration of striated muscle after injury He points out that the only portions of the muscle which take part in the regeneration are the nuclei and the small accumulations of

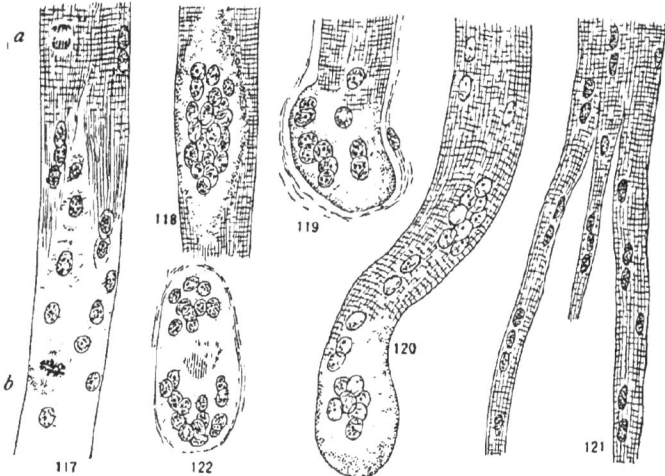

FIGS. 117–122.—Various stages of regeneration after wounding in striated muscle: Fig. 117, injured muscle after three days, showing proliferation of nuclei and formation of protoplasmic cells, Fig 118, multinucleate masses resulting from proliferation; Figs 119, 120, "muscle buds" at ends of injured fibers, Fig 121, regenerated fibers, Fig. 122, giant cells, inclosing a piece of necrotic muscle fiber From Ziegler, '01.

granular undifferentiated cytoplasm, as he terms it, which surround them. From these parts the new muscle cells arise by division of the nuclei and growth of the granular cytoplasm (Fig 117), these cells form multinucleate masses either along the course (Fig. 118) or at the injured end of the fibrillar substance (Fig. 119) From the cytoplasm of these cells new fibrillar substance arises in continuity with the old (Figs 120, 121). When these cells are not in contact with living muscle substance, as at b in Fig. 117, they form multinucleate "giant cells" (Fig 122), and these do not give rise to new fibrillar substance, but usually die sooner or later. Even if Minot is correct in maintaining that the fibrillar substance has no capacity for regeneration, it is of interest to note that the new fibrillar substance seems to arise in continuity with the old, while isolated cells apparently do not produce fibrillar substance.

The conclusion that there is no dedifferentiation involved in such cases is, I believe, not warranted by the facts The point of importance is that during the earlier stages of their developmental history the muscle cells produced granular cytoplasm and nuclear substance and grew and divided, but later began to give rise to fibrillar substance and the proportion of this substance to the nuclei and granular "undifferentiated" cytoplasm increased enormously After injury, however, the activity of the muscle cells changes, and they produce more granular cytoplasm and more nuclear substance In short, they have returned to a kind of activity characteristic of early stages of embryonic development What is this if it is not dedifferentiation? The fact that the old fibrillar substance degenerates instead of regenerating is quite irrelevant. The question is not whether all parts of the cells are capable of regeneration, but whether the cells can again resume a kind of activity characteristic of an earlier stage of development, and the process of regeneration of muscle and various other tissues in man and the higher animals leaves no doubt that they possess this capacity. Even in the outgrowth of new nerve fibers from the central stump of a cut nerve there is a return to a process of growth and development which is normally characteristic of an earlier stage of development Champy maintains that dedifferentiation occurs in tissues cultivated outside the organism in nutritive media—the method often termed explantation—and has described at length the changes in cultures of kidney cells [1] Regression and dedifferentiation certainly occur to a greater or less extent in most tissues of man and the higher animals, but the apparent inability of the cells of one tissue to give rise to other tissues indicates that,

---

[1] See Champy, '13, '14, and earlier papers which are included, together with many other references bearing upon this question, in the bibliographic lists of these papers.

at least under the usual conditions, regression does not bring the cell back to a completely undifferentiated stage.

It is of course true that in some tissues, such as the skin, the more highly differentiated cells show no capacity for dedifferentiation, but die and are replaced by division and growth of cells which remain throughout life in a more or less embryonic condition   In such cases there is no evidence of regression and dedifferentiation, but its absence in the one tissue does not justify the conclusion that it is absent in another.   Dedifferentiation and regression in tissue cells are undoubtedly associated with rejuvenescence in the higher as well as in the lower organisms, and tissue regeneration, whether a feature of normal life or the result of injury, must bring about some degree of rejuvenescence in the parts concerned

After a period of hibernation, tissue regeneration is often very extensive (Monti, '05) and may involve tissues which usually show but little regeneration.   In such cases the large proportion of young cells in the body must render the animal as a whole, though not necessarily all parts of it, appreciably younger than before hibernation.   In fact, the periodic cycle of activity and hibernation in various forms is in many respects similar to an age cycle.   It is probable that the rejuvenescence begins during the hibernation period when the animal is living upon its own substance, like the starving planarian, and that this change leads sooner or later to renewed division and growth of cells.   At the same time, other cells doubtless die and are later replaced by the younger cells

Other periodic changes, particularly in the glandular tissues, show the essential characteristics of an age cycle   In the pancreas cell, for example (see pp. 189-191), the loading of the cell is both morphologically and physiologically similar to senescence, and the discharge to rejuvenescence.   In such cases the changes occur in individual cells without cell reproduction.

The cells of the nervous system in man and many animals are believed to persist throughout life, and to possess no appreciable capacity for regression and dedifferentiation beyond their ability to regenerate the nerve fibers which arise from them.   Doubtless this belief is correct, so far as visible structural changes or measureable metabolic changes are concerned; but is there not reason to believe that the effect of a change in mental occupation or of a vacation after long-continued mental labor in a particular field is in some slight degree a rejuvenescence of the nerve cells? Many facts indicate that a reasonable variety in mental occupation is a factor in retarding mental senility What we often call mental fatigue may be something much less evanescent than fatigue in the ordinary sense, but recovery may occur in time. Verworn ('09, p 557) has drawn a distinction between fatigue, resulting from accumulation of substances which retard metabolism, and exhaustion, resulting from lack of oxygen or other substances necessary for metabolism. Recently Dolley ('14) has maintained that both of these changes may bring about senility in the nerve cell. Exhaustion, I believe, resembles senility as death from asphyxiation resembles death from old age. In both exhaustion and senility the rate of oxidation may be decreased, but the factors involved and the condition of the organism in the two cases are very different. Recovery from exhaustion is then not the same sort of change as rejuvenescence except as it involves increase in rate of oxidation. Fatigue and recovery constitute a cycle resembling much more closely the age cycle As I have pointed out in chap viii, it is impossible to draw the line sharply between age changes and various other periodic or cyclical changes in the organism, and, although the nervous system is without doubt a highly stable tissue, the very definite physiologically regressive changes which occur in recovery from mental fatigue or from long-continued mental activity of a particular kind suggest that changes closely approaching rejuvenescence occur. Even here development is not always and only progressive, as Minot and many others would have us believe, but is made up of progressive and regressive changes with the balance greatly in favor of the former.

The occurrence of rejuvenescence in connection with starvation in planarians raises the question whether any changes in this direction are associated with starvation in the higher animals The metabolism of starvation in man and the higher vertebrates has been extensively studied by many investigators,[1] and there is

---

[1] See the bibliographies in the the article by Weber, "Über Hungerstoffwechsel," *Ergebnisse d Physiol*, I, 1902, in the paper by Pembrey and Spriggs, '04, and in Benedict's studies of starvation metabolism in man (Benedict, '07, 15)

general agreement that the rate of metabolism falls rapidly during the early stages of starvation to a more or less constant level   In the later stages of starvation the well-known premortal increase in nitrogen elimination occurs, which most authors believe to be due to increased breakdown of tissue substance after the reserves of fat have largely disappeared   In Benedict's latest study of starvation-metabolism, covering a fasting period of thirty-one days in the human subject, the oxygen consumption, carbon-dioxide production, and heat production per kilo of body-weight show a slight increase toward the end of the period, and other investigators mention slight changes of the same sort, but whether these facts have any significance in connection with rejuvenescence is not yet clear. While considerable loss of weight occurs before death, in no case is there a degree of reduction comparable to that observed in the lower invertebrates   Apparently the higher animals are unable for some reason to use their own tissues as a source of nutrition to any such extent as the lower forms.   Probably this inability is due in large part to the relatively high physiological stability of the tissue components, but other factors may also be concerned

While there is no distinct indication of any rejuvenescence during the starvation period, it has often been noted that the body-weight after starvation becomes greater than before   Von Seeland ('87) found this to be the case in fowls with periodic starvation   The increase in weight was due primarily to increase in proteids and not to deposition of fat   Noé ('∞) obtained similar results by periodic starvation of rabbits and mice.   In man also a starvation period is often followed by an increase in vigor and body-weight, and starvation, properly controlled, is believed by many to possess a certain therapeutic significance.

The injurious effects of overnutrition in man are commonly supposed to be due in large measure to the accumulation of fat or to intoxications.   The possibility must, however, be admitted that overnutrition may actually increase the rate of senescence to some slight extent by increasing the deposition in the cellular substratum, not only of fat, but of other substances which aid in decreasing the general rate of metabolism   Instances of longevity in man on a low diet are not lacking, and much has been written during recent years of the perils of overeating

In certain bacterial diseases, such for example as typhoid fever, a very great decrease in body-weight may occur, and it is often observed that the body-weight becomes greater and the person apparently more vigorous after recovery than before the illness.

These various facts viewed in the light of the effects of starvation and reduction in the lower invertebrates indicate that, even in man, reduction by starvation or other means may bring about some degree of rejuvenescence through the breakdown and elimination of constituents of the cellular substratum. During reduction in these cases the rejuvenescence is potential rather than actual, and it becomes apparent only when recovery occurs. But rejuvenescence by reduction is limited in the higher animals, for reduction in these forms soon ends in death, so that there is at present no immediate prospect of our being able to rejuvenate ourselves to any great degree, or to retard senescence or delay death to any great extent by any such means Under certain conditions long-continued or periodic starvation may bring about an appreciable rejuvenescence. but it is not in any sense a cure-all for human ills. There is not the slightest doubt that certain recent books and articles on the therapeutic value of starvation, written by laymen who have experimented on themselves, have done great harm to many persons. Certainly no one who desires to subject himself to experiment of this kind should do so without submitting first to a thorough medical examination and to medical observation and control during the experiment. Where weakness or organic disease exists, such experiments may be only a means of aggravation and so hasten, rather than delay, death And even if such diseases as typhoid fever do in some cases accomplish a slight degree of rejuvenescence, no one will be inclined to regard them as an unmixed good. In too many cases they serve only to develop or aggravate weaknesses or to prepare the way for other infections, and so to shorten life rather than to prolong it

A recent study of the susceptibility to the cyanides and to lack of oxygen of fishes during starvation. by Mr M. M. Wells,[1] seems to indicate that, as regards the effect of starvation, the fishes

---

[1] Mr Wells, formerly an assistant in the Department of Zoology of the University of Chicago, has not yet completed his investigations, but very kindly permits the citation of certain of the results obtained

occupy a position intermediate between the higher vertebrates and the lower invertebrates, such as *Planaria* Thus far Mr Wells has found that the susceptibility to cyanide and lack of oxygen decreases early in starvation and remains more or less constant during the first month or six weeks and then undergoes a rapid increase and may become as high as that of well-fed growing individuals of much smaller size than the starved animals at the beginning of the experiment. Apparently the rate of metabolism falls early in starvation and remains relatively low for several weeks while decrease in weight goes on, but after several weeks the rate begins to rise and may reach that of animals which are physiologically much younger than the starved animals were at the beginning. During the first part of the period the starved fishes behave as regards rate of metabolism like the warm-blooded animals, but later a rise in rate occurs like that which the planarians show from the beginning Any attempt at interpretation of these results must at present, however, be little more than a guess. The experiments suggest that after removal or transformation of certain constituents of the substratum the cells begin to burn themselves up at an increasingly rapid rate as in *Planaria*, and so a much greater degree of rejuvenescence occurs, at least in some tissues, than in the mammals

It has long been known that frogs and salamanders may live for long periods of time without food and may undergo a considerable degree of reduction during starvation. In his studies of the effects of starvation on members of this group Morgulis ('11, '13) has found that protracted starvation has a distinctly rejuvenating effect. After starvation the animals grow more rapidly. use a larger percentage of the nutrition in growth, and attain larger size than those continuously fed. Contrary to von Seeland (p. 298), Morgulis finds that intermittent starvation has a stunting effect, but suggests that in his experiments the animals did not completely recover between starvation periods.

In man and the higher vertebrates and probably also in the higher invertebrates, such as the insects, individuation and differentiation have progressed so far that after the earlier stages of development any considerable degree of reduction or regression is impossible under ordinary conditions without endangering in one way or another the continued existence of the whole mechanism. But the facts indicate that even in such organisms some degree of regression and rejuvenescence may occur

LENGTH OF LIFE AND DEATH FROM OLD AGE

When the rate of metabolism becomes so low in consequence of advancing senescence that the cell or organism can no longer synthesize its metabolic substratum in sufficient amount to compensate the losses, atrophy begins and must sooner or later end in the destruction of the physiological mechanism, which is death.

In a complex organism like man, different cells and tissues grow old at different rates, and death from old age of the organism as a whole does not by any means imply the death of all its cells Death of cells apparently from old age occurs from early stages of development throughout the whole life history, and we also know that most of the cells of the body do not die when death of the individual occurs. The individual dies when some tissue or organ which is essential for its continued existence reaches the point of death, and since the parts are incapable of dedifferentiation and a new individuation, the other organs or cells die sooner or later because of lack of nutrition or oxygen, or because of the accumulation of toxic products of metabolism.

So-called physiological death in the higher animals is then due to the breakdown of the physiological mechanism of the individual at some essential point, and not to the simultaneous death of all parts As regards this fact different authorities are agreed, but wide differences of opinion exist as regards the organ or organs responsible for breakdown of the mechanism. Muhlmann ('oo. 'ro, '14) and Ribbert ('o8) maintain that physiological death is essentially a death of the brain, Lorand ('11), that the glands of internal secretion are primarily responsible, and Demange ('86) and Metchnikoff ('03, '10) regard arteriosclerosis as the most important factor in death.

Without attempting any extended discussion of these and other views. it may be pointed out that the growth of the central nervous system begins and is completed earlier, and that its development is apparently more continuously progressive, with less rejuvenescence, than that of other organs. Even in starvation the nervous system shows little or no reduction. There is, therefore, some reason for believing with Muhlmann and Ribbert that death from old age uncomplicated by disease or incidental factors is primarily a death of the nervous system, and both the histological characteristics of the nerve cells and the physiological condition of the nervous system in cases of extreme old age afford support to this view. Even in invertebrates as low in the scale as annelids, Harms ('12) has observed that the first structural changes preceding natural death occur in the cephalic portion of the central nervous system.

But death from old age alone without any complicating factors is undoubtedly rare, and it is very difficult to determine in any given case whether complicating factors are present or not; consequently it is not possible to assert positively that natural death is in all cases death of the brain or nervous system, although the evidence points in that direction.

In various insects and in certain fish, e g , the salmon, death occurs almost at once after extrusion of the sexual products. In such cases the factor immediately concerned in bringing about death is probably exhaustion rather than old age, although the organism is undoubtedly in an advanced stage of senescence when sexual maturity is attained. In certain insects and some other invertebrates which do not feed in the adult stage natural death is probably a death from starvation.

The natural length of life of organisms must depend on a variety of factors, such as specific constitution of protoplasm, rate of senescence, continuity of progressive development, or in other words the degree of rejuvenescence during the life history, functional activity, perhaps the amount and in some forms probably also the character of food In general it represents the length of time from the beginning of senescence in the early stages of development to the stage where the rate of metabolism is so low that the physiological mechanism disintegrates Commonly the life of the organism is very much longer than that of many of its constituent cells, but it is probable that the extreme limit of life of the individual is determined by the length of life of its shortest-lived essential organ or tissue, and this must be the organ or tissue which is least subject to or capable of regression and rejuvenescence and whose development is consequently most continuously progressive. In the higher animals this organ is unquestionably the central nervous system. This line of evidence, therefore, lends further support to the view that natural death is a death of the nervous system.

In the warm-blooded vertebrates, where rejuvenescence plays a minor part in the life history, the length of life in a particular species is a more or less definite length of time, because the rate of metabolism is largely independent of external conditions and the rate of development and senescence is therefore determined largely by internal factors which are more or less constant for the species. In the cold-blooded animals, however, where rate of metabolism is dependent on external temperature, senescence can unquestionably be retarded, and so the length of life increased, by low temperature. Moreover, in many of these animals long-continued starvation and extensive reduction may occur with complete recovery, and there is no doubt that under such conditions a greater or less degree of rejuvenescence and consequently an increase in length of life may occur in some cases. As regards the lower invertebrates, it was shown in an earlier chapter that senescence may be retarded or inhibited for a long time and probably indefinitely by the simple means of underfeeding. This is of course not possible in the higher animals, for their most stable tissues undergo senescence to some extent even under these conditions.

Among the lower animals and the plants cell death occurs, as in the higher forms, as the end of progressive development, and death of the many-celled individual may occur if progression and senescence are not balanced by regression and rejuvenescence. Even in the unicellular forms reproduction by fission brings about some degree of rejuvenescence, and it is probable that nuclear and cell division in general accomplish the same result to some slight degree. When cells lose the capacity to divide they differentiate grow old, and sooner or later die. In short, the only conclusion warranted by the facts is that death is everywhere the final result of progressive development, if the process goes far enough, but in many organisms progressive development is interrupted by regressive processes connected with repair, reproduction, lack of food, or other conditions, and the death point is never attained by the individual, although even in such forms death of cells, apparently from old age, may be a characteristic feature.

The appearance of death in the course of evolution as the end of the life history of the individual is to be regarded as a result of the increasing physiological stability of the substratum of the organism and the increasing degree of individuation which the greater stability makes possible These changes determine a greater degree of continuity of progressive development and senescence and so less frequent and less extensive regression, reproduction, and rejuvenescence.

As the evolution of the individual advances with its increasing differentiation and more intimate correlation of parts, death as the termination of the individual life history becomes more and more inevitable.

SOME THEORIES OF LENGTH OF LIFE

Most authors who have discussed senescence have regarded death as merely the final termination of the processes of senescence, whatever their view concerning the nature of these But certain of the theories advanced which concern themselves particularly with the problem of the length of life require special mention here.

Some thirty years ago Weismann ('82, '84) first stated his view that the cause of death lies in the limitation of capacity for cell reproduction. In the unicellular organisms, according to Weismann, this capacity is not limited, therefore the protozoa do not die   In the multicellular organism, however, only the germ cells retain the capacity for unlimited division; in the somatic cells the number of possible cell divisions has been limited by the action of natural selection, which determines in general that life shall not continue long after the reproductive period is completed. In later writings ('92, '04) Weismann has elaborated this idea further, but without essential change   The theory concerns itself with the evolution of length of life and of death rather than with the problem of the nature of the physiological processes involved. Death must of course have occurred before the length of life could be subjected to the action of selection. Weismann maintains, however, that death is not a fundamental characteristic of life, but an adaptation which has arisen "because unlimited duration of the life of the individual would be a senseless luxury " In other words, death appeared at some time as a chance variation which was inherited and was of such value to the organic world that through the action of natural selection it has become universal in multicellular organisms Death was possible in these forms because somatic and germ cells were separated, while in the unicellular forms they are one and the same cell

The problems of death and length of life find no solution in these speculations The occurrence of death is simply assumed as the foundation of the theory. But it is not true that all multicellular forms necessarily die. As I have endeavored to show, many forms, both plants and animals, may escape death by reproduction and rejuvenescence in exactly the same way as do the protozoa On the other hand, there is every reason to believe that if the protozoa live long enough without reproduction they too die of old age and the germ cells of the multicellular forms also apparently undergo senescence and die of old age if rejuvenescence is not initiated by fertilization (see pp. 403–6). The evidence also indicates that death occurs in general soon after the period of sexual reproduction is over, not because of advantage to the species, but because sexual maturity is a physiological feature of relatively advanced age. Progressive development, which ends in death, except where interrupted by regression, is far advanced when sexual reproduction begins And, finally, it is rather remarkable that natural selection should have succeeded so completely, as Weismann believes it has, in eliminating the species in which death does not naturally occur

A theory of length of life of a very different sort, based primarily upon calorimetric investigations on various domestic mammals and man, has been advanced by Rubner ('08, '09). From the available data Rubner has calculated the total energy requirement in calories for a doubling of body-weight after birth and the requirement per kilogram of body-weight for the whole period of life after growth is completed in a number of the domestic mammals and man. The total calories required for the doubling of weight are given in Table VI, and the total calories per kilogram of body-weight for the period after completion of growth in Table VII

The totals for all except man show a rather close agreement in each table, and while Rubner admits that the data on which these figures are based are not in all cases satisfactory, he concludes from the figures that the amounts of energy required, first, for the doubling of weight in growth and, secondly, for the maintenance of each kilogram of body-weight during adult life, are the same in all species in the tables except man   Man uses a much greater

TABLE VI

Horse	4 512	Pig		3,754
Cow	4,243	Dog		4,304
Sheep	3,936	Cat	.	4,554
Man	28,864	Rabbit	.	5,066

TABLE VII

Man	725,770	Dog	.	163,900
Horse	163,900	Cat		223,800
Cow	141,090	Guinea-pig.		265,500

amount of energy in both cases, i e., a much smaller percentage of the energy of food is concerned in growth and maintenance of body-weight in man than in the other mammals   These results of his calculations lead Rubner to suggest that the living substance can undergo only a certain number of atomic rearrangements before becoming exhausted and breaking down   According to this view, life is terminated by the completion of a complex chemical reaction.

While I do not regard myself as qualified to criticize the methods of calculation, or the data on which these are based, though they may be open to criticism at certain points, Rubner's general conclusion demands consideration on general biological grounds.   Assuming the validity of the data and methods of treatment, considerable uniformity in energy requirement in the mammals is to be expected, for they are closely related to each other, the rate of metabolism is not widely different in different species, and progressive development is not to any great extent interrupted by regression and rejuvenescence.   The facts scarcely warrant us in going beyond the conclusion that development is a similar process in all these mammalian species.   If life is terminated, not by the completion of a complex reaction, as Rubner suggests, but by changes in the substratum which retard metabolism, the domesticated mammals might certainly be expected to require somewhere near similar amounts of energy to attain the death point.

Rubner fails entirely to take into account the fact that in all the species under consideration the length of life of different cells is very different. Some die after a life which is short compared with the life of a whole organism, and are replaced by others, so that in some tissues growth and development continue throughout the life of the animal. Other cells apparently persist as long as the animal lives, and it is probably these, e.g., the cells of the nervous system, which are primarily responsible for natural death, as suggested above. Rubner's theory also does not admit the possibility of rejuvenescence except in connection with fertilization, nor does it show how the starting-point of the complex reaction is again attained at the beginning of each generation. As regards the exceptional position of man, Rubner believes that the human living substance is different from that of other mammals and requires a much larger amount of energy for a given amount of growth. These data compare man with domesticated mammals; if it were possible, it would be of considerable interest to determine whether the energy requirements are the same in wild as in domesticated animals It seems probable that they would be higher in the wild forms

In a number of papers Loeb has discussed the nature of the processes which bring about death in the mature egg when it is not fertilized and has described certain methods by which its life can be prolonged. In two papers, however (Loeb, '02, '08), he has dealt with the problems of death and length of life in a more general way. The starfish egg, if not fertilized, dies, usually within a few hours after maturation, but if it is prevented by lack of oxygen from undergoing maturation its life may be prolonged for days. From these facts Loeb concludes that natural death in these cases is due to specific destructive processes which are set going by maturation. These processes cannot be identical with the processes underlying development, because they are inhibited or delayed by the fertilization of the egg

In the second paper he uses the temperature coefficient of the length of life of sea-urchin eggs at high temperatures as a basis for his conclusions   To determine the temperature coefficient of length of life Loeb subjects lots of freshly fertilized eggs of sea-urchins to different temperatures above that in which they normally develop, and then, by removing portions of each lot at intervals to room temperature and allowing them to develop, he finds the length of time at the high temperature which is just necessary to prevent the eggs from developing into normal swimming larvae. The ratio of these times for different temperatures is the temperature coefficient. These experiments give a temperature coefficient of approximately 1,000 for 10° C , i.e., it requires only about one-thousandth as long at 30° as at 20° C to injure the eggs so that they do not produce normal larvae   The temperature coefficient of the length of life of unfertilized eggs Loeb finds to be about the same.

The temperature coefficient of embryonic development in the sea-urchins is 2 86 for 10° C., which means that a rise in temperature of 10° increases the rate of development 2 86 times. This is about the usual temperature coefficient of chemical reaction at these temperatures

Loeb's argument is that if the processes which determine development and those which determine length of life are identical, they must have the same temperature coefficient, and since they do not, he concludes that they must be different   Death is therefore not the final result of development, but of specific processes quite distinct from the developmental processes   He also attempts to account for the supposed large numbers of individuals in the animal life of cold waters on this basis, at 10°, for example, animals develop about one-third as rapidly but live one thousand times as long as at 20°; therefore the number of individuals alive at any given time must be much greater at the lower than at the higher temperature.

There are several objections to this line of argument. In the first place, the processes which immediately determine death may be very different from those which underlie development, and still death may be the result of the developmental processes, because these bring the organism into a condition where the death changes can occur   Loeb, himself, admits this when he says that the destructive processes which bring about death in the unfertilized egg are set going by the maturation process   Maturation is a normal feature of the life history of the egg, and to say that it leads to death is merely to say that the end of the developmental history is death.

As regards the conclusions drawn from the temperature coefficient of length of life, Loeb assumes that death from high temperature is identical with natural death from old age, although there is no evidence that this is the case   Certainly there is little reason for believing that the death of embryos in early stages or of larvae is the same thing as the death from old age of full-grown animals Death in these early stages, however it occurs, is undoubtedly due to processes different from the developmental processes, but it is at the same time an indication that something has gone wrong and not in any sense a natural physiological death   To make an accidental process of this kind the basis for conclusions concerning length of life and physiological death under natural conditions is certainly not warranted until convincing proof that the two are identical is presented   Loeb has failed completely to show that the processes which bring about death at high temperature have anything to do with physiological death in nature and he has presented no evidence to show that physiological death is not the result and final stage of development.

CONCLUSION

As regards the relation between senescence, death, and rejuvenescence, the higher animals and man differ from the lower organisms in the limitation of the capacity for regression and rejuvenescence under the usual conditions   Senescence is therefore more continuous than in the lower forms and results in death, which is the final stage of progressive development.   These characteristics of man and the higher animals are connected with the evolutionary increase in the physiological stability of the protoplasmic substratum and the higher degree of individuation which results from it   Nevertheless, some degree of rejuvenescence occurs, even in man, and different tissues differ as regards their capacity for rejuvenescence, the central nervous system being apparently least capable of regressive changes. This characteristic of the nervous system suggests the probability that the natural or physiological length of life in these forms is determined primarily by the length of life of the nervous system and that physiological death is primarily the death, as the final stage of senescence, of the nervous system. This view is supported by various facts of observation

Physiological or natural death is not something which has originated in the course of evolution from the lower to the higher forms. All organisms, from the lowest to the highest, from the simplest to the most complex, undoubtedly die of old age, unless senescence is compensated by rejuvenescence. In the lower forms the death point may never be attained under the usual conditions because the low stability of the substratum and the consequent low degree of individuation permit the frequent occurrence of a high degree of rejuvenescence. In the higher forms death becomes inevitable and necessary because the capacity for rejuvenescence is limited by the greater stability of the substratum. For his high degree of individuation man pays the penalty of individual death, and the conditions and processes in the human organism which lead to death in the end are the conditions and processes which make man what he is The advance of knowledge and of experimental technique may make it possible at some future time to bring about a greater degree of rejuvenescence and retardation of senescence in man and the higher animals than is now possible, but when we remember that the present condition of the protoplasmic substratum of these organisms is the result of millions of years of evolutionary equilibration, we cannot but admit that this task may prove to be one of considerable difficulty.

REFERENCES

BENEDICT, F. G.

1907   "The Influence of Inanition on Metabolism," *Carnegie Inst Publ* , *No. 77*.

1915   "A Study of Prolonged Fasting," *Carnegie Inst Publ., No 203*

CHAMPY, C

1913.   "La différenciation des tissus cultivés en dehors de l'organisme," *Bibliogr. Anat* , XXIII

1914.   "Notes de biologie cytologique. Quelques résultats de la méthode de culture de tissus III, Le rein," *Arch. de zool. exp* , LIV.

DEMANGE.
    1886   *Étude clinique et anatomo-pathologique de la vieillesse.*

DOLLEY, D H
    1914.   "On a Law of Species Identity of the Nucleus-Plasma Norm for
         Nerve Cell Bodies of Corresponding Type," *Journal of Comp.
         Neurol*, XXIV.

HARMS, W.
    1912.   "Beobachtungen uber den naturlichen Tod der Tiere. I Mitt.
         Der Tod bei *Hydroides pectinata* Phil., nebst Bemerkungen uber
         die Biologie dieses Wurmes," *Zool. Anzeiger*, Bd. XL

LOEB, J.
    1902   "Über Eireifung, naturlichen Tod und Verlangerung des Lebens
         beim Seesternei," *Arch. f. d. ges. Physiol.*, XCIII.
    1908   "Uber den Temperaturkoeffizienten fur die Lebensdauer kalt-
         blutiger Tiere und über die Ursache des naturlichen Todes,"
         Arch. f. d. ges. Physiol., CXXIV.

LORAND, A.
    1911.   *Das Altern, seine Ursachen und seine Behandlung.* Leipzig

METCHNIKOFF, E.
    1903.   *The Nature of Man.* English translation New York and London
    1910.   *The Prolongation of Life.* English translation. New York and
         London

MINOT, C. S.
    1908.   *The Problem of Age, Growth and Death.* New York.
    1913   *Moderne Probleme der Biologie.* Jena

MONTI, R.
    1905.   "Il rinnovamento dell' organismo dopo il letargo." *Monitore Zool.
         Ital.*, XVI.

MORGULIS, S
    1911.   "Studies of Inanition in Its Bearing upon the Problem of Growth,"
         Arch. f. Entwickelungsmech, XXXII.
    1913.   "The Influence of Protracted and Intermittent Fasting upon
         Growth," *Am. Nat.*, XLVII.

MÜHLMANN, M
    1900.   *Uber die Ursache des Alters.* Wiesbaden.
    1910.   "Das Altern und der physiologische Tod," *Sammlung anat u.
         physiol. Vortr*, XI
    1914.   "Beitrage zur Frage nach der Ursache des Todes," *Arch. f. Pathol.*
         (Virchow), CCXV.

NOÉ, J.
    1900.   "La réparation compensatrice après la jeune," *Compt. rend de la
         Soc. biol.*, LII.

PEMBREY, M S., and SPRIGGS, E I
    1904. "The Influence of Fasting and Feeding upon the Respiratory and Nitrogenous Exchange," *Jour. of Physiol.*, XXXI

RIBBERT, H
    1908 *Der Tod aus Altersschwache* Bonn

RUBNER, M.
    1908. *Das Problem der Lebensdauer und seine Beziehungen zu Wachstum und Ernahrung.* Munchen
    1909. *Kraft und Stoff im Haushalte der Natur* Leipzig

SEELAND, VON.
    1887. "Über die Nachwirkung der Nahrungsentzichung auf die Ernahrung," *Biol Centralbl.*, VII.

VERWORN, M.
    1909 *Allgemeine Physiologie.* V. Auflage. Jena.

WEISMANN, A.
    1882. *Über die Dauer des Lebens* Jena
    1884 *Über Leben und Tod* Jena
    1892. *Das Keimplasma.* Jena.
    1904. *Vortrage uber Descendenztheorie.* II Auflage. Jena.

ZIEGLER, E.
    1901. *Allgemeine Pathologie* X. Auflage. Jena.

PART IV

GAMETIC REPRODUCTION IN RELATION TO THE AGE CYCLE

CHAPTER XIII

ORIGIN AND MORPHOLOGICAL AND PHYSIOLOGICAL CONDITION OF THE GAMETES IN PLANTS AND ANIMALS

THE THEORETICAL SIGNIFICANCE OF GAMETIC ORIGIN

The question of the origin of the gametes or sex cells derives its chief importance from the germ-plasm theory, first advanced by Galton ('72) and Jäger ('77) and later developed by Weismann ('85, '92), which postulates the continuous existence of a germ plasm independent of the soma—that is, of other parts of the organism—except for nutrition, and giving rise to the gametes. If such a germ plasm exists and is continuous from generation to generation we should expect to find in at least some organisms indications of the separate existence of germ plasm and soma, even in early stages of development. An early segregation of the germ plasm from the somatic cells has been recorded for various animals and these facts have commonly been regarded as affording support to the germ-plasm hypothesis. Other facts, such as the formation of gametes and the occurrence of regeneration from apparently differentiated cells in some animals and in plants, forced Weismann to assume the existence of a "supplementary germ plasm" which was supposed to exist in the nuclei of many differentiated cells and which might be "activated" under the proper conditions and give rise to new embryonic cells, or even to gametes. The existence of this supplementary germ plasm may be assumed wherever it is necessary for the theory, so that a vicious circle is established.

But when we consider the facts apart from theoretical considerations, we find that the gametes appear to be integral parts of the organism when they arise, that they become highly specialized and differentiated cells, and that fertilization, whatever the nature of its mechanism, initiates a process of dedifferentiation and rejuvenescence which is followed by another period of differentiation and senescence. This and the two following chapters are concerned with the development of this point of view.

THE ORIGIN OF THE GAMETES IN PLANTS

Thus far no evidence has been discovered among the plants of an early separation of the primitive germ cells from other so-called somatic portions of the organism, such as has been described for various animals (see pp 323–33) No *Keimbahn* or germ path exists in the plants, that is, the germ cells cannot be followed through the developmental history as cells or protoplasmic regions distinct from other parts of the body

In that group of the green algae known as the *Conjugales,* which includes *Spirogyra* and the desmids, in the diatoms, and in most of the ciliate infusoria among the animals, the cell which constitutes the body of the organism becomes the gamete without any or with comparatively little visible structural change, two such cells conjugate, and their contents fuse to form the zygospore

In other algae and in those fungi in which gametic reproduction is known to occur, the gametes are always more or less different both in morphological structure and behavior from other parts of the organism, but they originate from the plant body and to all appearances are the most highly specialized parts of the species, and, finally, in most cases, show a high degree of sexual differentiation, as the following figures show   Fig 123 shows the young egg cell of *Volvox,* Fig. 124 a *Volvox* spermatozoid, Fig 125 the oogonium and antheridium of the alga *Oedogonium* with female and male gametes, Fig 126 the sex organs of *Chara* with the single egg in the oogonium, and Fig. 127 a spermatozoid of *Chara.* In Fig. 128 the sex organs of the fungus *Saprolegnia* and their relation to the vegetative part of the plant are shown   In all these cases the gametes show the same sort of sexual differentiation as in the multicellular animals.   In the mold *Mucor,* however, the ends of two hyphae enlarge and come together, and a gametic cell is separated from each (Fig 129), but the two cells are not, so far as known, sexually differentiated   These two cells increase in size (Fig 130) and unite to form the zygospore (Fig. 131)   In none of these cases is there any trace of an early segregation of the germ cells from the rest of the plant.   The sex organs and germ cells appear only when the plant attains a certain physiological condition.

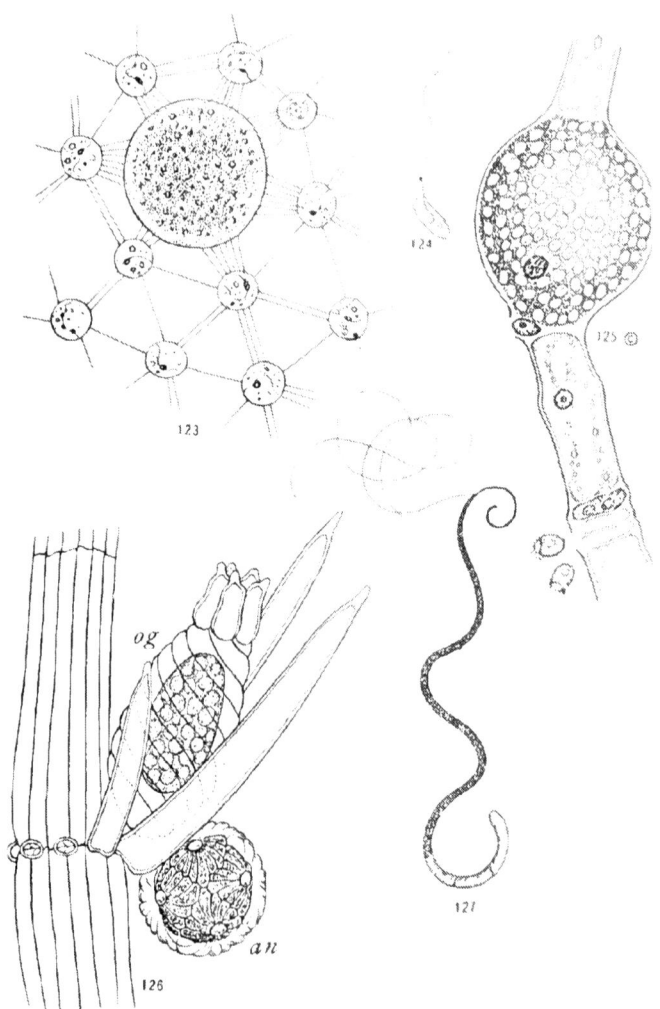

FIGS. 123-127.—Gametes of various algae: Fig. 123, young egg cell of *V. aureus*, connected with surrounding vegetative cells by numerous plasmatic strands (from Klein, '89); Fig. 124, spermatozoid of *Volvox aureus* (from Klein, '89); Fig. 125, part of filament of *Oedogonium*, showing oögonium with large egg and below the antheridia, from two of which spermatozoids have escaped (from Coulter, etc., '10); Fig. 126, branch of *Chara*, bearing oögonium, *og*, containing a single egg and antheridium, *an* (after Sachs, from Coulter, etc., '10); Fig. 127, spermatozoid of *Chara* (from Belajeff, '94).

In the mosses and ferns the separate history of the germ cells
may in the male extend back to an early stage in the development
of the male sexual organ, the antheridium, where the spermatogenous cell or cells become separated from the cells of the
antheridial wall.   Fig. 132 shows the stage of development of the
antheridium in which the spermatogenous cells first become segregated in *Riccia*, one of the liverworts.   After their segregation

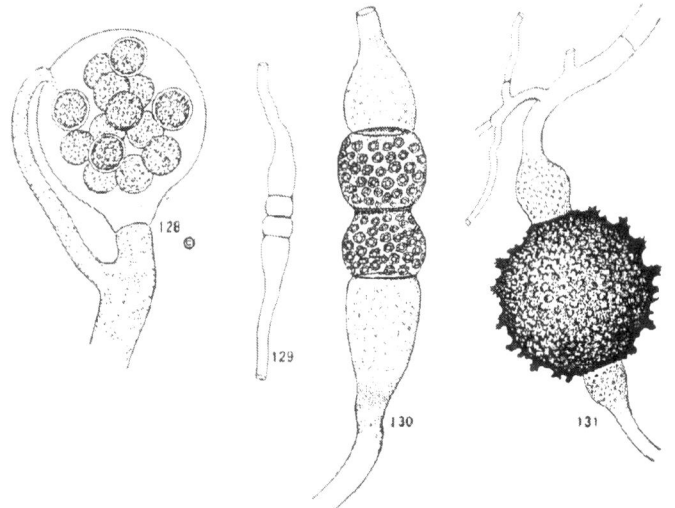

Figs. 128–131.—Gametes of fungi: Fig. 128, oögonium of *Saprolegnia*, containing several eggs and antheridial tube piercing its wall in fertilization (from Coulter,
etc., '10); Figs. 129–131, three stages in formation and union of gametes in *Mucor*
(from Brefeld, '72).

the spermatogenous cells undergo numerous divisions and finally
give rise to spermatozoids.

The female gamete, on the other hand, is not separated from
other non-gametic cells until the last division preceding fertilization.
Figs. 133–39 show the development of the archegonium of *Riccia*.
The divisions of the central cell in Fig. 135 produce the four neck
canal cells and the ventral cell (Fig. 137). Fig. 138 shows the
division of the ventral cell which gives rise to the ventral canal

cell and the egg. The fully developed archegonium con
the egg *o*, is shown in Fig. 139. The canal cells take no
reproduction, but degenerate before fertilization.

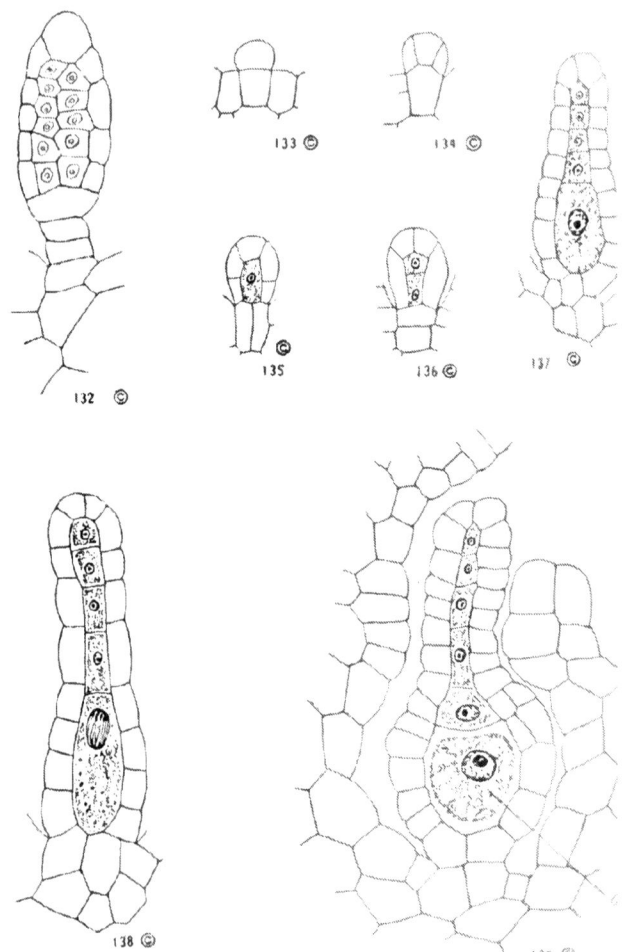

FIGS. 132–139.—Stages of gamete formation in the liverwort *Riccia*: 1
antheridium in stage at which spermatogenous cells become segregated fro
of wall; Figs. 133–139, formation of archegonium and egg, *o*, in *Riccia*. From C
etc., '10.

In the seed plants the whole gametophyte generation is greatly reduced and represents scarcely more than specialized male and female organs of the plant. In the lower seed plants, the gymnosperms, a considerable number of nuclear divisions may occur in the development of the gametophyte, and the female gamete is separated from other cells at some stage of this development. In the male gametophyte of the gymnosperms the number of divisions varies, but is always small, and in the course of these divisions the male gamete is separated from non-reproductive cells.

And finally in the angiosperms, which represent the final stage in reduction of the gametophyte, the development of the male gametophyte—the mature pollen grain—from the microspore consists, with one exception, of only two nuclear divisions, of which the first separates the primary spermatogenous cell from the tube nucleus and the second divides the spermatogenous nucleus into two male gametes, so that the male gametophyte contains only three nuclei (Fig. 140).

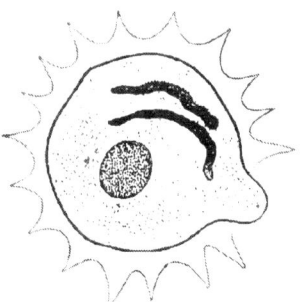

FIG. 140.—Pollen grain of *Silphium terebinthinaceum*, showing rounded vegetative nucleus and the two elongated male nuclei. From Merrell, '00.

The course of development of the female gametophyte, which is the embryo sac within the ovule, is indicated in Fig. 141. The nucleus of the megaspore (*A*) divides and the two daughter nuclei pass to opposite poles (*B*); a second division occurs in each (*C*), and a third follows (*D*), so that eight nuclei are present, four at each pole, but without cell boundaries. Two nuclei, one from each group of four, move toward the middle of the embryo sac and fuse to form the primary endosperm nucleus. About the three nuclei at the micropylar end (the upper end in the figures) three naked cell bodies arise, and these three cells are the egg and the two synergids (*E*). The three nuclei at the opposite pole form the three antipodal cells which are usually ephemeral but may persist. Thus the germ

plasm is segregated only at the last division preceding the fin
differentiation of the egg.

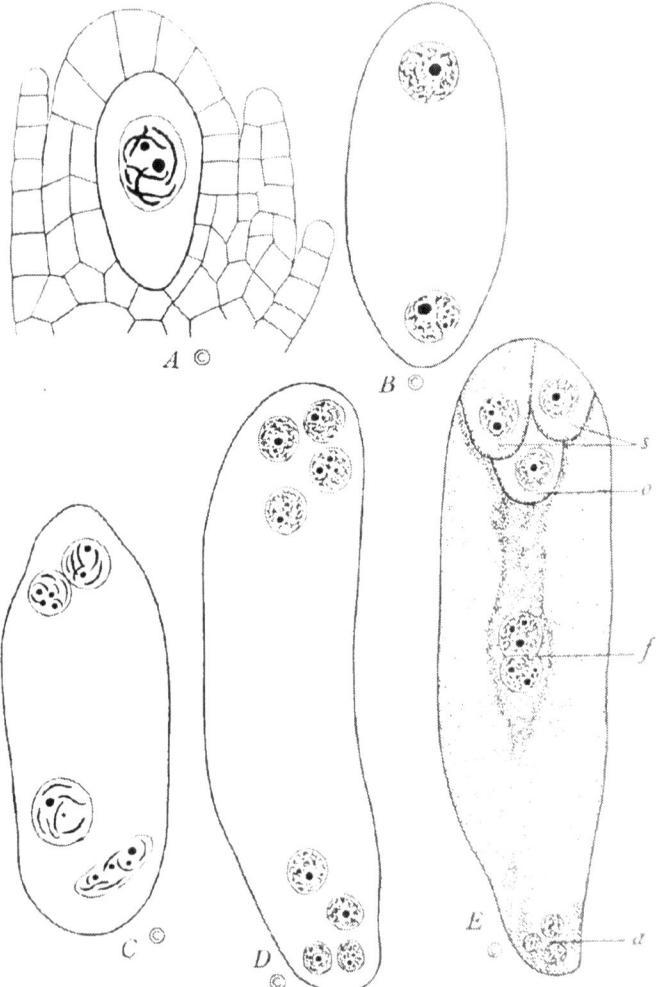

FIG. 141.—Development of female gametophyte and formation of egg in th
higher seed plants: A, megaspore in the ovule; B, first division; C, second division
D, third division; E, mature gametophyte: o, egg; s, synergids; a, antipodals;
primary endosperm nucleus. After Coulter, etc., '10.

The whole process of development of the gametes in the plants bears all the marks of a highly specialized process, far removed from anything which occurs in unspecialized embryonic cells, and nowhere do we find a separation of the gametic from the somatic material before the later or final stages of the developmental process.

The occurrence among mosses, ferns, and seed plants of what is known as apogamy, i e , the formation of a sporophyte without fertilization from a vegetative cell of the gametophyte instead of from the egg,[1] is of interest in this connection. In apogamous ferns the embryo apparently may rise from any vegetative cell of the prothallium, which is the gametophyte, and in seed plants it may arise either from the synergids or the antipodals of the embryo sac, or from both In some cases also among angiosperms sporophytes may arise from cells of the nucellus or of the integument adjacent to the embryo sac. These cells are not even parts of the gametophyte, but belong to the sporophyte generation, yet in the region of the embryo sac they may produce embryos and sporophytes as does the egg. In such cases the gametophyte generation is omitted from the life history.

All of these cases of non-sexual development from vegetative or "somatic" cells of the sporophyte—the generation which usually develops from the fertilized egg—indicate that the capacities of the egg are not fundamentally different from those of other cells of the gametophyte and of some cells of the sporophyte. It is of course easy to assume with the Weismannians that, in spite of their visible differentiations, all such cells contain an undifferentiated germ plasm, but, so far as scientific analysis is concerned, this assumption is equivalent to begging the whole question A simpler view and one much more nearly in accord with the facts of observation and experiment is that which is held by most botanists, viz , that many, or in some plants all, specialized or differentiated cells may under proper conditions lose their specialization and become embryonic and so give rise to new individuals [2]

[1] See Winkler, '08, for a general survey and bibliography of the subject.

[2] In the usual course of development all the cells of the gametophyte have the reduced or haploid number of chromosomes like the animal egg after maturation,

It was shown in an earlier chapter (pp. 245-47) that dedifferentiation undoubtedly occurs very commonly in plants, especially in connection with adventitious and experimental reproduction. The new plants thus formed from cells previously differentiated as parts of other plants possess the capacity to form gametes   In other words, gametes may very often arise from cells which form differentiated parts of the plant body, and there is no evidence of the continuous existence of any germ plasm in the theoretical sense in such cells.

To sum up, we find in the plants no indication of continued or early segregation of germ plasm from somatic plasm. In most cases the gametes are not separated from somatic cells until the final stages of their developmental history, and on the other hand differentiated cells, in many cases every cell of the plant, may undergo dedifferentiation and redifferentiation into new individuals capable of producing gametes   Either all the cells of the plant contain germ plasm or there is no continuity of germ plasm in the plant. The facts point to the second of these alternatives   The gametes arise in the course of development like other specialized parts, and like these also possess a definite history of differentiation.

THE ORIGIN OF THE GAMETES IN ANIMALS

In many of the unicellular animals, as in the unicellular plants, the cell which constitutes the organism becomes the gamete. In others the gametes are different in form from the vegetative stages,

the process of reduction occurring in the formation of the spores which give rise to the gametophyte   But in various mosses and ferns apospory may occur, i e , the gametophyte may arise from other cells of the sporophyte without the occurrence of chromosome reduction, in which case the cells of the gametophyte, including the egg, possess the full or diploid number of chromosomes   Where the gametophyte possesses the haploid number of chromosomes, apogamy gives rise to a sporophyte with the haploid number, half the number characteristic of sporophytes, but when the gametophyte cells are diploid, the sporophyte which arises apogamously or parthenogenically possesses the full number   Various other combinations of apospory, apogamy, parthenogenesis, and fertilization have been recorded.   In certain mosses, for example, the aposporous formation of diploid gametes, followed by fertilization and the development of a tetraploid sporophyte, has been observed (Marchal, '07, '09, '11, '12)   The number of chromosomes is evidently not connected in any essential way either with the differentiation of sporophyte and gametophyte or with the formation of the gametes, since any of these stages may possess either the diploid or haploid number and sometimes spermatozoa and eggs approaching in morphological differentiation those of the multicellular forms appear   In the multicellular animals the process of gamete formation differs in certain respects from that in the plant   There is in the animal no developmental history with cell division, growth, and differentiation between maturation and fertilization, corresponding to the gameto-phyte generation in plants.   The gametic cells are segregated from other cells long before the maturation divisions occur   Since the germ-plasm theory has found its adherents chiefly among zoologists, it is natural that the attention of zoological investigators should have been attracted to the question of the early segregation of the germ cells from the somatic cells   If the germ plasm is really a distinct and separate entity independent of the soma and is con-tinuous from one generation to another, we should expect the germ cells to be segregated from the somatic cells at the beginning of embryonic development.   Thus far, however, no case has been discovered in which such a segregation occurs, although in various animal groups a more or less complete segregation apparently does occur at an early stage of development.   In other groups, among the animals, no indication of such segregation has ever been ob-served, although theoretical considerations have led many zoolo-gists to believe that even in such cases a segregation occurs, but without visible differences between germ cells and other cells.

To discuss this subject at length is beyond the present purpose, but some of the more important cases of early segregation must be briefly considered.[1]   Perhaps the most striking case of early segre-gation of germ cells is that in the parasitic worm *Ascaris megalo-cephala*, first described by Boveri and later confirmed by other investigators, but recently denied by Zacharias [2]   As every zoolo-gist knows, the process of segregation of the germ cells in this species begins at the first cleavage of the egg and is accompanied by the peculiar process of "diminution" of the chromatin in the somatic cells   Diminution, which occurs first in one cell of the

---

[1] For general surveys of the subject with bibliographies see Korscheldt and Heider, '02, pp 368–77, Waldeyer, '06, Felix and Buhler, '06, Hacker, '12a, '12b, Hegner, '14c

[2] Boveri, '87, '99, '04, zur Strassen, '96, Zacharias, '13, Zoja, '96

two-cell stage, consists in the separation of the large club-shaped ends of the chromosomes, their exclusion from the nucleus of the following resting stage, and their gradual disappearance in the cytoplasm. At the same time the remaining portions of each chromosome break up into a number of smaller chromosomes and in following divisions of this cell similar small chromosomes appear, and the nuclei of the resting stages are relatively small and poor in chromatin. In the other cell, however, diminution does not occur, the chromosomes retain their original form and large size, and the resting nucleus is large and rich in chromatin In the second cleavage this cell gives rise to one cell which undergoes diminution and one which does not, and in the third and fourth cleavages also one cell remains with chromatin undiminished. In the fifth cleavage the undiminished cell divides into two equal cells, and these are, according to Boveri and others, the primitive germ cells Here then we can trace the line of descent of the germ cells, the germ path (*Keimbahn*), from the first cleavage. The germ path and the fates of the various cells which undergo diminution are indicated in Fig. 142.

The process of early segregation of germ cells in *Ascaris* has been very generally regarded as constituting almost a demonstration of the continuity and independence of the germ plasm, but as a matter of fact it is far from being anything of the kind. In the first place, while it seems fairly certain that the reproductive organs of *Ascaris* do arise from the undiminished cell line of descent, it is not known whether these cells give rise merely to the germ cells or to the walls of the reproductive organs as well. In the latter case the germ path of early cleavage has not resulted in the segregation of germ plasm from the soma, but merely in the segregation of different organs, for the walls of the reproductive organs are not germ plasm.

Moreover, the whole process is very different from what we should expect in a segregation of germ plasm from the soma If the germ plasm is a distinct entity, why should it not become segregated in the first division instead of in the fourth? The first four cleavages are really segregations into different cells, not simply of germ plasm, but of various parts of the body, as Fig 142 shows

The diminished cell S_1 of the two-cell stage produces a definite part of the ectoderm, and the cells S_2, S_3, and S_4 of following generations each have a definite fate. In other words, various portions of the soma or body are segregated before the so-called germ plasm.

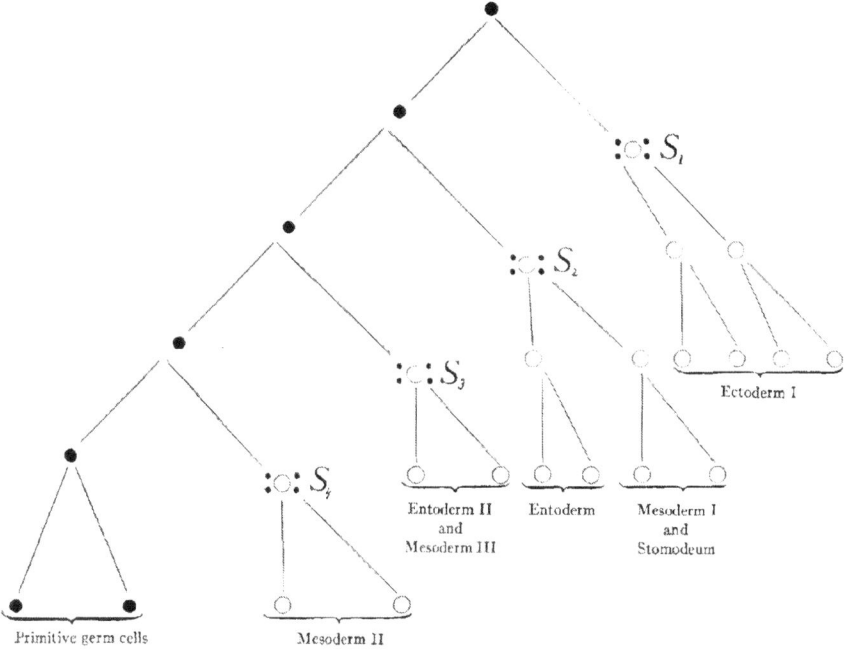

Fig. 142.—Diagram of the cell lineage in the early cleavage of *Ascaris megalocephala:* the black circles represent cells before chromatin diminution and the primitive germ cells which do not undergo diminution; the unshaded circles with four black dots about them represent the cells which undergo diminution, and the unshaded circles alone, the cells after diminution. The further history of the various groups of cells is indicated by the words, "ectoderm," etc. After Boveri, '10.

The undiminished cells show in all cases a slower rate of division than those in which diminution has occurred, and there is no evidence to show that the differences in the behavior of the chromatin are anything more than visible indications or expressions of differences in rate of metabolic activity. It is quite possible that the undiminished cells become germ cells because they have a low rate of metabolism and are not involved in the early differentiations, but differentiate later.

A recent study of modified cleavage made by Boveri ('10) on polyspermic and centrifuged eggs of *Ascaris* has proved beyond a doubt that the occurrence or non-occurrence of chromatin diminution in a nucleus depends, not upon its qualitative constitution, but upon its cytoplasmic environment. If this is true, persistence of the undiminished condition is not a segregation of preformed germ plasm, but a nuclear reaction to cytoplasmic conditions. The "germ path" is a feature of the cytoplasm, not of the nucleus, and the cytoplasm is not, properly speaking, a part of the germ plasm at all, but represents the soma of the cell. Which nuclei shall

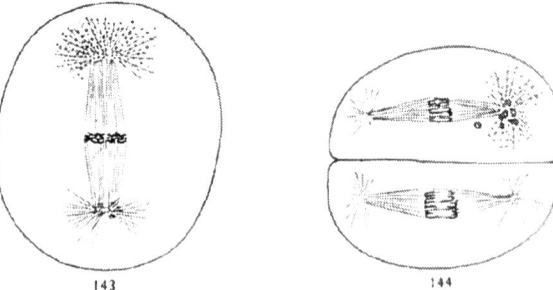

FIGS. 143, 144.—First and second division in egg of *Cyclops*, showing at one pole of spindle the granules which mark the germ path. From Amma, '11.

become the nuclei of germ cells is determined, not primarily by the nuclei themselves, but by the soma of the cell; the germ plasm is not then an independent entity, but is determined by correlative factors, like any other part of the organism, except the apical or head region.

Häcker ('97, '02) has described a germ path for *Cyclops* and other copepod crustacea, and his observations have been confirmed by Amma ('11). The germ path in this case is characterized by certain granules which appear at one pole of the first cleavage spindle (Fig. 143), pass into one of the two daughter cells, and later aggregate into larger masses and disappear. At the second division (Fig. 144) and also at the third and fourth divisions similar granules appear at one pole of the spindle of the cell to which the granules passed in the preceding division, and in each case pass into one of the two daughter cells, which continues the germ path   But in the cell of the fifth generation the granules appear all around the mitotic figure and pass into both daughter cells, which are according to Häcker the primitive germ cells   Here the germ path is characterized, not by peculiar nuclear features, but by cytoplasmic differentiations which are products of metabolism· the germ cells are evidently an integral physiological part of the organism.   Somewhat similar germ paths have been described for various other crustacea.

The early segregation of the primitive germ cells in *Sagitta* has been noted by several authors, and Buchner ('10) has recently discovered the beginning of the germ path in the granules resulting from the degeneration of a nutritive cell taken up by the egg in the ovary, again a cytoplasmic not a nuclear basis of segregation, although the granules in this case may be of nuclear origin.   In a discussion of other cases Buchner concludes that determination of the germ path in this way is of very general occurrence.

In many insects a distinct germinal path with early segregation of the primitive germ cells has been observed.   Among the diptera all forms carefully examined show some sort of germ path.   In the gnat *Chironomus*, for example (Hasper, '11), the primitive germ cell is segregated in the second cleavage (Fig 145), and in the fly *Miastor* (Kahle, '08; Hegner, '12, '14a, '14c) the segregation of the mother germ cell occurs in the third cleavage, one nucleus of this cleavage becoming imbedded in a peculiar cytoplasmic region at the posterior end of the egg, and giving rise later to the germ cells, while all the other nuclei undergo a process of diminution of chromatin somewhat similar to that occurring in *Ascaris*.

A cytoplasmic germ-path determinant in the form of a peculiar granular cytoplasmic region at the posterior pole of the egg, which during cleavage becomes nucleated and separates off as the primitive germ cells, has recently been described for several chrysomelid beetles, including the potato beetle, by Hegner ('09, '11, '14a). This author concludes with Boveri that the cytoplasm, not the nuclei, determines which cells shall become germ cells, but this

means that the germ cells are probably determined in essentially the same way as other parts of the organism In various other insects also a germ path has been described. In certain hymenoptera Hegner ('14b) finds that the granules of the polar cytoplasmic region are derived from the disintegrated nucleus of a nutritive cell taken up by the egg during its growth, an origin very similar to that which Buchner described in the case of *Sagitta*.

In all these cases among the inverte-brates the factors determining what shall become germ cells and what somatic structures apparently exist in the cytoplasm and not in the nuclei. Moreover, the cytoplasmic regions which determine the germ cells are not directly related to the cytoplasm of pre-existing germ cells, but very evidently are simply regions where certain special metabolic conditions exist Cells arising from these regions become germ cells, just as those arising from other regions become one part or another of the body. It is of interest to note that very generally the germ cells arise from regions of the egg with a relatively low metabolic rate. They very commonly divide more slowly than other cells. In fact, it seems possible that this low metabolic rate, rather than any specific character, determines that they shall not take part in the early development of the body, because other cells react

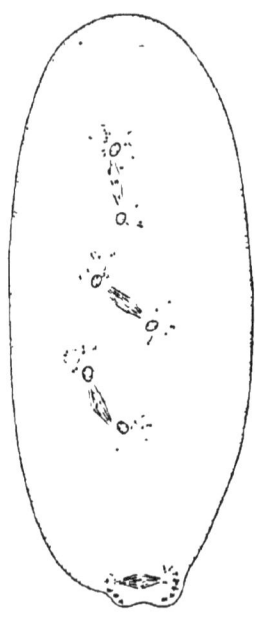

FIG 145 —Early cleavage of *Chironomus*, a gnat the spindle at the lower end of the egg represents the primitive germ cell, the cytoplasm about this spindle separates with it from the remainder of the egg and divides into two cells, each of which divides farther From Hasper, '11

more rapidly than they do They are, so to speak, left behind and only later become an active functional part of the organism

Among the vertebrates comparatively early segregation of the primitive germ cells is apparently of wide occurrence in fishes, amphibia, and reptiles. More than thirty years ago Nussbaum ('80) described the early differentiation of the sex cells in fishes and amphibia. Later, Eigenmann ('92, '96a) described the early segregation of germ cells in fishes and found that the primitive germ cells in the fish *Cymatogaster* were segregated in the fifth cell generation of cleavage, and Wheeler ('00) found a relatively early differentiation of the germ cells in the lamprey. Two years later Beard ('02), as the result of his work on selachians, reached the conclusion that the germ cells are independent unicellular organisms which pass a part of their life in the multicellular sterile soma This conclusion rests on the occurrence in embryonic stages of certain large cells seen by various investigators in certain regions of the embryo and which are described as migrating to the position of the sexual organs and later becoming the germ cells Since Beard's paper, a large number of similar observations have been made by various authors on fishes, amphibia, and reptiles.

As regards all these data on germ-cell segregation in the vertebrates, the first question is the correctness of the observations Much time has been devoted to the observation of these cells in the embryonic stages and but little to the details of their later fate Moreover, the extensive migrations described from various regions of the embryo to the position of the sexual organs are in all cases inferences from the examination of fixed and stained material But granting that the observations are correct, the segregation of the germ cells is no earlier in most cases than that of many other parts of the body, and such cases afford no valid evidence against the view that the germ cells are integral, specialized parts of the body like other organs. In most cases these early germ cells in vertebrates are. like those of invertebrates, apparently cells with a lower rate of metabolism than other parts of the embryo Often they retain yolk granules later than other cells, and in all respects appear to be less active during early stages (Eigenmann, '96b).

At present the only conclusion possible from all these observations on germ paths and germinal segregation is that while the data, if correct, as they probably are in at least many cases, do indicate that in various forms the germ cells become more or less distinctly segregated from other cells at early stages of development, they do not in any way constitute a valid argument for the independence and continuity of the germ plasm.

Moreover, there are many animals in which up to the present time no indication of early segregation of germ cells has ever been found by any investigator. In some of these forms, e g., certain flatworms and the polychete annelids, the sex organs appear only at a certain stage of development, or periodically, and before or between the periods of their occurrence no traces of anything representing germ cells can be found   The assumption has often been made that in such cases the germ plasm is segregated in certain cells, but that these cells possess no characteristic visible features distinguishing them from other cells or tissues   In the turbellaria, for example, the parenchyma has often been regarded as an "indifferent" tissue representing the germ plasm   But the only justification for terming such tissues as the turbellarian parenchyma indifferent or undifferentiated tissues lies in the fact that they give rise to germ cells and in reconstitution to various other parts Morphologically they are not undifferentiated, but possess definite histological characteristics quite different from those of cells or tissues which are really embryonic or undifferentiated, and when other tissues or organs arise from them they first lose these characteristics and become embryonic and then undergo a new differentiation   Moreover, when they undergo such changes their rate of metabolism becomes higher, an indication that they are undergoing dedifferentiation and becoming younger   They may be less highly specialized than certain other tissues of the organism, but only theoretical grounds can prevent us from admitting that where the germ cells arise from such tissues they arise from differentiated functional parts of the organism by a process of dedifferentiation and redifferentiation.

In the tapeworm *Moniezia*, for example, the sex cells arise from the parenchyma, and apparently any parenchymal cells which lie within the region involved in the production of sex cells may undergo dedifferentiation and take part in the process. Even the large muscle cells may give rise to testes, as indicated in Figs 146 and 147. In such cases the muscle fiber undergoes degeneration, the vacuoles disappear, and the nucleus begins to divide, apparently at first amitotically.

In some of the lower animals new individuals arise agamically or can be produced by experimental isolation of pieces from regions of the body which do not contain sex organs, yet these individuals are capable of producing sex cells. To assume that these regions of the body contain germ plasm in the Weismannian sense ready to develop into ovaries or testes when necessary is simply to beg the question. To all appearances germ cells develop in such cases from more or less differentiated cells of the region involved by a process of dedifferentiation and redifferentiation, and the assumption of a pre-existent germ plasm is entirely unnecessary.

It is scarcely probable that the germ plasm is a totally different thing in animals and plants. In the preceding section it has been pointed out that for a very large number of plants the development of

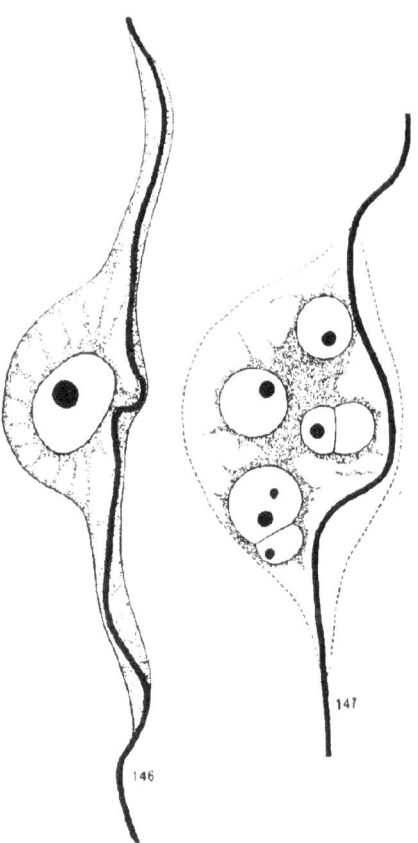

FIGS. 146, 147.—Formation of a testis from a muscle cell in *Moniezia:* Fig. 146, large muscle cell with single fiber; Fig. 147, transformation of muscle cell into testis.

germ cells from differentiated functional cells of the plant body has been experimentally demonstrated. This fact in itself creates

a presumption in favor of a similar origin in animals, and the purpose of the present section is to show that the facts themselves
when correctly analyzed, point to the same conclusion. The
assumption of the existence of supplementary germ plasm, i e
of portions of germ plasm in the nuclei of all or certain somatic cells
or tissues, not only finds no support in the data of observation and
experiment, but deprives the germ-plasm hypothesis of all scientific
value. It is undoubtedly true that the more highly specialized
cells of an organism, be it animal or plant, do not so readily undergo
dedifferentiation and redifferentiation under altered correlative
conditions and so do not so readily give rise to germ cells or other
parts as do the less highly specialized cells, in fact, many cells,
especially in the higher forms, are probably incapable of such
change, but this does not constitute adequate grounds for the belief
that germ plasm and soma are independent entities

Summing up, it appears that the facts afford no adequate
grounds for regarding the germ cells as anything else than an
integral part of the organism specialized in a certain direction like
other parts   But in spite of the complete absence of any trace of
early segregation of germ cells in many organisms, in spite of the
fact that the egg cytoplasm, not the nucleus, is apparently responsible in most if not in all cases of early segregation, in spite of our
ignorance in many cases whether the so-called primitive germ cells
really give rise only to gametes, and, finally, in spite of the remarkable conception of the organic world to which the germ-plasm
theory leads us—in spite of all these difficulties, the view that these
processsess of early specialization in the egg constitute a spatial
morphological segregation of the independent germ plasm from the
body or soma still finds supporters, as is evident from the most
recent consideration of the subject by Hegner ('14c).

THE MORPHOLOGICAL CONDITION OF THE GAMETES

Minot ('08) has maintained on morphological grounds that the
animal egg is an old cell approaching death, but has not so far as I
am aware, expressed any opinion regarding the condition of the
spermatozoon, although, according to his theory that increase in
the proportion of cytoplasm to nuclear substance is a fundamental

factor in senescence, the spermatozoon should be a very young cell, for it is almost without cytoplasm in most cases. I have called attention to various lines of evidence which indicate that both egg and spermatozoon are highly differentiated, old cells (Child, '11), and Conklin ('12, '13) has expressed himself as in essential agreement with this view.

The process of formation of the gametes in its morphological aspects is very evidently a process of specialization and differentiation. The fully developed gametic cells are among the most highly specialized cells, if not the most highly specialized cells of the multicellular organism, but the primitive germ cells from which they arise are minute cells without any morphological structure beyond that common to cells in general, and with a high metabolic rate—in short, with all the visible characteristics of embryonic or unspecialized, undifferentiated cells The process of development of the gametes from such cells is a process of specialization and morphological differentiation of the same sort as that which occurs in other cells of the organism Morphologically the fully formed gamete certainly bears no resemblance to an embryonic cell. A few figures will serve to emphasize this point.

In Figs. 123–31 (pp. 317–18) the sex organs and gametes of some of the algae and fungi are shown The gametes are readily distinguished from the vegetative cells and in most cases appear to be more highly specialized and differentiated than those. Male gametes, the spermatozoids of a few plants from other groups, are shown in Figs. 148–53 Fig. 148 is the spermatozoid of a liverwort; Fig. 149, a horse-tail, *Equisetum,* Fig. 150, a fern. Fig. 151, a cycad, *Zamia,* Fig. 152 is the spermatozoid or generative nucleus of the sunflower, Fig. 140 (p 320) shows the pollen grain of *Silphium,* another composite with the two elongated generative nuclei or spermatozoids, and Fig. 153, a fully developed spermatozoid of the same plant. These male cells are different in various ways, but most of them possess a well-developed motor apparatus of one kind or another.

The differentiation of the male gamete among the animals is perhaps more uniform than among plants, but there are many animal species with aberrant forms of spermatozoa. Figs. 154–57,

161, and 166 show more or less "typical," fully deve
spermatozoa from various invertebrate and vertebrate species

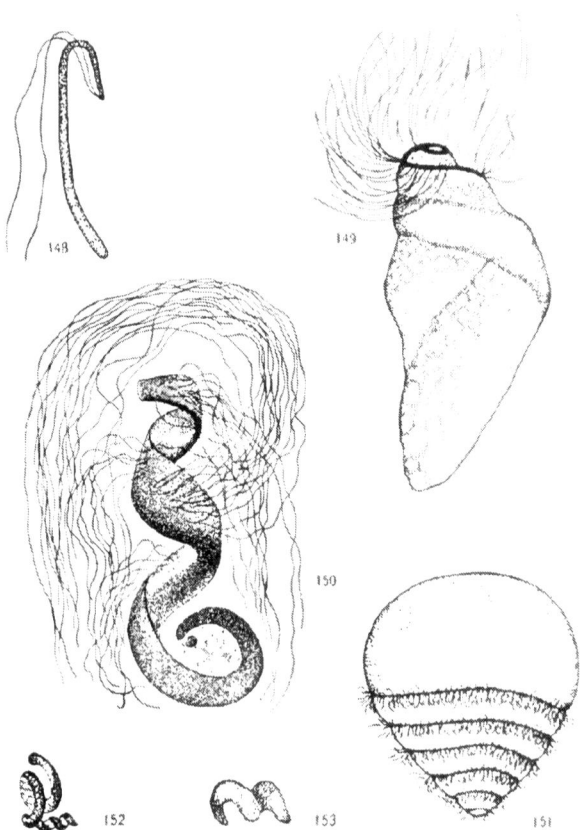

FIGS. 148–153.—Male gametes of various plants: Fig. 148, *Sphaerocarp
restris*, a liverwort (from Land, unpublished); Fig. 149, *Equisetum* (from Sharp
Fig. 150, *Nephrodium*, a fern (from Yamanouchi, '08); Fig. 151, *Zamia*, a cycad
Webber, '01); Fig. 152, *Helianthus*, sunflower (from Nawaschin, '00); Fig. 1:
phium (from Merrell, '00).

in Figs. 158–61 four developmental stages of the guinea-pig spe
tozoon are given. A few of the aberrant spermatozoan f
among animals are shown in Figs. 162–72. Figs. 162–64 are

three species of turbellarian worms, forms related to *Planaria;*
Fig 165 is the non-motile spermatozoon of the nematode worm
Ascaris megalocephala; Figs. 166 and 167 show the two forms of
spermatozoa found in certain snails; Figs. 168, 169, and 170 are

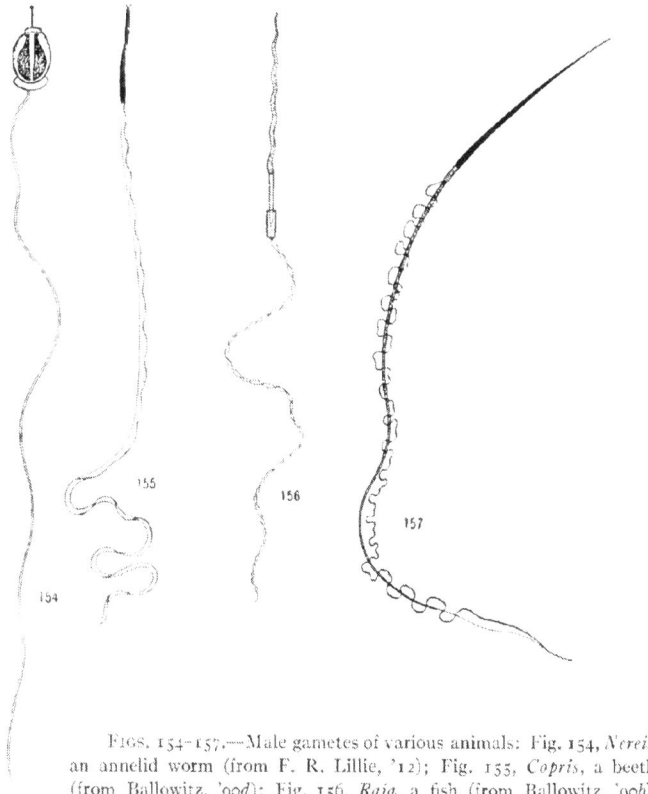

Figs. 154-157.—Male gametes of various animals: Fig. 154, *Nereis,*
an annelid worm (from F. R. Lillie, '12); Fig. 155, *Copris,* a beetle
(from Ballowitz, '90d); Fig. 156, *Raja,* a fish (from Ballowitz, '90b);
Fig. 157, *Triton,* a salamander (from Ballowitz, '90b).

from various species of crustacea, and Figs. 171 and 172 from
arachnids, but Fig. 171 perhaps represents a stage of spermatozoan
development rather than the mature form.

Usually the male gamete in both plants and animals is highly
motile, and the course of its development is to a large extent a

differentiation of the motor mechanism from a cell of the usual so
But in some cases, as in the angiosperms among plants (Figs.
153), in *Ascaris* (Fig. 165), and in the
crustacea (Figs. 168–70) among animals,
the male gamete is almost or quite non-
motile. Even in such cases, however,
it is none the less a highly specialized
cell. In the angiosperms among plants
a morphologically differentiated cytoplasmic mechanism is absent, but the
history, form, and behavior of the
nucleus attest its specialization. In
Ascaris (Fig. 165) the peculiar structure
of the cell shows that it has departed
far from the generalized form of the
embryonic cell. In the crustacean spermatozoa (Koltzoff, '06a) the skeletal or
supporting structures are extensively
developed, but according to Koltzoff
('06b, '08), such structures are present
in other spermatozoa also. Ballowitz'
('86–'08) extensive studies of the finer
structure of the spermatozoa also
demonstrate the morphological complexity of these remarkable cells. In
the more highly differentiated forms
there remains no trace of the ordinary
amorphous cytoplasm of the cells from
which they arise: all has either undergone breakdown as a source of energy
or has been transformed into the fibrillar
or other structures of the spermatozoon.

The development of the female
gamete follows a very different course,
but is none the less a process of specialization and morphological differentiation. Figs. 123, 125, 126, and 128

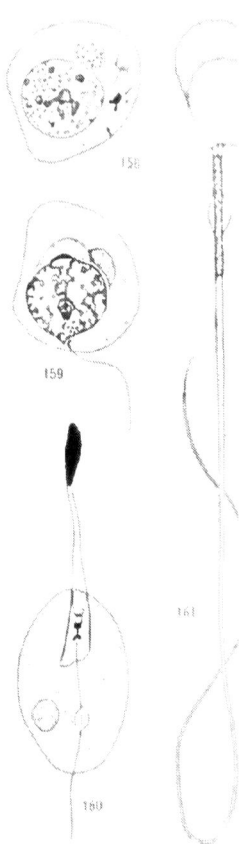

FIGS. 158–161.—Develop-
ment of spermatozoon f
spermatid in the guinea-
Fig. 158, beginning of tr
formation; Fig. 159, begin
of development of tail; Fig.
side view after formation
the thin flat head, Fig.
mature spermatozoon. Fr
Meves, '99.

(pp. 317-18) show the female gametes in some of the algae and fungi. The development of the female cell in the liverwort *Riccia*

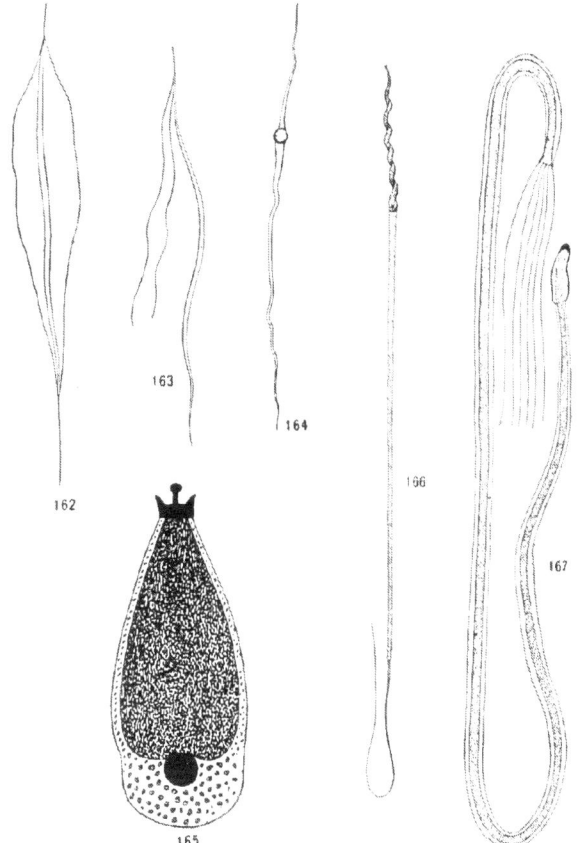

FIGS. 162-167.—Some peculiar forms of spermatozoa from the lower invertebrates: Fig. 162, *Plagiostomum*, a turbellarian (from Böhmig, '90); Fig. 163, *Castroda*, a turbellarian (from Luther, '04); Fig. 164, *Mesostomum*, a turbellarian (from Luther, '04); Fig. 165, *Ascaris megalocephala*, nematode worm (from Scheben, '05); Figs. 166, 167, the two forms of spermatozoa in *Paludina*, a snail (from Meres, '03).

is outlined in Figs. 133-39. Fig. 173 shows the archegonium of the fern *Nephrodium*, containing the large egg; Fig. 174 is the fertilized egg of the cycad *Zamia;* Fig. 175, the archegonium of a conifer, *Torreya taxifolia*, containing the large egg: incidentally this figure also shows the pollen tube with the two small male nuclei near the tip. The development of the female gamete in the angiosperms is outlined in Figs. 141, *A–E* (p. 321). Fig. 176 is the embryo sac of the sunflower at the time of fertilization, and Fig. 177, that of the coneflower, another composite, at the same stage. The eggs in all these plants are manifestly highly specialized cells which have undergone great changes from the embryonic condition.

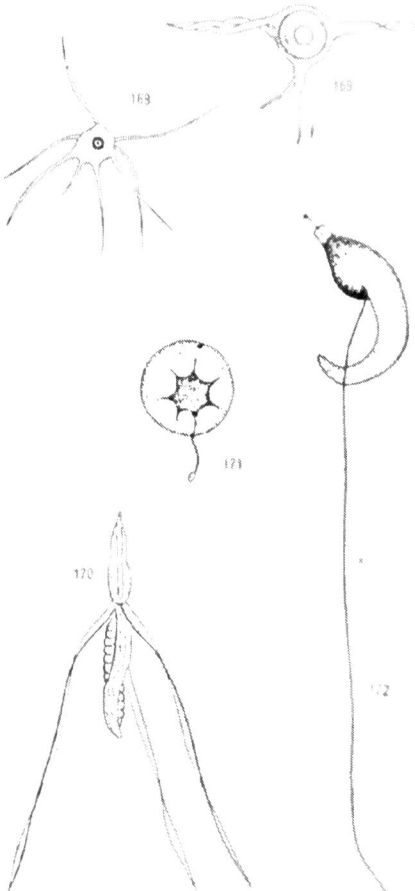

The animal egg usually exhibits an even greater degree of morphological specialization than that of the plant because it is loaded to a greater or less degree with granules or masses of yolk substance which becomes available as a nutritive supply at the beginning of embryonic development. The accumulation of yolk is often so great that the egg cell attains an enormous

FIGS. 168–172.—Peculiar forms of spermatozoa from the arthropods; Figs. 168, 169, 170, *Pinnotheres*, *Maja*, and *Munida*, all crustacea (from Koltzoff, '06); Figs. 171, 172, *Acantholophus*, *Agalena*, both spiders (from Bösenberg, '05).

size, the bird's egg representing the extreme of development in this direction. Since the period of growth and differentiation of

the animal egg as a single cell involves so much more extensive
and conspicuous change than in the plant, it has attracted much
attention and the course of oögenesis has been described for many
animal species. The following figures include characteristic stages
in the differentiation of a few animal eggs. Figs. 178-80 show
the egg of the fresh-water hydra, first at the beginning of its
growth as a small cell lying between the cells of the ectoderm
(Fig. 178); secondly, as a large amoeboid cell in the ovary
(Fig. 179); and, thirdly,
as a full-grown egg, still
in the ovary, with large
yolk spheres in the
cytoplasm. Figs. 181
and 182 show the primi-
tive germ cells and the
final stage of oögenesis
in the liver fluke *Fasciola
hepatica*, a parasitic flatworm. In most of the
flatworms the egg
accumulates little or no
yolk within its own
cytoplasm, but other
nutritive cells contain-
ing yolk are inclosed in
the capsule with it be-
fore it is extruded. In
these forms the egg cell
itself remains of small

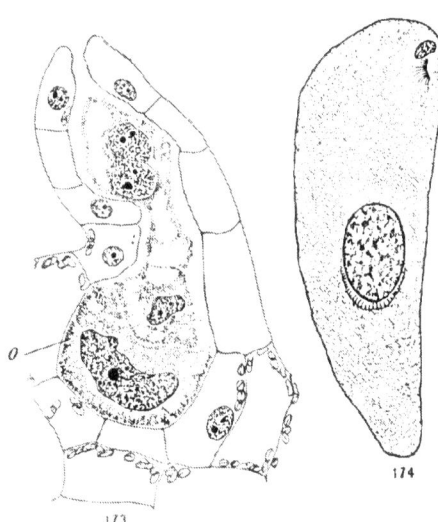

FIGS. 173-174.—Fig. 173, archegonium of *Nephrodium*, a fern, containing the egg, *o* (from Yamanouchi, '08); Fig. 174, fertilized egg of *Zamia*,
a cycad (from Webber, '01).

size and its growth history is relatively simple. In this and in
various other animals the egg as it grows develops a stalk (Fig. 182)
by which it is connected with the ovarian wall and through which
it probably receives most or all of its nutrition. Fig. 183 shows
an ovary of the bryozoan *Plumatella fungosa*, with eggs in various
stages of growth and differentiation. These eggs develop successively from the primitive cells, and each egg in turn is displaced
by the growth of another behind it.

The interesting oögenesis of *Sternaspis scutata*, a peculiar annelid, is shown in Figs. 184 and 185. The eggs arise on the walls of certain blood vessels and as they grow stalk containing a loop of the blood vessel, so that b directly through the basal end of the egg. Fig. 184 shows the egg at the beginning of yolk formation: the cyto- plasm contains a few yolk granules and shows a strongly radiate structure centering about the vascular loop. In the full-grown egg the cytoplasm is loaded with numerous large yolk spheres (Fig. 185) except at the basal end, where there is an area of granular cytoplasm. At this stage the egg becomes free from the stalk, which undergoes atrophy and resorption.

A different type of oögenesis is shown in Fig. 186, an ovarian tubule from the water beetle *Dytiscus margi-nalis*. Here growing

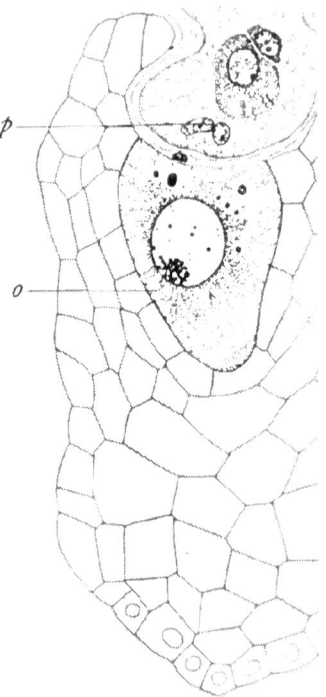

FIG. 175.—Female gametophyte o conifer, showing the egg, *o*, and above tube with the two male nuclei, *sp*. I and Land, '05.

eggs alternate with groups of so-called nurse cells, which food supply and are used up during the growth of the egg

Three stages of ascidian oögenesis are shown in Fig The first, the young ovotestis, the animals being herma with a young egg cell at the left, the second, the growin rounded by its follicle from which the so-called test c

which enter the cytoplasm of the egg and serve as food—are beginning to arise. The third figure (Fig. 189) shows a segment of the
egg at a still later stage with follicle and test cells in the peripheral
cytoplasm and yolk masses forming below them. Figs. 190, 191

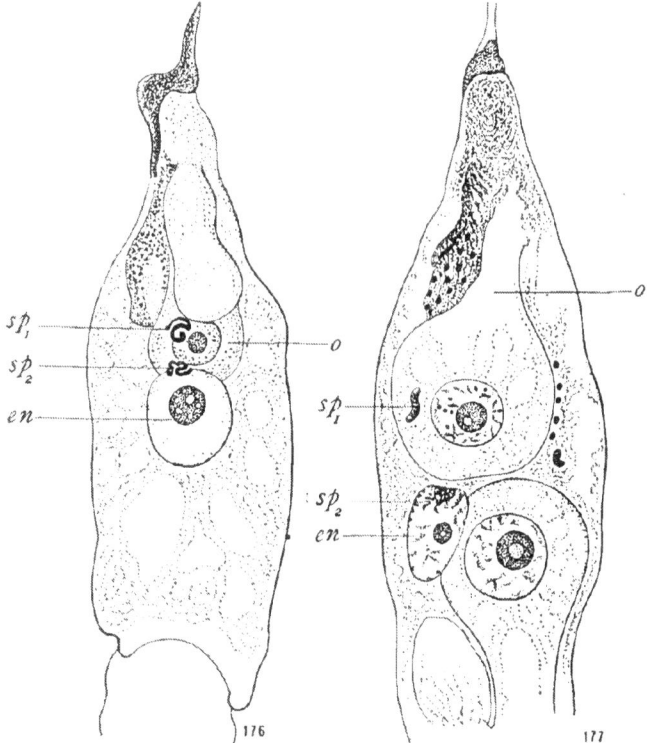

FIGS. 176, 177.—Embryo sacs of *Helianthus* (sunflower) and *Rudbeckia* (coneflower) at time of fertilization, showing egg, *o*; two male nuclei, *sp₁, sp₂*; embryo sac
nucleus, *en*. From Nawaschin, '00.

are two stages in the oögenesis of a fish egg, the first showing the
young egg at the beginning of yolk formation, the second, a later
stage in which the cytoplasm is loaded with numerous yolk spheres.

In various invertebrate groups the same individuals produce at
different times parthenogenic eggs, i.e., eggs which develop without

fertilization, and zygogenic eggs which require fertilizatie
development. It is a fact of great interest that in such
parthenogenic eggs usually differ morphologically from t
genic eggs. In *Sida crystallina*, one of the cladoceran crus
example, the parthenogenic eggs are smaller and contain

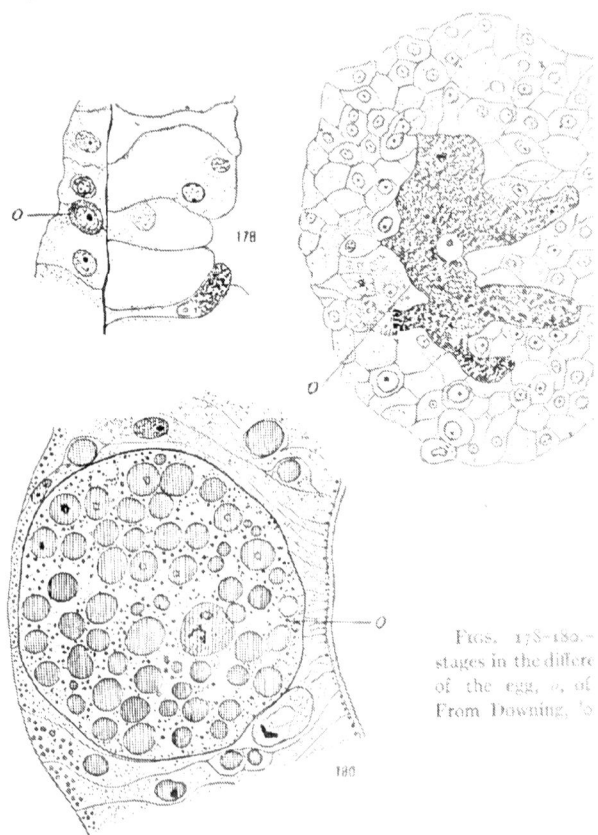

Figs. 178-180.—
stages in the differe
of the egg, o, of
From Downing, 'o

than the zygogenic eggs. Fig. 192 shows an ovarian tube
species containing various stages of parthenogenic oögene
primitive cells (*pc*), formed at the upper end of the tub
the period of division is over arrange themselves in group
(*g*, *g*) of which the third from the upper end develope

egg (*o*) and the other three become nurse cells, which supply the egg with nutrition. Three of these nurse cells thus contribute to the formation of one parthenogenic egg   The zygogenic egg, however, uses up not only three nutritive cells, but often several other cell groups, including the young egg cells, i e , a much larger amount of nutritive material contributes to its formation than to that of the parthenogenic egg.   Fig 193 shows the lower end of an ovarian

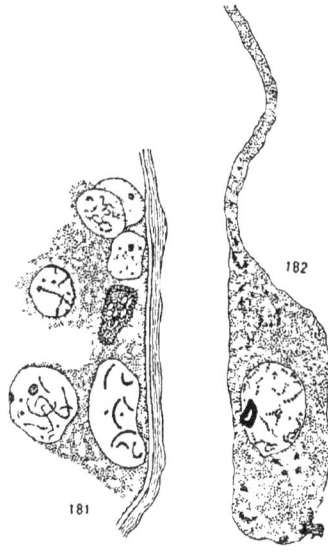

tubule containing a zygogenic egg. It is much larger than the parthenogenic egg and contains more yolk

Among the insects, the plant lice also produce both parthenogenic and zygogenic eggs.   In this case the difference between the two kinds of eggs is very marked, the parthenogenic egg being much the smaller and containing little yolk (Fig 194) as compared with the zygogenic egg (Fig 195). Even the nurse cells, which here form a sort of gland with which the egg cell is connected by a protoplasmic strand, are larger and more highly developed in the latter case   Similar differences have been observed in other forms producing the two kinds of eggs.   If the process of oogenesis is a pro

Figs 181, 182 —Primitive germ cells and full-grown egg of *Fasciola* (liver fluke), with stalk of attachment. From Schubmann, '05.

cess of differentiation and senescence, we must conclude that in these cases the parthenogenic egg does not proceed so far in development as the zygogenic egg   Morphologically it is evidently less highly differentiated and younger

Among the bees, however, where eggs which produce males, i e., the drones, apparently develop parthenogenically, while the females, both workers and queens, develop from fertilized eggs, no characteristic morphological differences between the partheno

genic, male-producing, and the zygogenic, female-producing
have, so far as I am aware, been described.   But the morph
differences in the daphnids and plant lice are evidently e

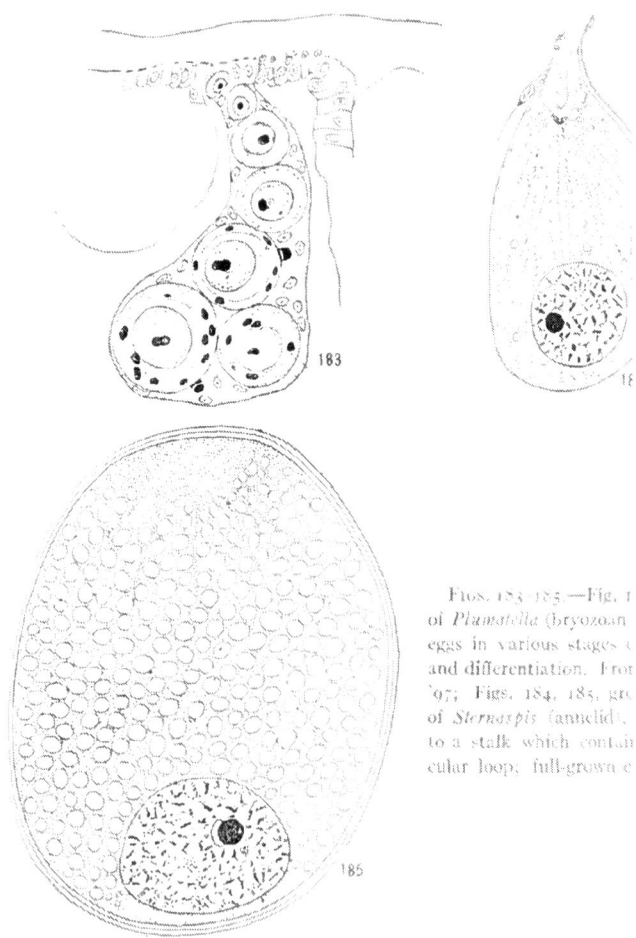

FIGS. 183-185.—Fig. 1
of *Plumatella* (bryozoan
eggs in various stages a
and differentiation. From
'97; Figs. 184, 185, gro
of *Sternaspis* (annelid),
to a stalk which contain
cular loop; full-grown e

and it is possible either that much less conspicuous morph
differences exist in the bees, or that the physiological diff
are so slight as to be morphologically inappreciable; p

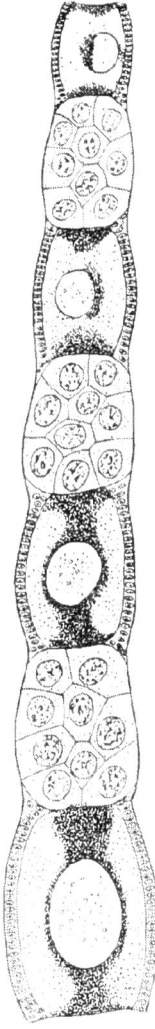

FIG. 186.—Part of an ovarian tubule of *Dytiscus* (beetle), showing eggs alternating with groups of nutritive cells: the dark regions of the eggs are dense aggregations of granules derived from the nutritive cells. From Korschelt, '91.

the physiological condition of the bee's egg is so near the boundary line between parthenogenesis and zygogenesis that slight differences suffice to determine it one way or the other.

Many other interesting cases of oögenesis might be added to the few described here, but the fact that the formation of the female gamete in organisms is a process of growth and morphological differentiation requires no further evidence.

The gametes then in both plants and animals are to all appearances the final stages of a period of growth and differentiation. Except in a few of the unicellular organisms where body and gamete are the same cell, the gametes are highly specialized cells, different from any other cells of the body and bearing not the slightest resemblance to embryonic or undifferentiated cells. Of course it is possible to assume with Weismann and others that, in addition to the oögenic and spermatogenic protoplasm which is responsible for the differentiation, the cells each contain "undifferentiated germ plasm," but we can find neither morphological nor physico-chemical support for such an assumption. Not only is such germ plasm not visible, but from a physico-chemical point of view it is difficult to conceive how it could continue to exist through the course of differentiation of the

gametic cells. The only conclusion in agreement with the fa
is that the gametes are physiologically integral parts of
organism, that they are, like other parts of the organism, more

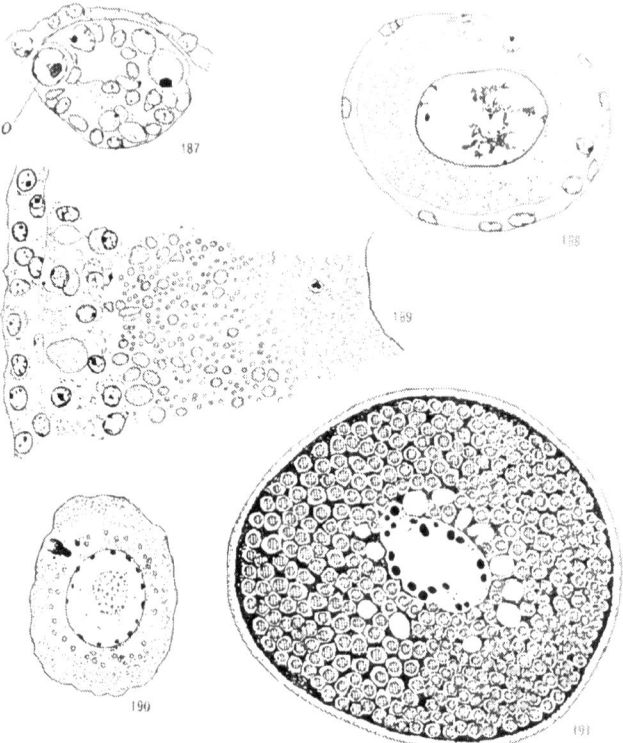

FIGS. 187–191.—Oögenesis of ascidian and fish: Fig. 187, ovotestis of young
of *Distaplia* (ascidian) with primitive egg cell, *o*; Fig. 188, growing egg with
cells and follicle; Fig. 189, portion of half-grown egg, showing follicle, test cells,
formation of yolk (from Bancroft, '09); Figs. 190, 191, Two stages in the gro
and differentiation of the egg of *Rhombus* (fish) (from Cunningham, '97).

less highly differentiated cells, and that, like other parts th
undergo differentiation because of the conditions to which th
are subjected in the organism and not because of peculiar, inher
properties.

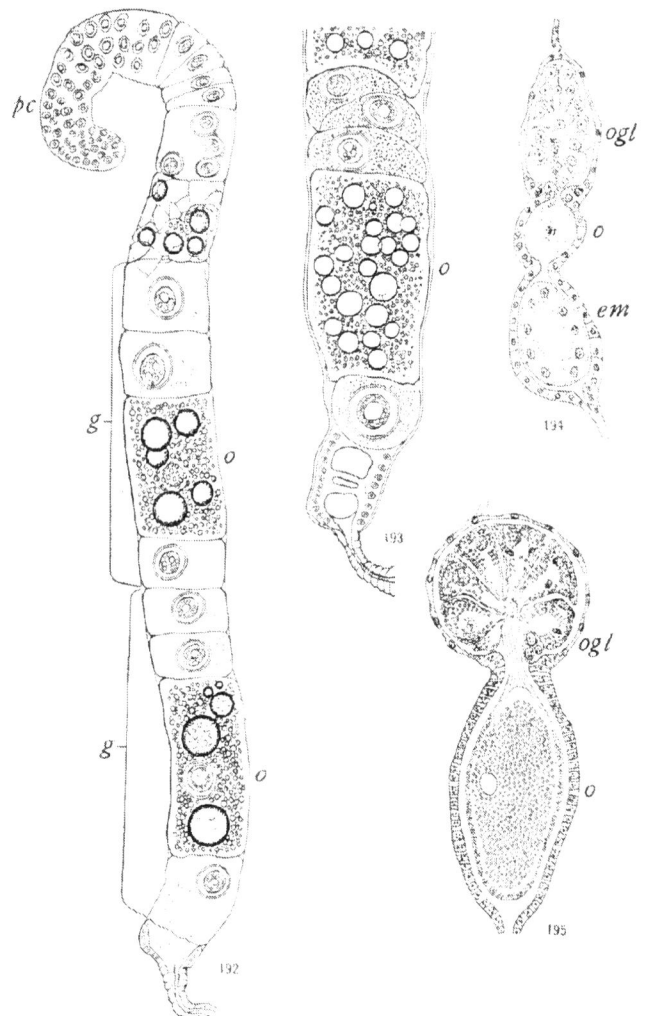

FIGS. 192-195.—The differentiation of parthenogenic and zygogenic eggs: Fig. 192, ovarian tubule of *Sida* (daphnid crustacean), showing primitive germ cells, *pc*, and groups, *g g*, of eggs, *o*, and nurse cells; Fig. 193, part of a tubule containing a zygogenic egg, *o*; Fig. 194, ovarian tubule of *Melanoxanthum* (plant louse), showing nutritive gland, *o gl*, parthenogenic egg, *o*, and embryo, *em*; Fig. 195, ovarian tubule of *Melanoxanthum*, showing nutritive gland, *o gl*, and zygogenic egg, *o*. Figs. 192, 193, from Weismann, '77; Figs. 194, 195, from Tannreuther, '07.

THE PHYSIOLOGICAL CONDITION OF THE GAMETES

If the gametes are highly differentiated cells — the final stages of a period of growth and progressive development — they must be physiologically in an advanced stage of senescence. Their rate of metabolism and rate of growth must have been high at the beginning of the period of differentiation and have undergone decrease during this period.

As regards these points, our positive experimental knowledge is very slight, but various facts of observation point very clearly to certain conclusions. Growth has ceased in the fully developed gametes, but the earlier stages of their development are periods of rapid and extensive growth, and in the plants there is usually more or less cell division in the earlier stages of gametic development. In the female gamete growth is usually considerable, often very great in amount. In many of the lower plants the cytoplasm of the egg becomes loaded with nutritive substance, as in the case of the yolk-bearing animal egg, but in the higher plants development follows a different course and the embryo obtains its food to a large extent from other cells. The rate of growth in the developing gamete is apparently higher in the earlier than in the later stages, but I am unable to cite any exact observations upon this point.

The course of development in the male gamete usually differs very widely from that in the female. Growth occurs, but it is much less in amount, and instead of the accumulation of inactive substance in the cytoplasm, a transformation of the cytoplasm into a morphological mechanism, usually motor in function, occurs. In the fully developed male gamete, as in the female, growth has ceased. In most cases the general metabolic substratum of the cell has to a large extent or wholly disappeared and the cell has very evidently progressed as far as is possible in a certain direction.

As regards the metabolic condition of the gametes of plants, G. Maige ('09, '11) has shown that the rate of respiration decreases in the anther during the development of the pollen grain from the spore. The rate of respiration in the pistil, however, is usually higher than in the anther and frequently increases during the development of this organ. The changes of rate in the embryo sac alone have not been determined, but it seems probable that the

high rate and the increase in rate in the pistil as a whole are associated with the reproductive processes concerned in the formation
of the ovules and embryo sacs within them, processes which involve
much more extensive growth than the development of the pollen
grain The volume and weight of these parts in relation to total
volume and weight of the pistil increases as development goes on,
and this change is undoubtedly sufficient to account for the increase
in respiratory rate in the whole pistil in those cases where it occurs.
Probably the rate of respiration in the embryo sac decreases as its
development proceeds Fertilization occurs and embryonic development begins in the seed plants without any considerable period
of rest, and this fact may also play a part in determining a high
respiratory rate in the pistil during the later stages of its existence

Determinations of the rate of oxygen consumption or production
of carbon dioxide or other metabolic products have not been made
for different stages of gametic development in animals, but as
regards the egg there can be little doubt that the rate of metabolism
decreases as development proceeds and that in the fully developed
egg very little chemical activity is going on The male gamete, on
the other hand, usually shows very great motor activity, often continuing over a long period of time, and at first glance there may
seem to be little reason for regarding it as a physiologically old
highly specialized cell, approaching death It must be remembered, however, that, except in some of the less highly differentiated
male cells of the unicellular organisms and the lower plants, the
motor activity of the sperm is wholly or in large degree due to
external stimulation In this respect the sperm resembles volun-
tary muscle In both cases the fully differentiated cell or tissue is
capable, when stimulated, of a very high rate of reaction, perhaps
higher than that in the sperm mother cell or the embryonic muscle
cell, but it is certain that the self-determined inherent rate of metabolic change without stimulation in the differentiated cell is a much
more exact measure of its physiological condition or its stage of
senescence as compared with the embryonic cell. In the "resting"
muscle and in the motionless spermatozoon the metabolic rate is
undoubtedly lower than in the undifferentiated cells from which
they arose.

It is a question of some interest whether the energy expended in the movements of the spermatozoon is derived entirely from its own substance or whether in any case it obtains nutritive material from the fluids in which its movement occurs. It is difficult to understand how some of the more highly specialized forms of animal spermatozoa can contain a sufficient amount of material to furnish energy for their long-continued activity. If the spermatozoon does obtain nutrition from the external world after its isolation from the parent body, it may perhaps undergo some degree of senescence even during this period.

Tests of the susceptibility to cyanide of various developmental stages of the gametes have given uniform results. Thus far I have made susceptibility tests on the female cells of the starfish and sea-urchin, of various marine annelids, and of the fish *Tautogolabrus* and upon both female and male cells of the nematode worm *Ascaris megalocephala*. *Ascaris* is a particularly favorable form for tests of this sort, first, because ovaries and testes are tubular organs lying in the body cavity and can readily be removed; secondly, because all stages in the development of the male and female gametes can be obtained from a single individual of the proper sex at any time, and, thirdly, because the spermatozoa are non-motile. In both male and female the primitive mother cells in the uppermost or innermost portion of the tubular testis or ovary, where growth and cell division are still occurring, show very high susceptibility like that of embryonic cells; lower down in the tube, where the growth and development of the gametes begin, the susceptibility begins to decrease, and the decrease is progressive as gametic development proceeds, until in the fully developed gamete the susceptibility is exceedingly low. In a potassium cyanide solution, o oo5 mol., the primitive female mother cells underwent the death change and disintegrated almost at once, the earlier stages of the growth period in fifteen to thirty minutes, somewhat later stages in one to two hours, while the fully formed eggs showed in most cases no changes until after twenty-four to forty-eight hours in the solution and did not actually disintegrate for several days. Numerous other stages were tested, and in all cases the susceptibility was found to undergo a progressive decrease. The male cells show essentially the same progressive change in susceptibility, although it is very difficult to determine with certainty when death occurs in the mature spermatozoon

In the other forms examined attention has been directed chiefly to the female cells, because the different stages of development are readily distinguishable by size and because in the male the cells are minute, the different stages being in most cases less readily distinguishable in the living cells, except under very high powers, and finally the spermatozoa are motile and it is practically impossible to eliminate the motor activity without injuring the sperm or altering its physiological condition   In all cases where female cells were examined the results are similar to those with *Ascaris* cells   The susceptibility of the primitive mother cells is high, approaching that of embryonic cells, and decreases progressively during development of the gamete, and that of the full-grown egg is exceedingly low—lower than that of most differentiated cells. Wherever the stages of spermatogenesis could be clearly distinguished the same results have been obtained for the non-motile stages

The susceptibility to cyanide of conjugating infusoria (*Colpidium*) is very distinctly lower than that of non-conjugating and dividing stages (see p. 381).   The conjugating stages in these animals are comparable to the fully developed gametes of multicellular forms, and their low susceptibility indicates that their rate of metabolism is lower and they are physiologically older than other stages.

If the susceptibility method can be trusted, and a large and increasing volume of evidence indicates that it can, the development of the gametes in animals is associated, as the decrease in susceptibility indicates, with a decrease in rate of metabolism—a process of senescence—and the fully developed gamete is physiologically an old cell approaching death

Chemical analysis of heads of spermatozoa,[1] so far as it throws any light on the question, indicates that at least some spermatozoa

---

[1] The literature of the subject, including the pioneer work of Miescher and A P. Mathews' analyses (Mathews, '97), is discussed by Burian, '04, '06. Recently Steudel ('11a, '11b, '13) has made new analyses with improved methods.

are highly specialized and that this specialization has been in the direction of a chemical simplification, at least during the later stages. Apparently the proteid constituents may undergo more or less breakdown during spermatogenesis. According to Burian, this process of breakdown of the proteid constituents may differ in degree in different spermatozoa. So far as our knowledge goes the spermatozoa of vertebrates, except the fishes, contain typical proteids as constituents of their nucleoproteids, while in the fishes these are replaced by the simpler histones or the still simpler protamines, and in some cases the histones are formed during spermatogenesis, the protamines in the fully developed spermatozoa. The nucleoproteids of the nuclei of other cells of the body sometimes contain typical proteids, sometimes histones, in combination with the nucleic acid, but the process of proteid breakdown does not go as far as the formation of protamines From this point of view, the differentiation of spermatozoa is apparently not fundamentally different from that of other cells, but some spermatozoa seem to be more highly specialized than other cells.

As regards the eggs, it is evident that, at least in those cases where they contain yolk, a progressive change in chemical constitution of the whole cell must occur during the course of differentiation: the most striking feature of this change is the increase in lipoids, which form an important constituent of the yolk Concerning changes in chemical constitution of the egg nucleus we know practically nothing.

THE SIGNIFICANCE OF MATURATION

At some point in the life history between successive generations of gametes the process known as maturation occurs. In most cases, both in animals and in plants, the process of maturation consists of two nuclear and cell divisions during which the number of chromosomes in the nucleus is decreased one-half more or less (haploid number). In fertilization the normal or diploid number is restored by the union of the two gametes each with the haploid number. In spite of years of investigation and discussion, cytologists appear to be almost as far as ever from an agreement as to what really occurs in the maturation divisions, indeed, it is still a question whether the maturation divisions or either one of them are in any way fundamentally different from other nuclear divisions. They are believed by many to be of great importance in heredity, but until the problem of their cytological character is solved any consideration of their significance for heredity must remain in the field of speculation

The question of the physiological significance of maturation has attracted little attention, but as a matter of fact it is in the answer to this question that we shall find the key for the solution of the other problems which have arisen in connection with maturation At least one of the maturation divisions, the so-called heterotypic division—but whether the first or the second, opinions differ—has commonly been supposed to be distinguished from ordinary divisions by the behavior of the chromosomes, and much has been made in a theoretical way of this difference But with the extension of our knowledge, one feature after another which was believed to be characteristic of the maturation division has been found in other divisions which have nothing to do with the development of the gametes The peculiar behavior of the chromatin, consisting in premature division and agglutination of chromosomes to form rings or other figures, which has been regarded as a characteristic feature of the so-called "heterotypic" maturation division, has been observed by Häcker, Bonnevie, and others in cleavage stages of various forms, has also been found in the cells of malignant tumors, and has been experimentally induced by the use of ether and chloroform and as a result of injury to the parent body [1] Hacker is inclined to believe that this heterotypic behavior of the chromosomes indicates a low degree of differentiation, hence its occurrence in gametic history, in early cleavage, and in cancer cells which are often regarded as a product of dedifferentiation Hacker was led to this conclusion by his belief, based on theoretical grounds, that the gametes are undifferentiated cells containing germ plasm, but from a physiological point of view both the stages in gametic history where maturation occurs and the early cleavage stages are stages of relatively high differentiation

[1] Bonnevie, '08, Farmer, Moore, and Walker, '04, Hacker, '00, '04, '07, Schiller, '09.

It is evident that whatever the cytological or hereditary significance of the chromosome behavior in maturation, this behavior must have a physiological basis, it must be associated with certain physiological conditions. The discovery of similar behavior in other cells and the experimental production of it serve at least to pave the way for the determination of its physiological significance. The fact that the "heterotypic" behavior can be experimentally induced by means of narcotics seems to show that its occurrence is connected with a low rate of metabolism In maturation, both in plants and in animals, it occurs at the end of a developmental period. In most plants with alternation of generations the maturation divisions occur in the formation of the spores, and a more or less extended period of dedifferentiation, cell division, and progressive development, i e., the gametophyte generation, occurs between maturation and fertilization In animals, on the other hand, no cell division occurs between maturation and fertilization. But the important point is that in all cases the maturation divisions occur in cells which are in an advanced stage of developmental history and physiologically old and which therefore possess a low metabolic rate. The occurrence of heterotypic behavior in cancer cells is probably likewise due to a low metabolic rate, though not in consequence of differentiation and advanced age, but because of partial asphyxiation or intoxication of certain cells in the rapidly growing cell mass

According to this conception, then, the peculiar characteristics of the maturation divisions find their physiological basis in a low metabolic rate which may result from differentiation and senescence or be induced experimentally or otherwise Other features of maturation which indicate a low metabolic rate are the absence of the usual nuclear growth between the first and second divisions and, in animal eggs, the slow progress of maturation and its frequent cessation until a further stimulation from without occurs, and the very slight influence of the nuclear division upon the cytoplasm, the cytoplasmic divisions resulting in the formation of the minute polar bodies and leaving practically the whole volume of the egg intact.

In the animal egg, where maturation occurs after the enormous growth of the egg cell is completed, the process appears to be initiated either by the physiological or physical isolation of the egg cell from its source of nutritive supply in the parent body, or often by its extrusion from the body into water, or in many cases only after the spermatozoon has entered the egg. In most cases the egg is incapable of even the maturation divisions, except after some degree of excitation, and in some eggs the isolation from the parent body is sufficient, while others require the additional stimulation of extrusion into water, and for still others the further change result-ing from entrance of the sperm is necessary. In the formation of the megaspore and microspore in plants and in the spermatogenesis of animals the period of growth between other divisions and matura-tion is slight or practically absent, and with rare exceptions the cells divide equally in the maturation divisions. Whether in these cases also the maturation divisions are initiated by a stimulation of the cells from without is not known, but the probability suggests itself that they occur as the result of a physiological or physical isolation of the cells

From this point of view the maturation divisions appear to be divisions occurring in relatively old differentiated cells as a reaction to physiological or physical isolation from the parent body, or to this factor in combination with others   Their peculiar features are apparently associated with the low metabolic rate in the cells concerned. In the mosses and ferns the spores resulting from the maturation divisions undergo rejuvenescence and begin a new developmental and vegetative cycle without fertilization, but in the seed plants the degree of rejuvenescence is apparently slight in most cases and the divisions few in number, and in animals, except in the case of parthenogenic eggs, rejuvenescence occurs only after fertilization.

CONCLUSION

In the present chapter the attempt has been made to show that the developmental history of the gametes affords no adequate grounds for the belief that germ plasm is something independent of the rest of the organism.   There is no proof of the "segregation of the germ plasm" as an independent entity in embryonic develop-ment, but the germ cells are very evidently determined like other parts of the body by correlative factors   Moreover, the course of development of the gametes bears every indication of being a progressive differentiation and senescence, not fundamentally different from that of other organs of the body, and the fully developed gametes are physiologically old, highly differentiated cells, which are rapidly approaching death and in most cases actually do die soon after maturity unless fertilization occurs.   Whatever their significance for inheritance may prove to be, the peculiar features of the maturation divisions are apparently associated with the condition of advanced physiological age and low metabolic rate in the cells where they occur   These cells, whether they are the spore mother cells of plants or the gamete mother cells of animals, are advanced stages of a period of progressive development and must undergo dedifferentiation and rejuvenescence before they can enter upon a new period of development.   In the plants this may occur to a greater or less extent without fertilization in the development of the gametophyte, but in the gametes of animals, with the exception of parthenogenic eggs, dedifferentiation and rejuvenescence occur only after fertilization.

REFERENCES

Amma, K.
   1911. "Über die Differenzierung der Keimbahnzellen bei den Kopepoden," *Arch. f. Zellforsch.*, VI

Ballowitz, E.
   1886–1908   The following is a partial list of this author's papers on the structure of spermatozoa   "Zur Lehre von der Struktur der Spermatozoen," *Anat. Anz*, I, 1886, "Untersuchungen uber die Struktur der Spermatozoen," *Arch f. mikr. Anat*, XXXII, 1888, "Fibrillare Struktur und Contractilitat," *Arch f d. ges. Physiol*, XLVI, 1890; "Untersuchungen uber die Struktur der Spermatozoen," *Arch f mikr. Anat*, XXXVI, 1890, "Das Retzius'sche Endstuck des Saugetierspermatozoen," *Internat Monatsschr. f Anat u Physiol*, VII, 1890, "Untersuchungen uber die Struktur der Spermatozoen   Die Spermatozoen der Insekten," *Zeitschr f. wiss. Zool.*, L, 1890, "Die Bedeutung der Valentinschen Querbander am Spermatozoenkopf der Saugetiere," *Arch f. Anat u. Physiol.*, Anat. Abt., 1891, "Weitere Beobachtungen uber den feineren Bau der Saugetierspermatozoen," *Zeitschr f wiss. Zool.*, LII, 1891; "Die innere Zusammensetzung des Spermatozoenkopfes

der Saugetiere," *Centralbl f Physiol.*, V, 1891; "Weitere sperma-tologische Beitrage," *Internat. Monatsschr f. Anat u. Physiol*, XI, 1894, "Uber die Spermien des Flussneunauges (*Petromyzon fluviatilis L*) und ihre merkwurdige Kopfborste," *Arch f. mikr. Anat.*, LXV, 1904, "Die Spermien des Batrachiers *Pelodytes punctatus* Bonap," *Anat. Anz*, XXVII, 1905, "Über einige Strukturen der Spermie des *Spelerpes fuscus* Bonap," *Anat Anz*, XXVIII, 1906; "Zur Kenntnis der Spermien der Cetaceen," *Arch. f. mikr. Anat*, LXX, 1907, "Uber den feineren Bau der eigenartigen aus drei freien. dimorphen Fasern bestehenden Spermien der Turbellarien," *Arch f mikr Anat.*, LXX, 1907; "Die kopflosen Spermien der Cirripedien (*Balanus*)," *Zeitschr. f. wiss. Zool.*, XCI, 1908

BALLOWITZ, K.
1894. "Zur Kenntnis der Samenkorper der Arthropoden," *Internat. Monatsschr. f. Anat. u. Physiol*, XI

BANCROFT, F. W.
1899 "Ovogenesis in *Distaplia occidentalis* Ritter (MS) with Remarks on Other Species," *Bull of the Mus of Comp Zool. Harvard*, XXXV.

BEARD, J.
1902 "The Germ Cells: Part I, *Raja batis*," *Zool. Jahrbucher; Abt. f Anat u. Ont.*, XVI

BELAJEFF, W
1894. "Uber Bau und Entwickelung der Spermatozoiden der Pflanzen," *Flora*, LXXIX

BOHMIG, L.
1890. "Untersuchungen uber rhabdocolen Turbellarien: II, Plagio-stomina und Cylindrostomina Graff," *Zeitschr. f. wiss Zool*, LI.

BOSENBERG, H
1905. "Beitrage zur Kenntnis der Spermatogenese bei den Arachnoiden, *Zool. Jahrbucher; Abt. f. Anat u. Ont*, XXI.

BONNEVIE, KRISTINE
1908. "Chromosomenstudien. II, Heterotypische Mitose als Reifungs-charakter, *Arch. f Zellforsch*, II

BOVERI, T.
1887. "Uber Differenzierung der Zellkerne wahrend der Furchung des Eies von *Ascaris megalocephala*," *Anat. Anz*, II.
1899. "Die Entwickelung von *Ascaris megalocephala* mit besonderer Rucksicht auf die Kernverhaltnisse," *Festschrift f. von Kupffer*. Jena.

BOVERI, T.

> 1904. *Ergebnisse uber die Konstitution der chromatischen Substanz des Zellkernes.* Jena

> 1910 "Die Potenzen der *Ascaris*-Blastomeren bei abgeanderter Iurchung," *Festschrift zum 60 Geburtstag R Hertwigs*, III

BRAEM, F.

> 1897. "Die geschlechtliche Entwickelung von *Plumatella fungosa*," *Zoologica*, X

BREFELD, O

> 1872. *Botanische Untersuchungen uber Schimmelpilze* Heft I

BUCHNER, P.

> 1910 "Die Schicksale des Kernplasmas der Sagitten in Reifung, Befruchtung, Ovogenese und Spermatogenese," *Festschrift zum 60. Geburtstag R. Hertwigs*, I.

BURIAN, R

> 1904 "Chemie der Spermatozoen, I," *Ergebn. d. Physiol*, III
> 1906. "Chemie der Spermatozoen, II," *Ergebn. d. Physiol*, V

CHILD, C. M

> 1911 "A Study of Senescence and Rejuvenescence Based on Experiments with Planarians," *Arch. f Entwickelungsmech*, XXXI

CONKLIN, E G.

> 1912. "Cell Size and Nuclear Size," *Jour. of Exp Zool*, XII
> 1913 "The Size of Organisms and of Their Constituent Parts in Relation to Longevity, Senescence and Rejuvenescence," *Pop Sci Monthly*, August

COULTER, J M, BARNES, C. R., and COWLES, H C.

> 1910. *A Textbook of Botany.* New York

COULTER, J M, and LAND, W. J. G

> 1905. "Gametophytes and Embryo of *Torreya taxifolia*," *Bot Gazette*, XXXIX

CUNNINGHAM, J. T.

> 1898. "On the Histology of the Ovary and of the Ovarian Ova in Certain Marine Fishes," *Quart Jour of Micr. Sci.*, XL

DOWNING, E R

> 1909. "The Ovogenesis of Hydra," *Zool Jahrbucher, Abt f Anat u Ont*, XXVIII

EIGENMANN, C.

> 1892. "On the Precocious Segregation of the Sex Cells of *Micrometrus aggregatus*," *Jour. of Morphol*, V
> 1896a "Sex Differentiation in the Viviparous Teleost *Cymatogaster*," *Arch f Entwickelungsmech*, IV.

EIGENMANN, C.
    1896b. "The Bearing of the Origin and Differentiation of the Sex-Cells of *Cymatogaster* on the Idea of the Continuity of the Germ Plasm," *Am Nat*, XXX

FARMER, J B , MOORE, J E S., and WALKER, C. E.
    1904 "Über die Ähnlichkeit zwischen den Zellen maligner Neubildungen beim Menschen und denen normaler Fortpflanzungsgewebe," *Biol. Centralbl* , XXIV.

FELIX, W , and BUHLER, A.
    1906. "Die Entwickelung der Keimdrusen und Ausfuhrungsgange," *O Hertwigs Handbuch der vergleichenden Entwicklungslehre*, Bd. III, T. 1. Jena.

GALTON, F.
    1872. "On Blood-Relationship," *Proc. Roy. Soc.*, XX

HACKER, V.
    1897. "Die Keimbahn von *Cyclops*," *Arch f mikr Anat* , XLIX
    1900. "Mitosen im Gefolge amitosenahnlicher Vorgange," *Anat. Anz.*, XVII.
    1902. "Uber das Schicksal der elterlichen und grosselterlichen Kernanteile," *Jen. Zeitschr. f. Naturwiss* , XXX
    1904. "Über die in malignen Neubildungen auftretenden heterotypischen Teilungsbilder," *Biol Centralbl* , XXIV.
    1907. "Die Chromosomen als angenommene Vererbungstrager," *Ergebn. u Fortschr. d. Zool.*, I.
    1912a. Kapitel "Zeugungslehre" in A Langs *Handbuch d Morphol. d wirbellosen Tiere*, Bd. II. Jena.
    1912b *Allgemeine Vererbungslehre*, II Auflage. Braunschweig

HASPER, M.
    1911. "Zur Entwicklung der Geschlechtsorgane von *Chironomus*," *Zool. Jahrbucher; Abt. f. Anat. u. Ont* , XXXI

HEGNER, R W.
    1909. "The Origin and Early History of the Germ Cells in Some Chrysomelid Beetles," *Jour of Morphol* , XX.
    1911 "Experiments with Chrysomelid Beetles: III, The Effects of Killing Parts of the Eggs of *Leptinotarsa decemlineata*," *Biol. Bull* , XX.
    1912. "The History of the Germ Cells in the Paedogenetic Larvae of *Miastor*," *Science*, XXXVI
    1914a. "Studies on Germ Cells: I, The History of the Germ Cells in Insects with Special Reference to the *Keimbahn*-Determinants, II, The Origin and Significance of the *Keimbahn*-Determinants in Animals," *Jour. of Morphol* , XXV

HEGNER, R W
    1914*b* ' Studies on Germ Cells. III, The Origin of the Keimbahn-
        Determinants in a Parasitic Hymenopteron, *Copidosoma*," *In it*
        Anz, XLVI
    1914*c*. *The Germ-Cell Cycle in Animals* New York.

JAGER, G
    1877   "Physiologische Briefe," *Kosmos*, I

KAHLE, W
    1908   "Die Paedogenese der Cecidomyiden," *Zoologica*, XXI

KLEIN, L.
    1889   "Morphologische und biologische Studien uber die Gattung
        Volvox," *Jahrbucher f. wiss Bot*, XX

KOLTZOFF, N. K.
    1906*a*. "Studien uber die Gestalt der Zelle I, Untersuchungen uber
        die Spermien der Decapoden," *Arch f mikr Anat*, LXVII
    1906*b*. "Über das Skelett des tierischen Spermiums," *Biol. Centralbl*,
        XXVI.
    1908. "Studien uber die Gestalt der Zelle II, Untersuchungen uber
        das Kopfskelett des tierischen Spermiums, *Arch f. Zellforsch*, II

KORSCHELT, E
    1891. "Beitrage zur Morphologie und Physiologie des Zellkernes," *Zool
        Jahrbucher, Abt f. Anat. u. Ont.*, IV

KORSCHELT, E, and HEIDER, K.
    1902   *Lehrbuch der vergleichenden Entwicklungsgeschichte der wirbellosen
        Tiere.* Allgem. Teil, I Lieferung   Jena.

LILLIE, F. R.
    1912. "Studies of Fertilization in *Nereis* III, The Morphology of the
        Normal Fertilization of *Nereis*," *Jour. of Exp Zool*, XII

LUTHER, A
    1904   "Die Eumesostominen," *Zeitschr. f. wiss. Zool*, LXXVII

MAIGE, M.
    1909. "Recherches sur la respiration de l'etamine et du pistil," *Rev gén
        de bot*, XXI.
    1911. "Recherches sur la respiration des différentes pièces florales,"
        Ann. des sci nat, *Bot*, (9) XIV

MARCHAL, ÉL, et MARCHAL, ÉM.
    1907. "Aposporie et sexualité chez les mousses I," *Bull. Acad. Roy de
        Belgique;* Cl des Sci
    1909. "Aposporie," etc. II, *Bull. Acad Roy de Belgique;* Cl des Sci.
    1911   "Aposporie," etc III, *Bull. Acad Roy de Belgique;* Cl. des Sci.

MARCHAL, ÉM.

  1912. "Recherches cytologiques sur le genre *Amblystegum*," *Bull. Acad Roy de Belgique,* Cl des Sci

MATHEWS, A. P.

  1897 "Zur Chemie der Spermatozoen," *Zeitschr. f. physiol. Chem.,* XXIII.

MERRELL, W. D

  1900. "A Contribution to the Life History of *Silphium*," *Bot. Gazette,* XXIX

MEVES, F.

  1899. "Über Struktur und Histogenese der Samenfaden des Meerschweinchens," *Arch f mikr Anat,* LIV

  1903. "Über oligopyrene und apyrene Spermien und uber ihre Entstehung, nach Beobachtungen an *Paludina* und *Pygaera*," *Arch f mikr Anat,* LXI.

MINOT, C S.

  1908. *The Problem of Age, Growth and Death*   New York.

NAWASCHIN, S

  1900 "Uber die Befruchtungsvorgange bei einigen Dicotyledoneen," *Berichte d deutsch. bot. Gesell.,* XVIII.

NUSSBAUM, M

  1880. "Zur Differenzierung des Geschlechts im Tierreich," *Arch. f mikr. Anat.,* XVIII

SCHEBEN, L.

  1905. "Beiträge zur Kenntnis des Spermatozoons von *Ascaris megalocephala*," *Zeitschr f. wiss Zool.,* LXXIX.

SCHILLER, J

  1909 "Über künstliche Erzeugung "primitiver" Kernteilungsfiguren bei *Cyclops*," *Arch. f. Entwickelungsmech.,* XXVII

SCHUBMANN, W

  1905. "Uber die Eibildung und Embryonalentwicklung von *Fasciola hepatica* L ," *Zool. Jahrbucher, Abt f. Anat. u. Ont,* XXI

SHARP, L W.

  1912. "Spermatogenesis in *Equisetum*," *Bot. Gazette,* LIV

STEUDEL, H.

  1911a. "Zur Histochemie der Spermatozoen " I. Mitt *Zeitschr. f. physiol. Chem.,* LXXII

  1911b "Zur Histochemie," etc II Mitt *Zeitschr f. physiol Chem,* LXXIII

  1913. "Zur Histochemie," etc III Mitt *Zeitschr f. physiol. Chem,* LXXXIII.

ZUR STRASSEN, O.

    1896 "Embryonalentwicklung der *Ascaris megalocephala*," *Arch f Entwickelungsmech* , III

TANNREUTHER, G W.

    1907 "History of the Germ Cells and Early Embryology of Certain Aphids," *Zool Jahrbucher, Abt. f. Anat u. Ont* , XXIV

WALDEYER, W.

    1906. "Die Geschlechtszellen," O Hertwigs *Handbuch der vergleichenden Entwickelungslehre*, Bd. I, T I Jena

WEBBER H J

    1901 "Spermatogenesis and Fecundation of *Zamia*," *U S Dept of Agric* , *Bureau of Plant Industry, Bull. No. 2.*

WEISMANN, A

    1877. "Beitrage zur Naturgeschichte der Daphnoiden," T II, III und IV, *Zeitschr. f wiss Zool* , XXVIII

    1885. *Die Continuitat des Keimplasmas als Grundlage einer Theorie der Vererbung.* Jena

    1892. *Das Keimplasma.* Jena

WHEELER, W. M

    1900. "The Development of the Urogenital Organs of the Lamprey," *Zool Jahrbucher; Abt. f Anat u Ont* , XIII

WINKLER, H

    1908. "Uber Parthenogenesis und Apogamie im Pflanzenreiche," *Progressus rei bot.*, II.

YAMANOUCHI, S.

    1908 "Spermatogenesis, Oogenesis and Fertilization in *Nephrodium*," *Bot. Gazette*, XLV

ZACHARIAS, O

    1913 "Die Chromatin-Diminution in den Furchungszellen von *Ascaris megalocephala*," *Anat. Anz* , XLIII

ZOJA, R

    1896. "Untersuchungen uber die Entwicklung der *Ascaris megalocephala*," *Arch. f. mikr. Anat* , XLVII.

CHAPTER XIV

CONDITIONS OF GAMETE FORMATION IN PLANTS AND ANIMALS

In all organisms the production of the gametes or sexual cells, the condition known in the higher forms as sexual maturity, is apparently associated with certain other physiological conditions which, at least in the higher animals, are characteristic of relatively advanced stages of development. The present chapter is an attempt to establish a general foundation for the interpretation of the various data of observation and experiment This foundation is in brief the view that the production of gametes is simply one feature of the orderly development of the organism and is therefore associated with certain conditions in other organs and is related to processes of differentiation and senescence in the organism as a whole

CONDITIONS OF GAMETE FORMATION IN THE ALGAE AND FUNGI

It was formerly believed that the essential factors determining reproduction, and particularly gametic or sexual reproduction in plants were internal, and that external factors had but little to do with the process But various investigators, and particularly Klebs, have demonstrated that the sequence of events in the life cycle of plants can, to a very large extent, be controlled by external factors. Klebs's work along this line has been discussed in chap x in connection with agamic reproduction (pp 249-52), and here only certain points which concern the formation of gametes need be considered. Klebs mentions the fact that where spore formation or gamete formation or both occur in cultures of *Vaucheria* and *Saprolegnia*, in addition to what he calls growth, which is what I have called vegetative reproduction, these more specialized reproductive processes occur on the older parts of the plant body and the vegetative on the younger He also concludes that the attainment of a certain concentration of the organic substances in the plant is an essential condition for such reproductive processes and that for gametic reproduction the concentration must be higher

364

than for spore formation According to Klebs, these differences in concentration concern primarily the nutritive substances, but it seems probable that the protoplasm of the cells may also be involved I have endeavored to show that vegetative reproduction in consequence of the regressive changes associated with it retards or inhibits the progress of senescence (pp 237–55). The conditions which bring about the formation of gametes in Klebs's experiments decrease or check vegetative growth, and the cells of the plant accumulate organic substance and so attain a condition of greater physiological age with a lower rate of metabolism than during active vegetative reproduction Apparently spore formation occurs at an earlier, and gamete formation at a later, stage of this process of senescence.

In the algae and fungi, with their low degree of individuation, certain parts of the plant may under certain conditions become old while others remain young, and in such cases gamete formation and vegetative reproduction may occur simultaneously, the one in the older, the other in the younger, parts. The results of Klebs's experiments do not then indicate that the plant has no definite life history, but merely that because of its capacity for vegetative reproduction it can be prevented indefinitely from attaining the later stages. But when it, or a part of it, attains these stages, the more specialized reproductive processes appear, and the formation of gametes is apparently characteristic of a more advanced stage than spore formation. Even after gamete formation, however, the plant does not necessarily die, but under the proper conditions may resume vegetative reproduction or spore formation In those cases where gametic reproduction may be induced before vegetative reproduction has continued for any considerable length of time it is probable that the conditions bring about premature aging and the plant very soon attains a certain physiological state which under other conditions may arise only after a long time or not at all.

The process of aging in these lower plants is then very intimately associated with external conditions Under certain conditions progressive senescence and gamete formation under others a balance between senescence and rejuvenescence, with continuous vegetative reproduction, may occur A life cycle exists as a possibility for the lower plant, and gamete formation is a feature of its later stages, but since physiological progression may be experimentally accelerated, retarded, or inhibited by controlling the relation between progression and regression, the life cycle does not appear as a definite, uniform, internally determined sequence of events such as occurs in the higher animals

CONDITIONS OF GAMETE FORMATION IN MOSSES AND FERNS

In mosses and ferns the life cycle is complicated by an alternation of sporophyte and gametophyte generations, each of which possesses a characteristic different structure   The gametophyte produces sexual organs in which the gametes develop, and the gametes after fertilization give rise to the sporophyte which produces asexual spores, and these produce another gametophyte generation.   In mosses the gametophyte is the vegetative generation, and the sporophyte does not lead an independent life but develops upon the gametophyte   In the ferns, on the other hand. both the sporophyte, the fern plant, and the gametophyte, the prothallium, lead an independent vegetative life

In both mosses and ferns the production of sexual organs and gametes on the gametophyte occurs only after a certain period of vegetative activity which may vary in length with external conditions; in other words, gamete formation seems to be characteristic of a certain physiological condition which does not exist in the early life of the gametophyte but arises only later   This condition evidently corresponds to the condition of sexual maturity in the higher animals   Moreover, after producing sex organs and gametes the gametophyte dies, except where parts of it produce new gametophytes asexually.

Vegetative agamic reproduction in the gametophytes occurs very widely and in a great variety of forms among both mosses and ferns and leads directly to the formation of new gametophyte individuals   In certain species, or under certain external conditions, vegetative reproduction of the gametophyte may continue indefinitely, and sex organs and gametes do not appear or appear very rarely.   This is conspicuously the case in many of the so-called true mosses, the *Bryales*, in which the degree of individuation in the gametophyte is evidently very slight, and vegetative reproduction occurs by the isolation of leaves, branches, specialized gemmae etc., and in many cases from single cells of various regions of the gametophyte. In many such species sex organs and gametes appear only occasionally, or very rarely, and vegetative propagation of the gametophyte may continue indefinitely.

If the viewpoint developed in preceding chapters has any foundation in fact, we must believe that in every one of these vegetative reproductions a new individuation and some degree of reconstitutional change in the cells involved occur. And again, if this is the case, the new individuals resulting from reproduction are, at least to a slight degree, younger physiologically than the individual of which they originally formed a part. The result of continued vegetative reproduction, whether it is induced by external factors or determined by a low degree of individuation in the species, is then to prevent the gametophyte generation from attaining physiological maturity; consequently the specializations and morphological differentiations characteristic of maturity, viz., the development of sex organs and gametes, do not take place, or take place only rarely when individuals in consequence of external or internal conditions happen to reach maturity.

Various botanists have suggested that in such cases the vegetative reproduction is the consequence of the failure to produce sex organs and gametes, but the facts point to the opposite conclusion—that the continued vegetative reproduction with the accompanying reconstitution simply prevents the individual from attaining maturity. Whether in any case the capacity for gamete formation has been lost or is disappearing, can be determined only after the most extensive and intensive research. But the low degree of individuation accounts without difficulty for the preponderance of vegetative reproduction, and there is no reason for believing that a loss in the capacity for gamete formation has occurred. Failure to produce gametes in such cases probably means only that the individual never attains the physiological condition of which that particular process is a feature.

The occurrence of apogamy in the ferns[1] indicates, as already pointed out (p 322), that there is no segregation of germ plasm

---

[1] Farlow, '74, de Bary, '78, Heim, '96, Farmer and Digby, '07, Woronin, '8, Winkler, '08.

in the gametes alone. Apparently the sporophyte may arise from any vegetative cell of the gametophyte. But the fact that apogamous development of a sporophyte often begins as a transformation of the sex organs either antheridia or archegonia, or is correlated with the incomplete development or degeneration of the sex organs or of the eggs, suggests that some sort and some degree of phys iological correlation exists between apogamy and formation of gametes. It seems not improbable that the degree of individuation is in such cases not quite sufficient to carry the organism through the entire cycle, and the physiological isolation of vegetative cells in the stages near maturity leads to reproduction of a sporophyte, i e , the vegetative cells have the same developmental capacity as the egg, but are less specialized and so do not require fertilization. Up to the present, however, other aspects of the process of apogamy have received much more attention than its physiology and relation to the individuation of the organism in which it appears, and any attempt at physiological interpretation must at present be a mere guess.

CONDITIONS OF GAMETE FORMATION IN THE SEED PLANTS

In the mosses, ferns, and related forms the two generations, the asexual sporophyte and the gametophyte which produces sexual organs and gametes, are more or less distinct and separate organisms with different morphological structure and different habit In the seed plants, however, the sporophyte generation has become by far the most conspicuous feature of the life cycle, and the gametophyte generation is reduced to the pollen grain and the embryo sac of the flower. The flower is commonly defined as an axis or shoot of which some parts bear sexual organs The flower, like the vegetative shoots, arises from an agamic bud, but this bud is evidently more highly specialized than the vegetative buds, for its parts are variously modified and differentiated in various directions into the parts of the flower Moreover, the axis which produces the flower usually does not continue to grow for a long time, or indefinitely, but the growth is narrowly limited and the development of the flower ends under the usual conditions in death. Evidently the flower represents the most advanced or the highest stage in the differentiation of the plant body Both morphologically and physiologically it is a much more highly differentiated and special-ized system than the vegetative axes of the plant

This being the case, we should expect to find the flower as the final stage of development, as the expression of maturity of the plant Among the flowering plants this appears in general to be the case. The young plant grows, produces new vegetative axes, and in most cases becomes what the zoologist would term an asexual colony, but after a longer or shorter period of such vegetative growth and reproduction, varying in different plants from a few weeks to many years, flower buds appear in place of certain or all of the vegetative buds, gametes are produced, and seeds are formed In many plants vegetative growth ceases when flowering occurs, and flowering is followed by death of the whole plant, except the seeds, but in others the sequence may be repeated an indefinite number of times during the life of the plant.

To all appearances then these plants have a definite life history, vegetative growth and reproduction of vegetative axes being characteristic of the earlier stages and the development of flowers and gametic reproduction of the later stages. In those plants where the sequence is repeated periodically, different shoots or axes, that is, different plant individuals, are concerned in each period. Moreover, it is a well-known fact that in general cuttings from plants in bloom or ready to bloom are likely to bloom earlier than cuttings from plants which are still in the stage of active vege-tative growth. Such facts indicate clearly that flowering is an expression of internal conditions which are characteristic of a rela-tively advanced stage in the life of the plant or in a seasonal or other period of metabolic activity and growth

But certain facts of observation and experiment have often been regarded as pointing to a somewhat different conclusion. First among these is the familiar fact, to which attention has already been called (pp. 239-44), that many plants live and grow indefinitely without sexual reproduction. This is true, not only of many rhizome plants, in which the rhizome or rootstock grows con-tinuously and produces new buds and roots, and from time to time branches, while at the other end death continually advances, but it apparently holds for at least many other plants as well Propagation by cuttings may be continued for a large number of generations and probably indefinitely in many plants, and some plants are not known to reproduce sexually in nature.

Many of our cultivated plants have been bred agamically, either wholly or to a large extent, for a long period of years. The banana is one of the most conspicuous examples, the sugar cane another, and in various species of willow and poplar and many plants grown from bulbs or tubers, e g., the potato, the agamic method of propagation is the usual one.

Mobius ('97) has brought together a large number of these cases, and has considered particularly those in which agamic propagation for a longer or shorter time was apparently followed by the deterioration or the dying out of the stock. In many cases parasitic diseases are responsible for this result, in other cases climatic or other external factors, and Mobius concludes that there are no grounds for believing that agamic propagation necessarily results in an aging, deterioration, and death of the stock.

Mobius has also discussed the facts bearing on the question whether continued agamic propagation may lead to loss of the power of gametic reproduction and concludes that, in at least most cases, gametic reproduction is prevented by external factors and agamic reproduction takes its place. It is an undoubted fact that plants which do not reproduce sexually usually show a high degree of agamic reproductive capacity of one form or another While it is not possible at present to analyze most of these cases, they all fall readily into line with the view that gametic reproduction is characteristic of a certain relatively advanced stage of the life history of the individual, and that the individual cannot attain this stage under conditions which bring about a continued or periodic breaking up, physiologically speaking, into new individuals. If conditions in nature or under cultivation favor continued vegetative growth, new individuations continually occur and the reconstitutional changes connected with this continued agamic reproduction prevent any individual from attaining the condition of maturity. Or the conditions may decrease the degree of individuation of the species

by altering the rate of metabolism, or in some other way and so
lead to vegetative or other forms of agamic reproduction

From this point of view, the absence or rare occurrence of
gametic reproduction in various plants, either in nature or under
cultivation, is not in any sense the factor which determines increased
agamic reproduction, but the agamic reproduction prevents the
organism from attaining the physiological condition in which
gametic reproduction occurs   Teleological interpretation of such
cases is entirely unnecessary and beside the point.   Whether one
form of reproduction or another occurs depends upon the physiological condition of the individual   In the physiologically
young, immature individual, whether it be a unicellular plant, a
single plant axis, or a whole multiaxial plant, reproduction, when it
occurs, is agamic, while the formation of gametes occurs in the older,
mature individual

This conclusion may seem at first glance to conflict seriously with
certain other observational and experimental data concerning the
occurrence and experimental production of flowers.   Flowers appear
frequently, either as an anomaly in nature or under experimental
conditions, on plants which, as regards length of time from the seed,
as well as size and morphological condition, are in an early stage
of development and young.   The experimental investigations of
Vochting, Klebs, and others have demonstrated that the occurrence
of flowering may be controlled within wide limits by means of
various external conditions.[1]

Vöchting's experiments on *Mimulus tilingii* show very clearly
the significance of light for flowering.   In a certain low illumination
in which vegetative growth is possible the inflorescence begins to
develop, but the preformed flower buds cease their development at

[1] The following references will serve as a guide to the literature of the subject
Mobius ('97) presents and describes numerous facts, largely observational rather
than experimental, bearing upon the problem.   Diels ('06) has brought together many
cases of premature flowering or "nanism," both from his own observations and from
the literature.   The experimental investigations of Vochting ('03), Klebs ('03, '04,
'06), and others demonstrate that the occurrence of flowering may be controlled within
wide limits by means of external factors   Jost ('08, pp 439-46) gives a good general
survey of the subject   Additional references are Benecke, '06, Döposchig-Ühlár '12,
A Fischer, '05, Goebel, '08, pp 6, 10, 117, 190, Loew, '05   These papers contain
further references.

an early stage, and instead of flowers axillary buds become active and grow out into vegetative branches and the inflorescence is transformed into a vegetative complex and the formation of gametes does not occur. It should be noted that in this case it is only the later stages of flower development which are inhibited by the low light intensity. The specialization or change, of whatever character it may be, which determines the development of an inflorescence has occurred in these plants, but it stops at a certain stage and with its cessation new vegetative individuals arise in consequence of physiological isolation, and the vegetative life is resumed.

Klebs records similar results for various species and states that in all plants which do not possess a considerable volume of reserves a decrease in illumination suppresses the formation of flowers. According to Klebs, this influence of illumination on flowering is essentially a matter of photosynthesis Blue light, which decreases photosynthesis, acts like decreased illumination on flowering, while in red light, by which photosynthesis is less affected, flowering occurs.

Various other conditions—temperature, water, nutritive salts, etc.—have been found to influence the occurrence of flowering. In summing up his experiments on flowering plants in general Klebs says

For the formation of flowers the relations between the internal physico-chemical conditions must be different from those in which vegetative growth occurs. I believe that a quantitative increase in concentration of the organic substances, with all its physical and chemical consequences, plays an essential part in the transition from growth to reproduction All external factors may influence the occurrence of flowering favorably or unfavorably, according to their intensity, their interrelations with each other, and the specific nature of the plant, their effect depending upon the relations among the internal conditions which they bring about [1]

In a later paper Klebs states the results of his extensive experiments on *Sempervivum funkii* in somewhat more definite form. He says.

I begin with a vigorous, previously well-nourished rosette which is ready to bloom and make the experiments which determine its fate before or during the primordial stages of flower development. The results are as follows:

[1] Klebs, '04, pp 553-54

1. In bright light with active photosynthesis and intense absorption of water and salts active vegetative growth results

2. In bright light with active photosynthesis but with limited absorption of water and salts profuse flowering results.

3 With a medium water and salt absorption the intensity of photosynthesis determines whether vegetative growth or flowering shall occur When the production of organic substance is decreased, e g., in blue light, vegetative growth results, and when it is increased, flowering occurs [1]

These results have in general been confirmed by the observations and experiments of others, so that it seems to be a well-established fact that the development of flowers depends upon different metabolic conditions from those which determine vegetative growth. Observation and experiment agree, moreover, in indicating that flowering is determined by the accumulation in the plant of organic substances which, because of insufficiency of water and salts, are not completely transformed into metabolically active protoplasm or its products, and so do not simply produce growth, but rather a change in metabolic conditions in the direction of differentiation and senescence.

If the formation of a new vegetative tip, i e , a new vegetative axis, is the generalized form of reproduction in the flowering plant (cf. pp 238–39), then there can be no doubt that the flowering is a specialized type of reproduction   The flower certainly shows a much higher degree of differentiation of its parts than does the vegetative axis   Moreover, the metabolic conditions which favor flowering are conditions which cannot arise at once in a plant individual beginning its development and dependent upon external sources of nutrition   At least certain stages of metabolic history must be passed through before the plant is capable of being brought into the flowering condition   Authorities in general agree that a certain amount of vegetative growth must occur before the plant can be induced to bloom   In other words, the plant must apparently attain a certain stage of development, a certain physiological age, before flowering is possible   But this stage having been attained, the further metabolic conditions which favor flowering are similar in character to those which bring about morphological differentiation and senescence in animals, for they consist in the

[1] Klebs, '06, pp 105–6

accumulation of inactive or relatively inactive organic substances in the cells and consequently a decrease in metabolic rate. We see also that such internal conditions bring about a higher degree of differentiation in the plant than the conditions accompanying vegetative growth Moreover, the parts particularly involved in this differentiation—the inflorescence axis or the flower—do not under the usual conditions undergo any further vegetative growth, but, after their development is completed, die a natural death, and in many cases this natural death involves the whole plant, the seeds only remaining alive.

The evidence seems then to point very clearly to the conclusion that flowering in the plant is characteristic of an advanced stage in the life cycle—that the blooming plant is physiologically relatively old The conditions which prevent flowering and favor vegetative growth are simply such as keep the plant in a relatively young condition by preventing the accumulation of the organic substances and bringing about repeated vegetative reproduction in consequence of growth.

It may seem at first glance that the metabolic conditions in the flower are not in accord with the conclusion that the flower is the product of advanced age in the plant The flower, particularly in its earlier stages, is usually the seat of a very intense respiratory activity and often possesses a higher rate of oxidation than any other part of the plant.[1] If blooming is a feature of advanced age and if rate of oxidation is in any way associated with age, it would seem that we ought to find a low rate of oxidation in the flower Such a conclusion, however, ignores completely the fact that the formation of the flower is a complex reproductive process and unquestionably involves a greater or less degree of rejuvenescence which appears in increased respiratory activity, and that in the formation of the pollen grains in the anther and the ovules and embryo sacs in the ovary extensive reproduction again occurs. Moreover, in the developing flower the proportion of actively growing cells to the total weight is greater than in the vegetative portions of the plant, with the exception of the embryonic growing

[1] See A. Maige, '06, '07; G. Maige, '09, '11, and, for further references, Pfeffer, '97, Nicolas, '09

regions. In consequence of this condition the flower may be expected to show a relatively high rate of respiration

The accumulation of organic material and the relatively low metabolic rate in the vegetative parts of the plant are probably factors in making possible the high rate in the flower, which develops at the expense of the nutritive substances in other parts. The flower is a new individual or system of individuals, which arises under conditions of low metabolic rate in other parts, and such conditions favor the establishment in it of a high rate of metabolism and growth. Evidently the flower is a more stable structure than most of the vegetative parts of the plant and it undergoes rapid progressive differentiation and aging. These characteristics are also doubtless associated, on the one hand, with metabolic condition of advanced age in other parts and, on the other, with its own high metabolic rate.

In most flowers the rate of respiration decreases from relatively early stages onward, but in some cases it undergoes increase or remains almost constant up to the time of opening. These differences are probably associated with differences in the size and amount of growth of the ovary and its contents as compared with other parts of the flower. It was suggested in the preceding chapter (pp. 349–50) that the increase in rate of respiration in the pistil during its development is connected with the increasing bulk of the growing ovules and embryo sacs in proportion to the whole pistil. Since it is impossible to measure the respiratory rate of single gametophytes (pollen grains or embryo sacs) or gametes during their development, the available data on rate of respiration in the flower and its parts are incomplete for present purposes. In the case of the pistil particularly they represent measurements of rate in a complex system in which different parts attain their maximum activity at different times and differ in amount and rate of growth in different cases. Nevertheless, so far as the data are applicable they do not conflict with, but rather support, the view that the flower is a product of relatively advanced physiological age in the plant.

In those cases where blooming is periodically repeated in the life of the plant, as in perennials, it must be remembered that new phytoids are concerned and that each period represents the life history of a generation of phytoids. The life of the perennial, multiaxial plant is not comparable to the life of an individual animal, but is made up of innumerable life cycles with senescence and death of the more highly differentiated parts in each generation.

From this standpoint the cases of premature flowering are to be regarded simply as cases of prematurely established physiological conditions resembling those which usually arise only after a considerable period of vegetative activity It is impossible to consider these cases at length, and in many of them the determining conditions have not been analyzed. One interesting case recently recorded by Dôposcheg-Uhlár ('12) may, however, be mentioned. Bulbs of a species of *Begonia* could be made to produce either a vegetative shoot or an inflorescence at once according as they were allowed to produce roots or not. The roots provided for the entrance of water and salts and so made possible the transformation of the organic reserves in the bulb into protoplasm, and under these conditions complete rejuvenescence to the vegetative condition was possible. When, however, root formation did not occur, the metabolic conditions in the cells were those characteristic of an advanced stage of the life cycle under ordinary conditions and growth from the bulb resulted in the immediate development of the highly differentiated flower structure. The early flowering of various other plant species grown from bulbs is probably to be interpreted in the same way. The internal conditions in such cases are those of relatively advanced age

Numerous cases of the transformation of an inflorescence, a flower or some part of a flower. into a new vegetative axis have been recorded by various authors (see pp 246-47), and Klebs, Goebel, and others have induced this transformation by subjecting the young inflorescence or flower to external conditions favorable to vegetative growth.[1] As Goebel ('08, pp 117-18) suggests, these cases are undoubtedly to be interpreted as cases of return to a juvenile stage The external conditions have made dedifferentiation and rejuvenescence possible, even in the relatively highly differentiated flower.

[1] See the references given on p 246, and particularly Klebs,'03, '06.

Proceeding now to the last point in our consideration, the development of the flower is preliminary to the formation of the gamete The gametophytes develop as parts of the flower (see pp. 320 22, the pollen grains being the male, the embryo sac in the ovule the female gametophyte. Although these gametophytes are much reduced as compared with those of the mosses and ferns, yet their formation in the seed plants, as in the lower forms, is unquestionably the result of a specialized agamic reproductive process, i.e, spore formation. The gametophytes arising from the spore are certainly in the seed plants highly specialized organs or organisms. Their development differs widely in the two sexes and in both is very different from anything else in the development of the plant (see Figs. 140, 141, pp. 320, 321)

It is in these highly specialized organs, or individuals, as we choose to call them, that the gametes are formed. The whole history of the plant leading up to the formation of the gametes is a history of specialization and differentiation of parts, and we have therefore every reason to regard the gametes as among the most highly specialized and differentiated cells produced by the plant.

CONDITIONS OF CONJUGATION IN THE PROTOZOA

According to Weismann all protozoa are potentially germ cells. Maupas in his investigations on the ciliates reached the conclusion that conjugation results from internal factors which, during the period of agamic reproduction, bring about a progressive senescence of the stock ending in death unless conjugation occurs. Conjugation in some way rejuvenates the animals and so makes possible a new series of agamic generations. But the investigations of recent years, as noted in chap. vi, have forced a change in view [1]

On the one hand, the breeding experiments of Calkins, Enriques, Woodruff, and Jennings have demonstrated that at least some races of *Paramecium* and other ciliates can be bred agamically for hundreds or thousands of generations, and probably indefinitely, without the occurrence of conjugation and without loss of vigor, provided the proper conditions are maintained in the medium

[1] Among the more important references are those given in the footnotes on p 130, see particularly Woodruff, '14, Jennings, '12, '13

On the other hand, Enriques, Jennings, Woodruff, Baitsell, and others have shown that conjugation may be induced experimentally. According to Jennings, different races show great differences in their capacity or tendency to conjugate, some conjugating every few weeks, others at intervals of a year or more, or not at all But in those races which conjugate readily conjugation occurs, "not as a result of starvation, but at the beginning of a decline in nutritive conditions after a period of exceptional richness that has induced rapid multiplication. At the time of conjugation the animals are often in good condition and multiplication may still be in progress" (Jennings, '10, p 298). As regards these points Calkins is in essential agreement with Jennings. In his experiments with a single race Zweibaum found that conjugation may be induced in a great variety of ways, provided a certain nutritive condition exists in the animals. This condition is brought about by keeping animals which have been richly fed for some weeks in a medium with less food and then removing to a medium containing almost no food. Differences in the methods of Jennings and Zweibaum may be due to differences in the races used for experiment, but there is general agreement that decreased nutrition favors the occurrence of conjugation. Woodruff has recently brought about conjugation experimentally in the *Paramecium* culture which has been bred agamically for nearly five thousand generations, and Baitsell has also found that the occurrence of conjugation in other infusoria can be experimentally controlled

These recent investigators agree in general that conjugation is not the result of a progressive senescence, and so does not represent the end of the life history   Calkins and Gregory maintain further "that the progeny of an ex-conjugant is not a homogeneous race, but consists of differentiated individuals which give rise to pure lines, some of which conjugate, others do not. In other words, some *Paramecia* are potential germ cells, others are not." Woodruff, however, disputes this conclusion and holds that the occurrence or non-occurrence of conjugation depends on environmental conditions

In chap. vi facts are cited which indicate that some degree of senescence occurs during the life of each generation and some degree of rejuvenescence, at least in the cytoplasm, in each agamic reproduction, and the periodic process of endomixis and the reproductive rhythms associated with it were interpreted as periods of senescence, death, and replacement of the meganucleus. Since Woodruff and Erdmann ('14) have demonstrated, not only that endomixis occurs periodically, but that it has no relation to the occurrence of conjugation, we must conclude that the progressive senescence of the meganucleus which results in endomixis is not the essential factor concerned in bringing about conjugation. Moreover, since conjugation is not a feature of an internally determined invariable life cycle, but is rather associated with and dependent upon certain environmental conditions, at least to a high degree, it seems probable that the physiological conditions of conjugation are primarily cytoplasmic rather than nuclear, for the cytoplasm is more affected than the nucleus by the environmental conditions.

Since cytoplasmic rejuvenescence occurs with each agamic reproduction, it is evident that the physiological age of the cytoplasm attained in each generation may depend, at least in part, upon the frequency of reproduction. With abundant food and favorable medium the reconstitution associated with one reproduction is scarcely completed before another reproduction occurs. Under such conditions the degree of physiological senescence between two successive fissions must be less than when the interval between reproductions is longer. Consequently certain conditions which retard growth and agamic reproduction, but which are not so extreme as to bring about either complete quiescence or starvation and reduction, favor the attainment of a more advanced cytoplasmic age by the individuals of each generation. Under these conditions the parts continue to exercise their special functions for a longer period before undergoing regressive changes in connection with reproduction, and the advance of senescence in each generation may not be balanced by the rejuvenescence occurring in each reproduction, so that progressive cytoplasmic senescence of the race may occur. We need not expect, however, to find conspicuous morphological differences between such animals and those which are growing and reproducing rapidly. The differences can at most be merely those between physiologically older and younger individuals both of which have attained the adult form, and in organisms as simple as the ciliates would be more readily distinguishable physiologically than morphologically. But so far as I am aware, this point has not been considered by most students of protozoa. One author, Prowazek ('10), has stated that when cultures of *Colpidium* are prevented from dividing by insufficient nutrition, they rapidly become old. In his cultures, however, the animals were evidently starved, for they underwent reduction in size to a considerable extent and their susceptibility to atropin underwent a marked increase. These changes in size and susceptibility suggest that these cultures were undergoing reduction and increase in rate of metabolism in consequence of partial starvation (cf. chap. vii) instead of undergoing senescence. Nutrition seems to have been insufficient in this case to permit senescence to occur, for that the food should have been at least sufficient to prevent decrease in size

But the important point is that those conditions which favor a progressive senescence are the conditions which favor conjugation The facts from this point of view suggest simply that under conditions which favor rapid agamic reproduction the animals have no opportunity to attain maturity because of the frequent reconstitution and rejuvenescence. When agamic reproduction is retarded or inhibited, maturity is very soon attained and conjugation occurs

The occurrence of endomixis indicates, as I have pointed out, that the meganucleus undergoes senescence in spite of agamic reproduction If, at the time when the meganucleus is approaching death, the cytoplasm is physiologically young and in good metabolic condition, then apparently endomixis and recovery without conjugation occur, but if, at this time, the cytoplasm is also in a condition of advanced physiological senescence, then probably the physiological conditions for conjugation are present, and if conjugation is impossible, death may result. According to this view, endomixis results from progressive senescence of a single specialized organ, the meganucleus, and conjugation from the senescence of both meganucleus and cytoplasm.

If senescence is essentially a decrease in rate of metabolism, the stage of maturity must possess a lower rate of metabolism than the stage in which agamic reproduction is occurring While I have not as yet made a systematic study of the changes in susceptibility of ciliates with changes in medium and other conditions certain differences in susceptibility observed in a culture of *Colpidium* are of some interest in this connection.   This culture was at first undergoing very rapid agamic reproduction and the small recently divided individuals, as well as most of those in late stages of division, were more susceptible to cyanide than the larger, older individuals In the course of a few days an acute epidemic of conjugation occurred in the culture, and fissions almost ceased   conjugation was confined to the larger individuals of the culture   At this stage the small animals were most susceptible, the large, non-conjugating animals less susceptible, and the conjugating pairs least susceptible of all.   The low susceptibility of the conjugants indicates that they possess a lower metabolic rate and so are physiologically older than the other members of the culture

These experiments suggest that the occurrence of conjugation is associated with the attainment of a certain physiological age, a condition of maturity, with a relatively low rate of metabolism If this conclusion is correct, we must consider the question of the influence of external conditions upon the attainment of this maturity : is it possible to accelerate or retard its occurrence through cultural or other environmental conditions ? It is not to be expected that a sudden decrease in rate of metabolism induced by external conditions will bring about a normal maturity in a very young individual: such a change would simply retard or inhibit its development.   But when development has reached a certain stage and the organism is approaching maturity, then it is very probable that a slight decrease in metabolic rate, externally induced, may be sufficient in many cases to bring about or accelerate the change which under constant external conditions would have occurred much more slowly.   Some of the chemical agents which Zweibaum and others have used to induce conjugation may perhaps act in this way

As regards the different capacity or tendency of different races to conjugate, which has been discussed by Jennings, Woodruff, and

Calkins, it is possible at present only to point out certain probable factors concerned   In the first place, the rate and course of individual senescence or rejuvenescence under a given complex of conditions is probably different in different races of *Paramecium* and other forms, and the rate and course of individual senescence or rejuvenescence in a given race may differ under different conditions. Differences of this kind also appear to some extent in planarians. In *Planaria velata* the course of the age cycle depends upon the character of the food (see pp 169–75). With some kinds of food progressive senescence from generation to generation occurs and in a few generations death results, while with others rejuvenescence and senescence balance each other in each generation. Doubtless similar relations exist in *Paramecium* and other ciliates between character of food, rate of senescence in each generation, and degree of rejuvenescence in each reproduction. And it is not at all improbable that various other factors besides nutrition. e.g., many chemical agents, may influence the rate, degree, and course of development, senescence, and rejuvenescence

Whether, as Calkins believes, some races of *Paramecium* and other ciliates are not even potentially capable of conjugation can be determined only by extensive investigation, and then only with a certain degree of probability   It is of course conceivable that in organisms with great capacity for agamic reproduction the capacity to attain gametic maturity may not be realized under ordinary conditions (see chap. x), but as yet we have no adequate basis for maintaining that the potentiality is absent in such cases

In the higher animals a definite sequence of events is a fundamental characteristic of the life cycle, and it seems not wholly logical to maintain that a sequence is entirely absent in the simpler forms. We can scarcely doubt that an individual *Paramecium*, continuing to live without reproduction and with sufficient food for maintenance in a constant medium which does not inhibit metabolism, will undergo certain more or less definite changes, and will show a life history.   And it seems probable that if these changes proceed sufficiently far without interruption by reproduction or change in external conditions, the individual may attain maturity— the physiological condition in which conjugation occurs—or may even die of old age. But the more readily agamic reproduction occurs in consequence of either internal or external factors, the less likely is the life history of the individual to attain its later stages

In the case of the protozoa the question of progressive race senescence has occupied the minds of most investigators to the exclusion of individual senescence Apparently, however, the solution of the whole problem is to be found in the relation between individual senescence and rejuvenescence under different conditions If progressive senescence in a race, ending in conjugation or death, does not occur in a race bred agamically, it is not because the individuals do not undergo senescence, but rather because the cytoplasmic senescence in each generation is compensated by rejuvenescence in each agamic reproduction and because senescence of the meganucleus is compensated by the process of nuclear reorganization which Woodruff and Erdmann have called endomixis

CONDITIONS OF GAMETE FORMATION IN THE MULTICELLULAR ANIMALS

Our knowledge concerning the physiological conditions which determine the formation of gametes in the lower multicellular animals is as yet very fragmentary As regards many forms we do not even know whether sexual maturity occurs once or periodically in the life cycle, or whether its appearance is merely a reaction to external conditions. Observation of the animals in nature seems to indicate clearly enough that in general the formation of gametes occurs only when a period of vegetative growth, with or without agamic reproduction, is approaching or has reached its end In the case of the fresh-water hydra considerable experimental work has been done,[1] and most authors agree that low temperature determines sexual maturity, although different species appear to differ to some extent as regards the effective temperatures Nussbaum maintains that starvation or at least decrease in nutrition is the essential factor, but other authors do not agree with him. These results do not afford us any very deep insight into the physiology of gamete formation. They merely indicate that a relatively low rate of metabolism favors or even determines gamete formation, but whether gamete formation ever occurs without the aid of external

[1] R Hertwig, '06, Krapfenbauer, '08, Frischolz, '09, Nussbaum, '09, Koch, '11

factors which decrease metabolism we do not know. It may be that such processes as budding and the replacement of differentiated old cells by young cells from the interstitial tissue prevent progressive development in hydra beyond a certain point under the usual conditions, in which case low temperatures by decreasing the rate of metabolism may bring about essentially the same changes that would occur in further development determined by internal factors. In many if not in all of the coelenterates, however, there are indications that the formation of gametes is associated with an advanced stage of the life cycle

One of the most interesting cases is that of certain jelly-fishes or medusae belonging to the family Margelidae (Chun, '96; Braem, '08). These medusae reproduce agamically by budding, and buds arise in a definite order upon the proboscis and develop from the ectoderm alone instead of from both body layers, as do other coelenterate buds. The young medusa gives rise to these buds, but as it grows older sex organs begin to appear from the same body layer and in the same region as the buds and sometimes in place of them. Fig. 196 shows the proboscis of one of these medusae on which both buds and ovaries containing eggs are present. After the sex organs once appear the buds gradually cease to form and only gametes are produced in later stages.

In these medusae the same region and layer of the body and, so far as we can determine, cells of exactly the same character, give rise in the younger animal to agamic buds and in later stages to gametes Very evidently the physiological condition of these cells undergoes change during the life history of the animal. Braem regards this case as indicating that the agamic buds as well as the gametes arise from germ plasm, but it seems rather to indicate that gametes as well as agamic buds may arise from cells which are functional, more or less specialized parts of the organism, and that the gametes are more highly specialized cells and arise later in the life history than those which develop into buds

As regards the planarian worms a few facts are at hand. Attention has already been called (pp. 99, 125) to the fact that *Planaria dorotocephala* is not known to reproduce sexually at all in the locality where I have collected material. But in stocks which are kept in the laboratory under uniform conditions, provided with abundant food and prevented from undergoing fission, the animals often continue to grow until they are fully twice as large as the largest found under natural conditions, and a considerable number of these very large animals develop the hermaphroditic sexual organs characteristic of the species, become sexually mature, and lay eggs. Often

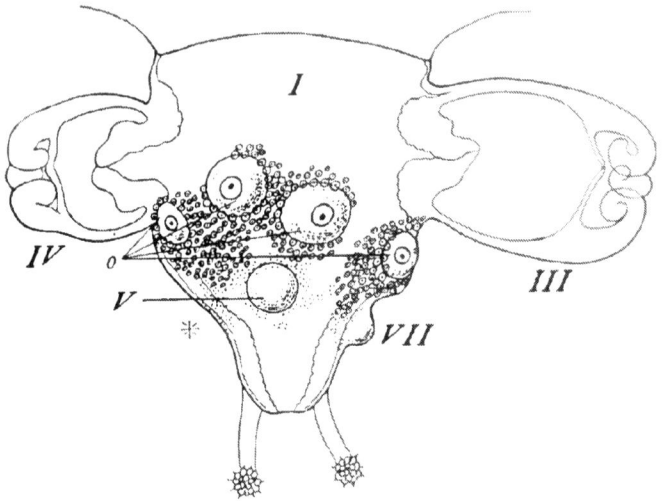

FIG. 196.—Manubrium of female *Lizzia* (jelly-fish), showing asexual buds and eggs: in addition to the four large eggs, *o*, those regions which are occupied by distinctly differentiated ovarial cells are indicated by drawing in cell outlines and nuclei in the dotted regions are cells which may become either buds or ovarian cells: roman numerals I, III, IV, V, VII, indicate buds in the order of their formation, bud I having already become free and buds II and VI being on the other side of the manubrium: the point * indicates the position where the eighth bud should appear. From Braem '08.

sexually mature animals can be made to undergo fission simply by transferring them to another perfectly clean aquarium without slime on its walls, and when the level of fission is anywhere near the openings of the sexual ducts, which lie a short distance behind the mouth, the openings and all the terminal organs disappear.

The very low susceptibility of the sexually mature animals to cyanides, as compared with that of the largest animals in nature indicates that physiologically they are very much older than the latter In consequence of continued feeding and growth and the absence of the reconstitutional changes connected with fission, these animals have evidently attained a stage of development which is not reached by the animals in nature.

The conditions in nature which prevent the animals from attaining the later stages of development and sexual maturity are less abundant food and consequently greater activity, which in turn determines more frequent fission, so that the animals are almost continuously undergoing reconstitution. Moreover, the animals are subjected more or less periodically to periods of partial starvation.   Insufficiency of food may arise from the rapid increase in numbers of the animals by fission during the summer, perhaps also from the slow reproduction of the food animals in winter These two facts, fission and repeated partial starvation, contribute to keep the animals physiologically young and so prevent them from attaining the age and physiological condition in which sexual maturity occurs

Planaria maculata becomes sexually mature in some localities and not, or only very rarely, in others (Curtis '02).   In the latter localities the factors which prevent the occurrence of sexual maturity are undoubtedly the same as those which produce the result in *P dorotocephala*, i.e., repeated fission and periodical or occasional partial starvation.

In a stock of *P. maculata* kept in the laboratory I found that sexually mature individuals, after egg laying, lose the sexual organs and undergo a considerable reduction in size.   During this period they take little or no food, but after a time begin once more to feed and grow, and if growth is rapid they may reproduce agamically, while if it is slow they may in some cases become sexually mature again without passing through any period of agamic reproduction

The differences in susceptibility of the animals at these different periods indicate that the sexually mature stages are physiologically older than others, and that after egg laying they undergo a considerable degree of rejuvenescence during the reduction, and once more begin to undergo senescence when they begin to feed.   Whether they remain asexual or become sexually mature depends on the amount and uniformity of the food supply and the rate of growth There is no question that in *P maculata*, as well as in *P. dorotocephala*, sexual maturity represents a condition of greater physiological age than the asexual stage.

The case of *P. velata* is somewhat different. Under the conditions where it is usually found in nature, as well as in the laboratory, this form unquestionably grows old, ceases to feed, and undergoes fragmentation in each generation without becoming sexually mature. Apparently sexual reproduction has no place in the life cycle of this species. If it were not for the fact that the animal stops feeding and ceases to grow before fragmentation occurs we might believe that the life cycle of the individual is simply interrupted as in *P. dorotocephala* and in many plants by the agamic reproduction, but as a matter of fact the period of development and growth is apparently completed before fragmentation begins. Thus far it has not been possible to induce sexual maturity experimentally in this species. It seems probable, however, that certain of the feeding experiments already described afford a clue to the understanding of this case. It was pointed out that the length of the growth period and the amount of growth before fragmentation differ very widely with different foods In other words, the rate of senescence differs according to character of food This suggests the possibility that with certain foods growth might continue and fragmentation be delayed until attainment of the stage of sexual maturity, but only further experiment can throw light upon the question.

As regards the parasitic groups of flatworms, the flukes and the tapeworms, there can be no doubt that formation of gametes and sexual reproduction is characteristic of an advanced stage in the life of the individual. Such parasites are subjected to but little change in external conditions, especially those living in the bodies of mammals, and yet they pass through a definite life history, ending in the development of gametes and, following this, the death of the individual. In some of the flukes the number of larval generations between the egg and the development of the sexual organs may differ according to external factors, but the relation between sexual maturity and relatively advanced age is unmistakable

In other animal groups in which agamic reproduction is a more or less characteristic feature of the life cycle—certain families of annelids, the bryozoa, and the tunicates—it is in general true that agamic precedes gametic reproduction in the life history, and in some of these forms, notably in certain annelids, agamic reproduction may apparently continue indefinitely under certain conditions without the attainment of sexual maturity.

Among the higher invertebrates, and among the vertebrates, the definite character and internal determination of the life history become in most cases even more apparent   In many forms, as in most of the insects, development ends in a single period of gametic production followed by death   In many other forms, after maturity is once attained, the production of gametes is periodic or continuous and the animal may live for a long time and may also undergo extensive growth, as do most of the mollusks after the first period of sexual maturity   In such cases growth, as well as gamete production, appears to be periodic, and the formation of gametes follows. at least in most cases, the growth period.

Periodicity of this sort in the organism is commonly associated with periodicity in the environment, e g , with seasonal or other periodic changes   The environmental periodicity may determine slight alterations of senescence and rejuvenescence as perhaps in the case of the mollusks, where growth periods ending with or followed by gamete formation occur or in other cases the activity of the sexual organs may be directly influenced by nutritive condition, temperature, etc.

That the vertebrates pass through a definite developmental history, with sexual maturity as a comparatively late stage, and that this history is primarily determined by factors within the organism rather than environmental conditions is sufficiently evident   Here agamic reproduction does not occur, except in a few cases in early embryonic stages, and the life history is without the complications which arise in lower forms to prevent, balance, or retard progressive development   Even among the vertebrates, however, the appearance of sexual maturity may be hastened or retarded by the character and amount of the food and by various other environmental conditions   The tadpoles of frogs and salamanders, for example, may be made to undergo metamorphosis into the adult form at a very small size or to attain giantism without metamorphosis by controlling the character of the food (Gudernatsch, '12, '14, Romeis, '14), and their development may be modified in various other ways. Even in man the age in years at which sexual maturity occurs varies somewhat widely with climatic and other factors   But none of these facts indicate anything more than that a certain physiological condition of the organism may be attained sooner or later according to the nature of the environment.

In various species among both invertebrates and vertebrates cases of premature sexual maturity may occur while the animal is still morphologically a larva, as in the so-called axolotl form of certain salamanders; or after sexual maturity in the larval stage the sex organs may disappear and the animal undergo metamorphosis to the adult form, after which new sex organs arise and a second period of sexual maturity occurs, as in certain ctenophores.

Evidently the sex organs may mature and produce gametes at various stages of morphological development, but we know nothing of the physiological conditions in these cases.   In the light of the facts already cited, however, it is probable that, whatever the morphological stage at which sexual maturity occurs, certain physiological conditions must exist in the organism which make its appearance possible and that these are conditions which ordinarily arise relatively late in development.   In other words, the cases of premature sexual maturity are probably cases of accelerated physiological senescence.

PARTHENOGENESIS AND ZYGOGENESIS

In several of the invertebrate groups, viz , the rotifers, the cladocera among the crustacea, and the plant lice and related families among the insects, the eggs of a single individual or of successive generations differ in behavior, some developing parthenogenically into females or males, and others zygogenically, i e., requiring fertilization for development.

Within recent years members of the crustacean group of cladocera, the daphnids, have been the subject of extensive investigation along these lines,[1] and while different authorities are not as yet in full agreement, evidence which points to a definite conclusion is accumulating

It is well known that the daphnid females produce three kinds of eggs, parthenogenic eggs which produce females, parthenogenic eggs which produce males, and zygogenic eggs which produce females Both the female- and male-producing parthenogenic eggs develop at once and are commonly known as "summer eggs." The zygogenic eggs, on the other hand, are surrounded by a thick shell and hatch only after a quiescent period which often, but not necessarily, coincides with the winter season, hence they are known as "winter eggs" The problem to which attention has been chiefly directed is that of the relative importance of external and internal factors in determining the production of these three kinds of eggs. Weismann believed that a fixed cycle of generations determined by inheritance existed in each species quite independently of external factors, according to this view a certain number of generations of parthenogenic females were produced, then males developed from parthenogenic eggs and zygogenic eggs were produced, which after a quiescent period developed into parthenogenic female-producing females, and these began the cycle anew

Later investigators have found that the cycle of generations is far from being hereditarily fixed and that it can be greatly modified by external factors. Under certain conditions, e g., with high temperature and abundant nutrition, parthenogenic reproduction may continue indefinitely Other conditions, such as low temperature and lack of food, favor the production of males and zygogenic eggs. In general. males and zygogenic eggs are produced under similar conditions Moreover, Woltereck has found that after producing males the females may again begin to produce females parthenogenically without producing winter eggs, and the same change may occur even after the production of winter eggs. Kuttner showed, however. that the cycle of generations may occur independently of change in external conditions.

[1] Some of the more important papers are the following Issakowitsch, '06, '08, Kuttner, '09, Langhans, '09, Papanicolau, '10a, '10b, '11, von Scharfenberg, '10, Strohl, '07, '08, Weismann, '80, Woltereck, '09, '11.

Woltereck's extensive investigations, together with the evidence from the work of others, seem to show very clearly that, while differences exist in different races and species, nevertheless a cyclical change affecting the character of the eggs produced does occur in these animals independently of external factors, although it may be modified by temperature, nutrition, and chemical constitution of the medium in which the animals live. Woltereck divides the cycle into three periods, the first including the early generations of females following the winter eggs. These females are predominantly parthenogenic and female-producing, at least until late in life, and external factors have no effect on the character of the eggs. After this follows a second period in which external conditions determine to a very large extent whether parthenogenic eggs producing females, or parthenogenic eggs producing males and zygogenic eggs are produced, and finally a third period occurs in which parthenogenic eggs producing males and female-producing zygogenic eggs appear independently of external conditions.

Von Scharfenberg and Papanicolau found that a change in egg character occurred, not only in the course of successive generations, but also in the course of single generations, i e., the eggs produced early in the life of a female are more likely to develop parthenogenically into females and those produced later in life into males or to be zygogenic winter eggs. In the earlier generations of a cycle the male-producing and zygogenic eggs appear later in the life of the individuals, in later generations earlier. Moreover, the same three periods appear more or less clearly in the reproductive cycle of the single females as in the cycle of generations.

This reproductive cycle appearing both in single individuals and in successive generations is in certain respects analogous to the cycle of agamic and gametic reproduction in many of the lower animals. In the early stages of the cycle the daphnids, although producing what we call eggs, are really reproducing agamically, since the eggs develop parthenogenically, but in later generations, as well as later in the life of the individual, they become sexually mature, and males and females appear and the eggs require fertilization. There seems to be a progressive change in physiological condition in these animals, both individually and in successive generations, which corresponds to the aging and the attainment of sexual maturity in other forms. The parthenogenic female-producing egg is apparently characteristic of the young animal and the earlier generations in a cycle, the parthenogenic male-producing egg and the zygogenic female-producing egg of a more advanced age in the individual and in the generations   Richard Hertwig ('12) in discussing these facts says: "It is therefore possible to speak in a double sense of an aging of the daphnids and of a change in the constitution of the eggs determined by it "

Woltereck has found that an individual may pass through more than one of these reproductive cycles.   Even after producing winter eggs, females may again pass through a labile period in which the character of the eggs can be influenced by external conditions and still later attain a condition in which the eggs are parthenogenic and female-producing in spite of external conditions. In other words, they become physiologically young again   But it has been shown in earlier chapters that such rejuvenescence occurs in many forms.   In the case of the daphnids it does not proceed as far as in many of the lower animals, for these may lose their sexual organs entirely and return to reproduction by budding or fission, while in the daphnids we find only a return from the production of zygogenic to the production of parthenogenic eggs

As regards the rotifers, in certain species of which parthenogenesis and bisexuality exist, the various investigators[1] still differ widely in their opinions as to the determining factors.   The effective factor in determining parthenogenesis and bisexuality is according to Maupas temperature, and according to Nussbaum nutrition, while Punnett finds that neither of these external factors is concerned, but that the character of the eggs is hereditarily determined Whitney regards the age of the family, that is, the position in the cycle of generations, as the important factor, although he admits the influence of external conditions   And, finally, Shull has demonstrated the influence ef external factors in the environmental medium, apparently of chemical nature, but believes that internal factors are also involved.   With such differences of opinion it

[1] Maupas, '91, M Nussbaum, '97, Punnett, '06, Shull, '10, '11a, '11b, '12, Whitney, '07, '12a, '12b.

seems at least probable that internal physiological conditions, which are not yet clearly recognized, are the real determining factors, and that the various external factors merely modify their action. As Woltereck ('11) has pointed out, there is every reason to believe that the relation between parthenogenesis and bisexuality is essentially the same in the rotifers as in the daphnids.

Parthenogenesis and bisexuality are also found among the plant lice and various other related forms among the hemiptera. In these cases, as in the daphnids, bisexuality appears later in the cycle than parthenogenesis, but concerning the influence of external conditions in modifying the usual course of events, our knowledge is fragmentary. Low temperature or lack of food may apparently at times induce bisexuality, as in the daphnids. All that we know suggests that in this, as in other cases, bisexuality is a feature of more advanced age than parthenogenesis, and that the aging may be accelerated or retarded, perhaps reversed, by external conditions.

The parthenogenic egg is apparently a less highly specialized, physiologically younger cell than the egg requiring fertilization. Morphologically it is less highly differentiated, at least in many cases, than the zygogenic egg (see pp. 342–46), and when isolated from the parent body it is capable of developing at once without fertilization (cf. pp 406–8) If such eggs are produced by animals in the earlier stages of their adult life history or by the earlier generation of a cycle, we are forced to the conclusion that the germ cells undergo differentiation and aging like the rest of the body. In short, the egg produced by the older organism is itself older and more highly specialized than that produced by a younger.

The physiological character of the action of external conditions in modifying the eggs can at present only be surmised Woltereck suggests that the differences in the eggs are due to differences in the intensity of assimilation in the ovary, high intensity determining parthenogenic female-producing eggs and low intensity bisexual eggs. A decrease in intensity of assimilation is, however, a characteristic feature of senescence and may result from internal as well as from external conditions. Apparently the external factors, whatever the exact mechanism of their action, either accelerate, retard, or reverse the life cycle of the whole animal and so affect the character of the eggs, or else they alter conditions in the ovaries so that eggs are isolated from the parent organism earlier or later in their development.

If the external conditions decrease the general metabolism, they may bring about physiological conditions which would arise without their action in more advanced stages of senescence, but if their effect is to increase metabolism, they may make the animal somewhat younger physiologically by increasing breakdown and elimination, or they may at least retard or inhibit senescence. In this manner the character of the eggs may be influenced through the physiological condition of the whole animal.

It is probable, however that the physiological age and condition of the egg do not necessarily correspond in all cases to the physiological age of the egg-producing organism. Under certain conditions, such as abundant nutrition or high temperature, the development of successive eggs may be so rapid that each egg is forced down the ovarian tubules and isolated before its growth is completed, even though the animal itself is physiologically old. Such an egg must be physiologically younger than one which undergoes more growth before isolation   Probably the action of external factors in determining parthenogenesis and bisexuality is sometimes of this character, and a high rate of egg production results in younger eggs, a low rate of egg production in older eggs.

Summing up, this point of view seems to afford a basis for reconciling the apparently conflicting data, and for further analytic investigation.   The parthenogenic egg in the daphnids and rotifers is apparently physiologically younger and less highly differentiated than the zygogenic; the physiological age, both of the individual and of the race, and probably also the rate and conditions of egg production, are factors in determining whether parthenogenic or zygogenic eggs shall be produced, and, finally, external factors act by accelerating, retarding, or reversing the course of the life history in the individual or race, or by influencing the rate and other conditions of egg production in the ovary

It seems to be definitely determined that among the bees the males arise from parthenogenic eggs, the females from fertilized

eggs, as Dzierzon maintained more than sixty years ago.[1] The
queen bee is apparently capable of producing drone eggs at any
time, or at least repeatedly, during her life   It is conceivable that
all eggs produced by the queen are potentially parthenogenic and
so male-producing, but that when fertilized they produce females
(see pp. 344–45), but if the parthenogenic eggs are physiologically
different from the zygogenic in this case, it seems probable that the
former are at least slightly younger than the latter when they
leave the ovary   If, as suggested above, not only the physiological age of the animal, but the conditions in the ovary determining
the rate of egg production—the abundance of nutrition, etc —are
factors in the determination of parthenogenic and zygogenic eggs,
old queens may produce parthenogenic or young queens zygogenic
eggs under certain conditions.   Only under fairly constant external
conditions could a definite, fixed relation between physiological
condition of the egg and physiological age of the parent be expected.

   In certain of the parasitic flatworms—the digenetic trematodes
—two or more larval generations occur between the fertilized egg
and the adult stage.   The first of these larval generations arises
from the egg as a single individual which contains within its body
certain cells known as germ cells.   Each of these germ cells develops
within the parent body into a larval individual of the second generation, and in many cases these larvae likewise contain germ cells
which give rise to a third larval generation: sometimes the process
may continue still farther, but in any case the final larval generation
undergoes transformation into a single adult individual and becomes
sexually mature.

   The germ cells in the bodies of these trematode larvae have
commonly been regarded as eggs, and the development of the second
and following larval generations as cases of parthenogenesis.   The
observation of Cary ('09) that these germ cells resemble parthenogenic eggs in giving rise to a single polar body before beginning
development gives further support to this view   If these cells are
actually parthenogenic eggs or approach such eggs in their characteristics, their appearance during or immediately after the embryonic

<hr />

[1] The latest studies on the subject, Nachtsheim, '13, Armbruster, '13, give an
extensive bibliography

period seems to conflict with the conclusion reached in the present chapter that the formation of gametes is a feature of relatively late stages in the life history of the individual. This conflict, however, is apparent rather than real Each larval generation has a life history of its own not essentially different from that of other animals: during this period it undergoes progressive differentiation and growth, but the rate of growth decreases and the larva finally dies, apparently of old age I have determined the changes in susceptibility to cyanides of two of the larval generations of certain species and have found that a marked and rapid decrease in susceptibility occurs in each generation and that the early stages of each generation show a much higher susceptibility than the late stages of the preceding generation This means that each generation undergoes a rapid senescence and that rejuvenescence occurs during each reproduction, but there is some evidence that progressive senescence from generation to generation also occurs to some extent

During the earlier stages of the life of a larva the cells which later become germ cells undergo division and so increase in number, but they do not become mature and begin independent development into new individuals until a relatively late larval stage of larval life is reached. The period of reproduction through the germ cells is in fact a feature of advanced age in the life of the larva. The cells resemble eggs in possessing a low metabolic rate before beginning development because they are parts of a physiologically old body and it is probable that the occurrence of a maturation division with the formation of a polar body is connected with this condition (see pp. 353–56). What we commonly call the life history of these worms is then in reality a series of life histories with alternating periods of senescence and rejuvenescence. Each period of senescence is accompanied in its later stages by reproduction through cells which resemble parthenogenic eggs more or less closely, but only in advanced age of the final generation, the adult form, do sexual maturity and fertilization occur. Certain other points in these life histories are of interest in connection with the problem of the life cycle, but this brief consideration is perhaps sufficient to show that the peculiar larval reproduction of these species is a feature of advanced age like gametic reproduction in other forms

It is apparently true for both animals and plants that the production of gametes is associated with certain internal conditions which are characteristic of an advanced physiological age. But since the course of the age cycle may be accelerated, retarded, or reversed by the action of external factors, the formation of gametes in the lower organisms, where the influence of external factors is relatively great, may often appear to be largely dependent upon these external factors Not only is gamete production a feature of relatively advanced age, but in some cases the physiological age of the egg—parthenogenic or zygogenic character—apparently depends to some extent on the physiological age of the parent.

The association of gamete formation with advanced physiological age is a fact of great importance, for it indicates that the "germ plasm" is an integral physiological part of the organism and that the formation of the gametes is the final stage of a period of progressive development in the reproductive cells. In the earlier stages of the life history of the organism isolated cells or cell masses may react to isolation by dedifferentiation and reconstitution to a new individual, i.e , agamic reproduction occurs The parthenogenic egg is apparently a cell which has undergone a considerable degree of differentiation as a gamete, but has not lost the capacity to react to isolation by dedifferentiation and reconstitution. And, finally, the zygogenic gamete has attained a stage of differentiation and senescence in which it is no longer capable alone of reacting to isolation, but can undergo dedifferentiation and reconstitution only when fertilization occurs. If there are any cells in the organism which do not contain "undifferentiated germ plasm," the gametes certainly seem to be among those cells

REFERENCES

ARMBRUSTER, L.
　　1913. "Chromosomenverhaltnisse bei der Spermatogenese solitärer Apiden (*Osmia cornuta* Latr.)," *Arch. f. Zellforsch* , XI

BARY, A. DE.
　　1878. "Uber apogame Farne und die Erscheinung der Apogamie im Allgemeinen," *Bot Zeitung*, XXXVI

BENECKE, W

1906 "Einige Bemerkungen uber die Bedingungen des Bluhens und Fruchtens der Gewachse," *Bot. Zeitung*, LXIV, Abt. II

BRAEM, F

1908. "Die Knospung der Margeliden, ein Bindeglied zwischen geschlechtlicher und ungeschlechtlicher Fortpflanzung," *Biol Centralbl.*, XXVIII.

CARY, L R

1909 "The Life History of *Diplodiscus temporatus* Stafford," *Zool Jahrbucher, Abt f Anat u Ont.*, XXVIII

CHUN, C.

1896. "*Atlantis;* Biologische Studien uber pelagische Organismen: I, Die Knospungsgesetze der proliferierenden Medusen," *Bibliotheca Zool.*, VII, 19.

CURTIS, W. C.

1902. "The Life History, the Normal Fission and the Reproductive Organs of *Planaria maculata*," *Proc. of the Boston Soc. of Nat. Hist*, XXX.

DIELS, L.

1906. *Jugendformen und Blutenreife im Pflanzenreich.* Berlin

DÖPOSCHEG-UHLÁR, I.

1912 "Fruhblute bei Knollenbegonien," *Flora*, CIV.

FARLOW, W. G

1874. "An Asexual Growth from the Prothallus of *Pteris cretica*," *Quart. Jour of Micr Sci.*, XIV

FARMER, J B, and DIGBY, L

1907. "Studies in Apospory and Apogamy in Ferns," *Annals of Bot*, XXI

FISCHER, A

1905. "Uber die Blutenbildung in ihrer Abhangigkeit vom Licht und die blutenbildenden Substanzen," *Flora*, XCIV

FRISCHOLZ, E.

1909 "Zur Biologie von *Hydra*," *Biol Centralbl.*, XXIX

GOEBEL, K.

1908. *Einleitung in die experimentelle Morphologie der Pflanzen.* Leipzig

GUDERNATSCH, J. F.

1912. "Feeding Experiments on Tadpoles I, The Influence of Specific Organs Given as Food on Growth and Differentiation," *Arch. f Entwickelungsmech*, XXXV.

1914. "Feeding Experiments on Tadpoles· II, A Further Contribution to the Knowledge of Organs with Internal Secretion," *Am. Jour. of Anat*, XV.

HEIM, C.
   1896. "Untersuchungen an Farnprothallien," *Flora*, LXXXII

HERTWIG, R
   1906. "Über Knospung und Geschlechtsentwickelung von *Hydra fusca*,"
       Biol. Centralbl , XXVI
   1912. "Über den derzeitigen Stand des Sexualitatsproblems nebst
       eigenen Untersuchungen," *Biol Centralbl.*, XXXII

ISSAKOWITSCH, A
   1906 "Geschlechtsbestimmende Ursachen bei den Daphniden," *Arch.*
       f. mikr. Anat., LXIX.
   1908. "Es besteht eine zyklische Fortpflanzung bei den Daphniden
       aber nicht im Sinne Weismanns," *Biol. Centralbl.*, XXVIII.

JENNINGS, H S
   1910. "What Conditions Induce Conjugation in *Paramecium?*" *Jour. of*
       Exp. Zool , IX.
   1912. "Age, Death and Conjugation in the Light of Work on Lower
       Organisms," *Pop. Sci. Monthly*, June.
   1913 "The Effect of Conjugation in *Paramecium*," *Jour. of Exp Zool* ,
       XIV.

JOST, L.
   1908 *Vorlesungen uber Pflanzenphysiologie:* II Auflage   Jena

KLEBS, G.
   1903. *Willkurliche Entwicklungsanderungen bei Pflanzen*   Jena.
   1904. "Über Probleme der Entwickelung," *Biol. Centralbl.*, XXIV.
   1906. *Über kunstliche Metamorphosen.* Stuttgart.

KOCH, W
   1911. "Über die Geschlechtsbildung und den Gonochorismus von *Hydra*
       fusca, Über die geschlechtliche Differenzierung und den Gono-
       chorismus von *Hydra fusca*," *Biol. Centralbl* , XXXI.

KRAPFENBAUER, A.
   1908 *Einwirkung der Existenzbedingungen auf die Fortpflanzung von*
       Hydra. Inaugural Dissertation. Munchen

KUTTNER, O
   1909 "Untersuchungen uber Fortpflanzungsverhaltnisse und Vererbung
       bei Cladoceren," *Internal Rev. d. ges Hydrobiol. u. Hydrogr.*, II.

LANGHANS, V. H
   1909 "Experimentelle Untersuchungen zu Fragen der Fortpflanzung,
       Variation und Vererbung bei Daphniden," *Verhandlungen d*
       deutsch. zool. Gesell

LOEW, O
   1905 "Zur Theorie der blutenbildenden Stoffe," *Flora*, XCIV

MAIGE, A
> 1906 "Sur la Respiration de la fleur," *Compt. rend Acad Sci* , CXLII.
> 1007. "Recherches sur la respiration de la fleur," *Rev gén de bot* , XIX

MAIGE, G.
> 1909. ' Recherches sur la respiration de l'étamine et du pistil," *Rev gén de bot* , XXI
> 1911. "Recherches sur la respiration des différentes pièces florales," *Ann des sci nat , Bot* , (9) XIV.

MAUPAS, E
> 1891. "Sur la Déterminisme de la sexualité chez l'*Hydatina senta*," *Compt rend Acad Sci* , CXIII

MOBIUS, M.
> 1897. *Beitrage zur Lehre von der Fortpflanzung der Gewachse* Jena

NACHTSHEIM, H
> 1913. "Cytologische Studien uber die Geschlechtsbestimmung bei der Honigbiene (*Apis mellifica* L)," *Arch f Zellforsch* , XI

NICOLAS, G
> 1909. "Recherches sur la respiration des organes vegetatifs des plantes vasculaires," *Ann des sci nat. Bot* , (9) X.

NUSSBAUM, M
> 1897. "Die Entstehung des Geschlechtes bei *Hydatina senta*," *Arch. f. mikr. Anat* , XLIX
> 1909 "Über Geschlechtsbildung bei Polypen," *Arch. f d ges Physiol.*, CXXX

PAPANICOLAU, G
> 1910a. "Uber die Bedingungen des sexuellen Differenzierung bei Daphniden," *Biol. Centralbl* , XXX
> 1910b. "Experimentelle Untersuchungen uber die Fortpflanzungsverhaltnisse der Daphniden," *Biol. Centralbl.*, XXX
> 1911. Anhang. *Biol Centralbl* , XXXI

PFEFFER, W
> 1897 *Pflanzenphysiologie*, Zweite Auflage, I, Band.

PROWAZEK, S.
> 1910 "Giftwirkung und Protozoenplasma," *Arch. f. Protistenkunde*, XVIII

PUNNETT, R. C
> 1906. "Sex-Determination in *Hydatina*, with Some Remarks on Parthenogenesis," *Proc. Roy. Soc B* , LXXVIII.

ROMEIS, B

1914 "Experimentelle Untersuchungen uber die Wirkung innersekretorischer Organe II, Der Einfluss von Thyreoidea- und Thymusfutterung auf das Wachstum, die Entwicklung und die Regeneration," *Arch. f Entwickelungsmech*, XL, XLI

SCHARFENBERG, U. VON.

1910 "Studien und Experimente uber die Eibildung und den Generationszyklus von *Daphnia magna*," *Internat Rev d. ges. Hydrobiol u. Hydrogr.* Biol. Supplement.

SHULL, A. F.

1910 "Studies in the Life Cycle of *Hydatina senta* I, Artificial Control of the Transition from the Parthenogenetic to the Sexual Method of Reproduction," *Jour of Exp. Zool*, VIII.

1911a "Studies, etc · II, The Rôle of Temperature, of the Chemical Composition of the Medium and of Internal Factors upon the Ratio of Parthenogenetic to Sexual Forms," *Jour of Exp. Zool*, X.

1911b. "The Effect of the Chemical Composition of the Medium on the Life Cycle of *Hydatina senta*." *Biochem Bull*, I.

1912. "Studies, etc III, Internal Factors Influencing the Proportion of Male Producers," *Jour of Exp. Zool.*, XII

STROHL, H.

1907. "Die Biologie von *Polyphemus pediculus* und die Generationszyklen der Cladoceren," *Zool. Anz.*, XXXII.

1908. "Polyphemusbiologie, Cladocereneier und Kernplasmarelation," *Internat Rev d ges Hydrobiol. u Hydrogr*, I

VOCHTING, H

1893. "Uber den Einfluss des Lichtes auf die Gestaltung und Anlage der Bluthen," *Jahrbucher f wiss Bot.*, XXV.

WEISMANN, A.

1880. "Beitrage zur Naturgeschichte der Daphnoiden, VII," *Zeitschr f. wiss Zool.*, XXXIII

WHITNEY, D. D.

1907. "Determination of Sex in *Hydatina senta*," *Jour. of Exp Zool.*, V.

1912a. "'Strains' in *Hydatina senta*," *Biol Bull*, XXII

1912b. "Weak Parthenogenetic Races of *Hydatina senta* Subjected to a Varied Environment," *Biol Bull*, XXIII

WINKLER H

1908. "Uber Parthenogenesis und Apogamie im Pflanzenreiche," *Progressus rei. bot*, II.

WOLTERECK, R.

1909. "Weitere experimentelle Untersuchungen uber Artveranderung · speciell uber das Wesen quantitativer Artunterschiede bei Daphniden," *Verhandlungen d deutsch zool Gesell*

WOLTERECK, R

    1911.   "Uber Veranderung der Sexualitat bei Daphniden," *Internat. Rev. d ges Hydrobiol u Hydrogr.*, IV

WOODRUFF, L. L

    1914.   "On So-called Conjugating and Non-conjugating Races of *Paramecium*," *Jour of Exp Zool* , XVI

WOODRUFF, L. L., and ERDMANN, RHODA.

    1914.   "A Normal Periodic Reorganization Process without Cell Fusion in *Paramecium*," *Jour. of Exp Zool* , XVII.

WORONIN, HELENE

    1908.   "Apogamie und Aposporie bei einigen Farnen," *Flora*, XCVIII

CHAPTER XV

REJUVENESCENCE IN EMBRYONIC AND LARVAL DEVELOPMENT

If the gametes are physiologically old cells, rejuvenescence must occur during embryonic development, for the organism when it begins its active independent life at the end of the embryonic period is certainly very much younger in every respect than the gametes before fertilization. It now remains to consider the evidence bearing upon this point. This evidence is chiefly zoological rather than botanical, for in most of the plants the early embryonic stages cannot readily be isolated for experimental purposes.

THE EFFECT OF FERTILIZATION

To attempt any consideration of the problem of fertilization itself would lead us too far afield; moreover, no well-established and generally accepted theory of fertilization has as yet emerged from the great mass of often conflicting experimental data and opinions It is the effect of fertilization rather than the process itself with which we are primarily concerned.

Whatever the nature of the process, it is a self-evident fact that the union of the two gametes is usually the starting-point of a new period of activity and change in the resulting cell It is true that in some cases among both plants and animals fertilization is followed after a short period of activity by a quiescent period, but we know that in certain of these cases the cessation of activity is due to incidental or external factors, such as the presence of an impermeable shell or envelope of some sort which cuts off the supply of oxygen or water, or otherwise interferes with dynamic activity until it is removed in one way or another, or gamete formation may occur at seasons of the year or under external conditions which retard or inhibit metabolic activity. In the delayed germination of plant seeds,[1] in the quiescent encysted periods of certain protozoa

---

[1] See, for example, Crocker, '06, '07, '09, and references to literature in these papers

after union of the gametes, and in the cessation of development of the "winter eggs" of flatworms, rotifers, crustacea, and insects, the presence of shells or envelopes of some sort is undoubtedly the chief factor in retarding or inhibiting the metabolic activity Even in those animal eggs which, like some seeds, must before they will hatch be subjected to certain external conditions, such as freezing temperature or desiccation, or in the case of *Branchipus*, the fairy shrimp, apparently to both, there is good reason to believe that the effect of these conditions in altering or disintegrating the egg envelope is much more important than any effect which they may have upon the protoplasm itself. These, however, are cases of the cessation of development rather than of its failure to begin

There are some cases where gametic union does not result in a period of increased activity and where internal rather than external factors seem to be responsible. Jennings ('13), for example, has found that in *Paramecium* the effects of conjugation are by no means uniform, for many of the ex-conjugants show decreased rather than increased activity and some die, while others do exhibit an increased rate of growth and division. It is probable that this lack of uniformity in the results of gametic union is connected with the fact that the body and the gamete are the same cell. Different individuals become specialized in different directions and the physiological effect of gametic union must vary widely, for in some cases the two protoplasms are incompatible in some way, or a summation of their physiological defects occurs, while in others the result is the opposite In the multicellular organisms, however, where the gametes develop as specialized parts of the body more or less remote from the influence of factors external to the organism, their course of development and consequently the effects of their union are much more definite and uniform, but even here the results of gametic union may vary to some extent, although increased dynamic activity following union is the usual result

There are in fact very few exceptions to the rule that gametic union is followed by increased dynamic activity, and it is probable that most, if not all, of these exceptions will prove to be apparent rather then real. We may say then with Loeb that fertilization in some way saves the life of the gametes. If the gametes are highly differentiated, physiologically old cells, approaching death, an increase in dynamic activity can scarcely mean anything else than the beginning of a period of rejuvenescence and dedifferentiation

The increase in the dynamic activity of the sea-urchin egg after fertilization has been determined in various ways by various investigators.[1] Lyon found that the susceptibility of the eggs to cyanide was greater after than before fertilization. Measurements of the oxygen consumption of the egg of the Neapolitan sea-urchin (*Strongylocentrotus lividus*) by Warburg showed that after fertilization the oxygen consumption was between six and seven times as great as before, and Loeb and Wasteneys found that in an American sea-urchin (*Arbacia punctulata*) the fertilized egg consumed three to four times as much oxygen as the unfertilized.[2] In a study of heat production in the sea-urchin egg Meyerhof finds the heat production per hour between four and five times as great in fertilized as in unfertilized eggs.

In the starfish egg, however, according to Loeb and Wasteneys ('12), the oxygen consumption is about the same before and after fertilization. This difference in behavior between starfish and sea-urchin eggs is undoubtedly connected, as Loeb ('11) suggested, with the fact that in the starfish the extrusion of the eggs from the ovaries into sea-water starts the maturation divisions, while in the sea-urchin maturation has occurred and the egg is quiescent when the sperm enters it. But the unfertilized starfish egg dies very soon unless, according to Loeb, its oxidation processes are inhibited by lack of oxygen or by cyanide.[3] As a matter of fact, the starfish egg is almost a parthenogenic egg, as Mathews ('01) has shown. By experimental means its development can readily be initiated without fertilization. But, left to itself, it is apparently not quite able to begin normal development; something goes wrong and death soon follows. The unfertilized sea-urchin egg, on the other hand, which remains almost quiescent after extrusion from the

[1] Loeb, '10, Loeb and Wasteneys, '10, '11, Lyon, '02, Meyerhof, '11, Warburg, '08, '10

[2] There are certain sources of error in the method used for determining oxygen consumption which make it possible that these values are too high, but that an increase occurs cannot be doubted

[3] Loeb, '11, Loeb and Wasteneys, '12

ovary and does not begin development until the sperm enters, may live for a week or more.   The death of the unfertilized starfish egg is not comparable to death from old age in organisms in general, but is the result of the peculiar physiological condition of the egg almost on the boundary line between parthenogenesis and zygogenesis   The conclusions concerning natural death which Loeb has drawn from the behavior of this egg are certainly not applicable to death from old age (see pp. 307–9).   A few other eggs show somewhat similar behavior, but in all of them a more or less similar physiological condition exists and their behavior cannot be made the basis for conclusions as to the nature of death in general.

In experiments of my own the susceptibility of various animal eggs to cyanide before and after fertilization has been tested, both by observing the occurrence of the death changes and by determining the limits of recovery in a given concentration.   The sea-urchin egg and the eggs of *Nereis*, *Chaetopterus*, and *Hydroides*, among the annelids, are all somewhat more susceptible to cyanide after fertilization than before, although the difference is not very great.   In the starfish egg, however, the susceptibility increases markedly in unfertilized eggs when maturation begins, and there is little or no further change on fertilization.   Since increased susceptibility means increase in rate of metabolism, these results agree in general with those obtained by other methods, although the increase in susceptibility to cyanide is not as great as might be expected if the rate of oxidation increases from three to six times with fertilization The results with the starfish egg indicate, as Loeb suggested, that here the chief increase in rate of oxidation occurs with maturation.

PARTHENOGENESIS

The naturally parthenogenic egg is evidently a cell which possesses the capacity to react to its physiological or physical isolation from the parent body or from the former source of nutrition or to the change of conditions associated with its extrusion from the body by the initiation of a normal development.   Although oxygen consumption and susceptibility of parthenogenic eggs before and after isolation have not been determined, the observations on the starfish egg which is on the verge of parthenogenesis and the very evident increase in activity in parthenogenic eggs during and after maturation leave no room for doubt that the physiological changes which occur in zygogenic eggs after the entrance of the sperm occur in parthenogenic eggs independently of the sperm   Moreover, among animals most parthenogenic eggs undergo only one maturation division before beginning development.   It was also pointed out in chap. xiii that in many cases parthenogenic eggs are apparently less highly differentiated morphologically, and younger physiologically, than zygogenic eggs of the same species.

The obvious conclusion in the light of the various facts is that eggs which are capable of parthenogenic development in nature are less highly specialized as gametic cells than those which require fertilization.   They react to isolation by undergoing dedifferentiation and reconstitution into new individuals, and in this respect they resemble the pieces from the bodies of many lower animals, such as *Planaria*, which undergo reconstitution when isolated. The capacity of parts of the body for reacting to physiological or physical isolation by dedifferentiation varies inversely as the degree of physiological stability of the structural substratum (see pp 39–42).   But physiological stability of the substratum apparently increases during individual development and also during the course of evolution, and often varies to a considerable extent in related species   Since the development of the primitive egg cell into an egg is apparently subject to the same laws as the development of other parts of the body, the parthenogenic egg must represent an earlier stage of development than the zygogenic egg of the same species   But it does not by any means follow that the eggs of all species would develop parthenogenically if they were isolated at a sufficiently early stage   Since the bodies of different species and the different tissues of the same individual possess very different degrees of reconstitutional capacity, we must expect to find differences of the same sort in eggs   Moreover, since the formation of gametes is characteristic of relatively late stages in the individual life history, we should expect a rather high degree of physiological stability in the eggs of most species and parthenogenesis in comparatively few.   As a matter of fact, parthenogenesis occurs only here and there among organisms, but it is of interest to note that it is relatively frequent in the lower plant s, the algae and fungi. To what extent it may occur among the lower animals is not fully known, though apparently it appears c hiefly as a characteristic of certain groups without relation to their s ystematic position. Finally, we cannot expect to find parthenogenesis ne cessarily associated with a high degree of reconstitutional capa city in other parts of the body, for the physiological condition of the primitive germ cells from which eggs are formed, the rate of gr owth of the egg, the character and amount of its nutrition, and dou btless many other factors, must be concerned in determining whether it shall be parthenogenic or zygogenic.

From this point of view the parthenogenic egg is a cell which has undergone more or less development as a gamete but still retains the capacity to initiate dedifferentiation and reconstitution independently of union with a male gamete In t his respect it resembles the less highly specialized cells of other tiss ues rather than the gametes.

Much evidence has accumulated to show that in the higher seed plants reproduction of a new sporophyte generation very often occurs in various other ways than by the fertilization of a zygogenic egg. In some cases the reproductive cell is not the egg cell, but a vegetative cell of the gametophyte and the reproductive process is known as apogamy; in other cases the maturation divisions characteristic of spore formation do not occur, i e , there is apospory, but a gametophyte containing a parthenogenic egg is formed, in still other cases the reproductive cell is not even a part of the gametophyte, but a cell of the nucellus which corresponds to the sporangium There can be little doubt that in such cases the reproductive cell does not attain the specialized condition and advanced age characteristic of the zygogenic egg. The final stages of progressive development are omitted in one generation or the other.

THE EXPERIMENTAL INITIATION OF DEVELOPMENT

Through the extensive investigations of Loeb, Delage, Bataillon, and many others during the last twenty years it has been demonstrated that the eggs of various species of animals which in nature require fertilization for their development can be induced experimentally to develop without fertilization   General agreement has not yet been reached as to the nature of the changes concerned in the initiation of development, but there can be no doubt that the increased metabolic activity which in nature follows fertilization may be brought about by the action of certain experimental conditions   A great variety of agents and conditions have been employed in these experiments. Harvey ('10) has tabulated the different methods. A few of these methods bring about in certain species a normal, orderly development like that which occurs after fertilization   With many of the so-called parthenogenic agents, however, and in some species with all, the changes which are initiated differ more or less widely from normal development.   In some cases development may proceed more or less normally through the earlier stages, but ends in death at or before a certain stage; in others the forms produced are clearly abnormal from the beginning, in still others only a few divisions, or only changes in the membrane, occur before death   In certain cases also some degree of differentiation without any cell division results from the use of these agents.

All of these experimental effects have very commonly been regarded as initiation of development, but if the term "development" means anything, it means an orderly series of events leading to a certain definite result.   The course of events and the result attained are subject to more or less variation, and it is not always possible to make a sharp distinction between what is and what is not development.   Nevertheless, it is evident that many of these experimental treatments of the egg do not initiate development, but a change which lacks some of the essential features of development and soon leads to death.   To maintain that any experimental agent or condition which brings about some degree or kind of cellular activity in the egg initiates development is to lose sight entirely of the fundamental characteristics of development; and to use such experimental data indiscriminately as a basis for conclusions concerning the nature of fertilization is certainly not a justifiable procedure   It cannot be doubted, however, that development in the strictest sense is initiated experimentally in certain

cases and by certain methods, and no criticism can detract from
the importance and interest of this fact

The questions which have been most widely discussed in connection with this field of investigation, viz , the nature of the
changes produced in the egg and the manner in which the experimental conditions act to produce them, are outside the range of
the present discussion.   The point to which I desire particularly
to call attention is the difference in the reaction of the eggs of
different animals to the experimental conditions.   Some eggs react
readily to a variety of experimental conditions and give 100 per
cent, or nearly, of normal embryos or larvae, while others, even in
the most favorable cases, give only a small percentage of normal
forms, or react only to certain experimental conditions, and still
others are refractory to all methods and have never been known
to develop except when fertilized   In the egg of the starfish, for
example, which is on the verge of natural parthenogenesis, development can apparently be initiated by almost any slight stimulus,
while the egg of the sea-urchin is somewhat less susceptible to the
various agents and conditions employed to initiate development,
and many other eggs are only slightly or not at all susceptible
Our knowledge along this line is as yet somewhat fragmentary, for,
although changes of some kind and degree have been experimentally
induced in the eggs of many different species of invertebrates and a
few vertebrates, no systematic comparative study along these lines
has yet been attempted.   But that great differences in the capacity
to begin development without fertilization exist in different eggs
is a demonstrated fact, and the probability that these differences
are associated with the different degrees of specialization and differentiation of eggs at once suggests itself.   If the eggs of different
species represent various degrees of specialization, all gradations
from natural parthenogenesis through the various degrees of susceptibility to experimental parthenogenic agents to the strictly
zygogenic condition, in which the egg reacts only to the entrance
of the sperm, must be expected to occur.   Apparently some eggs
can be aroused from their quiescent condition and started along the
course of development in a great variety of ways, some of which may
differ widely from the process of fertilization, while others can be

aroused only by experimental conditions which approximate more closely the conditions of fertilization, and still others only by fertilization itself, or conditions essentially identical with it   Moreover, it is by no means certain that the conditions concerned in fertilization are exactly the same in all cases.   The morphological differences in the gametes of different species show clearly enough that the course of gametic development is not always the same, and the assumption that the action of the sperm is always the same seems to be unjustified.   The result is, of course, essentially similar in all cases, i e , increased metabolic activity, transformation of nutritive substances, and cell division, but different factors or combinations of factors may be concerned in producing it in different cases.   The differences in the reaction of different eggs to the experimental parthenogenic agents suggest that various degrees of specialization exist in the process of fertilization itself   The conception of the gametes as highly specialized, physiologically old cells places the whole problem of the initiation of development by either experimental or natural means in a new light

OXYGEN CONSUMPTION AND HEAT PRODUCTION DURING EARLY STAGES OF DEVELOPMENT

The first stage of development is a period of repeated cell division, the cleavage period, during which the proportion of active cytoplasm and nuclear substance increases at the expense of substances which were accumulated in the egg during its growth and have been previously inactive; or in some organisms, where the egg itself contains but little nutritive material, it becomes dependent at an early stage on nutriment from without.

Authorities are generally agreed that during at least some part of this period an acceleration in the rate of metabolism occurs.[1] According to Warburg and Loeb and Wasteneys the oxygen consumption of sea-urchin eggs increases during the course of cleavage. In the egg of the mollusk *Aplysia limacina* Buglia found that the oxygen consumption decreased slightly while carbon-dioxide production remained uniform during the earliest stages of cleavage, but in later embryonic stages both underwent a marked increase

[1] Buglia, '08, Loeb and Wasteneys, '11, Meyerhof, '11, Warburg, '08, '10.

and finally became nearly uniform again in early larval stages
Meyerhof has shown that the heat production of the sea-urchin
egg increases steadily up to the larval stage; at the sixty-four-cell
stage it is about twice as great as during the first hour after fertil-
zation, when the larva begins to swim it is three times as great,
and at a stage four hours later, four times as great.   Heat production in the *Aplysia* embryo decreases during the first few cleavages,
then increases rapidly to the larval stage, when it becomes nearly
uniform, i e , the changes in heat production in *Aplysia* are essentially parallel to the changes in oxygen consumption and carbon-
dioxide production as determined by Buglia.

All of these data indicate that at least the oxidation processes
increase in rate during the earlier stages of development, and the
general behavior of the developing embryo, the increase in the
amount of metabolically active cytoplasm and nuclear substance,
and the decrease in amount of yolk where yolk is present suggest
that not merely oxidation but metabolic activity in general
undergoes a marked increase during this period.   In short, this is a
period of physiological rejuvenescence.

CHANGES IN SUSCEPTIBILITY DURING EARLY STAGES

Lyon ('02) found that the susceptibility to cyanide of the sea-
urchin egg underwent a gradual increase during the course of
cleavage, and I have determined the susceptibility to cyanide during early development in a number of animal species.   In these
experiments the susceptibility was measured in most cases by the
limits of recovery, that is, the length of time in the cyanide solution at which recovery ceased to occur on return to water.   It was
also possible in most cases to determine the survival time by
observing the death changes in the cyanide   A part of the results
of these experiments appear in the following tables   For the sake
of simplicity only the average survival times are given, viz., the
average length of time in cyanide necessary to prevent any visible
degree of recovery after return to sea-water.   These tables serve
merely to give a general idea of the changes in susceptibility and
do not show the differences or the different rates of change in the
susceptibility of different regions of the embryos

In both starfish and sea-urchin the susceptibility increases very greatly, and more in the starfish than in the sea-urchin, up to the early gastrula stage and then begins to decrease slightly as the larval structure begins to develop   At this stage the cells have lost the differentiation of the egg, the chemically active protoplasm has undergone great increase at the expense of the inactive substance and has attained the maximum, and from this stage on the developing organism begins to grow old

TABLE VIII

STARFISH (*Asterias forbesii*)
KCN o or mol

Stage of Development	Average Survival Time in Hours and Minutes
Unfertilized egg undergoing maturation	11 30
30 minutes after fertilization . .	11 30
2–8 cells	10 30
64–128 cells . . .	5 30
Blastulae before movement	1 15
Early gastrulae	1 35
Advanced gastrulae . .	1 20
Young bipinnaria larva . .	3 00

TABLE IX

SEA-URCHIN (*Arbacia punctulata*)
KCN o 005 mol.

Stage of Development	Average Survival Time in Hours and Minutes
Unfertilized egg	8 15
20 minutes after fertilization	6 45
4–8 cells	5 45
Late cleavage .	3 30
Early gastrulae . .	2 15
Advanced gastrulae	3 00
Prepluteus	3 30

In this connection it is of great interest to note that in the starfish and sea-urchin and various other species the late blastula and early gastrula stages appear to be critical stages in development under many experimental conditions, e g , in experimental parthenogenesis, in many hybrids and under the action of various external agents. Development may proceed with little or no disturbance up to these stages and then stops or becomes abnormal. If these stages are passed successfully, further development is likely to follow its usual course. It is easy to see why, if anything is wrong, it should become evident during these stages, for they represent the period when the intrinsic metabolic activity of the cells is greater than at any other period of the life history, and the physical condition of the protoplasm which is of course correlated with the high rate of metabolism must likewise be most susceptible to change at this time. Internal or external factors, which produce little or no effect when the metabolic and protoplasmic susceptibility is lower, may at this time bring about changes which either lead to death or profoundly modify the further course of development.

The different behavior of the two eggs in relation to fertilization which was mentioned in an earlier section (pp 405–6) appears in the tables The starfish egg shows scarcely any increase in susceptibility just after fertilization, while in the sea-urchin egg the increase is marked.

TABLE X

Nereis limbata

KCN 0 005 mol.

Stage of Development	Average Survival Time in Hours and Minutes
2–4 cells	13 45
Early gastrulae . . .	11 30
Early larvae hatching . .	. . 7 30
Larvae 8 hours after hatching . . .	. 3 30
Larvae with two pairs of setae	45
Full-grown larvae . .	. . . . . 1 40
Advanced larvae . .	. 2 30

In *Nereis*, an annelid worm, the susceptibility increases up to the larval period and during this period begins to decrease. Undoubtedly the great increase in susceptibility in the early larval stages is due in part to the appearance and increase of motor activity and functional stimulation. The larva is a highly organized animal with sense-organs and muscles, and its rate of metabolism is higher than that determined by conditions existing within its cells because it reacts to external stimuli But even during the larval period very considerable changes in susceptibility occur which must belong to the age cycle. In the earlier larval stages the animal is still growing young, while in the later stages it is growing old.

Between *Nereis* and another annelid, *Arenicola cristata*, an interesting difference exists. During the period of rejuvenescence the *Nereis* embryo obtains its nutritive material from the yolk in the egg, but this material is used up before the end of the larval period, and metamorphosis from the larval to the adult form does not occur unless the larva can obtain food from without The egg of *Arenicola*, however, contains sufficient yolk to carry development completely through the larval period and metamorphosis to the stage of a worm with five or six segments, after which food from without is necessary In both these forms the embryonic period of increase in susceptibility, i e , of rejuvenescence, ends at about the stage when the last of the yolk is used up: the *Nereis* embryo continues to grow younger only up to the larval stage, while rejuvenescence in *Arenicola* continues through the larval stage, the metamorphosis, and up to the six-segment stage of the worm. During this period yolk is being transformed into chemically active nuclear substance and cytoplasm, and the proportion of chemically active to inactive substance increases to a certain point where the accumulation of new structural substance, together with any part of the old that may remain, balances the synthesis of active protoplasm.

Susceptibility determinations have been made for only two other species of annelids, *Chaetopterus pergamentaceus* and *Hydroides dianthus*, and in both rejuvenescence takes place during the embryonic period, as in *Nereis*, but the stage at which rejuvenescence gives place to senescence was not determined in these forms.

Among the vertebrates the eggs of two species of fish have been used for susceptibility determinations In contrast to the holoblastic egg of the starfish, sea-urchin, and annelid in which the yolk is in all or some of the cells and the whole egg divides, the fish eggs are meroblastic, most of the yolk being separated from the active protoplasmic part of the egg, and only the latter divides In such eggs the embryo begins at a rather early stage to feed on the yolk outside its own cells, and its relation to the nutritive supply becomes similar to that of the animal developing from a holoblastic

egg which has used up all its yolk   It is a point of some interest
to determine at what stage the embryonic period of rejuvenescence
ends in such cases.   The survival times for these two forms are
given in Tables XI and XII.

TABLE XI

Fundulus heteroclitus

Saturated Phenyl Urethane in Sea-Water

Stage of Development	Length of Time after Fertilization in Hours and Minutes	Average Survival Time in Hours and Minutes
2 cells .	3 30	11 45
Advanced periblast	24	4 30
Embryo just appearing	45	5 30
Embryo with 3–4 somites	69	6 00
Embryo with heart beating	117	7 30
At time of hatching..	408	2 00

TABLE XII

Tautogolabrus adspersus

KCN o 005 mol

Stage of Development	Length of Time after Fertilization in Hours and Minutes	Average Survival Time in Hours and Minutes
15 minutes after fertilization	0 15	10 45
1–2 cells	0 50	10 10
4–8 cells .	2	7 30
Many cells ..	5	6 35
Periblast .. .	7	5 45
Embryo just appearing. ..	20	0 45
Heart beating .	42	0 15
Newly hatched .	55–60	0 20

Phenyl urethane was used instead of cyanide in determining the
susceptibility of the *Fundulus* egg, because the membrane of this
egg is impermeable to cyanide, as it is to many other substances, so
that even in high concentrations development is not retarded, while
for phenyl urethane the permeability is practically complete.

Rejuvenescence occurs in *Fundulus* during the early stages of
development, as indicated by the increase in susceptibility, but
as soon as the embryo begins to form, it gives place to senescence.
The great increase in susceptibility between establishment of the

heart-beat and hatching is probably due in part to increased functional activity and stimulation, but it may be largely the consequence of the increasing lipoid content of the nervous system in connection with medullation of the nerves, a change which would increase the relative concentration of phenyl urethane in the nervous system and so might intensify its action (see pp. 75-76). In the vertebrates particularly these changes in the nervous system make the use of the susceptibility method with highly fat-soluble substances difficult in the later stages of development. If this second increase in susceptibility is due to the increase of fatty substances in the nervous system, it of course does not mean that a second period of rejuvenescence occurs, but rather that the susceptibility to phenyl urethane is not a measure of the metabolic condition at this stage. In all probability senescence and decrease in metabolic rate continue from the stage where the susceptibility first begins to decrease.

In *Tautogolabrus* the period of increasing susceptibility continues up to the time of hatching, and almost all of the increase occurs before movement or special function of organs begins. At the periblast stage, where *Fundulus* shows the highest susceptibility, *Tautogolabrus* has undergone only half of its increase and the total increase of susceptibility in the latter is about twice that in the former. These differences between the two forms are undoubtedly associated with differences in the course of development. The second column of Tables XI and XII shows that *Tautogolabrus* develops three or four times as rapidly as *Fundulus*, and its development up to the time of hatching occurs very largely at the expense of nutritive material in the protoplasmic part of the egg, but little of the separate yolk mass being used during this stage, while in *Fundulus* most of the yolk is used before hatching It is also evident that the protoplasms of the two species differ widely in capacity for growth, for the egg of *Fundulus* is very much larger and the adult usually much smaller than that of *Tautogolabrus*. Apparently the differences between the two eggs determine that the degree of rejuvenescence is much greater and that the period of rejuvenescence extends to a much later stage of development in *Tautogolabrus* than in *Fundulus*.

In the frog and salamander, the only other vertebrates for which embryonic susceptibilities have been determined, the changes are very similar to those described for other forms. From the time of fertilization on, through cleavage, gastrulation, and the formation of the embryo, and somewhat beyond the stage of hatching, the average susceptibility increases   As in the fishes, the results in the later stages are perhaps complicated by the increased metabolic activity connected with the functional activity of special organs and with movement, or by changes in the nervous system, but as regards the earlier stages this is certainly not the case.

All of these data, as well as those on oxygen consumption, are in full agreement with the observed facts of development   It is well known that as cleavage goes on the rate of cell division is accelerated and other developmental changes proceed more and more rapidly up to a certain stage.   In general the rejuvenescence of certain parts of the embryo, and particularly of the apical region. where the metabolic rate is originally highest, proceeds more rapidly than that of other parts and is completed earlier

THE MORPHOLOGICAL CHANGES DURING EARLY DEVELOPMENT

The morphological changes during the period of increasing susceptibility consist in an increase of nuclear as compared with cytoplasmic substance and in the decrease and disappearance of the yolk in the cytoplasm and the increase of the amorphous, undifferentiated, or embryonic cytoplasm; often also, particularly in the later stages, the new morphological features connected with the new process of differentiation begin to appear.   The increase, both absolute and relative, in total nuclear volume is a characteristic feature of embryonic development in animals and is evident from observation. It has often been stated that the nuclear volume or nuclear substance increases in geometrical progression during this period, but measurements. so far as they have been made, indicate that this is by no means always the case.   Godlewski ('08) has found that in the sea-urchin from the four-cell to the sixty-four-cell stage the nuclear volume does increase almost in geometrical progression, while from the sixty-four-cell stage on there is but little further increase.   During the period of nuclear

increase there is no increase, but rather a decrease, in total cytoplasmic volume, for the nuclear substance is formed at the expense
of the cytoplasm or of substances contained in it, consequently
the relative increase in nuclear substance is somewhat greater than
the absolute. According to Erdmann ('08), the nucleoplasmic
relation, that is, the volume of the nucleus in relation to the volume
of the cytoplasm, undergoes very great increase from the four-cell
stage to the gastrula in the sea-urchin, and the volume of the
chromosomes, in relation both to cell volume and to nuclear volume,
also increases during this period.   Conklin ('12), in a study of the
mollusk *Crepidula*, also finds an increase in total nuclear volume
during cleavage, though by no means so great as that found in the
sea-urchin.

   The change in the nucleoplasmic relation during this period is
evidently in the reverse direction from that which it underwent
during the growth period of the gametes. Undoubtedly the
increase in relative nuclear volume during early development is, as
Conklin points out, an important factor in the acceleration of metabolic activity, but it is not the only nor even the primary factor,
for the acceleration may begin before the nuclear increase, and
under other conditions acceleration of metabolism may occur without such increase   The increase in nuclear volume is an indication
rather than a cause of the metabolic changes which the embryo is
undergoing during this period.   Moreover, as regards the spermatozoon, entrance into the egg constitutes a sudden and enormous
increase in cytoplasmic volume, yet the spermatozoon undergoes
regressive changes as well as the egg.   The general significance of
the nucleoplasmic relation for the problem of age is considered in
chap. xvi (see also pp. 284-86).

   In most animal eggs the cytoplasm contains more or less fatty
substance—the yolk—in the form of granules, droplets, or large
masses, and in such eggs the most conspicuous cytoplasmic change
during the early stages of development is the gradual disappearance
of this yolk.   But even in eggs which contain no visible yolk the
cytoplasm becomes more homogeneous in appearance, and cytoplasmic strands, granules of various sorts, and other structural
features of the egg disappear wholly or in part.   At the same time

that these regressive processes are going on, progressive changes
are occurring and new structural features are beginning to appear
In some embryos these do not become visible or conspicuous until
the regressive changes are far advanced, while in others, such, for
example, as certain annelids and mollusks, in which larval forms
differentiate very early in development, they may begin to appear
during the first few divisions following fertilization, or some of the
structural features of the egg may be carried over into the larva.
In short, both the degree and rate of morphological regression, as
well as the degree and rate of rejuvenescence during early stages,
vary greatly in different forms

LARVAL STAGES AND METAMORPHOSIS

In many animals the form hatching from the egg is widely
different, both in structure and in behavior, from the adult, and is
known as a larva: sooner or later this form undergoes either a
gradual or a somewhat abrupt transformation or metamorphosis
into the adult form   The question as to the nature of larval
metamorphosis and the internal and external conditions which
determine it has been much discussed, and various hypotheses
have been advanced.   Here, however, the purpose is only to present
a few suggestions rather than to attempt extended discussion.

In the first place the term "larva" is a loose biological term with
little physiological significance.   The larva is merely a form different from the adult and appearing before it in the life history.   But
the larva of an annelid which develops during the first few cell
divisions after fertilization is very different from the larva of an
insect or a frog which appears only after thousands of divisions and
extensive differentiation.   The larval form may represent an
earlier or a later stage in the developmental history

In many invertebrates, e g., in the annelid *Nereis*, the larval
form develops during the period of rejuvenescence.   So far as I
have been able to determine, the eggs or embryos of all species
in which the larval form arises very early possess a strongly marked
axial gradient and individuation progresses rapidly, while in those
where the larval period occurs at a later stage the gradient is much
less clearly marked in early stages and develops only gradually.

The larval form of the annelids, mollusks, crustacea, and some other invertebrate groups represents chiefly the head and anterior regions of the body, and metamorphosis consists, not only in changes in the parts already formed, but in the addition of new segments from a growing region just in front of the posterior end. The fully developed larva of the annelid *Nereis*, for example, consists of the head and the first three segments, as indicated in Fig. 197, and during the transformation of this free-swimming form into the worm new segments are added successively at the posterior end. In this and

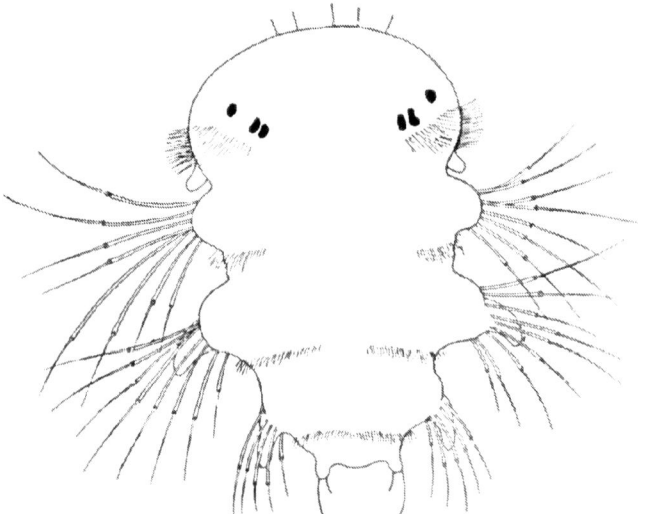

FIG. 197.—Trochophore larva of *Nereis*. After E. B. Wilson, '02

in other related species the axial gradient, which is so clearly marked during prelarval stages, becomes less and less distinct in the larva, until, as metamorphosis approaches, the growing region at the posterior end shows the highest metabolic rate of any part of the body. These changes enable us to gain some insight into the process of formation of new segments. The head-region undergoes rejuvenescence and begins senescence before other parts, so that in the larval stage its metabolic rate begins to decrease before that of the more posterior regions. But even before its metabolic rate begins to decrease, the rate in more posterior regions is increasing more rapidly than in the head, and the result is a partial physiological isolation of the posterior region and the formation of a new segment   Similarly, physiological isolation of the posterior region from the first segment results in the formation of the second, and isolation from the second in the formation of the third.   But by this time the rate of metabolism in the head-region is decreasing, and a little later it begins to decrease in the first, then in the second and the third segments.   Sooner or later this process leads to partial physiological isolation of the posterior end and, if food is present to provide energy and substance for growth, another segment is added posteriorly, and so on.

In the crustacea the process is essentially similar.   In the lower crustacea the earliest larval stage represents, as in *Nereis*, the head, and three segments with their appendages, and new segments are added successively at the posterior end.   Fig. 198 shows a stage in the metamorphosis of the fairy shrimp *Branchipus*.   The original larval form in this case consisted of the head and the first three segments to which the three pairs of large appendages are attached in the figure, and to this new segments are successively added at the posterior end.   The figure shows a stage in which a large number of segments have already formed, but are not yet fully developed.   .

In the insects and vertebrates the formation of the segments occurs before hatching, but is in all probability a similar process. The changes called metamorphosis in the insects belong to a much later stage of development   Here the larval form, which has fed and grown for a time and has acquired a large nutritive reserve, undergoes transformation into the mature form, the imago, during the pupal stage which usually shows little or no movement and does not feed.   In this case the changes seem to be the result of aging of certain of the larval organs in consequence of which growth and development of certain parts previously inhibited now becomes possible.   In some insects many of the larval organs actually die and undergo complete resorption or degeneration.   In some other invertebrates parts of the larva die and are cast off bodily when metamorphosis begins

Apparently in all these cases metamorphosis is a parti logical disintegration of the individual resulting from the axial gradient during the earlier stages of developmen the aging and death of certain larval organs. Where

FIG. 198.—Larval metamorphosis of *Branchipus* (fairy shrim

period occurs at a very early stage of development a we axial gradient and a relatively high degree of individu present at the beginning, or at a very early stage, of development.

Metamorphosis in the amphibia is evidently a process associated with progressive development and physiological senescence, and it may be hastened or delayed by external factors which accelerate or retard development, but the physiological factors immediately concerned in bringing about the changes which occur are still obscure   Metamorphosis unquestionably results in a higher degree of physiological integration, particularly in the higher amphibia, the frogs and toads, in fact, it is in a sense a new integration within the previously existing individual.   In the substitution of physiologically younger for older organs and parts, which apparently occurs in amphibian metamorphosis, differences in metabolic rate may play a part, but our knowledge is at present too incomplete to permit definite conclusions.

EMBRYONIC DEVELOPMENT IN PLANTS

In most plants embryonic development takes place within special organs of the parent plant, and the embryonic stages are not accessible to physiological investigation as are those of many animals   Moreover, the plant ovum does not in most cases accumulate a large supply of nutritive substance within its own body, but is nourished by other cells   Only in certain algae and fungi, where embryonic development occurs apart from the parent body, is there any considerable accumulation of nutritive material in the egg itself.

So far as I am aware, no determinations of oxygen consumption, carbon-dioxide production, or susceptibility have been made upon the embryonic stages of plants, but observation indicates clearly enough that the metabolic changes during these stages are not fundamentally different from those in animals.   Fertilization in the plant, as in the animal, initiates an increased activity in the previously quiescent ovum, repeated division occurs with an absolute and relative increase of nuclear substance, and, where nutritive substances are present in the egg, they gradually disappear.   As in the animal, the cells resulting from the successive divisions become more or less completely "embryonic" or undifferentiated in appearance, and from such cells the new plant individual arises. There is, in short, every visible indication of a process of regression and rejuvenescence in the early stages of plant development. The youngest stage physiologically is probably earlier in some and later in other plants, as in different animals, but, as pointed out in chap. x, certain parts in most plants remain physiologically young for a long time, or indefinitely, and well-marked differentiation and senescence are confined to other parts.

THE DEGREE OF REJUVENESCENCE IN GAMETIC AND AGAMIC REPRODUCTION

In gametic reproduction the organism begins its life history as a single cell resulting from the union of two highly specialized, old cells, and the earlier part of this history is a period of dedifferentiation, cell division, and rejuvenescence. In many cases of agamic reproduction also the life history begins with a single cell, but in many others the reproductive body is a cell mass often containing various differentiated organs. Evidently in those cases where a single specialized cell is the starting-point, the degree of reconstitutional change involved in the formation of a new individual is in general greater than where the individual arises from a large mass of cells, for in the latter case some of the cells or organs are incorporated as parts of the new individual with but little change. It has been shown in chap. v, for example, that in *Planaria* the degree of reconstitution and rejuvenescence varies inversely as the size of the isolated piece: in the large piece, while certain cells may become embryonic, these rapidly differentiate and grow old and the total rejuvenescence is slight, while in the smaller piece the cells undergo more change and the total rejuvenescence is greater in amount. In the single cell which gives rise to a new individual the changes are still greater, and the degree of rejuvenescence of the whole must also be greater, because the reconstitutional changes are very extensive and involve the cell as a whole. Moreover, if it is true that the gametes are more highly specialized than single cells which reproduce agamically, we must conclude that the degree of rejuvenescence is in general greater in gametic than in any form of agamic reproduction, that is, in multicellular organisms.

If, however, the same degree of rejuvenescence occurs in successive agamic generations, even though it is much less than that occurring in gametic reproduction, the agamic process may be repeated indefinitely without race senescence. The failure of agamic reproduction after a larger or smaller number of agamic generations is not due to the fact that there is less rejuvenescence connected with it than with the gametic reproduction, but rather to the fact that under the existing conditions senescence in each agamic generation is not entirely compensated by rejuvenescence in each reproduction, and race senescence results   In such cases of course a substitution of gametic for agamic reproduction will rejuvenate the race and make possible a new series of agamic generations.   This course has from time to time been followed with the potato, when a particular race has seemed to show signs of decrease in vitality or commercial value, and often with good results. There is, however, every reason to believe that a change of the right kind in conditions of cultivation would accomplish the same result without breeding from the seeds instead of the tubers. Doubtless the gametic process affords a less difficult and more rapid method of accomplishing the desired result, but it is probably not the only method.

In many organisms, under the ordinary conditions of nature. senescence is evidently not completely compensated by the rejuvenescence occurring in agamic reproduction, and progressive senescence of the race or colony occurs.   This is apparently the case among both plants and animals, but, as already pointed out, experimental investigation has shown for many of these cases that under the proper conditions progressive senescence does not occur, and these results make it probable that we shall find this true for many other cases.   It may be, however, that in some forms senescence progresses in spite of agamic reproduction and independently of external conditions. and if so the agamic period must in any case sooner or later come to an end in such forms   Perhaps some of the higher animals, where agamic reproduction occurs only as polyembryony or in the early stages of postembryonic life, constitute cases of this sort

The point of chief importance is, however, that the difference between agamic and gametic reproduction is, as regards the relation between senescence and rejuvenescence, one of degree rather

than of kind, and that there is much more difference in this respect
between different forms of agamic reproduction than between
agamic reproduction from single cells and small cell masses and
gametic reproduction. From the physiological point of view the
reproductive process is fundamentally the same wherever it occurs
in nature: it is in all cases the reconstitution of a new organism from
a part of one previously existing, but the starting-point of the new
individual and consequently the degree of reconstitution and the
result differ in different forms and with different conditions.

CONCLUSION

It is only necessary to point out the close agreement between
all the different lines of evidence in indicating that the early stages
of development from the egg in both animals and plants constitute
a period of rejuvenescence in every sense. Minot ('08) has already
advanced this view on the basis of the changes in the nucleoplasmic
relation, but has failed to present any of the physiological evidence
in support of it   The nucleoplasmic relation is a rather unsafe
criterion of physiological age, but it is interesting to see that in the
present case it leads to the same conclusion as the physiological
evidence.

From this point of view gametic reproduction differs from
agamic only in the greater degree of specialization of the reproductive cells and the special conditions necessary to initiate the process of dedifferentiation and rejuvenescence   The same periodic
changes, the same life cycle and age cycle, occur in both. We
can dispense entirely with that remarkable conception, the germ
plasm of the Weismannian theory, and say that germ plasm is
any protoplasm capable under the proper conditions of undergoing
dedifferentiation and reconstitution into a new individual of the
species. Reproduction, whether it is the process of reconstitution
in a piece experimentally isolated from an animal or plant body,
or the process of development from the fertilized egg, is fundamentally the same physiological process and involves both regressive
and progressive changes, both rejuvenescence and senescence

A recent attempt by Godlewski ('10) to compare the process of
regeneration with gametic reproduction requires mention here

Godlewski found that in the earlier stages of regeneration the epithelial cells of amphibia show an increase in cytoplasmic in relation to nuclear volume as compared with the cells of differentiated normal epithelium, and that the nucleoplasmic relation gradually approaches the norm as regeneration proceeds   From these facts he concludes that the earlier stages in regeneration correspond to the period of oogenesis, and particularly that stage of it in which the egg cytoplasm increases in amount, while the later stages of regeneration correspond to the period of embryonic development in which nuclear substance undergoes relative increase These conclusions only serve, I think, to show how unsafe the nucleoplasmic relation is as a criterion of physiological condition. It is probable that the first effect of stimulation and increase in metabolic rate in these cells is some degree of hypertrophy (pp. 43–44) with increase in the relative volume of cytoplasm, but this is soon followed by divisions with increase in relative nuclear volume   This is the period of dedifferentiation and rejuvenescence and corresponds not to the growth period of the egg, but to the period of rejuvenescence in embryonic development, while the later stages of regeneration correspond to the period of morphogenesis and senescence in the later stages of development.

REFERENCES

BUGLIA, G
    1908.　"Sullo scambio gassoso delle uove di '*Aplysia limacina*' nei vari periodi dello sviluppo," *Arch di fisiol.*, V.

CONKLIN, E G
    1912.　"Cell Size and Nuclear Size," *Jour. of Exp Zool* , XII

CROCKER, W.
    1906.　"Rôle of Seed Coats in Delayed Germination," *Bot Gazette*, XLII
    1907.　"Germination of Seeds of Water Plants," *Bot. Gazette*, XLIV
    1909.　"Longevity of Seeds," *Bot. Gazette*, XLVII.

ERDMANN, RHODA.
    1908.　"Experimentelle Untersuchung der Massenverhaltnisse von Plasma, Kern und Chromosomen in dem sich entwickelnden Seeigelei," *Arch. f Zellforsch* , II

GODLEWSKI, E , Jr.
    1908.　"Plasma und Kernsubstanz in der normalen und der durch aussere Faktoren veranderten Entwicklung der Echiniden," *Arch f. Entwickelungsmech.*, XXVI.

Godlewski, E , Jr.
   1910. "Plasma und Kernsubstanz im Epithelgewebe bei der Regeneration
          der Amphibien," *Arch. f Entwickelungsmech* , XXX

Harvey, E. N
   1910. "Methods of Artificial Parthenogenesis," *Biol Bull* , XVIII.

Jennings, H. S
   1913. "The Effect of Conjugation in *Paramecium*," *Jour of Exp Zool.*,
          XIV.

Loeb, J
   1910. "Die Hemmung verschiedener Giftwirkungen auf das befruchtete
          Seeigelei durch Hemmung der Oxydationen in demselben,"
          Biochem Zeitschr., XXIX
   1911. "Auf welcher Weise rettet die Befruchtung das Leben des Eies ?"
          Arch. f. Entwickelungsmech , XXXI.

Loeb, J., und Wasteneys, H.
   1910. "Warum hemmt Natriumcyanide die Giftwirkung einer Chlor-
          natriumlosung fur das Seeigelei ?" *Biochem Zeitschr.*, XXVIII.
   1911. "Sind die Oxydationsvorgange die unabhangige Variable in den
          Lebenserscheinungen ?" *Biochem. Zeitschr* , XXXVI
   1912. "Die Oxydationsvorgänge im befruchteten und unbefruchteten
          Seesternei," *Arch. f. Entwickelungsmech.*, XXXV.

Lyon, E. P.
   1902. "Effects of Potassium Cyanide and of Lack of Oxygen upon the
          Fertilized Eggs and the Embryos of the Sea Urchin (*Arbacia
          punctulata*)," *Am. Jour of Physiol* , VII

Mathews, A. P.
   1901. "Artificial Parthenogenesis Produced by Mechanical Agitation,"
          Am. Jour. of Physiol , VI.

Meyerhof, O.
   1911. "Untersuchungen uber die Warmetonung der vitalen Oxydations-
          vorgange in Eiern, I–III," *Biochem. Zeitschr.*, XXXV

Minot, C. S.
   1908. *The Problem of Age, Growth and Death.* New York

Warburg, O.
   1908. "Beobachtungen uber die Oxydationsprozesse im Seeigelei,"
          Zeitschr f. physiol. Chem., LVII
   1910. "Über die Oxydationen in lebenden Zellen nach Versuchen am
          Seeigelei," *Zeitschr. f physiol Chem.*, LXVI.

Wilson, E. B.
   1892. "The Cell-Lineage of *Nereis*," *Jour. of Morphol.*, VI.

PART V

THEORETICAL AND CRITICAL

CHAPTER XVI

SOME THEORIES OF SENESCENCE AND REJUVENESCENCE

The present chapter makes no attempt at a complete historical review of the various ideas and theories concerning the nature of the age process: it is merely a brief critical consideration, in the light of the preceding experimental data, of some of the more recent theories and suggestions

SENESCENCE AS A SPECIAL OR INCIDENTAL FEATURE OF LIFE

The popular belief, which is of course based on the phenomena of old age and death in man and the higher animals, is that the process of aging is a wearing out and death a final breakdown of the organic mechanism, or some essential part of it. This idea has from time to time found scientific support, chiefly among those who have considered the problem of senescence primarily in relation to man. Among the earlier authorities of the modern era in science Lotze ('51, '84) is one who holds this view, and recently Magnus-Levy ('07) has expressed the same opinion. While the phenomena of senile atrophy in extreme old age in man and the higher animals may perhaps be interpreted as in some sense a wearing out (see pp. 288–89), they represent only the final stages of senescence and are the result of what has happened during the earlier life of the organism. Both man and animals grow old throughout the course of progressive development, as the decrease in rate of metabolism indicates.

Speculative attempts have been made to show that age and death are associated in some way with the reproductive function. Weismann regards the limitation of life as an adaptation which has arisen by the action of natural selection, because continued life of the individual after the reproductive period is a "senseless luxury" for the species Weismann's views are discussed in another chapter (see pp 304–5). In opposition to this hypothesis Goette ('83) maintains that reproduction is the real cause of age and death of the parent individual and at the same time brings about rejuvenescence in the offspring The foundation of Goette's hypothesis is the fact that reproduction in many of the simpler organisms involves a disintegration of the original individual and the origin of new individuals from its parts or certain of them According to von Hansemann ('93, '09), it is the atrophy of the sexual organs, the final elimination of the germ plasm, which brings about the changes of old age ending in death These hypotheses are little more than guesses based on observation of the life histories of various organisms.

Various authors have suggested that conjugation and fertiliza-tion bring about rejuvenescence in some way. Maupas ('88, '89) believed that the infusoria grow old and may finally die of old age in the course of repeated agamic reproductions and that conjuga-tion renews their capacity for growth and division, but later investigators do not confirm these conclusions (see pp. 136-45) Bernstein ('98) suggests that certain internal conditions whose nature is unknown act as inhibitors of the growth impulse, and that their effect increases during life and finally brings about death. Fertilization, however, weakens or inhibits the inhibitors, and growth proceeds anew until again gradually inhibited. According to Buhler ('04) the molecular constitution of the organic substance undergoes gradual change during life and becomes less and less capable of metabolism, and fertilization re-establishes the original constitution. Rubner ('89) has advanced a very similar view. These hypotheses are merely statements of a supposed fact and do not throw any light upon the problem of the nature of the processes concerned in either senescence or rejuvenescence.

The idea that age and death are the results of an intoxication, a poisoning of the organism in one way or another, has been ad-vanced by various authors, among whom Metchnikoff ('03, '10) has received most attention According to Metchnikoff man is slowly poisoned by resorption of the products of bacterial activity in the large intestine. One result of this intoxication is arterio-sclerosis; another is that some of the phagocytes, the white blood corpuscles, under the influence of the poisons depart from their proper function as scavengers and protectors of the tissues and begin to devour the cells of the highest organs of the body, even those of the nervous system While Metchnikoff's ideas have aroused great popular interest, largely because of his scheme for prolonging life by preventing the intestinal intoxications, they have received little support among scientists The evidence for the universal or almost universal occurrence of chronic intoxication in man, and of arteriosclerosis as a result of it, is far from convincing, and the hypothesis of the action of the phagocytes under such conditions has proved even less acceptable. At best Metchnikoff's hypothesis is not widely applicable, for many animals which possess no large intestine grow old and die. But, as is evident from his statement that natural death occurs very rarely, Metchnikoff is really concerned with certain pathological aspects of advanced life in man and not at all with the problem of physiological senescence. While his ideas may or may not be of practical value, they have no general theoretical significance.

According to Jickeli ('02) metabolism is an incomplete process and injurious substances accumulate in the cell because of this incompleteness of metabolism. The secretions of cuticular substances, cysts, cellulose membranes, etc., the formation of hair, feathers, and various other products of cellular activity represent these injurious substances of which the cell attempts to rid itself by excretion, or the body by giving rise to parts which are sooner or later cast off. In other cases the cells react to the accumulation of injurious substances by increased rate of division, which results in increase of surface and so in greater possibility of excretion The accumulation of the injurious substances brings about senescence and death, and excretion by the cell, or the casting off of parts by the organism, is a process of rejuvenescence. This hypothesis is based entirely on a teleological conception of the cell and the organism and cannot be regarded as in any real sense physiological, although in his fundamental idea that senescence results from accumulation of substances in the cell and rejuvenescence from their elimination Jickeli approaches my own position. But for him the substances concerned are not the protoplasmic substratum of the cell, but something "injurious" which remains in the cell only because metabolism is an incomplete process, and the cell and the organism are all the time struggling, apparently with superhuman intelligence, to rid themselves of their burdens.

More recently Montgomery ('06) advanced a somewhat similar hypothesis. He believed that waste products accumulate in the cells as life continues and that some of them are toxic. Senescence and death are the result of the insufficiency of the excretion process. Reproduction is in general an escape or separation of some parts from "an empoisoned mass," and the part which is thus separated is capable of repeating the life history But Montgomery does not make it clear why the part or parts which separate as reproductive elements do not carry their share of the poisonous substances with them This is the most important point, for if the reproductive elements do not free themselves from these poisons they, as well as other parts, must die, and there seems to be no reason except a teleological one why parts should separate as reproductive elements at all. Here, as in Jickeli's hypothesis, certain cells free themselves, voluntarily as it were, from the poisonous substances which are killing the organism. The chief difference between Jickeli and Montgomery is that for the one rejuvenescence is an excretory process and may occur in somatic as well as in reproductive cells, while the other maintains that only the reproductive elements rejuvenate, and that they somehow leave the poisonous substances behind in the body or in a residuum.

SENESCENCE AS A RESULT OF ORGANIC CONSTITUTION

Most of those who have considered the problem of age from any general viewpoint have maintained that the conditions which determine senescence and death are found in the physiological constitution of the organism. Seventy years ago Johannes Muller ('44) expressed this opinion; some forty years later Cohnheim ('82) took the same position, and in more recent years this view has found numerous supporters

Butschli's suggestion ('82) that death is due to the exhaustion of the supply of a certain substance—the "life ferment"—which is gradually used up during life; and that the protozoa and the germ cells of multicellular forms do not die because they are capable of producing the substance anew, is not much more than a statement that death is the result of life without rejuvenescence Cholodkowsky ('82), on the other hand, suggested that death was rather the result of the multicellular condition with its accompanying differentiation. In such organisms the struggle for existence among the parts which Roux ('81) believed to be of such fundamental importance in organic life must lead finally to the death of the whole.

The change in the relation between surface and volume in the cell and the organism during growth has often served as the foundation for speculations concerning growth and its cessation, aging and death, and cell division. Since the volume of the cell or the organism increases more rapidly than its surface, and since nutrition and oxygen enter through the surface, it is argued that as the cell or the organism increases in size the amount of nutrition and oxygen which can enter through the surface must become less and less adequate for the needs of the growing cell mass. Sooner or later a stage may be reached where only the superficial parts of the cell receive sufficient nutrition, and finally the death of the cell may result from the starvation of the parts farthest from the surface Various authors, among them Herbert Spencer, Bergmann and Leuckart, and later Verworn, have called attention to the biological importance of this relation between surface and volume and have employed it as a basis for theoretical considerations concerning one aspect or another of life. Recently Muhlmann ('oo, '10, '14) has advanced a theory of senescence and death based upon this principle. According to Muhlmann growth brings about senescence and death because it leads sooner or later to starvation of the parts of the cell or the organism farthest from the surface. In the unicellular forms the nucleus reacts to the extreme stage of starvation by division, which is followed by cell division, and so an increase of nutritive surface is produced. but in multicellular organisms, where the cells do not separate from each other, cell division only leads to further growth and so to starvation, which is most extreme in the part farthest from the surface Old age is then a condition of starvation which according to Muhlmann is most extreme in the central nervous system, the part farthest removed from the nutritive surfaces, and death is consequently primarily a death of the nervous system. Death for Muhlmann is not only the cessation of life, as it occurs in man and the higher animals, but the division of the cell is the death of the individual cell   The changes in the cells during their development, the appearance of metaplasmic structural substances, which is usually regarded as differentiation, Muhlmann interprets as a dedifferentiation and regression from the embryonic condition and as a secondary result of the gradual starvation of the cells.

As regards the biological importance of the relation between surface and volume, I am not aware that it has been proved in any case to be a fundamental factor in limiting growth.   Growth is not simply a matter of nutrition: in the higher animals a very definite limit of size exists, no matter how great the supply of nutrition, and in many lower animals extensive reconstitutional growth may occur. even in a stage of extreme reduction from starvation.   On the other hand, the growth of embryonic cells may be inhibited by correlative influences from other parts, even though an abundant supply of nutrition is present.   In many cases animal eggs receive their nutrition chiefly or wholly through a minute fraction of their surface (see Figs 184, 185, p. 345) yet are able to attain an enormous size as compared with other cells of the body.   Similarly, in many cells of the multicellular body, the nutritive surface is evidently only a small fraction of the total surface of the cell, e.g., in many glandular tissues, yet life and function continue   And in the unicellular infusoria food enters through a definite mouth and passes into the entoplasm. where a nutritive surface is formed about each food particle.   In such cases the external surface of the cell has no relation to its capacity for ingesting food.   Oxygen doubtless enters through the cell surface, but it undoubtedly enters more or less rapidly according to conditions in the cell.   In fact, the whole theory of the biological importance of the relation between surface and volume rests rather upon a process of logic than upon the data of observation and experiment, and when we examine the behavior of cells and organisms it is difficult to find adequate support for it

As regards Mühlmann's hypothesis, the conclusion that old age is an advanced stage of cell starvation rests chiefly upon assertion rather than proof.   As a matter of fact, in starvation the nervous system loses less than other tissues, while in old age, according to

Muhlmann, it suffers most of all. That accumulation of structural substance and so-called metaplasm in the cells is the result of a gradual starvation is difficult to believe in view of the fact that during actual starvation in the lower animals these substances may disappear to a greater or less extent. And the fact that cell division can be inhibited by starvation is scarcely in agreement with Muhlmann's assertion that cell division results from starvation of the nucleus Muhlmann regards all that is commonly called progressive development as a regression or involution from the embryonic condition and maintains that the only progress is the reproduction of embryonic cells, but here again we have merely assertion, not evidence. In what way progress is involved in the reproduction of embryonic cells he does not attempt to show And his assertion that cell division and the cessation of life are both death leaves the idea of death without any physiological significance, for cell division and the cessation of life are certainly two very different processes In the one an increase in metabolism apparently occurs, while in the other metabolism ceases.

More than twenty years ago Richard Hertwig ('89) advanced the opinion, based on studies of certain protozoa, that "depression" and "physiological degeneration" of the cell—conditions supposedly more or less closely identical with senescence and natural death—are associated with an increase in the size of the nucleus relatively to the cytoplasm, and in later papers ('03, '08) he has attempted to show that the nucleoplasmic relation, i.e., the size ratio of nucleus to cytoplasm, varies and regulates itself within definite limits for each particular kind of cell and that its variation is an index of the functional condition of the cell This idea has been further developed by some of his students and others, but has also been rather widely criticized, and many investigators have not been able to find the definiteness of relation which Hertwig believes to exist. Conklin ('12), for example, concludes from an extensive study of the nucleoplasmic relation in the development of the mollusk *Crepidula*, that it is neither a constant nor a self-regulating ratio and not a cause of cell division, as Hertwig believes, but rather a result As a matter of fact differentiation and senescence in the higher animals are associated in most tissues with an increase in the relative volume of the cytoplasm rather than of the nucleus. Hertwig assumes that the cell is able to regulate its own nucleoplasmic relation, at least within certain limits, but the origin and nature of the nucleoplasmic tension which he postulates as the basis of this regulation, as well as the physiological mechanism of regulation, remain obscure. In short, the hypothesis has not a physiological foundation and apparently is not in complete agreement with the facts.

Minot's views, which are fully stated in his recent publications (Minot, '08, '13), are almost diametrically opposed to those of Hertwig, as regards the direction of change in the nucleoplasmic relation during senescence. Minot attempts to show that the growth and differentiation of the cytoplasm are the fundamental factors in senescence and death In the young cell the amount of cytoplasm in relation to the amount of nuclear substance is least, but during development it increases and undergoes differentiation, "cytomorphosis " occurs, and brings about senescence.

According to Minot this is a universal law, but his evidence is taken almost entirely from the higher animals. In many of the lower animals no marked proportional increase in the amount of cytoplasm occurs during development, and in the plants differentiation is in general accompanied, not by increase in the cytoplasm, but by vacuolization. Therefore the size relations of the cytoplasm and nucleus, while they may serve to some extent as an index of age in the higher animals, cannot by any means be regarded as a universal factor in senescence But the differentiation of the cytoplasm undoubtedly is a very important factor in senescence, and as regards this point my own view agrees closely with Minot's

The changes in the substratum of the cells are merely the conditions or one aspect of senescence, they are not senescence itself, for that is a change in the dynamic processes of the organism which ends in their cessation Minot, however, has not told us what senescence is nor how the cytoplasmic changes bring it about I have attempted to show that senescence is a decrease and rejuvenescence an increase in rate of metabolism associated with changes in the cellular substratum which themselves result from the relation between substratum and metabolism (Child, '11, '14). In his latest paper Minot has criticized this view on the ground that if it were correct we must be growing alternately old and young While I am quite ready to admit that this is to a certain extent the case, it does not by any means follow, as Minot has asserted, that every change in metabolic rate is either senescence or rejuvenescence. Undoubtedly it is often impossible to draw a sharp line of distinction between the age changes and many other periodic changes in the organism (see pp. 187-93), yet in general senescence and rejuvenescence are relatively slow and gradual changes in metabolic rate associated with certain changes in the cellular substratum, which do not undergo rapid reversal or regression Minot's criticism is quite beside the point There is nothing in his own theory that is in conflict in any way with the idea that senescence and rejuvenescence, viewed in their dynamic aspects, are changes in rate of metabolism, for it is concerned with certain conditions and indications of senescence in the cells rather than with the process of senescence itself.

According to Minot, dedifferentiation and rejuvenescence do not occur in the body cells. At various points in the present book (see especially chaps v-vii, x, xii) I have endeavored to show that dedifferentiation and rejuvenescence occur very widely in body cells. No further discussion, therefore, is necessary here Minot believes, however, that the egg differs from all other cells in that it undergoes rejuvenescence after fertilization The basis for this conclusion is the increase during this stage in the amount of nuclear substance in relation to cytoplasm As regards the occurrence of rejuvenescence in the embryo, I am in essential agreement with him, but my conclusions are based on the changes in metabolic rate rather than size relations of nucleus and cytoplasm Minot, however, has made no mention of the spermatozoon According to his view it should be one of the youngest cells in existence, since it possesses in most cases practically no cytoplasm. As a matter of fact, however, it shows none of the characteristics of a young cell. It is if anything more highly specialized than the egg, and has ceased entirely to grow, moreover, when it enters the egg it loses its morphological characteristics and to all appearances also undergoes dedifferentiation and rejuvenescence into an ordinary nucleus. It would be of interest to know how Minot regarded this cell.

Delage ('03) believes that age and death are the result of differentiation. In the course of differentiation the cells lose the capacity for reproduction and finally for growth, and no cell is able to live indefinitely without either growing or dividing. The idea that cell reproduction prevents or retards senescence seems to be involved in this view, but Delage does not attempt to develop it

Jennings has recently advanced a view very similar to that held by Delage. Age and death, according to Jennings ('12, '13), are the result of the increased differentiation of the higher organisms The infusoria do not necessarily die or undergo progressive race senescence, as Maupas believed. In the more complex and highly organized body of the higher animals the greater degree of differentiation brings about loss of capacity to carry on the fundamental vital processes, and so death finally results Jennings fails to note that the higher organisms differ from the protozoa, not merely in the degree of structural differentiation, but in the absence or limitation of agamic reproduction. As I have endeavored to show (pp 136–45), it is the repeated process of reproduction rather than their low degree of differentiation which prevents progressive race senescence and death in the protozoa. Each division brings about some degree of rejuvenescence, which may balance the senescence during the interval between divisions. Doubtless the capacity of the protozoa to reproduce agamically and their low degree of differentiation are associated with each other as results of a common cause, but it is the repeated interruption of progressive development by regression that prevents or retards old age and death

It remains to consider certain hypotheses which concern themselves more directly with the metabolic aspects of the age changes. In his *Allgemeine Biologie* (1899), Kassowitz has attempted a general consideration of biological phenomena on the basis of a theory of metabolism which assumes that all metabolism consists in the synthesis and destruction of the protoplasm molecule. All non-protoplasmic (metaplasmic) substances, such for example as fat, glycogen, starch, etc , which appear in the cell, must first have formed part of the protoplasm molecules, and their formation is the result of chemical decomposition of these molecules   When the cells are strongly stimulated, as they are during active function, the protoplasmic molecules break down into substances which are eliminated from the cell, such as carbon dioxide and the nitrogenous excretion products.   This Kassowitz terms active breakdown.   But even when the cells are not stimulated and functionally active to any marked degree, protoplasmic breakdown still occurs, although slowly and incompletely, and this inactive breakdown gives rise in large part to the metaplasmic substances which accumulate in the cell.   The metaplasmic substances are, according to Kassowitz, either quite incapable of further change in the cell after they are once formed, or must be slowly transformed by the action of enzymes before they can again take part in the synthesis of new protoplasmic molecules.   The presence of these metaplasmic substances in the cell interferes with the passage of oxygen to the labile molecules and with the transmission of stimuli and so favors further inactive, as opposed to active, breakdown of protoplasmic molecules   Consequently, when metaplasmic substances appear in the cell, the inactive breakdown increases and this in turn leads to further accumulation of metaplasm and so on.   The result is a decrease in functional activity and, sooner or later, death.   From this point of view senescence and death are the result of a progressive increase in the inactive breakdown and the metaplasmic substances formed by it.   Death from old age finds its determining factors in the chemical and physical constitution of protoplasm.

In this theory the ideas of the accumulation of substance in the cell and its effect upon metabolism as a basis for senescence is very clearly and fully developed.   And while there are various reasons for dissenting from Kassowitz' theory of metabolism based on the labile protoplasmic molecule (see pp 13–18) and from the sharp distinctions made between active and inactive breakdown and between protoplasm and metaplasm, we can agree with him that senescence and death are fundamental features of life and are associated with an increase in stability of substratum of the cell.

As regards rejuvenescence, Kassowitz is much less clear, although he has in his ideas a satisfactory foundation for a theory of rejuvenescence   In referring to Weismann's ideas concerning the immortality of the protozoa, he points out that since a rapid growth of protoplasm precedes each cell division, and since growing protoplasm with its large volume of active breakdown is an unfavorable substratum for the accumulation of metaplasm, therefore when such growth occurs the organism may frequently remain young. He apparently fails entirely to note that, according to his own hypothesis, elimination from the cell of metaplasmic substances should make the cell more capable of active breakdown, and so younger.

Enriques ('07, '09) lays stress upon the decrease in assimilatory capacity, and this capacity he believes decreases as differentiation increases   Death is not a necessary consequence of life, for the unicellular forms and also many plants may continue to live indefinitely.   Enriques cites some chemical analyses of plants in support of his view that the nitrogenous substances become "diluted" during development by the deposition in the cells of carbohydrates. Moreover, he finds that the changes in the nitrogenous substances precede the changes in other substances, and this confirms his belief that the assimilatory capacity of the cells decreases, for the nitrogenous substance is the assimilating substance.   In other words, a decrease in the proportion of chemically active protoplasm occurs during development   My own views are in essential agreement with those of Enriques, but I have endeavored to proceed a few steps farther and to show how rejuvenescence occurs and its significance in retarding and preventing senescence and death

Conklin ('12, '13) has expressed himself as in essential agreement with my own conclusions concerning the nature of senescence and rejuvenescence, but he lays particular emphasis upon the interchange between nucleus and cytoplasm as the fundamental condition of constructive metabolism, and concludes that "anything which decreases the interchange between nucleus and protoplasm leads to senility; anything which increases this interchange renews youth."   This conclusion seems to me not sufficiently broad in one sense and too broad in another.   It can scarcely be doubted that at least some degree of cytoplasmic or nuclear senescence may occur independently of the metabolic interchange between nucleus and cytoplasm, perhaps as a result of colloid or other changes in the substratum. Such a change will doubtless decrease nucleo-plasmic interchange, but this decrease will be secondary rather than primary in the senescence process Nucleoplasmic interchange depends upon the metabolic conditions in the cytoplasm and in the nucleus and may be altered by changes in either or both The primary metabolic changes of age must occur throughout the proto-plasm On the other hand, to say, as Conklin does, that anything which decreases nucleoplasmic interchange leads to senility and anything which increases it renews youth is manifestly not true, for low temperature may decrease and high temperature increase the interchange, but such metabolic changes do not, properly speaking, constitute senescence and rejuvenescence, although they may in some cases result sooner or later in one or the other.

The advances during recent years in our knowledge of the colloids and the very natural and entirely justifiable desire to apply the principles and conclusions of colloid chemistry to the living organism have led various authors to suggest that senescence in organisms is fundamentally a colloid change. In chaps i, ii, and viii I have called attention to these colloid changes and their impor-tance for the problems of senescence and rejuvenescence It can scarcely be doubted that the colloid substratum of the organism does undergo changes which are not essentially different from those in non-living colloids and that such changes play an important rôle in the process of senescence. They are perhaps, as I suggested (pp. 49–50), the primary changes in embryonic protoplasm which lead to decrease in metabolic rate and so initiate the processes of differentiation and senescence But something more than these changes is involved in at least most cases of senescence, for differ-entiation occurs, new structural substances are produced and accumulate in the cell, and its metabolic activity often becomes very different in character from that of the embryonic cell. While these changes may depend in large measure upon colloid changes, it is probable that changes in the chemical constitution of the substratum may also contribute to its increasing stability and so play a part in senescence.

The occurrence of rejuvenescence has not, so far as I know, been considered in connection with the suggestions that senescence is a colloid change, but from this point of view rejuvenescence would naturally be regarded as a reversal of the change concerned in senescence in consequence of altered conditions As I have pointed out (pp. 56–57), however, rejuvenescence is not necessarily a reversal of senescence, but rather, to a large extent at least, the substitution of a new substratum or protoplasm for the old, which may serve in greater or less part as a source of energy and of material. Here certainly chemical decomposition and synthesis are the important factors, although reversible colloid changes may be concerned to some extent.

Life is not entirely a matter of colloid condition, nor is it entirely a matter of chemical reaction; it is rather in the interrelations between chemical reaction and colloid substratum that we find the fundamental characteristics of life. If, as I have attempted to show, the age cycle is life itself, viewed from a certain standpoint, we must look to these interrelations for any adequate conception of the changes of senescence and rejuvenescence.

THE CONCEPTION OF GROWTH AS AN AUTOCATALYTIC REACTION AND THE RESULTING THEORY OF SENESCENCE

Within the last few years various authors[1] have suggested that growth is essentially an autocatalytic reaction. Loeb has made this suggestion in several papers concerning the process of nuclein synthesis in the developing egg, and Robertson, Wolfgang Ostwald, and Blackman have attempted to show that the processes of growth in general follow the laws of autocatalysis. An autocatalytic reaction is one in which one or more of the products of the reaction act as catalyzers and so increase the velocity of the reaction. In such a reaction the velocity of the transformation at any instant is proportional to the amount of material undergoing change and to the amount of material already transformed. This remains true until products of the reaction begin to decrease its velocity. The curve of such a reaction is in general an S-shaped curve, like Fig 199, at first concave to the axis of ordinates as the velocity of reaction increases and finally becoming convex to this axis as the velocity decreases.

[1] Blackman, '09, Loeb, '06, '08, '09, Wolfgang Ostwald, '08, Robertson, '08a, '08b, '13.

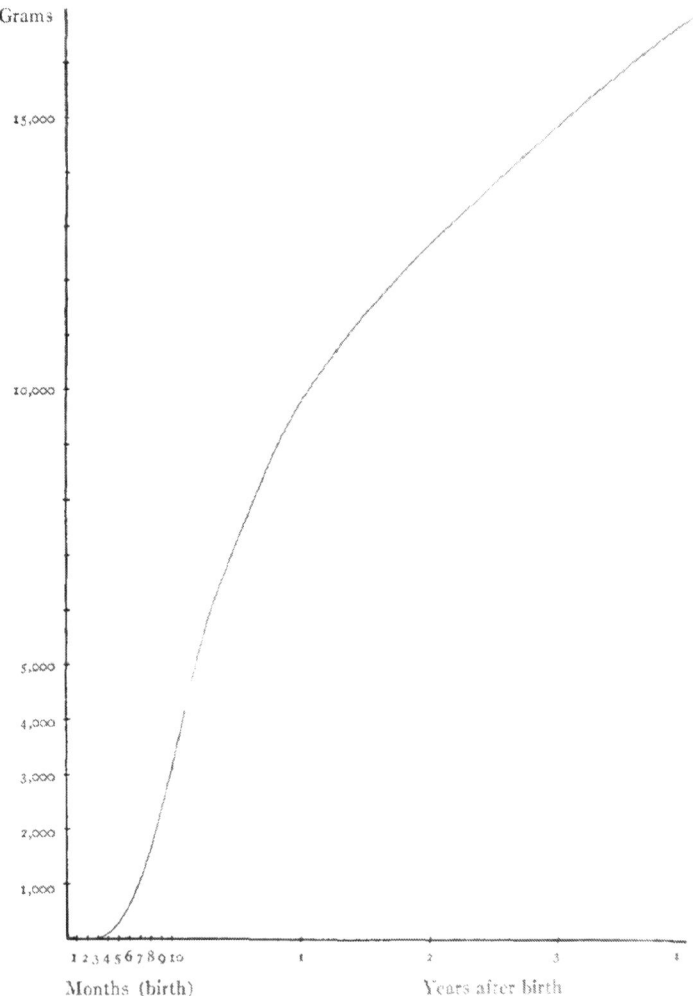

Fig. 199.—Curve of human growth for the embryonic period and the first for years after birth, drawn from the absolute increments of weight in Table XIII; eac vertical interval indicated on the axis of ordinates represents an absolute increase weight of 1,000 grams; on the axis of abscissae the ten short intervals at the left repr sent the nine months of the embryonic period and the month of birth, and each the following intervals represents one year.

If growth is a process of this kind, the rate of growth must increase up to a certain maximum as growth proceeds and then, after maintaining this maximum for a longer or shorter time, must decrease. Both Robertson and Ostwald present a great variety of data from various sources to support their conclusions. and many of Ostwald's curves are very characteristic curves of autocatalysis. Robertson has attempted to show further that in any growth-cycle of an organism, tissue, or organ, the maximum increase in volume or weight in a unit of time occurs when the total growth of the cycle is half completed From this point of view senescence consists merely in the retardation during the later stages of a growth-cycle of the rate of reaction by the accumulation of the products of reaction. Senile atrophy and death are not a feature of the reaction and must be due to special conditions not directly connected with growth. Rejuvenescence, so far as it occurs, must consist of a reversal of the reaction and consequently a removal of the accumulated products which were responsible for the retardation

The foundation upon which this conception of growth rests consists of the observational, statistical data of the increments of growth or of certain growth-components, such as weight, length, water-content, etc., in various organisms. Ostwald has shown that the absolute increments of growth or growth-components show very generally an increase during the earlier and a decrease during the later portion of the growth-cycle under consideration and so when graphically presented appear as an S-shaped curve like the curve of autocatalysis Robertson's conclusions rest on the same basis as Ostwald's. Stated in general terms these results mean simply that up to a certain point, the larger, or heavier, or longer the organism becomes, the greater its absolute increase in a given time. but beyond that point the absolute increase in a given time becomes smaller, although the total size, or weight, or length is still increasing

The same statistical data may be handled in another way. From the absolute increments we may determine the relative increments of weight, length, etc., that is, the increase in a given period of time in proportion to the weight or length at the beginning of that time. This relative increment may be expressed as a percentage of the total weight or length at the beginning of each per and may be called for convenience the percentage increment. 1 percentage increments for different periods enable us to comp the activity of the organic substance per unit of weight or len in adding to the weight or length in each period, and we find t in growth the percentage increments may decrease while absolute increments are still increasing. In other words, as grov proceeds, the absolute increment in grams or millimeters n become greater, but the growth-activity of each unit of weight length already present is decreasing.

TABLE XIII

WEIGHTS OF THE HUMAN EMBRYO AND OF THE CHILD DURING THE FIRST FOUR YEARS AFTER BIRTH

Age		Weight in Grams	Absolute Increment	Percentage Increment
2 months		4	. . . . .	. . . . .
3	"	20	16	400
4	"	120	100	500
5	"	285	165	137.5
6	"	635	350	123
7	"	1,220	585	92
8	"	1,700	480	39
9	"	2,240	540	32
10	" (birth)	3,250	1,010	45
½ year		5,620	2,370	73
¾ "		7,350	1,730	31
¾ "		8,820	1,470	20
1 "		9,920	1,100	12.5
1¼ "		10,720	800	8
1½ "		11,520	800	7.5
1¾ "		12,020	500	4.3
2 "		12,020	600	5
3 "		14,820	2,800	14.5
4 "		16,320	1,500	11.2

An example from among the data used by Ostwald will make matter clear. Table XIII gives in the second column the weig in grams of the human embryo at monthly intervals from second month to birth, as determined by Fehling, and of the c after birth at intervals of three months during the first two y and of one year each during the third and fourth years, as de mined by Camerer. The third column of the table gives the absol increments in grams for each period as determined from the differences in weight, and the fourth column the percentage increments, i.e., the increments expressed as percentages of the total weight at the beginning of each interval. It is evident at once that the absolute increments in the third column increase during the first seven months of the embryonic period, and that after birth there is at first an increase and then a decrease, with slight irregularities. But the percentage increments show an increase only from the third to the fourth month and afterward a decrease. In comparing the increments before and after birth it must be remembered that the time intervals from birth to two years are three times and those from two to four years twelve times as long as those before birth, so that we must divide the increments given in the table for these periods by three and by twelve respectively to make them comparable to the increments for the embryonic period.

If from the growth-increments we plot a curve of growth, using the time intervals as abcissae and the increments as ordinates, the form and direction of the curve will be very different, according as we use the absolute or the percentage increments The curve which results when the absolute increments are used is shown in Fig. 199.   This is an S-shaped curve and is similar to the curve of an autocatalytic chemical reaction.   Ostwald and Robertson have used the absolute increments in their studies of growth and have obtained similar curves for a variety of data.

But if we use the percentage increments the curve is of the kind shown in Figs. 200 and 201   Fig. 200 is the curve for the embryonic period and Fig. 201 for the period after birth, the former being on a larger scale than the latter in order to show its character more clearly This method of graphic presentation of the data gives a descending curve, which expresses the fact that the rate of increase in weight as a percentage of total weight decreases from a very early period on The other data of growth used by Ostwald and Robertson give essentially similar results, with here and there slight irregularities resulting from larval moultings, changes in relation to environment, etc.   Donaldson's and Minot's curves of rate of growth were also drawn from percentage increments.[1]

[1] See Donaldson, '95, Minot, '91, '08, and also pp 274–77 above

Evidently there must be no conflict between the conclusi
which we may draw from the two kinds of increments or the
kinds of curves, since both are obtained from the same statist

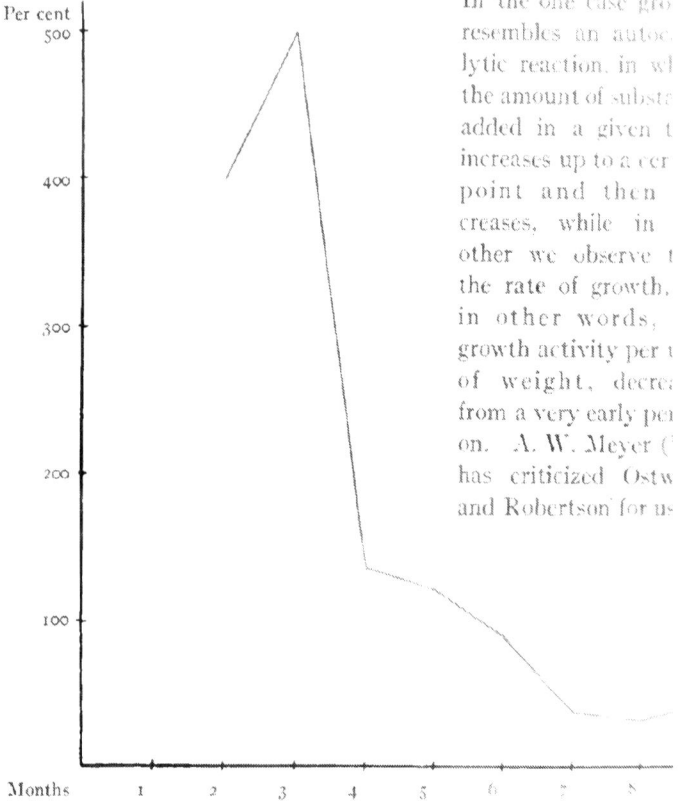

In the one case gro
resembles an autoc-
lytic reaction, in wl
the amount of substr
added in a given t
increases up to a cer
point and then
creases, while in
other we observe t
the rate of growth,
in other words,
growth activity per u
of weight, decre:
from a very early per
on. A. W. Meyer (
has criticized Ostw
and Robertson for us

FIG. 200.—Curve of human growth for the embryonic period and the mont
birth, drawn from the percentage increments of weight in Table XIII: each vert
interval indicated on the axis of ordinates represents an increment of 100 per cen
weight, and each horizontal interval on the axis of abscissae, one month.

absolute instead of percentage increments of growth as the ba
of their curves. This criticism is somewhat beside the point, fo
must be remembered that the absolute and relative increme
represent simply different aspects of the same process.

The general resemblance of the growth process to an autocatalytic reaction is self-evident: in the first place one result of growth is an increase in the amount of protoplasm, and the greater the amount of protoplasm the greater the amount of growth in a given time. Or more specifically, assuming what is undoubtedly true, that growth is dependent directly or indirectly upon the presence of certain enzymes, then it is evident that greater amounts of growth are possible as growth proceeds, for the necessary enzymes are one of the products of growth.

Doubtless certain reactions concerned in growth are autocatalytic reactions, but it seems obvious that growth is very much more than an autocatalytic reaction and that certain processes which do not follow the laws of autocatalysis are much more important in relation to the more conspicuous characteristics of growth than those which do or seem to. Growth produces other substances besides active protoplasm or enzymes, viz., substances which play little or no part in bringing about further growth, but form

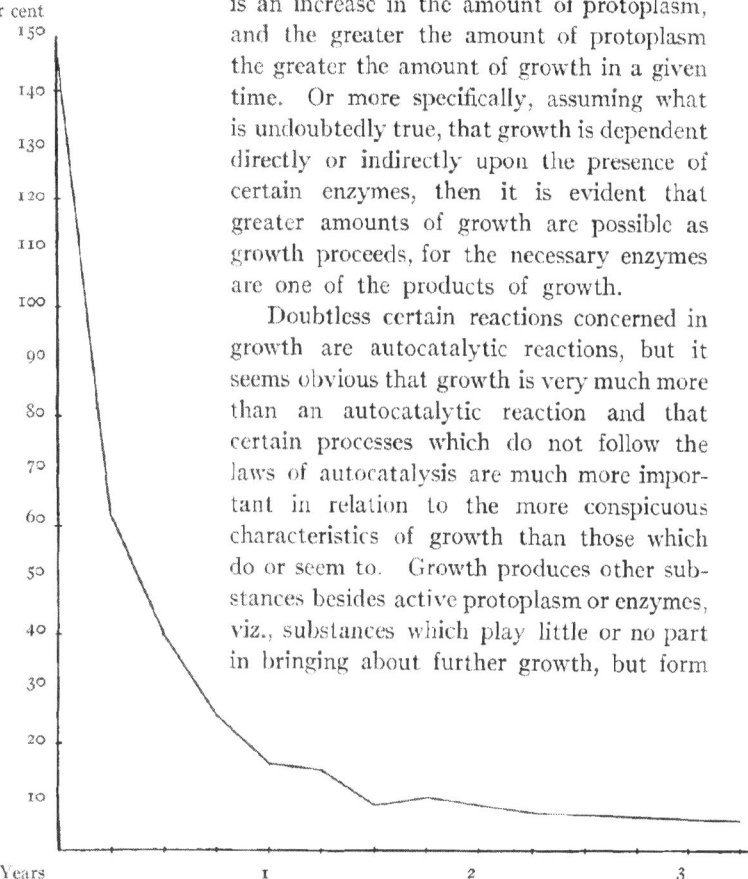

FIG. 201.—Curve of human growth from birth to three years, drawn from the percentage increments of weight in Table XIII: each vertical interval indicated on the axis of ordinates indicates an increment of 10 per cent in weight, each horizontal interval on the axis of abscissae, three months.

more or less stable structural constituents of the organism. As growth proceeds, the proportion of these substances to the total weight or volume undergoes more or less continuous increase and the proportion of active substance to total weight or volume becomes less and less. Consequently the percentage increment of growth decreases more or less continuously from the beginning of these changes, and the absolute increment, while at first increasing, must sooner or later decrease It is, in fact, not the increase in the autocatalyst of growth, but the increase of other products of reaction and the transformation of active protoplasm into other less active forms which retards growth, and these changes are going on and the proportion of these substances is increasing more or less continuously from the beginning of the growth period. Enriques ('09), in a critique of the autocatalytic theory of growth, has emphasized the fact that in consequence of differentiation a "dilution" of the actively growing substance occurs and the rate of growth decreases, until finally the total growth is insufficient to balance the losses, and senile atrophy occurs. Senescence, senile atrophy, and death result from changes of this kind, not from the autocatalytic changes, and there is no need of assuming, as the adherents of the autocatalytic theory of growth are forced to do, that the conditions which determine senile atrophy are different from those which are concerned in growth. Senile atrophy is in reality merely the necessary result of continued growth in organisms with a relatively stable substratum

Growth is not a simple chemical reaction and cannot be considered as such: it is a complex physico-chemical process in which changes in the physical character of the substratum as well as chemical conditions are concerned. The rate of growth is determined, not simply by the laws of autocatalysis, but by a complex of factors of different kinds. The decrease in the absolute growth-increment in later stages does not represent approach toward a chemical equilibrium, but rather a continued dilution and physical change of the protoplasm

The question whether reduction and dedifferentiation are reversals in the chemical sense of growth and differentiation has already been raised (see pp. 38, 56). If it were possible to regard the whole life cycle of the organism as a reversible chemical reaction it would doubtless simplify very greatly our conception of living things. But the organism cannot be compared to a chemical reaction; it consists of a multitude of chemical reactions and physical changes interrelated and localized and controlled by their relations to a peculiar physical environment or substratum, which in turn is the product of the reactions and is modified by them Many factors not concerned in simple chemical reactions *in vitro* are present in living organisms, and to ignore them can only result in failure to gain an adequate conception of what life is

Recently Robertson ('13) has attempted to develop the autocatalytic theory of growth still farther and to show that lecithin, or the substances of the phospholipine group to which lecithin belongs, are the autocatalysts of growth. Robertson points out that two kinds of autocatalytic growth are possible, one the autostatic in which the autocatalyst is decreasing in amount, the other the autokinetic in which it is increasing in amount. He believes that the early period of embryonic development in which the nuclear substance is increasing and the yolk decreasing is of the autostatic type, while the later period of cytoplasmic growth and differentiation is of the autokinetic type These two periods correspond in general to the periods which I have distinguished as the periods of rejuvenescence and senescence in the life cycle The grounds for his conclusion that lecithin is the autocatalyst are: first, that the amount of lecithin in the sea-urchin egg decreases during early stages of development (Robertson and Wasteneys, '13); secondly, that lecithin added to the sea-water retards, or, as he believes, may even reverse, the development of the sea-urchin in early stages; thirdly, that lecithin accelerates the growth and development of amphibian larvae in later stages preceding metamorphosis.

It is of course true that the amount of lecithin decreases during early embryonic development, for the yolk is rich in lecithin, and during this period yolk is the source of nutrition, and it is also true that the formation of nuclear substance undergoes marked acceleration at the same time, but there is also increase in the volume of active cytoplasm. In contrast to the period of senescence there is during this period of rejuvenescence an increase in concentration, so to speak, of the active substance of the organism at the expense of the yolk, and this increase in concentration is continuous throughout the period, which is brought to an end, not by the decrease in lecithin, specifically, but by the disappearance of the yolk as a nutritive supply If the organism obtains nutrition from without. the formation of both nuclear substance and cytoplasm may go on for a long time, but sooner or later the gradual "dilution" of the protoplasm begins to make itself felt. It may be that the synthesis of the nuclein of the nucleus is, as Loeb has suggested, an auto-catalytic reaction, but the important point is that any attempt to interpret the period of early embryonic development as a whole in terms of autocatalysis fails to take account of features of great biological importance.

As regards Robertson's further evidence, his experiments on the retardation of development by means of lecithin must be pre-sented in much more complete form before they can be regarded as convincing. To establish as a fact a change so important as the reversal of embryonic development requires extended and careful experimentation. There is no evidence, from Robertson's descrip-tion, of anything more than a toxic effect of the lecithin preparation, and for the present we can only regard his conclusion as based on very inadequate evidence.

While the autocatalytic theory of growth is interesting and doubtless of value as regards certain aspects of growth, it is at best only a partial theory and can never be applied to the growth process as a whole The great periodic changes in growth during senescence and rejuvenescence not only do not follow the laws of autocatalytic reactions, but are determined by a complex of factors of which some are only indirectly connected with chemical reactions of any kind. From the laws of simple chemical reactions alone we can never hope for anything more than partial and inadequate interpretations of the complex biological processes, such as growth and reduction, differentiation and dedifferentiation, senescence and rejuvenescence.

REFERENCES

BERNSTEIN, J.
    1898. "Zur Theorie des Wachstums und der Befruchtung." *Arch f Entwickelungsmech*, VII.

BLACKMAN, F. F
    1909 "The Manifestations of the Principles of Chemical Mechanics in the Living Plant," *Report of the 78th Meeting of the Brit Assoc for the Adv. of Sci*

BUHLER, A.
>   1904. "Alter und Tod," *Biol. Centralbl.*, XXIV.

BUTSCHLI, O.
>   1882. "Gedanken uber Leben und Tod," *Zool. Anzeiger,* V.

CHILD, C. M.
>   1911. "A Study of Senescence and Rejuvenescence Based on Experiments with Planarians," *Arch f Entwickelungsmech ,* XXXI
>   1914. "Starvation, Rejuvenescence and Acclimation in *Planaria dorotocephala*," *Arch f. Entwickelungsmech.*, XXXVIII.

CHOLODKOWSKY, N.
>   1882. "Tod und Unsterblichkeit in der Tierwelt," *Zool. Anzeiger*, V.

COHNHEIM, J.
>   1882. *Vorlesungen uber allgemeine Pathologie.* II. Auflage. Berlin.

CONKLIN, E. G
>   1912. "Cell Size and Nuclear Size," *Jour. of Exp Zool ,* XII
>   1913. "The Size of Organisms and of Their Constituent Parts in Relation to Longevity, Senescence and Rejuvenescence," *Pop. Sci Monthly,* August.

DELAGE, Y.
>   1903 *L' Hérédité et les grandes problèmes de la biologie.* Paris.

DONALDSON, H. H.
>   1895. *The Growth of the Brain.* London.

ENRIQUES, P.
>   1907. "La morte," *Rivista di Scienza.* Ann. I.
>   1909. "Wachstum und seine analytische Darstellung," *Biol. Centralbl.*, XXIX

GOETTE, A.
>   1883 *Über den Ursprung des Todes.* Hamburg

HANSEMANN, D. VON.
>   1893 *Studien uber die Spezifital, den Altruismus und die Anaplasie der Zellen.* Berlin.
>   1909 *Descendenz und Pathologie.* Berlin.

HERTWIG, R
>   1889 "Über die Kernkonjugation der Infusorien," *Abhandlungen d. Bayer. Akad. d. Wissensch ,* II. Kl., XVII.
>   1903 "Über Korrelation von Zell- und Kerngrosse und ihre Bedeutung fur die geschlechtliche Differenzierung und die Teilung der Zelle," *Biol. Centralbl ,* XXIII.
>   1908. "Über neue Probleme der Zellenlehre," *Arch f Zellforsch ,* I.

JENNINGS, H. S.
>   1912. "Age, Death and Conjugation in the Light of Work on Lower Organisms," *Pop Sci Monthly,* June

JENNINGS, H. S

1913   "The Effect of Conjugation in *Paramecium*,' *Jour of Exp Zool*, XIV.

JICKELI, C F.

1902.   *Die Unvollkommenheit des Stoffwechsels.* Berlin.

KASSOWITZ, M.

1899   *Allgemeine Biologie.* Bande I und II. Wien

LOEB, J.

1906   "Weitere Beobachtungen uber den Einfluss der Befruchtung und der Zahl der Zellkerne auf die Saurebildung im Ei," *Biochem. Zeitschr.*, II

1908.   "Uber den chemischen Character des Befruchtungsvorgangs und seine Bedeutung fur die Theorie der Lebenserscheinungen," *Vortr u Aufs u. Entwickelungsmech.*, H II.

1909.   *Die chemische Entwicklungserregung des tierischen Eies* Berlin.

LOTZE, R. H.

1851.   *Allgemeine Physiologie des korperlichen Lebens.* Leipzig.

1884   *Microcosmus* IV. Auflage Leipzig

MAGNUS-LEVY, A.

1907.   Article "Metabolism in Old Age" in *Metabolism and Practical Medicine·* C von Noorden. Anglo-American issue Chicago

MAUPAS, E.

1888   "Recherches expérimentales sur la multiplication des infusories ciliés," *Arch de zool exp*, (2), VI.

1889   "La Rajeunissement karyogamique chez les ciliés," *Arch. de zool. exp*, (2), VII.

METCHNIKOFF, E.

1903.   *The Nature of Man.* English translation. New York and London

1910.   *The Prolongation of Life* English translation. New York and London

MEYER, A. W.

1914.   "Curves of Prenatal Growth and Autocatalysis," *Arch f. Entwickelungsmech*, XL.

MINOT, C. S.

1891.   "Senescence and Rejuvenation," *Jour of Physiol*, XII.

1908   *The Problem of Age, Growth and Death* New York.

1913.   *Moderne Probleme der Biologie.* Jena

MONTGOMERY, T. H., Jr

1906   "On Reproduction, Animal Life Cycles and the Biological Unit," *Transactions of the Texas Acad of Sci.*, IX.

458 SENESCENCE AND REJUVENESCENCE

MUHLMANN, M.
1900 *Uber die Ursache des Alters* Wiesbaden.
1910. "Das Altern und der physiologische Tod," *Sammlung anat u physiol Vortrage*, H XI
1914 "Beiträge zur Frage nach der Ursache des Todes," *Arch f Pathol* (Virchow), CCXV.

MULLER, J
1844 *Handbuch der Physiologie des Menschen.* IV. Auflage Coblenz.

OSTWALD, WOLFGANG.
1908 "Die zeitlichen Eigenschaften der Entwicklungsvorgange," *Vortr u. Aufs u. Entwickelungsmech* . H V

ROBERTSON, T. B.
1908a. "On the Normal Rate of Growth of an Individual and Its Biochemical Significance," *Arch. f Entwickelungsmech* , XXV
1908b. "Further Remarks on the Normal Rate of Growth of an Individual and Its Biochemical Significance," *Arch f Entwickelungsmech* , XXVI.
1913. "On the Nature of the Autocatalyst of Growth," *Arch f Entwickelungsmech.*, XXXVII

ROBERTSON, T B , and WASTENEYS, H.
1913. "On the Changes in Lecithin-Content Which Accompany the Development of Sea-Urchin Eggs," *Arch. f. Entwickelungsmech.*, XXXVII

ROUX, W.
1881. *Der Kampf der Teile im Organismus.* Leipzig

RUBNER, M
1909 *Kraft und Stoff im Haushalte der Natur* Leipzig.

CHAPTER XVII

SOME GENERAL CONCLUSIONS AND THEIR SIGNIFICANCE FOR BIOLOGICAL PROBLEMS

It remains only to review briefly in a connected way some of the more important conclusions of the preceding chapters and to make a few further suggestions as to their bearing upon certain biological problems. In the first place, a full consideration of the facts leads unmistakably to the conclusion that the age cycle is simply one aspect of the developmental cycle, or we might even say that the developmental cycle is an aspect of the age cycle. Senescence and rejuvenescence do not include special processes, they are merely certain aspects of the relations between the metabolic reactions and the protoplasmic substratum. The progressive changes with which physiological senescence is associated are changes in the direction of greater physiological stability of the protoplasm and decreased dynamic activity. The regressive changes which bring about rejuvenescence are not necessarily reversals in the chemical sense of the progressive changes, but rather a substitution of a new substratum for an old. As a structure built by man, when it is no longer suited to existing conditions, may be torn down and some parts of it used, together with new material, for building a new structure which meets the demands of the new conditions, so in organisms structural features built up under certain physiological conditions may under others be broken down, and some of their constituents may take part in the formation of a new structure.

Both progression and regression are undoubtedly going on at all times in the active organism, but under the usual conditions of vegetative life the progressive changes overbalance greatly the regressive because building material in the form of nutrition is being added. But while growth and progressive development, with its specialization and differentiation of parts, is the more conspicuous feature of the life cycle, reduction and regression are none the less essential parts of it. The life cycle consists of one or more periods of senescence and one or more periods of rejuvenescence.

459

When the organism is adding to its structural substance, and transformation from more active to less active physical and chemical conditions takes place, senescence occurs   When conditions change so that previously formed structure is wholly or in part broken down and replaced by a new structural substratum, rejuvenescence occurs.

Senescence occurs chiefly during the vegetative life of the individual, while rejuvenescence is usually associated with reproduction, although various other conditions, such as starvation in which extensive breakdown of previously formed structure occurs, may bring it about.   Reproduction may be defined as the regression or dedifferentiation and reconstitution into a new individual of a physiologically or physically isolated part of a pre-existing individual   In agamic reproduction the changes result from the isolation of the part without further external action, but in gametic reproduction specialization of the part concerned, i e., the gamete, has proceeded so far that the union of the two widely different cells is necessary—except in parthenogenic eggs—to initiate the regressive and reconstitutional changes.

The occurrence of reproduction of one kind or another depends on various physiological conditions, the degree of individuation, physiological age, etc.   In general the vegetative forms of agamic reproduction occur in relatively young organisms, the more specialized agamic reproductions, such as formation of spores, gemmules, etc., are characteristic of somewhat later stages with a lower metabolic rate, and finally gametic reproduction is a feature of relatively advanced age and the gametes are cells which have reached the end of their progressive developmental history, have no further function in the parent organism, and are cast off as waste products or remain as physiologically isolated quiescent cells Before their isolation they were integral physiological parts of the organism, and they represent a more highly specialized, physiologically older condition than those parts which when isolated develop agamically.

The degree of physiological integration or individuation increases in general and up to a certain limit with increasing stability of the structural substratum   In general, also, the greater the degree of physiological integration, the more continuous the progress of senescence and the less frequently does vegetative agamic reproduction occur. In the plants and lower animals conditions which decrease physiological dominance and integration bring about reproduction of one kind or another. Senescence is itself such a condition, and in many organisms senescence may result automatically in the physiological isolation of parts, or the disintegration of the individual into fragments or cells, and so in reproduction.

Senescence is a characteristic and necessary feature of life and occurs in all organisms, but in many of the lower forms it may be more or less completely balanced by rejuvenescence in connection with reproduction or other regressive changes, so that there is little or no progressive senescence from one generation to another, or in the case of colonial forms, such as multiaxial plants, of the colony as a whole. Life in such cases consists of brief alternating periods of progression and regression, of senescence and rejuvenescence, which in some cases apparently balance each other for an indefinite period, while in other cases a slow progressive senescence may occur, extending through many generations.

Death is the inevitable end of the process of senescence when regression and rejuvenescence do not occur. In the lower forms, where agamic reproduction is frequent, or where other conditions, such as starvation, bring about regression periodically or occasionally, death does not necessarily occur. But in the higher forms, where progression and senescence are more nearly continuous, the life of the individual usually ends in death, though even in these forms some degree of rejuvenescence may occur.

If these conclusions are correct, agamic and gametic reproduction are fundamentally similar processes, except for the fact that in gametic reproduction specialization of the reproductive cells has proceeded so far that the peculiar conditions associated with fertilization are necessary for the initiation of the process of regression and rejuvenescence. And if we accept this theory of reproduction, the Weismannian conception of germ plasm as a self-perpetuating entity, independent of other parts of the organism except as regards nutrition—in short, a sort of parasite upon the body—becomes not

only unnecessary but impossible. Germ plasm is any protoplasm
capable, under the proper conditions, of undergoing regression,
rejuvenescence, and reconstitution into a new individual, organism,
or part. In other words, germ plasm becomes merely an abstract
idea which connotes the sum-total of the inherent capacities or
"potencies" with which a reproductive element of any kind, natural
or artificial, agamic or gametic, giving rise to a whole or a part,
enters upon the developmental process. Germ plasm is then
merely another term for heredity The process of inheritance is
concerned in every case of reproduction, whether it be agamic or
gametic, partial or total, and both experimental reproduction and
agamic reproduction in nature present opportunities for the study
of the process and mechanism of inheritance, which have thus far
been almost entirely neglected, but which are not found in connection with the much more highly specialized process of gametic
reproduction. And, admitting that every reproductive element
of any kind is, before reproduction begins, an integral physiological
part of an organic individual, we may define heredity more briefly
as the capacity of a physiologically or physically isolated part for
reconstitution into a new individual or part.

It does not by any means follow from this theory of reproduction
and inheritance that all the characteristics of the individual shall
reappear in the following generation. Many individual characteristics which are the result of action of external factors or of
special functional activity of certain parts—such, for example, as
calloused areas in the skin, the functional hypertrophy or atrophy
from disuse of certain muscles, and many others—are evidently the
result of local quantitative changes in metabolism and as such
cannot be expected to alter at once the equilibrium of the whole
protoplasmic system in such a way that they will be reproduced
in following generations in the absence of the special conditions
which determined their first appearance. This is equally true for
agamic and for gametic reproduction Nevertheless, since every
reaction represents to some extent a reaction of the whole organism and no change is purely local or entirely independent of
other changes, it is conceivable that if the special external or functional conditions act in the same way through a sufficient number

of generations, they may in time bring about an appreciable lasting change in the whole system of such a kind that the characteristics produced by them will become hereditary. And if the cells which give rise to gametes are integral parts of the organism, such a change must sooner or later affect them as well as other parts. It is quite impossible to discuss at this time the great mass of evidence for and against the inheritance of these so-called acquired characters. In general, biologists have been slow to admit the possibility of such inheritance, largely because it conflicts with the Weismannian theory, but if we admit that the gametes are integral parts of the organism, there is no theoretical difficulty in the way of such inheritance. Whatever the theoretical possibilities may be, it is in my opinion quite impossible to account for the course of evolution and particularly for many so-called adaptations in organisms without the inheritance of such acquired characters, but since thousands or tens of thousands of generations may be necessary in many cases for inheritance of this kind to become appreciable, it is not strange that experimental evidence upon this point is still conflicting.

The morphological parallelism between the course of individual development and the course of evolution have long been familiar to biologists and have been the subject of much discussion and speculation. While departures from this parallelism are numerous and often conspicuous, nevertheless the so-called biogenetic law that embryology repeats phylogeny, i e , the development of the individual repeats evolutionary history, still remains a striking biological fact. Moreover, a physiological parallelism seems to exist to some extent. In the individual we see advancing diversity and specialization of function, apparently associated with increasing stability of the structural substratum, and in evolution a similar series of changes. The question at once arises: Can we not find a clue in individual development to certain factors concerned in evolution?

In earlier chapters I have attempted to show that individual development and senescence are associated with the increase in stability of the substratum, while regression and rejuvenescence involve a return to the original "undifferentiated" active protoplasmic condition. It is of course not necessary to assume that in all cases exactly the same condition is attained in each successive regression and rejuvenescence It is quite conceivable, indeed probable, that, in spite of the successive regressive changes in each generation, there may be some slight, more or less continuous, progressive change, which perhaps becomes appreciable only after many generations. Have we, in fact, any right to assume that the organism returns to exactly the same condition in each successive regression? Is it not probable that a gradual, progressive senescence of protoplasm has occurred in the course of evolution? These questions have already been touched upon in chap. viii, and here it need only be said that the facts point very definitely in the direction of an affirmative answer.

If protoplasmic senescence is the essential factor in progressive evolution, then evolution is, like individual development, to a large extent internally, rather than externally, determined. We can accelerate, retard, or alter the course of individual development experimentally, but in spite of all such changes it retains a remarkable constancy of character. Have we not in evolution a somewhat similar process, a progressive change, a secular differentiation and senescence of protoplasm along lines which are determined primarily by the constitution of protoplasm rather than by external factors? In our attempts to modify experimentally the course of evolution are we not merely bringing about minor changes in a process which, like individual development, is internally determined, rather than determining the essential factors in evolution? Here again the facts seem to suggest an affirmative answer.

If evolution is in some degree a secular differentiation and senescence of protoplasm, the possibility of evolutionary rejuvenescence must not be overlooked. Perhaps the relatively rapid rise and increase of certain forms here and there in the course of evolution may be the expression of changes of this sort Perhaps also those forms which have been, so to speak, left behind as the lower organisms in evolutionary progress are forms in which senescence and rejuvenescence more nearly balance than in those that have gone on.

Even if evolution is a process of this kind we must believe that environmental factors affect its course to a greater or less extent, as they do the course of individual development, and we must admit the possibility of sudden changes of considerable magnitude, so-called mutations, although even these may be determined by previously existing internal conditions, as, for example, metamorphosis in individual development which is primarily the result of internal factors And, finally, as our ability to control the process of individual development has increased so greatly with the advance in knowledge of experimental methods, we may perhaps expect that in the course of time our ability to control the evolutionary process may increase, although the difficulties involved in controlling and modifying to any very great degree internal conditions which are the result of millions of years of alternating progressive and regressive change will perhaps make progress in this direction slow

Senescence and rejuvenescence result from a combination of factors which is found nowhere except in organisms, but there is no reason to believe that any one of the factors which make up the complex is peculiar to living things Changes in the permeability of membranes and other changes in aggregate condition of the colloids, changes in proportion of active and inactive substance in chemical systems, changes in water-content—all these and many others occur in non-living as well as in living systems But we may make our basis of comparison broader than this and use for definitions somewhat more general terms than heretofore. In such terms senescence is a retardation resulting from continued dynamic activity under certain conditions in a system, and rejuvenescence an acceleration resulting from elimination or transformation of the retarding factors under altered conditions. These definitions still hold good for the organism, but they also apply to many other changes in nature. Senescence and rejuvenescence in this sense are going on all about us, in some cases with short, in others with very long, periods The age changes in the organism are merely one aspect of *Werden und Vergehen*, the becoming and passing away, which make up the history of the universe.

INDEX

INDEX

Lightning Source UK Ltd.
Milton Keynes UK
UKHW020635260820
368857UK00004B/373